WHO OWNS THE MEDIA?

Concentration of Ownership in the Mass Communications Industry

Benjamin M. Compaine

with

Christopher H. Sterling
Thomas Guback
J. Kendrick Noble, Jr.

Knowledge Industry Publications, Inc.
White Plains, New York

Communications Library

Who Owns the Media? Concentration of Ownership in the
Mass Communications Industry
edited by Benjamin M. Compaine

Library of Congress Cataloging in Publication Data

Main entry under title:

Who owns the media?

(Communications library)
Bibliography: p.
Includes index.
1. Mass media—Economic aspects—United
States. 2. Mass media—Political aspects—United
States. I. Compaine, Benjamin M. II. Series.
P96.E25W5   380.3'0973   79-15891
ISBN 0-914236-36-9

Printed in the United States of America

CONTENTS

List of Tables and Figures

For two of my favorites,
sister Suzanne and nephew Lawrence

Acknowledgement

This book grew out of an idea proposed by Efrem Sigel, editor in chief of Knowledge Industry Publications, Inc. Its rapid and successful completion is due in large measure to the cooperation of the three outside contributors: Ken Noble, Chris Sterling, and Tom Guback. Although already steeped in the intricacies of the topics on which they were asked to write, they still had to amass and analyze a prodigious amount of data under exceedingly short deadlines. Not only were these deadlines met, but follow-up questions and such chores as checking galley proofs were similarly handled thoroughly and expeditiously.

The contributors all worked from the same outlines, so that they would cover the same basic territory. Otherwise, they have taken an independent stance about their industry segments regarding concentration. In that sense, their viewpoints do not necessarily reflect my own or those of the publisher.

In addition, special note must be made of the many organizations and individuals who have given us permission to use statistical material that they had compiled and published. They are identified as the sources for the more than 100 tables that appear in the book. This information is often prepared at considerable expense to the research organization, but most of us who compile such data realize that the value of the information goes beyond its original appearance in one publication, and its reuse in a different context makes a work such as this possible.

Finally, I would like to give special mention to Heather Kirkwood, the senior staff attorney at the Federal Trade Commission in charge of that agency's media project. Her synthesis of antitrust law with the unique role of the mass media in society was invaluable in establishing a new context for understanding concentration in this industry.

This has been an exciting project. My hope is that this book is a useful contribution toward stimulating thinking and fresh approaches among readers.

Ben Compaine

Bedford, N.Y.
May 1979

Introduction

One company, General Motors, had more revenue in 1978 than all television and radio broadcasters, newspaper, periodical and book publishers combined. In fact, three manufacturing companies had greater sales than the publishing and broadcasting industries. This includes such "giants" as NBC, CBS, Knight-Ridder, Times Mirror, Reader's Digest, ABC and Time Inc. Exxon receives more revenue in a week than The New York Times Co. receives in a year.

Why, then, does Larry Pressler, a freshman U.S. Senator from South Dakota, call for the federal government to break up "media giants"? Why has Rep. Morris Udall (D., Ariz.) been actively promoting a law to limit the size of owners of the mass media? What has been the motivation behind Federal Communications Commission rulings affecting newspaper and broadcast ownership combinations? Why do respected media critics warn of possible insidious control over public opinion and government policy by media conglomerates?

The mass communications industry is unique in the American private enterprise system because it deals in the particularly sensitive commodity of ideas, information, thought and opinion. Especially since the development of the broadcast media, we have become aware of the power of being able to simultaneously reach millions of individuals in the country as well as throughout the world with a message or an image. The mass media are perceived as opinion makers, image formers, culture disseminators.

At the same time, the media in the United States have a degree of autonomy that exists nowhere else in the world. Although other nations have a relatively free press, the United States is unique in allowing all forms of transmission of information to be privately owned. There is no government ownership of any significant newspaper, magazine or book publisher, television or radio station or network, other than some specialized publications through the Government Printing Office. The telephone lines and satellites may be subject to some government regulation, but they are all privately owned.

Above all, the very foundation of our governmental system, the

Constitution, singled out the press for special treatment: "Congress shall make no law ... abridging the freedom of speech, or of the press. ..." It may be argued that this absolute prohibition was written in an era when a handful of weekly colonial papers, a few books and magazines, laboriously turned off hand presses at the rate of 200 sheets per hour, was the universe of the press. At the start of the Revolutionary War there were only 35 weekly newspapers in the colonies, going into a total of about 40,000 homes.[1] The *Connecticut Courant* had what was described as the "amazing circulation of 8000. ..."[2]

Yet the politicians of the era were not ignorant of the power of the press. Thomas Paine's *Common Sense* pamphlet sold 120,000 copies in its first three months, and his views spread to virtually every literate American.[3] This one publication is given much of the credit for helping to bring Patriots watching from the sidelines into the revolutionary movement. Paine's first *Crisis* paper was published in the *Pennsylvania Packet* and was picked up by most of the Patriot press in the other colonies: "These are the times that try men's souls," he began. Washington read the words to his soldiers a week before their midwinter victory at Trenton. The authors of the Bill of Rights were probably well aware of the power of the press when they wrote that document.

The media have evolved into big businesses, just as other small businesses have changed and expanded with the technology of the Industrial Revolution, the enormous population growth of the nation and the complexity of dealing in a massive economy. But today, some critics are expressing concern that the modern media are becoming increasingly concentrated in the hands of a small group of corporate executives who may try to control what and how information is gathered and distributed to the populace.

The concerns are legitimate, in that the intention of the First Amendment was to allow for diversity of opinion. The fear at the time was that only government might have the power to limit that diversity. But today, there is growing concern in some private and government quarters that the range of opinions to which the public has access is being limited by large media conglomerates. The purpose of this book is to help sort out perceptions from reality and to give a sense of perspective to the term "media monopoly." The book presents a wealth of empirical statistical data and research findings, so that readers can draw their own conclusions. But it also presents an analysis of each major industry segment. The interpretations made by the authors may be subject to debate, but the empirical data should be studied carefully by those who wish to support their own positions.

ISSUES

There are at least three explicit issues and two underlying assumptions involved in the area of media ownership. The overt issues are:

1) The degree of concentration within industry segments, especially on the local level. This is seen in the issue of one-newspaper communities.

2) The degree of conglomeration. Conglomeration refers to the tendency for large corporations with diversified non-media holdings to buy into the media industry as well. Westinghouse, RCA, Times Mirror and Gulf + Western are examples of these types of firms.

3) The extent of cross media ownership. Part of the conglomeration issue, the ownership of media in more than one segment of the mass communications industry by a single firm is perhaps the most potent issue. CBS, Time Inc., Newhouse and Hearst are among the many firms with holdings across media segments.

Implicit in the discussion of concentration are other concepts reflecting American political traditions:

1) Bigness is bad. This applies to concentration of ownership in industries other than the mass media. There is a sense, in part supported by some economists, that after reaching a certain size which brings optimal efficiencies or production, further growth of firms in an industry provides no further economic advantages to society. The key question which can rarely be answered definitively is, how can we tell when that optimal point has been reached?

2) Localism is desirable: control of information, news and ideas should be spread around as much as possible. Locally owned newspapers and broadcast stations, many book publishers, scores of independent film producers and distributors would supposedly provide greater access to diverse opinions than fewer owners controlling an identical number of media outlets.

GOVERNMENT INVOLVEMENT

In summarizing the interest of the Federal Trade Commission in media ownership, a senior official explained that "We're somewhat

more concerned about concentration in the media [than other indus-
tries] because they are not just economic concerns but First Amendment concerns as well."[4]

The Federal Trade Commission, which until 1978 had left inquiries
into media ownership mostly to the Federal Communications Commission and the Justice Department, became active in the process by
focusing on this last assumption. Should a stricter standard apply to the
media than to other industries "because of the media's position in
American society and the importance of having many channels available for speech?"[5]

At a symposium on media ownership sponsored by the FTC in
December 1978, FTC chairman Michael Pertchuck asked, "[Can] free
speech be separated from the economic structure that controls the
media?" Pertchuck sees competition as an alternative to regulation:
"Should the government promote diversity and independence to avoid
having to regulate?"

The Federal Communications Commission has long been involved in
the media ownership question through its responsibility to license
broadcasters of radio and television. For a while it also involved itself in
regulating cable and in the common or cross-media ownership of
broadcasters and newspapers. Both cable and broadcasting regulation
by the FCC are treated at some length in chapters 3 and 7.

With the exception of the motion picture industry (see chapter 5),
the Justice Department has seen little cause to bring broad antitrust
actions against the mass media industries. Individual firms have been
affected, as in the case where Times Mirror Co. had to divest itself of
the *San Bernardino* (Calif.) *Telegram* on the grounds that it would
lessen competition since that paper is located near Times Mirror's *Los
Angeles Times.* Perhaps the most important Justice Department industry-wide action outside of film was the 1945 Associated Press case,
which clearly placed newspapers and other media within the jurisdiction of antitrust legislation. (See chapter 2.)

More recently, however, the antitrust division of the Justice Depart-
ment investigated the merger between newspaper giant Gannett and
Combined Communications, with its extensive broadcast holdings.
However, a top Justice Department official admitted:

The antitrust laws do not flatly prohibit media conglomerates any
more than they prohibit other kinds of conglomerates. Under
present law, some measurable impact on competition in some
market must be proven before a merger or acquisition will be held
to violate the antitrust laws. Indeed, the courts have been
generally reluctant to condemn conglomerate mergers where such

an impact has not been shown, regardless of the social or other objections that have been asserted.[6]

The emphasis of proposed antitrust legislation in 1979 was toward restrictions on absolute size, in contrast to the Sherman Act standards of having to show a real lessening of competition in a particular market. A bill proposed by Sen. Edward Kennedy in 1979 would prohibit companies with $2.5 billion of sales or $2.0 billion in assets from merging with one another. Companies with $350 million in sales or $200 million in assets would have to prove that a merger would enhance competition or produce efficiencies. This would be a switch from current statute, which puts the burden of proof on the government to show anti-competitive trends.

However, few of the mass media owning firms are large enough to come under the absolute prohibition of merger limit of the Kennedy proposal. Moreover, it would not prohibit the acquisition of small firms, such as a small city newspaper, a modest-sized book publisher or a broadcast station. The type of merger which would be prohibited is the attempted takeover of McGraw-Hill by American Express Co. in 1979.

THE ECONOMIC NATURE OF INFORMATION

Although this book incorporates the work of economists, it is not an economist's approach to understanding media concentration.[7] One particular economic concept is worth highlighting, however. A "public good" to an economist is one which has essentially no marginal cost associated with adding distribution. The best example is a television broadcast. Once the fixed costs of production have been incurred and the show is sent out over the air, there is no difference in expense to the broadcaster if one household or 21 million households tune into the show. Thus, television (and radio) advertising is not sold at its marginal cost, since that is $0.00. Price always exceeds marginal cost.

The "product" of the media differs from most commodities, which are private goods. Oranges are an example. Every orange has a cost, each one adds weight in shipment. Selling more oranges means adding more orange trees, etc. There can be a real marginal cost — the expense of growing and shipping one more orange.

In print media, the informational content is really the public good, while the physical product — paper and ink — is a private good. In many cases, the cost of producing the first copy constitutes the bulk of total cost, just as in broadcasting the production is virtually the total cost. Costs of editorial staff, typesetting and plate making are all necessary whether the print run will be 100 or 100,000. The incentive, therefore, for broadcasters and publishers is to increase circulation or audience for a product, since that adds little or nothing to marginal costs while justifying higher marginal revenue from advertisers in the form of higher advertising rates. The public good aspect of information is what encourages television networks and syndicated shows, as well as the desire for a firm to trade up from stations in smaller markets to larger ones. News services and print syndicates are encouraged by the same economic facts.

On the other hand, the economics of a public good are not fostered by adding newspapers to a chain or magazines to a group, except to the degree that some articles prepared for one publication may be adapted for another. Thus, while public goods have a market structure different from private goods, the low or nonexistent variable costs in adding distribution to one publication have no impact on other publications produced by the same firm, undermining many arguments justifying the economic benefit of chain ownership.

CONCERNS FOR PUBLIC POLICY

The second of the underlying assumptions identified above summarizes one viewpoint: that local and diversely held ownership would permit greater accessibility to the media. That assumption, which is clearly the basis for FCC limits on the number of broadcast stations any individual or corporation can own, must be balanced against the reality of what happens to the *impact* of any idea — good or bad — if the message becomes lost in trying to reach a fragmented audience. For example, cable television has been suggested as the answer to overcoming the limited spectrum space for broadcasting. In many communities, the existence of a dozen or two dozen cable channels allows the cablecasters to open up one or two channels to an almost public utility function: anyone who has something to say may appear on a public access channel. But who is listening? There has been little in the way of measurement of audiences in cable communities, but it may be speculated that even with 20 channels, the bulk of the audience will be tuned in to a handful with mass audience appeal. The access and diversity symbolized by public access cable may be no greater, as it turns out, than handing out mimeographed leaflets at a busy intersection or speaking to passersby from a soapbox.

The point is that public policy concerning media ownership and concentration must first be rooted in a realistic assessment of the existing data. Second, it must be oriented not to some ideal good but to a pragmatic good. It may be, for instance, that relatively large corporations with strong capital underpinnings will better serve the public's need for diversity, risk taking and depth of information than would more numerous but smaller firms with weaker capitalization and less willingness to take on major projects that include risk.

At the same time, smaller firms have always found new niches, provided innovation and then, when successful, been acquired by larger firms, thereby establishing an incentive for more new firms to follow a similar path. This cycle is particularly evident in the magazine and book publishing businesses. There appears to be no dearth of entrepreneurs, as the numbers of new book, magazine, weekly newspaper publishers and even film producers make clear.

Public policy makers can take several approaches to the issue of media ownership. Lawmakers can tamper with the structure or business behavior of media companies but not the product — news, information, ideas. There is, for example, no question that government has the power to deal with flagrant abuses of the press freedom, e.g., libel or true restraint of trade collusion. These governmental powers, however, deal with the *potential* for abuse, rather than an accusation that the media owners as a group have already committed such abuses.

Thus, the following strategies are available:

1) A positive policy with implementing legislation which encourages the formation of new media businesses: tax incentives on investments; waiving selected wage, environmental or similar rules that inhibit small businesses and capital formation; modified inheritance levies that today encourage divestiture; postal and telecommunications tariff and service that put the smaller user in a status comparable to bulk users. This sort of encouragement would still be far less than the direct subsidies other western democracies provide their fledgling movie makers and publishers. But it is also far less of a direct government involvement in the media than in France, Canada, West Germany or Great Britain.

2) A negative policy of prohibition by size limitations in the absence of evidence of conscious anticompetitive behavior. This might be aimed at banning firms with media holdings of a certain size from acquiring additional media properties in other industry segments or additional properties in their main area of dominance.

3) Combining the first strategy with some sanctions discouraging growth by merger of dominant media firms, while at the same time allowing firms of all sizes and holdings to grow through start-ups. Thus, once a newspaper reaches a size in circulation or number of papers where further acquisitions might be anticompetitive, it may still be permitted to grow by starting additional newspapers in communities that do not have any. Or, if policy-makers are convinced that a two or three newspaper town is better than one, incentives may be offered that encourage start-ups in such situations.

OBJECTIVES OF THIS BOOK

This project was created to bring together in one place as much relevant data as possible on the nature and degree of competition and ownership in the mass communications business. *Mass communication* is defined as the process of the delivery of a single message to a large, heterogeneous and anonymous audience in different locations at the same time. It encompasses television and radio, newspapers, books, cable television, magazines and theatrical film. The *mass media* refer to the institutions and devices that carry out the process of mass communication.

The book is first an empirical look at the structure of mass communications, by isolating the traditional media segments, each in its own chapter. It should become readily apparent how artificial these traditional barriers are, as the names of certain firms come up in more than one chapter. The relationships among the media become inescapable when discussing competition in the dissemination of ideas.

A second objective of the book is to present the findings of other researchers on the subject of competition. To what extent, for example, are residents in cities with a single newspaper benefited or harmed by lack of competitive newspapers?

A third objective is to really look at the mass communications industry as a unit. To what extent is it able to perform its basic role of providing variety of opinion and entertainment, as well as reasonable access to those with intelligent and reasoned opinions, even if unpopular or unconventional? Most importantly, this book seeks to answer, who owns what in mass communications? Is the industry significantly more concentrated in its ownership in 1979 than in 1970 or 1950?

Finally, the next six chapters present an assessment of ownership trends in individual media segments. Each analysis, however, should be viewed as an interpretation of the data by one person. Authors were asked not to set forth hypotheses to prove or disprove, but to collect the best data they could compile. To the extent that the writers have added a convincing interpretation to the data, so much value is added for the reader. Others may wish to use the chapters as the basis for articles or debates with another point of view. This, too, is consistent with the objective of this book.

Limitations and Assumptions

This project did not attempt to take up in addition to its other objectives a full debate on what the proper role and responsibility of the media should be in American society. That has been the subject of several excellent books itself.[8] This book assumes a responsibility for the press of reasonable diversity, access, fairness and honesty, without debating what is "reasonable" and with the recognition that in the real world there are obvious instances where this does not occur.

This study, as many others, has been hampered by the lack of availability of financial data from privately owned firms. To the extent that they operate differently from those who must report their financial operations to the public, there may be some amount of bias in some of the data. This is not viewed as being critical, however.

The book has omitted possible communications industry segments such as recording and music publishing. It has been assumed that these are concerned primarily with music, which may contain ideas, but are not generally considered as major conduits of mass communications.

A final assumption is that the media industry will continue to exist within the basic private enterprise system, tempered by some governmental regulation in broadcast. This means that anyone has the opportunity to enter some segment of the industry, limited only by ingenuity, management skill and the ability to raise a minimum amount of capital.

* * *

The mass communications industry in the United States is deeply rooted in the economic system. In this context, media technology and institutions have developed a mass communications system that is unique in the world for its independence from government control, direct or indirect. Businesses and individuals in private industry have been motivated to improve printing presses, invent typesetters and computer-driven laser composition devices, radio and television broadcasting, then color reception, two-way cable transmission communications satellites, video cassettes — the list goes on. Thousands of businesses and institutions are involved. In many ways, we are faced not with a problem of concentration but with a problem in being able to cope with the vast diversity of forms and content of the mass media.

Although not all critics of the perceived trend to ownership concentration believe the solution lies in government control, inevitably any actions they suggest will have to be taken by the federal government. Before we get to that point, it would be well to first consider to what extent such concentration exists, in what form, with what effects. We might also benefit from agreeing on what in fact is concentration: should it refer to a geographical market, a media segment such as newspapers or books, or should it refer to the entire realm of mass communications? *Who Owns the Media?* takes a long first step in addressing these questions.

FOOTNOTES

1. Edwin Emery and Michael Emery, *The Press in America*, 4th ed. (Englewood Cliffs, N.J.: Prentice-Hall, 1978), p. 69.

2. Ibid., p. 70.

3. Ibid., p. 68.

4. "FTC to Take on Media Concentration," *Advertising Age*, July 24, 1978, p. 1. Statement is from Alan K. Palmer, deputy director of the Bureau of Competition.

5. Ibid., p. 94.

6. I. William Hill, "Justice Department Probes Gannett-Combined Merger," *Editor & Publisher*, March 24, 1979, p. 11. Quotes John H. Shenefield, assistant attorney general for antitrust.

7. For some of the better treatments on the subject by economists, see Bruce M. Owen, *Economics and Freedom of Expression* (Cambridge, Mass.: Ballinger Publishing Co., 1975); James N. Dertouzos, "Media Conglomerates: Chains, Groups and Cross Ownership," discussion paper prepared for the FTC Media Symposium, Washington, D.C., December 14-15, 1978; James N. Rosse, "Economic Limits of Press Responsibility," *Studies in Industry Economics*, Department of Economics, Stanford University, 1975.

8. See, for example, William L. Rivers and Wilbur Schramm, *Responsibility in Mass Communication*, rev. ed. (New York: Harper & Row, 1969); Commission on the Freedom of the Press, *A Free and Responsible Press* (Chicago: University of Chicago Press, 1948); Gerald Gross, ed., *The Responsibility of the Press* (New York: Simon & Schuster, A Clarion Book, 1966).

2

Newspapers

The newspaper industry in the United States was born on September 25, 1690 with the publication of the short-lived *Publick Occurrences Both Foreign and Domestick*. By 1978 the value of industry receipts was an estimated $14.8 billion, making it the largest segment of the mass media industry. As a comparison, value of receipts for periodical publishers was $6.6 billion and for book publishers, $4.8 billion.

GENERAL CHARACTERISTICS

With its origins dating back to the earliest colonial days, it should not be surprising that the newspaper industry is economically mature. However, Table 2.1 shows a growth that has kept pace with the overall growth of the economy since 1970, although compound growth since 1960 has lagged with a 7.4% annual rate of growth compared to 8.2% for the Gross National Product. Advertising revenue (Table 2.2) also kept up with general economic indicators in the 1970s as well as with the rate of increase in total advertising expenditures. But it is significant that circulation has been stagnant for years, with the daily circulation of 61.8 million in 1978 still below the peak of 63.1 million reached in 1973 (Table 2.3).

There were 1764 daily newspapers of general circulation in 1978, a level that has remained stable since the mid-1940s (Table 2.3). In addition, there were almost 10,000 other newspapers, including about 40 foreign language dailies, 90 professional, business and special service dailies, and 8000 less-than-daily-frequency newspapers. This chapter concentrates on the daily newspapers of general interest.

The newspaper industry is one of the country's largest manufacturing employers. As seen in Table 2.4 employment reached an estimated 386,000 in 1973, declined as the result of labor saving technology as well as the ensuing recession, and then bounced back in 1977 and 1978 to surpass the 1973 level. Even so, since 1960 employment has increased at a much lower rate than overall civilian employment.

Table 2.1   Value of All Newspaper Shipments Compared to Gross National
Product, Selected Years, 1960 to 1978 (Index: 1970 = 100)

Year	GNP (current billions)	Growth Index	Year to year % increase	Value of receipts (billions)	Growth Index	Year to year % increase
1960	$ 506.0	52	—	$ 4.1	59	—
1965	688.1	70	36.0	5.2	74	26.8
1970	982.4	100	42.7	7.0	100	34.6
1971	1,063.4	108	8.2	7.4	106	5.7
1972	1,171.1	119	10.1	8.3	119	12.2
1973	1,306.6	133	11.6	8.9	127	7.2
1974	1,412.9	144	8.1	9.6	137	7.9
1975	1,528.8	156	8.2	10.5	150	4.2
1976	1,706.5	174	11.6	11.7	167	12.0
1977	1,889.6	192	10.7	13.3*	190	13.7
1978	2,107.0	214	11.5	14.8*	211	10.4
Compound annual % increase 1960-1978	8.2			7.4		

*Estimates of *Industry and Trade Administration,* U.S. Department of Commerce.

Sources: GNP: U.S. Bureau of Economic Analysis.
Newspaper Shipments: U.S. Department of Commerce, *U.S. Industrial Outlook,* 1979.

Table 2.2   Newspaper Advertising Revenues Compared to Total Advertising
Expenditures and Gross National Product, Selected Years,
1945 to 1978 (Index: 1970 = 100)

Year	Total Advertising (millions)	Total Advertising Index	Total Newspaper Share (millions)	Newspaper Advertising Index	GNP Growth Index
1945	$ 2,875	15	$ 921	16	22
1950	5,710	29	2,076	36	29
1955	9,194	47	3,088	54	41
1960	11,932	61	3,703	64	52
1965	15,255	78	4,457	78	70
1970	19,600	100	5,745	100	100
1975	28,230	146	8,442	147	156
1976	33,720	175	10,022	174	174
1977	38,120	197	11,132	194	192
1978	43,740[a]	223	12,690[a]	221	214

a. Preliminary.

Sources: GNP: U.S. Bureau of Economic Analysis.
Advertising: McCann Erickson Advertising Agency, Inc., New York, N.Y.,
published by *Advertising Age.*

Production workers account for about two-fifths of this work force and the proportion has been declining.

Profitability

If interest in buying and owning newspapers is any positive indicator of the financial health of a business, the rapid rate with which newspapers are being bought at increasingly higher multiples of dollars per reader or earnings is a sign of a prosperous industry. Table 2.5 lists the revenues and profits for publicly held companies that derive a substantial portion of their revenue from newspaper operations. Net profit margins ranged from about 18.5% for the Thomson papers to 3.2% for The New York Times Company. Even so, the median percentage return on sales for this group was 9.6% in 1978, twice the median margin for the *Fortune* 500 industrial companies. Only the strike-afflicted Times Company was below the *Fortune* median.

Table 2.6 compares this group of newspaper firms with the median net profit margins for selected groups from the *Fortune* list for 1978. The newspapers equalled or outperformed all industry categories. Revenues and profits for 1978 were showing strong gains.

Table 2.3   Daily Newspapers Circulation in the U.S., Selected Years, 1920-1978

	Total Daily		Sunday	
	Number	Circulation	Number	Circulation
1920	2,042	27,791	522	17,084
1930	1,942	39,589	521	26,413
1940	1,878	41,132	525	32,371
1950	1,772	53,829	549	46,582
1960	1,763	58,882	563	47,699
1970	1,748	62,108	586	49,217
1971	1,749	62,231	540	49,665
1972	1,761	62,510	603	49,339
1973	1,774	63,147	634	51,717
1974	1,768	61,877	641	51,679
1975	1,756	60,655	639	51,096
1976	1,762	60,977	650	51,565
1977	1,759	61,712	668	52,079
1978	1,764	61,836	679	53,186

Sources: *Editor & Publisher International Year Book,* annual editions.
   1977 and 1978: Audit Bureau of Circulation.

Table 2.4   Newspaper Employment Compared to Total U.S. Civilian Employment, Selected Years, 1946-1978 (Index: 1960 = 100)

Year	Newspaper Employment (thousands)	Growth Index	Total U.S. Civilian Employment (thousands)	Growth Index
1946	248	76	57,039	86
1960	325	100	65,778	100
1965	345	106	71,088	108
1970	373	115	78,627	120
1971	370	114	79,120	120
1972	380	117	81,702	124
1973	386	119	84,409	128
1974	385	118	85,936	131
1975	379	117	84,786	129
1976	383	118	87,485	133
1977	393	121	90,546	138
1978	399[a]	123	93,200[b]	142

a. Estimate.
b. April average.

Sources: U.S. Bureau of Labor Statistics, *Employment and Earnings,* monthly.
        U.S. Industrial Outlook 1979.

Consolidation

By oligopolistic standards, the newspaper industry was still relatively diversely held, at least in 1972 (the 1977 Census of Manufacturers was not available when this was published in mid-1979). Whereas the four largest firms in the newspaper industry accounted for 17% of total dollar shipments in 1972, the four largest aircraft manufacturers controlled 59%, radio and television set manufacturers 49%, paper mills 24%, bread and cake bakers 29%. Between 1947 and 1972, concentration of ownership of newspapers by this measure actually decreased, while the eight largest increased from 26% of shipments to 28%. Also, Table 2.7 indicates that newspaper publishing was less concentrated than its allied publishing industries.

COMPETITION AND GROUP OWNERSHIP

This section looks at the effects the lack of competition may have in one-newspaper cities and what the roles of various group owners may be. A "group" is defined as the ownership of two or more daily newspapers in different cities by a single firm or individual. Newspaper competition refers to separate ownership of two or more general interest daily newspapers in the same city. It will be seen, however, that "competition" may also be given a broader definition.

Background

In the heyday of multi-newspaper cities and many independent owners, newspapers were thin — even big city papers were often only eight pages in 1900.[1] Type was still hand set until the Linotype came into widespread use about the same time. Many daily newspapers were designed to appeal to a select group, and there was a newspaper that expressed the political views of seemingly every faction that sprang up. Newspapers did not really compete for the same audiences. Bennett wrote in his first issue of the *Herald* in 1835:

> There are in this city at least 150,000 persons who glance over one or more newspapers every day and only 42,000 daily sheets are issued to supply them. We have plenty of room, therefore, without jostling neighbors, rivals, or friends, to pick up at least 20,000 or 30,000 for the *Herald*, and leave something for those who come after us.[2]

Today, a newspaper can grow primarily by taking a subscriber from another newspaper. Moreover, the cost of newer and faster presses, Linotypes and then other technology, and the demands of the new

Table 2.5   Revenue and Profit for Publicly Owned Newspaper-Owning Firms, 1978

	1978 Revenue (thousands)	Net Profit (thousands)	% Return on Sales
Affiliated	$ 159,801	$ 8,974	5.6%
Capital Cities	367,476	54,033	14.8
Dow Jones	363,601	44,248	12.1
Gannett	690,128	83,104	12.0
Harte-Hanks	184,560	15,737	8.5
Knight-Ridder	878,875	76,756	8.7
Lee	104,690	15,914	15.2
Media General	243,699	17,972	7.4
Multimedia	110,630	15,601	14.1
New York Times	491,558	15,550	3.2
Thomson[a]	306,476	56,559	18.5
Times Mirror	1,427,931	125,147[b]	8.8
Washington Post	520,398	49,720	9.6
Median			9.6
Fortune 500 Median			4.8

a. In Canadian dollars.
b. After profit from sale of forest products assets.
Sources: Company financial statements. *Fortune,* May 7, 1979.

advertisers in the 1880s for circulation, brought about economies of scale which demanded a newspaper sold at a low price to a mass audience. The cost of entry increased as well. Increased specialization required by the technology of 1900 reduced the extent to which newspapers could depend on job printing during off hours as a means of subsidizing competing newspapers.[3]

Improved transportation made it possible for a single paper to distribute to a larger territory, and the telephone and telegraph also aided the same papers in covering the further away suburbs. Advertisers could also depend on customers patronizing their stores from a broader area and could therefore make use of the broadened circulation. Other trends during the beginning of the 20th century, as identified by Mott, include:[4]

1) A decline in the political partnership which had demanded that each group have a newspaper representing its view resulted in a need for fewer newspapers.

2) Advertisers found it cheaper to buy space in one general circulation newspaper than in several with overlapping circulation.

3) The Associated Press' rules for new memberships, providing exclusive territorial franchises; made acquisition of a newspaper with membership the easiest way for a nonmember in the same market to join.

Table 2.6   Median Return on Sales, Selected *Fortune* 500 Manufacturing Industries, Plus Newspapers, 1978

Industry	Median Profit Margin
Newspapers*	9.6%
Broadcasting and Motion Picture production and distribution	9.6
Pharmaceuticals	8.7
Printing and Publishing	8.4
Mining	8.1
Office Equipment (incl. computers)	7.9
Tobacco	6.4
Paper and Wood Products	5.3
Motor Vehicles and Parts	4.2
Apparel	3.3
Food	2.8
All Industries	4.8

*Newspapers from Table 2.5.

Source: *Fortune*, May 7, 1979

Table 2.7   Share of Total Dollar Shipments by Largest Firms in Publishing
Industries, 1947 to 1972

Year	Newspapers	Periodicals	Book Publishing
1947			
4 largest companies	21%	34%	18%
8 largest	26	43	29
50 largest	N.A.	N.A.	N.A.
1958			
4 largest companies	17	31	16
8 largest	24	41	29
50 largest	51	69	69
1963			
4 largest companies	15	28	20
8 largest	22	42	33
50 largest	52	73	76
1967			
4 largest companies	16	24	20
8 largest	25	37	32
50 largest	56	72	77
1972			
4 largest companies	17	26	19
8 largest	28	38	31
50 largest	60	69	77

N.A.—Not Available.

Source: U.S. Bureau of Census, Census of Manufacturers.

Radio, then television, made inroads into newspaper functions.
Perhaps the most significant factor is that with increasing competition
from newer media, newspapers are still considered an important mass
medium.

Confidence in the future of the daily newspaper can be demonstrated
in no better way than in the rate at which firms are spending to acquire
new newspaper properties. In 1978, 53 daily newspaper properties
changed hands. Forty-six of these were purchased by group owners,
including five chains being purchased by larger chains, such as the
acquisition of Combined Communications, Inc. with its two papers, by
Gannett. But the total of new chain-owned properties also includes 33
papers previously owned by independent firms, continuing the trend of
the disappearance of the independent newspaper.[5] In 1923, for
example, there were 31 newspaper groups publishing 153 papers. By
1954, that number of chains had tripled to 95 and by 1978, 167 groups
published an aggregate of 1,098 newspapers accounting for 62% of all
daily newspapers.[6]

As newspaper groups have grown, competition among newspapers within cities has diminshed. Table 2.8 follows the steady decline in the number of cities with competing papers. In 1923, 502 cities had two or more competing newspapers. By 1979, only 36 cities, or 2.3% of all cities, had newspaper competition.

Table 2.8   Number of Cities with Daily Newspapers and Number of Cities with Competing Daily Newspapers, Selected Years, 1923 to 1978

Year	Number of Cities with Daily Papers	Cities with Two or More Dailies*	% of Total Cities with Two or More Dailies
1923	1,297	502	38.7
1933	1,426	243	17.0
1943	1,416	137	9.7
1953	1,453	91	6.3
1963	1,476	51	3.5
1973	1,519	37	2.4
1978	1,536	35	2.3

*Under separate ownership.

Sources: James Rosse, Bruce M. Owen, and James Dertouzos, "Trends in the Daily Newspaper Industry, 1923-1973," Studies in Industry Economics, No. 57, Dept. of Economics, Stanford University, p. 30, Table 9. 1978: *Editor & Publisher International Year Book, 1978.*

Table 2.9 identifies the cities with competitive newspapers. In addition to the 36 cities that have newspapers under separate ownership, another 20 cities have newspapers that operate under the agency shop provision of the Newspaper Preservation Act (see pp. 45-46). Thus, although in each case a single firm handles all business and production for the two papers, there are still separate firms that own and manage the papers themselves, presumably guaranteeing editorial independence. Based on hearings in 1979, it appeared likely that the competing dailies in Cincinnati would have their petition for an agency shop provision approved.

Thus, the newspaper industry is concerned with two related trends in ownership: 1) the apparently increased concentration of ownership, and 2) the decrease in intracity newspaper competition. Table 2.8, however, shows that, ironically, *more* cities had at least one daily newspaper in 1978 than at any time since 1923.

Table 2.9   Cities with Competing Newspapers, 1979

Competitive Newspaper Cities

Anchorage, Alaska
Little Rock, Arkansas
Los Angeles, California
Sacramento, California
Colorado Springs, Colorado
Denver, Colorado
Manchester, Connecticut
Washington, District of Columbia
Champaign-Urbana, Illinois
Chicago, Illinois
Slidel, Louisiana
Baltimore, Maryland
Boston, Massachusetts
Detroit, Michigan
Columbia, Missouri
Fulton, Missouri
St. Louis[1], Missouri
Las Vegas, Nevada
Trenton, New Jersey
Buffalo, New York
New York, New York
Cincinnati, Ohio[2]
Cleveland, Ohio
McAlester, Oklahoma
Oklahoma City, Oklahoma
Philadelphia, Pennsylvania
Scranton, Pennsylvania
York, Pennsylvania
Chattanooga, Tennessee
Cookeville, Tennessee
Austin, Texas
Dallas, Texas
Houston, Texas
San Antonio, Texas
Seattle, Washington
Green Bay, Wisconsin

Agency Shop Cities

Birmingham, Alabama
Tucson, Arizona
San Francisco, California
Miami, Florida
Honolulu, Hawaii
Fort Wayne, Indiana
Evansville, Indiana
Shreveport, Louisiana
Lincoln, Nebraska
Albuquerque, New Mexico
Columbus, Ohio
Tulsa, Oklahoma
Pittsburgh, Pennsylvania
Knoxville, Tennessee
Nashville, Tennessee
El Paso, Texas
Salt Lake City, Utah
Charleston, West Virginia
Madison, Wisconsin
Spokane, Washington

[1] The St. Louis papers have a common printing plant but sell all advertising and circulation independently. In February 1979 they announced they were considering combining these functions as well and thus would become an agency shop.

[2] Application for agency shop pending before Justice Department.

Source: *Editor and Publisher International Year Book, 1978,* plus additional reports.

CONCENTRATION OF OWNERSHIP

Concentration of ownership is not a recent trend in the United States newspaper business. According to Table 2.10, the largest 25% of newspaper firms actually accounted for a lower percentage of daily circulation in 1978 than in 1923. A similar breakdown of the largest 10% and 1% of firms shows a parallel decline.[7]

Moreover, in comparison to other developed countries, concentration of ownership in the United States is relatively diverse. Nixon and Hahn found that the 20 largest newspaper firms controlled 43.0% of circulation in this country. Next closest was Spain, with 54.9%. Canada had 88.5% in this top group and Ireland 100%.[8]

The desire to own groups of newspapers — for whatever reasons — has long been compelling. E.W. Scripps started his in the 1880s. By 1900, there were eight major chains, including Scripps-McCrae, Booth, Hearst, Pulitzer, and the Ochs papers. In 1908, Frank Munsey's assessment of the newspaper glut was:

> There is no business that cries so loud for organization and combination as that of newspaper publishing. The waste under existing conditions is frightful and the results miserably less than they could be made.[9]

Although the data in Table 2.11 clearly show a steady increase in the number of group owners and the number of dailies they control, no chain in 1978 held the potential impact in total circulation as did Hearst at its circulation peak in 1946. In that year, its newspapers had a combined circulation of 5.3 million, or 10.4% of total daily circulation. In 1978, the largest chain, Knight-Ridder, had a circulation of only 3.7 million, accounting for 6.1% of all daily circulation. As seen in Table 2.12 Gannett, with the largest number of dailies, still accounts for only 5.5% of daily circulation. The group of selected chains in Table 2.12 accounted for 20.4% of daily circulation in 1946 and 23.2% 32 years later.

Much of the activity of these groups over the years has involved swapping properties. As some chains have grown, others have shrunk or disappeared. The Hearst chain has either bought or established 42 dailies, merging some, selling others, suspending several. In 1940 there were 17 Hearst papers, leading all chains in combined circulation.[10] By 1978, there were only 10 Hearst newspapers (two small dailies having just been added), seventh in total circulation. At one time, Frank Munsey had six newspapers in New York, Washington, Baltimore and Philadelphia. They were all merged, sold or suspended.[11] The trend in groups since the end of World War II has been upward, but it should be

Table 2.10 Percentage of Total Daily Circulation Accounted for by Smallest 25% and Largest 25%, 10% and 1% of Newspaper Firms, Selected Years, 1923-1978

	Smallest 25%	Largest 25%	Largest 10%	Largest 1%
1923	2.2	82.5	64.9	22.6
1933	2.2	84.2	67.4	23.2
1943	2.2	84.3	66.6	22.4
1953	2.3	83.6	66.6	21.0
1963	2.4	83.0	65.7	22.1
1973	2.8	80.4	66.3	20.6
1978	3.0	78.9	61.3	19.8

Source: Rosse, et al, "Trends in the Daily Newspaper Industry 1923-1973," p. 28. 1978 data added by author.

Table 2.11 Number of Newspaper Groups and Dailies They Control, Selected Years, 1910 to 1978

Year	No. of Groups	No. of Dailies	Average Size of Group (number of papers)	% of Total Dailies Group-Owned	% of Daily Circulation of Group-Owned Dailies
1910	13	62	4.7	—	–
1923	31	153	4.9	7.5	—
1930	55	311	5.6	16.0	43.4
1933	63	361	5.7	18.9	—
1935	59	329	5.6	16.9	—
1940	60	319	5.3	17.0	—
1945	76	368	4.8	21.0	42.0
1953*	95	485	5.1	27.0	45.3
1960	109	552	5.1	31.3	46.1
1966	156	794	5.1	46.7	57.0
1970	157	879	5.6	50.3	63.0
1977	167	1,047	6.3	59.4	71.4
1978	167	1,095	6.5	62.5	72.2

*Before 1954, number of dailies may be overstated because morning and evening editions of some papers were counted as separate papers.

Sources: 1910-1970 — "Number of Dailies in Groups Increased by 11% in 3 Years," *Editor & Publisher,* Feb. 23, 1974, p. 9.
1977 — "167 Groups Own 1,047 Dailies: 71% of Total Circulation," *Editor & Publisher,* July 9, 1977, p. 10.
1978 — "Half of Daily Circulation in 20 Newspaper Groups," *Editor & Publisher,* Sept. 16, 1978, p. 21. Current to Sept. 1, 1978.

Table 2.12 Newspaper Circulation by Selected Group Owners, 1946, 1966, 1978

Group	1946	1966	1978
Gannett	1.2%	1.9%	5.5%
Knight	2.3	2.2	6.1
Ridder	1.1	1.8	
Hearst	10.4	4.4	3.0
Scripps-Howard	4.4	4.8	3.3
Newhouse	1.0	5.0	5.3
Total	20.4	20.1	23.2

Source: *Editor and Publisher International Yearbook,* 1947, 1967; A.B.C. audited circulation, Sept. 30, 1978.

pointed out that of the 167 groups at the end of 1978, one-third owned only two newspapers. At the other extreme, Table 2.13 lists the 10 largest newspaper publishing firms by circulation. These accounted for almost 39% of all daily circulation in 1978, although only 16.6% of total newspapers compared to 32% of circulation for the 10 largest in 1971.[12]

Measured by the number of newspapers owned, the Gannett chain is the largest, with 78 dailies, plus two in the U.S. Virgin Islands and Guam. Thomson is second and buying rapidly, with 67 papers in the U.S. in addition to the newspaper chains in Canada and Great Britain. (The parent Thomson Organization is also being funded by its recent bonanza in oil holdings in the North Sea.) The 15 top firms listed in Table 2.14, although numbering only 9.0% of all chains, own more than 25% of all newspapers.

The nature of newspaper chains has changed over the years. Whereas the early group owners such as Hearst, Scripps and Munsey concentrated on big city newspapers, the new breed of chains focus on the smaller city newspapers — often those growing around the older central cities. For example, the average circulation of Gannett's 78 U.S. papers is just over 45,000, compared to 234,000 for the Hearst papers (before their recent acquisition of the two small Texas dailies). The average size of Thomson's 67 papers is about 17,000.

Effects of Concentration

There is a difference of opinion between those who would agree with Munsey that concentration of ownership may improve newspapers, and those who believe that chain ownership results in fewer editorial "voices," hence more homogeneous newspapers and a general reduction in quality. This viewpoint is expressed by Villard, who wrote:

It cannot be maintained that the chain development is a healthy one from the point of view of the general public. Any tendency which makes toward restriction, standardization, or concentrating of editorial power in one hand is to be watched with concern.[13]

The conflict may be made more real by reviewing an exchange of opinions in the *Columbia Journalism Review,* involving the purchase of the *Honolulu Star-Bulletin* by Gannett. An evaluation of the changes made at that paper after Gannett came in noted that two reporters, including the Washington correspondent, were fired; 12 columns, such as the surfing column and a "Nautical Notes" feature, were eliminated, as were two comic strips; the Copley News Service was cancelled; a final edition was cancelled, moving up the final deadline 75 minutes; 30 printers lost their regular positions and were put on a "daily basis"; three engravers were laid off and overtime was eliminated.[14] Gannett brought in a new publisher who told reporters that the cuts were needed for economic reasons and that the Honolulu paper was fourth from the bottom in year-to-year revenue improvement in the Gannett chain.[15]

Table 2.13 Ten Largest* Newspaper Publishing Firms by Circulation, 1978

Firm	1978 Daily Circulation[1] (thousands)	Number of Daily Newspapers
1. Knight-Ridder	3,742	36
2. Gannett	3,412	78
3. Newhouse	3,281	31
4. Tribune Co.	3,199	10
5. Scripps-Howard	2,038	16
6. Dow Jones	1,920	20
7. Hearst	1,904	10
8. Times Mirror	1,880	6
9. Cox	1,365	17
10. Thomson	1,146	67
Total	23,887	291
% of total Daily Circulation	38.6	
% of all Daily Newspapers		16.6

*These are followed by Capital Cities, The New York Times Company, Murdoch, Central Newspapers and Freedom Newspapers.

[1] Includes papers owned December 31, 1978.

Source: Audit Bureau of Circulation six months ending Sept. 30, 1978.

In a response to this criticism, the managing editor of the *Huntington* (W. Va.) *Advertiser* (which became a Gannett paper as part of the 1971 deal with Honolulu) wrote that the same type of things happened when the *Star-Bulletin*, an independent paper, bought the *Advertiser.* But he claims that when Gannett took over, virtually every member of the news staff got a raise, lingering union problems were settled with three years back pay, and the dingy newsroom was renovated; reporters were given a voice in policy-making and choosing their own editor; there was greater editorial freedom for columnists and reporters, and ad salesmen were given commissions as well as salary. The Huntington papers were encouraged to do investigative reporting, even to the extent of damaging previously "untouchable" community leaders. The editor wrote that the paper is opening up communication channels with the community and providing more leadership.[16]

Whether or not group ownership improves or degrades a newspaper depends on the criteria that are established for making such judgments, the state of the newspaper when the new owner arrives and, more importantly, which chain is doing the buying. Many will agree that the Knight-Ridder organization has dramatically improved the editorial quality of the *Philadelphia Inquirer* and *Daily News* since purchasing them from independent owner Walter Annenberg. Gannett, as just seen, has a more mixed reputation, but generally gets high marks for the quality of its business and editorial personnel.[17] The first priority of the Ottaway newspapers is "to improve news content, editorial quality and public service – to reach high standards of excellence. . . ."[18]

On the other hand, the newspapers owned by the Thomson group are frequently criticized. Its late founder, Lord Thomson, once compared newspapers (and television stations) to a license to print money. His creed was to get the most work for the least pay.[19] There is one Thomson paper that is reportedly earning a 45% pretax profit. "You can't make money like that and still turn out a good paper," warns a West Coast publisher.[20]

To be sure, single newspaper ownership is no guarantee of integrity or quality. Annenberg, when he owned the *Inquirer* and William Loeb, publisher of the *Manchester Union Leader*, are examples of controversial owners of single papers. Peter Nichols, referring to Loeb's use of his newspaper to further his personal causes, wrote of the publisher's "florid, virulent style" in attacking those he opposes in his papers.[21]

Summing up the argument for group ownership, John C. Quinn, group vice president for news for Gannett, notes that while each local newspaper can be tailored to the needs of the local market, it is also part of an organization large enough to have its own national news organization – such as the Gannett News Service, which includes a Washington, D.C. bureau. Quinn also points out that of the 35 Gannett

Table 2.14 Largest Newspaper Groups by Number of Daily Newspapers in Group, 1978

	Firm	Number of Daily Papers
1.	Gannett	78
2.	Thomson	67
3.	Knight-Ridder	36
4.	Donrey Media	34
5.	Newhouse	31
6.	Freedom Newspapers	30
7.	Harte-Hanks Communications	23
8.	Walls Newspapers[1]	22
9.	Scripps League Newspapers	20
9.	Dow Jones	20
11.	Stauffer Communications	19
12.	Cox Newspapers	17
12.	Worrell Newspapers	17
14.	Lee Enterprises	16
14.	Scripps-Howard	16
	Total	446
	Total daily newspapers	1,764
	% of total newspapers	25.3

[1] Includes 16 Walls Newspapers plus six owned by Jefferson-Pilot, of which Mr. Walls is a stockholder and chairman of the board.

Sources: *Editor & Publisher International Year Book, 1978,* plus newspaper, trade journal and corporate reports of acquisitions and sales.

newspaper editorial boards that endorsed a Presidential candidate in the 1976 election, 22 favored Ford and 13 Carter, implying the local autonomy of each newspaper.[22]

Addressing an International Press Institute conference in 1972, Quinn explained:

Newspaper concentration may multiply the anxiety over evil; it also increases the capacity for good. And a publisher's instinct for good or evil is not determined by the number of newspapers he owns. A group can attract top professional talent, offering training under a variety of editors, advancement through a variety of opportunities. ... It can invest in research and development and nuts and bolts experience necessary to translate the theories of new technology into the practical production of better newspapers.

Concentrated ownership can provide great resources; only independent, local judgment can use the resources to produce a responsible and responsive local newspaper. That measure cannot be inflated by competition nor can it be diluted by monopoly.[23]

What Quinn says is not in error. Nor, however, does it prove his case, for it echos a standard argument to support concentration of business in general. The real argument hangs on the goodwill of the people in control. And whereas under individual or small group ownership a "bad" publisher has a limited capacity for poor service, a chain that is prone to milking its properties or throwing around its influence can infect numerous localities with poor or destructive journalism.

The potential danger of group ownership lies in the concentration of financial, political and social power in relatively few people.

The four largest chains — Knight-Ridder, Newhouse, Tribune Co. and Gannett — have 22% of daily circulation among them. Of these, the Newhouse chain is frequently mentioned in the same category as the Thomson group. They "chop budgets and staff, hold investment to a minimum, and wring the paper dry of profits," reported one analyst.[24]

Relatively little empirical research has been done on the effects of chain ownership alone. One study, however, did find evidence that, contrary to the assertions of editorial independence on the part of chain owners, "chain papers were more likely to support the favored candidate of the press in every election."[25] More crucial, however, was the finding that in endorsing Presidential candidates in the elections of 1960 through 1972, inclusive, non-chain papers were *less likely* to endorse any Presidential candidate and that the "vast majority of chains exhibited homogeneous endorsement patterns," that is 85% or more of the papers endorsed the same candidate.[26] The study did add, however, that chains spread out over several regions were "consistently less homogeneous in each of the elections,"[27] indicating that the small, personally managed regional chains tend toward tighter editorial control than the more visible national groups.

Some recent examples of chain owners exerting their unified influence on editorial policy included William Randolph Hearst Jr.'s demand that his papers support the Johnson-Humphrey ticket in 1964 (though he let each paper make its own decision in 1968 and they split 8-5 in favor of Nixon-Agnew). In 1972, James M. Cox required his nine newspapers, including the *Atlanta Journal* and *Constitution*, to endorse the Nixon ticket.[28]

Grotta, in a somewhat broader study of both competition and concentration of ownership, found that in the aggregate "there was no evidence that consumers received any benefits from concentration of ownership through chain acquisition of a daily newspaper," at least of those papers which went from independent to chain during the course of his study.[29]

Why the Chains Keep Buying

There are several reasons why independent newspapers are selling out and chain owners are interested in buying more.

Profit. First of all, they can be a profitable investment. The median profit for the publicly held newspaper groups in 1978 was 9.6%, about twice that of the largest publicly owned manufacturing businesses. It is true that many of the newspaper companies also include revenue and profit from non-newspaper properties, including newsprint and broadcasting properties. But among those at the top of the list — Speidel (when it was separate from Gannett) and Gannett — virtually all of their revenue was from newspaper production.

Scarce Commodity. Second, newspaper properties are attractive because they are a scarce commodity. With a finite market of good, potentially profitably properties, competition to buy them is strong. "Brokers keep calling me on the phone and asking, 'Well, are you ready?'" reports John Northrop, publisher of the *Washington* (Pa.) *Observer Reporter* (circ. 32,753).[30] The alternative of starting a new paper of any size is not attractive. There just are not that many areas that can support a paper and do not already have one. Cowles Communications spent three years trying to establish the *Suffolk Sun* in competition with *Newsday* on Long Island and gave up.

Professional Management. The third reason is that as profitable as newspapers can be, under the professional management of chains they can be even more so. The objective of a family-owned business is often different from one that is publicly owned or professionally managed. Minimizing taxes and cash in the till, rather than earnings per share or return on investment, may be the objective of private owners.[31] With the new technology paying handsome returns in labor savings, groups can afford to pay high multiples on a family-owned newspaper, expecting to increase profits very rapidly through production savings and other cost controls.

As a case in point, a newspaper broker tells of a deal in which a South Carolina newspaper changed hands for 60 times earnings, but the new owner doubled earnings in the first year and after two years had increased profit to the point where he had paid an effective 20 times earnings for the property.[32] Robert Marbut, president of the acquisition-minded Harte-Hanks chain, says he would pay "100 times earnings for a newspaper which wasn't making any money," if he thought it had the potential, under new management, to become a profit-maker.

Earnings can also be increased by bringing in professional managers and using the sophisticated business and financial services many of the chains make available. The Gannett group has a marketing team which is sent to any local paper in the chain to provide in-house consulting to find ways to boost circulation and advertising. Stock analyst Ken Noble explained why this makes a difference:

> I think the motivation of the earlier newspaper groups was essentially to be important people in the cities in which their operations were located. This orientation made them somewhat reluctant to be aggressive in pricing, advertising and circulation rates. The new managers have no such relationships.[33]

The synergy of group management is perhaps best illustrated in the unique nature of Gannett's Westchester-Rockland Newspaper group. A plant in White Plains, N.Y., prints seven of the dailies in the group, including three zoned editions of one of the papers. The papers, primarily afternoon editions, range in size from 10,000 to over 50,000. The papers have some separate editorial staff, but share a common building and production equipment and can afford technology that would be prohibitive to any one of the papers alone. Moreover, certain common features and advertising inserts are combined with local news and advertising, enabling each paper to be something more than it might be otherwise. It has what might be termed a "critical mass" needed for certain newspaper economies.

Cash. Finally, newspaper chains tend to generate large amounts of cash, not only from profits but from depreciation and amortization of goodwill. They also carry low debt in relation to invested capital and compared to other businesses. Times Mirror cut its long-term debt by 16% between 1971 and 1978 and long-term debt divided by equity dropped from 16% to 6%, while cash from depreciation and amortization rose 107%. Knight-Ridder reduced its debt/equity ratio from 18% to 8% and Gannett realized $25.2 million in cash in 1978 from depreciation and amortization alone.[34] In addition, tax laws allow firms to accumulate undistributed profits to buy other communications properties, and as such are exempt from tax provisions on excess accumulated profits. This encourages further acquisition.

On the other hand, Dertouzos reports that there exists little convincing evidence that being part of a group provides any advantage in gaining advertising. Most newspaper advertising is derived from local sources and the small amount of national advertising comes mostly through advertising agencies.[35] Similarly, few chains provide economies in purchasing supplies, and even labor negotiations tend to take place at the local level.

One classic argument critical of industrial bigness is that a national chain can afford to sustain a loss at some of its local operating units in a battle with local independent competition. This does not appear to have much meaning for newspapers, however. First of all, chains tend to buy papers in cities that have no direct local competition. Secondly, in those cities where chains are in head-to-head competition with independent owners, they have not fared particularly well, as with Hearst in Boston, San Francisco or Baltimore or Scripps-Howard in Cleveland and Cincinnati.

Table 2.15 samples some recent acquisitions and, where available, the price paid.

Strategies for Growth in Chains

Newspaper groups have adopted varying strategies for growth. They all recognize to some degree, however, that sizable gains must come through acquisitions, since internal profit growth from circulation and advertising gains and technology savings is slow — after the initial gain from the new technology. Other than this common factor, the chains have several distinct approaches.

Table 2.16 summarizes the size and relative importance of newspaper operations from most of the leading publicly owned newspaper groups, as well as estimates for several of the privately held groups.

Some groups, such as Times Mirror, Hearst, Newhouse, The New York Times Company and Capital Cities Communications, are multi-product firms, with newspaper revenues sizable, but only part of the total. In 1978, newspaper revenue accounted for only 44% of Times Mirror revenue, with other sizable contributions from book publishing (15%), newsprint and forest products (16%) and magazine, broadcasting, cable and other business (26%). The New York Times Company has diversified to the extent that newspaper revenues accounted for 70% of the total in 1977, compared to 83% in 1968.[36]

Other firms, which had stayed close to all newspaper chains, such as Gannett, Knight-Ridder and Scripps-Howard, have expanded broadcast holdings. Both Gannett and Knight-Ridder significantly increased this area of participation in 1978 and 1979 acquisitions.

Other chains bought into the broadcasting business much earlier. The Washington Post Co. had four VHF television stations in major markets and one AM radio station, together accounting for 12% of 1978 corporate revenue — and 23% of pretax operating income. Lee Enterprises received 27% of revenue from broadcast.

On the other hand, for most of its history Dow Jones, publisher of *The Wall Street Journal*, 19 daily Ottaway newspapers, *Barron's* as well as books and other information services, has stayed away from diversification into broadcasting because it "wanted to stay away from a government regulated industry. Future growth [in broadcasting] is conditional on the government license."[37] Only in 1978 did it change its position to a willingness to consider broadcast properties, perhaps

Table 2.15 Some Recent Mergers and Acquisitions in Daily Newspaper Industry

Purchaser	Property Purchased	Year	Price
Newhouse	Booth Newspapers	1976	$300 million
Gannett	The New Mexican (Santa Fe) (18,000 daily, 21,000 Sunday)	1976	300,000 shares of stock
	Valley News Dispatch (Pa.) (44,000 daily)	1976	$9.3 million
	Shreveport (La.) Times & Journal (146,000 daily)	1976	$62 million
	Monroe (La.) News-Star World (50,000 daily) + broadcast affiliates		
	Speidel Newspapers	1976/77	$170 million
	Combined Communications*	1978/79	approximately $320 million in stock
	Wilmington (Del.) News and Journal (140,000 daily)	1978	$60 million
Combined Communications (acquired by Gannett in 1979)	Cincinnati Enquirer (190,000 daily, 290,000 Sunday)	1975	$55 million
	Oakland (Calif.) Tribune (176,000 daily, 290,000 Sunday)	1977	$13.9 million (plus $2.8 million for Tribune Bldg.)
Rupert Murdoch	San Antonio (Tex.) Express-News (149,000 combined daily, 130,000 Sunday)	1974	$18 million
	New York Post (489,000 daily)	1976	$27-30 million
Dow Jones (Ottaway Group)	Joplin (Mo.) Globe (40,000 daily)	1976	$12.2 million
	Essex Newspapers Beverly (Mass.) Times Gloucester (Mass.) Times (12,000 daily) Newburyport (Mass.) News (9,000 daily) Peabody (Mass.) Times (4,000 daily)	1978	$10 million

looking ahead to possible easing of government licensing requirements.

Given these various strategies, newspaper groups have also adopted different approaches to newspaper acquisitions. Almost all would agree with the Times Mirror's Chandler that "all else being equal, the choicest property is one that has a market almost to itself."[38] Newhouse, Lee,

Table 2.15, cont. Some Recent Mergers and Acquisitions in Daily Newspaper Industry

Purchaser	Property Purchased	Year	Price
Harte-Hanks	Wichita Falls (Tex.) Record-News & Times (52,000 daily)	1976	$15 million (for remaining 72% share)
Knight	Ridder Newspapers (17 daily)	1973	$174 million
Capital Cities	Kansas City (Mo.) Star & Times (626,000 combined daily, 396,000 Sunday)	1977	$125 million
	Wilkes-Barre (Pa.) Times-Leader-News & Record (70,000 daily)	1978	$9 million
Lee Newspapers	Kansas City (Kan.) Kansan (25,000 daily, 26,000 Sunday)	1976	$2 million
	Bismarck (N.D.) Tribune (25,500 daily)	1978	$4.8 million for 53% interest
	Lindsay-Schaub Newspapers (130,000 combined circulation) Decatur (Ill.) Herald & Review Carbondale (Ill.) Southern Illinoisian Midland (Mich.) Daily News Edwardsville (Ill.) Intelligencer Huron Daily Tribune (Bad Axe, Mich.)	1979	$60.4 million
Donrey Media Group	Cleburne (Tex.) Times-Review (9000 daily, Sunday)	1976	N.A.
	Borger (Tex.) News-Herald (7500 daily)	1978	N.A.
	Vallejo (Calif.) Times Herald (30,000 daily, Sunday)	1976	N.A.
Hearst	Midland (Tex.) Reporter-Telegram (20,000 daily)	1978	N.A.
	Plainview (Tex.) Herald (9000 daily)	1978	N.A.
Times Mirror*	Hartford (Conn.) Courant	1979	$105.6 million

*Proposed July 1979.

Sources: *Editor & Publisher,* compilation of papers and acquisitions, January 6, 1979, January 1, 1977, December 27, 1975, December 28, 1974, plus publicly-owned company annual reports and press releases.

Gannett, Multimedia, Thomson, Harte-Hanks, Media General and Donrey Media are among the major chains that have all or virtually all of their newspapers in these "monopoly" markets and generally would not even consider the acquisition of a property that faces head-on competition.

Table 2.16 Interests of Major Newspapers Owning Firms and Revenues from Various Sources, 1978

Firm	Revenue (thousands)	% from Newspapers	% from Broadcast & Cable	% from Other Media	% from Other	Number of Daily Papers
Knight-Ridder	$ 878,875	94	2	—	4	36
Gannett[d]	690,128	97	2[d]	—	1	80[f]
Newhouse[d]	1,200,000	80	12	8	—	31
Tribune Co.	897,900[c]	78	10	—	12	10
Scripps-Howard[d]	471,900	95	e	5	—	16
Dow Jones	363,601	91[b]	—	9	—	20
Hearst[d]	556,600	60	10	20	10	10
Times Mirror	1,427,854	44	26[a]	15	16	6
Cox[g]	400,000	100	—	—	—	17
New York Times	491,558	62	2	36	—	10
Washington Post Co.	520,398	47	12	41	—	3
Capital Cities	367,476	42	36	22	—	6
Lee Enterprises	104,690	67	27	—	6	16
Media General	243,699	47	7	—	47	6
Harte-Hanks	184,560	82	18	—	—	26

a. Includes small portion from magazines and other information services.
b. Includes revenue from news services, *Barron's* weekly and *Book Digest,* acquired Aug. 10, 1978.
c. 1977.
d. Estimate.
e. Scripps-Howard Broadcasting is a separate, publicly owned firm.
f. Includes Guam and Virgin Islands.
g. Estimates of revenue from newspapers only. Cox Broadcasting, a publicly owned firm, is controlled by the Cox family, and its sale to General Electric for $467 million is pending in 1979. Cox Enterprises also is seeking to build an oil refinery.

Source: Knowledge Industry Publications, Inc. Compiled from annual reports. Estimates where indicated.

Other firms, however, are more willing to take on the challenge of big city competition, either for the potential big profits they could bring, the prestige involved, or perhaps both. Knight-Ridder, although it has numerous "monopoly" operations among its 33 newspapers, also faces strong competition in Philadelphia, Miami and Detroit. The New York Times Company has a chain of profitable small monopoly market newspapers in Florida, but has many problems in New York. The Washington Post Company accepted the challenge of competition in purchasing the *Trenton* (N.J.) *Times* in 1974. Times Mirror operates most of its newspapers in highly competitive markets. Time Inc., although not a newspaper chain, purchased the ailing *Washington Star* in 1978.

Why Independent Papers Keep Selling

For every purchase, there must be someone willing to sell. Privately held independent newspapers are being pressured to sell for several reasons.

Weak Management. One is rising costs, including the investment in new technology, wages, newsprint and presses. This calls for strict controls and profit planning, which small independents cannot always get because they cannot afford the managerial types who can provide them. "The groups are corralling the bright young people and giving them publisher titles," explains one independent publisher.[39] Groups, on the other hand, can have specialists who can set up control systems for each paper, without any one having to be burdened by full development costs. Likewise, the chains can have production specialists to help in evaluating technology.

Family Squabbles. Nor are some family managements prepared to deal with the realities of the "bottom line." Even at the relatively large *Oakland* (Calif.) *Tribune* (circ. 176,563), family problems led that paper to sell to Combined Communications in 1977. Both the father and grandfather of the present publisher were former U.S. senators and "were interested in politics." With the paper to use as a power base, "business was secondary." Some family members involved in management in 1976 still complained that the paper was being run "more for 'civic pride' than profit."[40] "The idea of a family-owned newspaper in the future is not probable," concludes the publisher of the family-owned *Louisville* (Ky.) *Courier-Journal.*[41]

Inheritance Taxes. Another factor is the estate difficulty. A valuable newspaper property which is privately held is a taxable asset in the estate when the principal(s) die. The estate must pay the tax on the value of the property. If the estate is not well endowed with cash or other marketable securities to sell, the heirs may be forced to sell the newspaper to pay the taxes on it. The 1976 Tax Reform Act, which changed the method of determining the valuation of an asset in an estate, may have been an added factor in some sales in 1976. There was some speculation that Dorothy Schiff's sudden decision to sell the *New York Post* to Rupert Murdoch (for a reported $27 million) was because of the new law which might have put her heirs "in a less favorable inheritance-tax position."[42]

Tax Rates. Another aspect of the tax structure encourages selling. Income tax rates are as high as 70%, while tax on capital gains is less than half of that. By selling the newspaper in a cash transaction, the seller pays only the lower capital gains tax. If the exchange is for stock in the purchasing firm, then the swap is tax free, until the seller decides to sell the purchasing firm's stock. Moreover, in this case, the seller may then control a substantial block of the buyer's stock. The Booth chain, for example, though already publicly owned and a group owner itself, was still controlled by the Booth family. It was made vulnerable to an outside take-over when it exchanged 17% of its stock with Whitcom Investment Co. to purchase *Parade*, the national Sunday supplement magazine. When Whitcom offered this block of stock for sale several years later, Newhouse interests purchased it, giving Newhouse a wedge from which he finally bought total control of Booth in the largest newspaper cash deal ever.[43]

High Offering Prices. Finally, and perhaps most important most often, independent and small chain publishers are simply being overwhelmed with offers and money. Robert B. Whittington, a vice president of the recently sold small Speidel chain, recalls feeling "like a virgin at a stag party" when hordes of publishers came wooing.[44] The *Valley News Dispatch* (cir. 42,093) in Western Pennsylvania, was sold to Gannett for $9.3 million, or $221 per subscriber. Gannett also bought the *Shreveport* (La.) *Times* (circ. 80,090), along with two smaller papers in Monroe, La. (combined circ. 50,872) for $61 million. When Newhouse bought Booth, the $47 per share offering price compared to a $23 a share the stock was selling for on November 5, 1975 on the over-the-counter market and about $30 a share about a week before the Newhouse offer in mid-October, 1976.

Such sums merely harden the attitude of some of the independent owners remaining. They are so tired of being courted that some have stopped attending publishers' conventions. One such publisher of several small papers deplores the concentration of ownership in a nationwide chain. William Block, whose family controls the *Pittsburgh Post-Gazette*, feels that "some chain papers tend to be more cautious about controversy. You tend to play it safe when you don't own the paper yourself."[45]

DECLINING COMPETITION AND THE "MONOPOLY" NEWSPAPER

Of more concern perhaps than the growth of chains *per se* is the decline of newspaper competition within individual markets. Where 502 cities had two or more competing newspapers in 1923, including 100 cities with three or more papers, by 1978 that had decreased to 35 cities, less than 3% of total newspaper cities, with competing dailies. And only two cities, New York and Philadelphia, had as many as three competing ownerships.

The 2.2% of U.S. cities, however, that had fully competing newspaper firms accounted for 28.3% of all daily newspapers sold. This was still a significant decline from 1923, when 88.8% of newspapers were sold in cities with multiple competing newspapers. Table 2.8 shows this steady decline in multi-newspaper city circulation.

It should not be surprising that larger cities are more likely to be able to support competing newspaper firms. Even at the peak of newspaper competition, many smaller towns had only a single newspaper. Table 2.17 confirms that competing papers are many times the size of monopoly newspapers.

The issue in declining competition is whether it reduces the quality of the editorial product, lessens the diversity of opinions available to the reader, and results in a monopoly price structure for the advertisers and subscribers.

Effects on Economic Structure

Ray described the newspaper industry as one that conforms to an economic pattern of imperfect competition: stabilization of prices for both advertising and circulation; price discrimination in charging different groups of advertisers or subscribers differing rates at the same time; and non-price competition.[46]

Owen, Rosse and Grotta all accepted Chamberlin's theory of monopolistic competition to explain what Rosse calls the "isolate" structure of the industry and what effect this has on newspaper structure.[47] Rosse prefers "isolated" rather than "local monopoly" because:

[A] typical member of the industry, alone in his city market, is isolated in the sense that cross-elasticities of demands for his

Table 2.17 Mean Circulation of Competing and Non-Competing Newspapers, Selected Years, 1923-1978

	Mean Circulation of Papers with no Direct Competition	Mean Circulation of Papers with Competition
1923	4,308	22,869
1933	8,077	48,123
1943	12,334	89,079
1953	18,278	134,977
1963	23,779	203,638
1973	28,033	235,313
1978	23,330	215,524

Source: James N. Rosse and James N. Dertouzous, "Economic Issues in Mass Communication Industries," paper submitted to Federal Trade Commission, Dec. 14-15, 1978, p. 57.

products with respect to prices charged by other newspaper firms or by competing media are certainly finite and generally quite small.[48]

Thus, an isolated form is distinguished from a true monopoly in that "not all demand cross-elasticities are zero."[49] Rosse proceeds to document that economies of scale do indeed exist in newspaper publishing, helping to explain this isolate character. In essence he largely substantiates what is widely known; i.e., the cost of producing 100,000 copies of a newspaper is not 10 times that of producing 10,000 copies. Nor is the cost for one firm to produce and sell 100,000 copies of a newspaper each day twice that of two firms each publishing competing papers selling 50,000 each.

There are several areas for publishers of newspapers to effect economies of scale. Perhaps most significant is the "first copy" cost. There is a sizeable fixed cost in editorial, typesetting, plate-making and other make-ready to produce the first issue off the press. Rosse indicates that for a small circulation daily, the first copy cost may be 40% of total revenue.[50] Clearly, the greater the number of newspapers which can then be printed (and sold), the lower the average cost per copy. Second, the cost of publishing additional pages declines as the number of pages increases at any constant level of circulation. This is true in part because the cost of running the press does not increase proportionally to the number of pages printed at the same time. Finally, the expense of distributing one newspaper in a given locale to a group of subscribers is less than several firms each covering that territory for the same number of total subscribers.

Advertisers also have an interest in the number of newspapers in their communities. Publishers derive 20% to 30% of revenue from circulation, which may not even cover the cost of the newsprint and ink used to print the paper. The bulk of newspaper revenue comes from advertisers, whose interest is in reaching an audience they believe consists of many potential customers. Publishers know that they can justify a higher charge to advertisers as their circulation increases. But because of the economies of scale just discussed, a single newspaper in a given location can typically offer an advertiser a lower rate than could competing papers reaching the same total market. This is recognized in part in the combination rates offered by a single publisher of morning and evening newspapers in a city. For example, in 1977 the Atlanta *Journal* had a published open line rate of $1.40, while the *Constitution*, under the same ownership, charged $1.36. But by running the same ad in both papers, the advertiser paid $2.00.

This declining long-run average cost curve, however, is balanced by other factors that produce a practical limit on the extent to which a newspaper can expand. First, a large metropolitan daily faces increased transportation cost and other distribution expense, which may actually increase as circulation extends over a wider geographical area. This can be overcome somewhat, but at a cost in fixed plant, through suburban printing locations. The more limiting factor, preventing unlimited national expansion, is the highly localized demand of newspaper content. As the newspaper spreads out, it must become less complete in covering the local news of various communities and serving the need of local advertisers who are more concerned with agate line rates than overall milline rate.* It is this need to specialize in providing services for a geographically segmented audience and advertiser which ultimately offsets the economy of scale effects and determines the geographical extent of local newspaper monopoly.

"Umbrella Hypothesis"

What has resulted, then, is not *intra*city newspaper competition, but *inter*city competition, as developed by Rosse's "umbrella hypothesis."[51]

The model recognizes that while few cities have more than one daily newspaper, these newspapers nevertheless compete with other newspapers. That is, most regions of the country have a metropolitan newspaper whose circulation extends well beyond the central city, perhaps for hundreds of miles. The circulation falls off as the distance increases, but within this circulation area are "satellite cities," each with its own daily circulation that goes beyond its borders. Dailies in these level two cities may have circulation in smaller communities, which may in turn have their own local dailies. Even within the smaller community, there may be weekly newspapers, "shoppers" and other specialized media.

Figure 2.1 illustrates how each level throws an "umbrella" over the lower levels. The level one papers draw advertising from national and regional advertisers, as well as local in-city stores. They are also the most subject to competition from broadcast media, since they compete for the major national and international news as well as the advertising revenue. Newspapers at the second and third levels compete with each other only in the fringes of their natural markets, but they must compete with the papers above them and below them.

---

*The agate line rate is the basis for the actual cost of advertising per line. The milline rate is a calculation used to compare the cost of advertising in newspapers of different circulation. It is the hypothetical cost of one line per million subscribers and is used similarly to the cost per thousand in magazines or broadcast advertising cost comparisons.

Figure 2.1 Rosse's "Umbrella" Model of Newspaper Competition

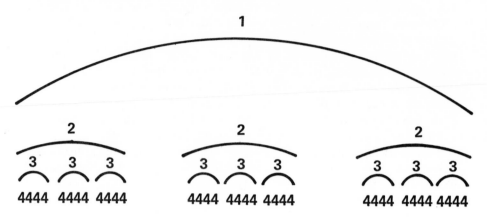

Key:
Level 1 — Newspaper in large metropolitan center
Level 2 — Newspapers in satellite cities
Level 3 — Local dailies
Level 4 — Weeklies and other specialized media

The second and third level newspapers are the ones that exist because of the needs of local readers and advertisers, which cannot be adequately fulfilled by the metropolitan daily. Even zoned editions of the big city papers cannot provide the complete coverage of local governments, school boards and sports teams, or the Main Street shopkeepers in the surrounding towns.

Moreover, it is metropolitan newspapers in particular that compete more than the smaller papers with the broadcast media. Local suburban newspapers, meanwhile, proliferate and absorb fringe area circulation. Thus, although newspapers may not have the head-to-head rivalries in the central cities as they did 75 years ago, they face more economic competition than the term "local monopoly" implies.

Clearly, the owner of a newspaper in the isolated market may still reap economic benefits, especially at the secondary and tertiary levels, where electronic media have less impact. In considering properties for acquisition, owners find that the choicest properties are the ones that have the immediate market to themselves, although Times Mirror Co.'s Otis Chandler may be overstating the case when he says these markets "give you a franchise to do what you want with profitability. You can engineer your profits. You can control expenses and generate revenues almost arbitrarily."[52]

Grotta, who accepts Rosse's contention of economies of scale, proceeds to ask if the larger forms that result from this natural tendency toward combination and merger are "more efficient in practice,"[53] especially in light of Samuelson's assertion that "imperfect competition may result in wastage of resources, too high price, and yet no profits for the imperfect competitors."[54] "Have consumers of the industry's products [the advertising space for the advertiser and copies of the newspaper for the reader] received any of the potential benefit . . . ?"[55]

Grotta found that "consumers receive no benefits from the assumed economies of scale" and that "consumers pay higher prices under monopoly with no compensating increase in quality or quantity of product."[56] Langdon, however, finds some conflicting evidence, at least concerning advertisers. Though concluding that "concentration of daily newspaper circulation in the hands of a single newspaper does appear to raise the general [national] and classified advertising rates to some extent," he tempers this by citing the lack of statistical results for retail advertising levels,[57] the area in which the consequences of monopoly power in a market could be expected to be the greatest.

He further states that milline rates for advertisers may actually decrease following a merger in a market, because of the "dominance of circulation over concentration"; that is, any increase in agate line rates is more than offset by the proportionately greater increase in circulation of the combined daily. This comes from the previously discussed economies of scale: the cost associated with publishing one newspaper with a given circulation is lower than those of two newspapers each with a portion of that circulation. The advertiser also avoids having to pay for duplicate readership of the competing papers.

Langdon's study does find that wage rates for newspaper employees tend to be lower in non-competitive situations.[58]

Cross-Media Ownership

The effects of non-competitive newspapers in a particular market may be mitigated by the existence of competing media, i.e., television, radio and magazines. What is potentially more insidious for readers and advertisers would be the situation where more than one medium in a locality is under the same ownership. This is reflected in concern about cross-media ownership.

Stempel studied the effects of a complete media monopoly in one small city, Zanesville, Ohio.[59] There, the city's only newspaper, radio station and television station were under the same ownership. Comparing Zanesville's residents with those who lived in similar cities with greater media diversity, Stempel found that:

1) Zanesville residents used the news media less and were less well informed than residents in comparison cities.

2) Zanesville residents got less news than residents in two comparison cities with competitive media.

3) Despite this, Zanesville residents used less non-local media than those they were compared with.

4) Nonetheless, public acceptance of the media was high.

Other studies yield conflicting findings on the effects of newspaper/broadcast affiliations. Litwin and Wroth found that media with concentrated ownership covered the news in greater depth because it had more resources. But Levin concluded that television stations owned by newspapers carried less locally originated programming. Although Anderson found that newspaper-owned television stations departed

Table 2.18 Commercial Broadcast Stations by Affiliation with Newspapers in Same Community, 1967, 1971

	1967			1971		
	Radio Only	TV Only	Both TV and Radio	Radio Only	TV Only	Both TV and Radio
Stations not affiliated with newspaper in same community	884	254	N.A.	890	294	N.A.
Stations affiliated with newspaper in same community (majority ownership)	230	15	201	194	16	183
Only station in community	104	2	13	77	1	12
Percent of total	45.2	13.3	6.5	39.7	6.3	6.6
Non-affiliated stations in same community	839	215	N.A.	798	264	N.A.
Communities with only one daily newspaper with ownership in:						
Only commercial radio station	76	N.A.	N.A.	53	N.A.	N.A.
Only commercial television station	N.A.	29	N.A.	N.A.	10	N.A.

N.A. — Not available.

Source: U.S. Bureau of the Census, *Statistical Abstract of the United States, 1978* (99th ed.), Washington, D.C., 1978, Table No. 985, p. 594.

more frequently from the norms of objectivity, otherwise he saw no differences in the news sources and practices of television stations owned by newspapers.[60] At best, it may be said that local cross-media ownership has a neutral effect on media content and operation. At worst, it has serious negative implications. No responsible research has established a beneficial relationship in having the newspaper and a broadcast property under the same ownership in a single market.

Although the effects may be in dispute, as a result of both FCC regulation and the general growth in the number of available broadcasting outlets, the number of distinct "voices," i.e., separately owned newspapers, AM, FM and television outlets, actually increased between 1950 and 1970 by 25%, with overall press control in the top 100 markets having peaked in 1940. Also in 1940, 23% of the broadcast voices were owned by newspapers in the same market. By 1950, the percentage had dropped to 3%.[61] (See Table 3.7 in chapter 3.) Table 2.18 shows the decline in situations where a newspaper owned the only radio and/or television station in a community. Instances where a community had only one television station owned by the only newspaper dropped by two-thirds from 1967 to 1971. In 1973, newspaper-affiliated television stations still accounted for 16.1% of all TV stations in the top 100 markets.[62] Under current FCC rulings, newspapers are prohibited from constructing or purchasing any broadcast facilities that would overlap their newspaper market.[63] Moreover, in March 1977, a U.S. Court of Appeals overturned an FCC ruling and ordered that even existing newspaper-broadcast combinations must be forced to split up. This would affect over 230 such combinations.[64]

Although Sterling warned that the trend of decreasing concentration may have reached its peak, he concluded:

> There appears to be a multiplicity of voices to be heard and read providing news and entertainment daily. When one adds in other media originating within most of these SMSA's, plus the many information and entertainment sources received but not originating in each market, the variety of voices and points of view is almost numberless.[65]

Effects on the Editorial Product

The most commonly expressed fear is that freedom of the press is endangered by less competition, hence less diversity of opinion. In fact, most studies have found that readers perceive little difference between competing and "isolate" newspapers, and researchers have found little to substantiate the view that lack of logical competition itself produces inferior journalism.

Nixon and Jones found few significant differences in content between competitive and non-competitive newspapers.[66] The one significant difference was in reporting news of accidents and disasters, in which case competing papers carried more such news. Another Nixon study found that nine types of news coverage were perceived by readers to be better after mergers than before. Overall, reader attitudes in Atlanta, Louisville, Minneapolis and Des Moines were slightly more favorable after merger eliminated head-on competition.[67]

In another study, Borstell found that competing dailies do not guarantee the "market place" of ideas which Ernst felt justified the need for competing newspapers. In examining pairs of competing papers in small cities, Borstell found only one pair that showed any tendency to compete by "issue," and there the competition was along partisan lines.[68]

A more recent study by Schweitzer and Goldman, partially replicating and extending an earlier project by Rarick and Hartman, further substantiated the body of research unable to find significant differences in competing and non-competing newspapers.[69] Schweitzer and Goldman studied the content and reader perception during a period of head-on evening competition in Bloomington, Ind., and contrasted this with a time when one of the papers was about to fold (moderate competition) and a period five months after one of the competing dailies closed down. They hypothesized that under conditions of intense competition, a daily newspaper would devote more of its non-advertising space to local content and sensational and human interest news and features than under conditions of non-competition. They further hypothesized that readers would perceive no difference in the quality of the two competing papers nor notice any difference in the amount of local news in the remaining non-competitive paper.

In fact, the findings substantiated none of their hypotheses. Local news content *did not* decline when competition ended, nor did the proportion of "immediate reward" items — sports, crime, accidents, etc. And, consistent with Nixon's previous study, the results confirmed that readers found no perceived difference in the surviving newspaper. Readers of the two papers were aware, however, of quantity differences in immediate reward items in the two papers. These findings support previous conclusions in similar studies of competing and non-competing newspapers.

Another study, looking only at differences in pairs of competing newspapers, found that, in fact, there are relatively few substantial variations, although "leading" newspapers in each pair did have some common characteristics.[70] Weaver and Mullins compared 46 newspapers in 23 markets, eliminating operations with joint operating agreements and match-ups where one paper had circulation more than twice its rival. Among the most significant findings of the Weaver and Mullins study were:

1) The amount of content in each of 20 editorial categories was almost the same.

2) Leading newspapers have a larger advertising hole.

3) Leaders used more news services.

4) The leader was more likely to be the newer paper.

5) In format, the trailing paper had larger pictures and fewer stories on page one.

Overall, the authors found "few content and relatively few consistent format differences." This dearth of difference among competing and within non-competing newspapers may have several explanations. It could indicate that the constraints of having to sell to a mass market dictate certain formulas that editors have honed over the years. Moreover, since editors often work their way up, moving from paper to paper, they share a common training ground that they all generally follow when they run a newspaper. There may also be an element of media responsibility that editors feel, particularly when they know they are the only newspaper in town. Publishers also may be particularly sensitive to accusations of abusing "monopoly" power, but they may have also learned that they must meet certain minimum standards to gain subscribers and the advertisers who want a decent circulation and rate. Certainly, it may be a combination of several or all of these or other factors. Perhaps it takes more than even two newspapers competing directly to provide the niche for a paper that can be more specialized, controversial or otherwise significantly different.

Most recently, Hicks and Featherstone added an important new aspect by studying the amount of content duplication in morning and evening papers in the same city under common ownership.[71] In the literature, the two papers would be considered to be a single "media voice," since it is hypothesized that the single owner would dictate content and editorial policy for both papers. Hicks and Featherstone compared the content of the two Newhouse-owned papers in New Orleans with that of another morning-evening combination owned by a small local chain in Baton Rouge and that of two newspapers in Shreveport, one of which is independently owned and the other owned by the Gannett chain. These two published under a joint operating agreement, however.

The study found that there was no significant difference in the non-advertising space (newshole) of the six papers, all clustering around the national average of 34% to 35%. The range was from 31% to 38%, with the independent Shreveport paper having the highest newshole, the evening Baton Rouge paper the smallest.

Perhaps more surprisingly, the study found remarkably little duplication in either news or editorial content among the papers in each city. In no case was there *any* duplication of editorials, columns, cartoons and letters. In hard news and local items, the Baton Rouge combination did have some statistically significant overlap, due in part to joint coverage of state capital news, but the Newhouse papers in New Orleans and the separate Shreveport papers had miniscule duplication. Noted the publisher of the New Orleans papers: "[The reporters on each paper] fight tooth and nail for stories; it is just as competitive as it would be with separate ownerships."

Hicks and Featherstone conclude that the concept of "media voice" might be modified, since in all three cities in their study readers did get two distinct newspapers "in terms of appearance, and no duplicated news. . . ."

ANTITRUST AND LEGISLATIVE ACTIVITIES

As part of the only industry specifically mentioned for protection in the Constitution, the newspaper has been largely, although not completely, immune from judicial and legislative tampering. One important case that did affirm the government's ultimate right to insure freedom of expression was the *Associated Press* case.[72] The AP, a cooperative financed by member newspapers to provide news accounts to all, had a policy of restricting competition by making it extremely expensive to buy a new membership in a city where there were already newspaper members. The government sued the Associated Press on antitrust grounds, and the AP's defense was the First Amendment, as well as the theory that newspapers were not covered by the Sherman Act since they were not engaged in interstate commerce. More important than the substantive ruling against the AP's restrictive practice, the Supreme Court's ruling clearly placed newspapers within the jurisdiction of antitrust legislation. It is surely in the government's power to *preserve* the free dissemination provided for in the First Amendment:

Freedom to publish is guaranteed by the Constitution, but freedom to combine to keep others from publishing is not. Freedom of the press from governmental interference under the First Amendment does not sanction repression of that freedom by private interests.[73]

With the rights of the government firmly established, the Justice Department brought an action against the two newspapers in Tucson, Ariz., which had formed a joint operating company to handle advertising, business and production matters, leaving editorial staffs and policy in the hands of the separate owners of the two papers. Forty-two other newspapers in 21 cities had similar joint operating agreements. Using *Tucson* as a test case, the government charged the two papers with price fixing, profit pooling and market allocation. In 1969, the Supreme Court upheld a summary judgment supporting the government's charge.[74] This ruling brought action on a bill which had been introduced in Congress in 1967 to protect such arrangements. So the Newspaper Preservation Act was passed in 1970, in effect exempting the 22 joint agreements from antitrust prosecution. The Act does, however, limit the right of future agreements, which must be approved by the Justice Department on a case-by-case basis. There are also sanctions for abuse of the legalized combination to prevent further competition in the market, but these have not been applied.

The proponents of this legislation argued that two separate editorial voices were a better alternative than the single voice that would exist if an otherwise marginal paper were merged into a single ownership. The opposing view, held by some independent newspapers, mostly small dailies, as well as *The New York Times* and the Newspaper Guild, was that prosperous suburban dailies and weeklies were replacing these failing metropolitan newspapers. The joint operating agreements could therefore lessen competition within the city and promote an unfair advantage over existing or potential rivals.

Critics of the Act have welcomed a lawsuit by the *Anchorage* (Alaska) *Daily News* to dissolve a joint operating agreement it has with the larger *Anchorage Times*. The litigation was the first such attempt to break an agreement and the *Daily News'* owner charged the *Times* with "monopoly, mismanagement and breach of contracts," all of which, it claimed, have lessened competition between the two newspapers and injured the *Daily News*.[75]

The *Daily News* formed the agreement with the *Times* in 1974, the first new agreement approved by the Justice Department since the Newspaper Preservation Act had been made law. It had to be judged "failing" to get that approval, and statements showed it to be losing $500,000 a year since 1969. Under the joint operating agreement, losses continued at about the same rate. The *Times,* with three times the circulation of the *Daily News*, sells advertising at one-half the milline rate of its competitor. In late 1978 the two papers agreed to dissolve the joint agency, and the *Daily News* established its own advertising, circulation and printing operation as of March 31, 1979.

While the number of cities with competing papers will increase by one with the Anchorage change, it is likely that the Justice Department will approve the application of the E.W. Scripps Co. to establish a joint operating agreement between its *Cincinnati Post* and Gannett's newly acquired *Enquirer*. The case involved the first time a public hearing was held under the Newspaper Preservation Act. Although the government attorneys, arguing before an administrative law judge, agreed with the Scripps position that the *Post* met the requirements of a failing newspaper, they went a step further by raising the question of whether a newspaper could truly be termed failing when the parent company might be financially benefiting from the tax write-offs accorded by the losses.[76] There is some speculation that should Scripps win its case in Cincinnati, it would seek a similar agency arrangement with its *Cleveland Press* property.

Another issue, involving the *New Orleans Times-Picayune*, concerned the legality of a morning-evening combined advertising rate offered by the owner of the two papers. Do not such rates, which may actually be cheaper in combination than for a single paper, invoke price discrimination to the disadvantage of a competitor of one of the combination's papers? The Supreme Court ruled the practice legal, thus making it that much more difficult for a single newspaper to compete with a morning-evening edition operation offering low combination rates.[77] Advertisers would tend to go into the morning-evening combination at a rate much lower than using a morning and evening from competitive firms.

Another antitrust suit involving a similar issue was filed in early 1977 by the owner of the *Sacramento* (Calif.) *Union* against McClatchy Newspapers, owner of the *Sacramento Bee, Fresno Bee* and *Modesto Bee* (all California) as well as several radio and TV stations. The suit contended that McClatchy Newspapers was illegally monopolizing the market by offering joint ad buys between the broadcast stations or discounts for advertisements in all three newspapers.[78]

Newspaper groups do have to show some sensitivity to antitrust laws, however. So far, the Justice Department has shown little activity concerning concentration of ownership, even as Gannett hits the 80-newspaper mark. For the most part, the chains have been careful not to buy papers that have overlapping distribution and thereby lay themselves open to charges of controlling all papers under the "umbrella."

For example, although Gannett's Westchester-Rockland Newspapers provide the basic local papers for a large contiguous areas in suburban New York City, they all compete under the dominating influence of the large metropolitan papers which are widely available in their territory.

On the other hand, Times Mirror was forced to sell its *San Bernardino* (Calif.) *Sun* and *Telegram* in 1970 because of an antitrust ruling based on the predominance of the *Los Angeles Times* in Southern California and the lessening of competition that would result if the relatively nearby San Bernardino papers were brought under the same ownership. The point that geographical proximity, not overall size of the chain, is the key to control, is underlined by the ready acquisition of the San Bernardino papers by Gannett.

There was some talk among industry analysts that Gannett's merger with Speidel Newspapers, announced months after Newhouse bought out Booth Newspapers, might provoke interest on the part of Congress or the Justice Department in the increased size of the chains, but there was no directly related activity. Separately, but simultaneously with these activities, Rupert Murdoch, the owner of a chain of Australian and British newspapers, received considerable visibility by following up his purchase of the *San Antonio* (Texas) *News* with a $27 million purchase of the *New York Post,* and ten days later the acquisition of the company that publishes *New York Magazine* and the weekly *Village Voice.* [79] In fact, the Justice Department did announce a "preliminary inquiry" into possible violations of antitrust statutes in Murdoch's New York purchases. The Federal Trade Commission held a public symposium on concentration of ownership of all the mass media in December 1978, and in the Congress Rep. Morris Udall (D., Ariz.) has been outspoken in his criticism of media concentration.

DISCUSSION

The issue of concentration of newspaper ownership and the proliferation of one newspaper firm cities tends to raise great passions among interested parties. It is easy to find examples on an individual case basis for some abuses these trends may create. On the other hand, stepping back from specific examples yields a more objective evaluation based on the full spectrum of evidence.

First, it should be clear that no newspaper or chain dominates the nation's news dissemination. Even the largest group accounts for less circulation than did the largest group in 1946. The control over total circulation by even the largest chains has changed little over the past 30 years. The three television networks, through their newscasts, would appear to have a far greater impact on control of news flow than any combination of newspaper chains.

Second, economists recognize that there are some benefits to being part of a chain-owned newspaper. But in addition to economic benefits, such papers have the opportunity to reduce their dependence on the wire services by being able to use news from the chain's own bureaus. A legitimate question, however, is how large a group has to be to maximize these advantages. If that could be determined, then it could be argued that further acquisitions by the chain yield no further social benefits.

The tendency toward one newspaper firm cities is largely economic and is due in large measure to the reluctance of advertisers, from whom newspapers derive the bulk of their revenue, to support competing newspapers when a single firm can provide the audience coverage they need more economically and hence at lower total advertising rates. A newspaper has never gone out of business for lack of editorial material. It needs readers so it can get advertisers. The sizeable first copy cost and the expense of distribution over a given territory tend to favor consolidation of newspapers in all but the larger cities.

Moreover, there is no empirical evidence that either chain-owned newspapers or newspapers in single firm cities as a group provide poorer service to readers or advertisers than independent or competing newspapers. Some newspapers — chain or independent — take advantage of their local monopoly status. But there are also examples of how a chain owner improves a newly acquired paper. Certainly the chain owner has the potential to dictate editorial policy. Some do in the endorsement of political candidates (although the question of how much real impact such editorials have is still unresolved) or in ordering certain articles to be printed. Other owners, however, use the same power to demand higher editorial standards. In the end, newspapers are a local product and must fulfill the needs of a community. Most chain owners appear to recognize this and give individual editors and publishers maximum latitude. Furthermore, even one newspaper communities appear to face intercity competition, as well as weekly and "shopper" newspaper rivals.

Perhaps the issue that has been least addressed and that should be a topic for further investigation is the role of the national news services and syndicators. A far more homogenizing effect on newspaper content than chain ownership may well be the standardization of national and international news through the Associated Press and United Press International, with The New York Times News Service a less frequently subscribed to supplement. Clearly the large expense in providing such around-the-world coverage explains the need for a small number of such services. Therefore, the question is, would even three or four newspapers in a single city be providing readers with anything more in national and international news than what is currently coming over the wires?

Policy Questions

With increasing interest on the part of various segments of the government in the media ownership question, there are a number of policy issues that must be addressed.

1) Should there be a limit to the number of newspapers or the total circulation controlled by a single owner? The Newspaper Guild is currently suggesting such a limit. But what is the logical basis for such a restriction? Is a chain with 60 small papers and 700,000 circulation better or worse for competition than a chain with six papers in competitive cities and 5 million circulation? Could the Justice Department or the courts successfully argue that controlling 10% of circulation is "too much" while a computer manufacturer is allowed to have 25% of its market?

2) Is there any way independent owners can be encouraged to hold onto their newspapers? Inheritance taxes on newspapers might be modified or capital gains taxes on such sales might be more heavily levied.

3) In what ways could incentives be given to encourage formation of new newspapers? A limit on newspaper acquisition by chains might be coupled with a provision to allow additional papers that are started by the chain. First-time publishers might be encouraged through other tax or loan incentives.

4) How can syndicators and news services be promoted? Is there an economic opportunity for another national news service? Is there justification for the territorial exclusivity many syndicators insist on? (When the short-lived *Trib* started up in New York in 1978, one of its problems was getting popular comic strips and other features that help attract many readers. Most of the best were already spoken for by the other metropolitan newspapers.)

5) To what extent does the prevailing method of using largely independent distributors affect a newspaper's circulation, and are there changes that could be made to make it easier for additional papers to enter a given market? For example, current laws and rulings prohibit a publisher from fixing the retail price of the newspaper sold through an independent distributor. While it is in the interest of the paper to keep the price low to encourage circulation (and hence attract advertisers), distributors are free to charge what they will, which in outlying areas may be substantially more than the printed price. (In northern Westchester County, N.Y., one distributor charges about 38 cents to deliver the daily *New York Times*, although the newsstands locally charge 20 cents — the list price.)

6) Could the Postal Service be relied on as an alternative means for home delivery at a competitive price? A new rural daily has been distributing home delivered papers by printing early in the morning and drop shipping at local Post Offices, which have the paper in most mail boxes in the territory by noon. But will continued increases in second-class rates make this option prohibitively expensive for a new daily?

There is little that government can do to remedy the decline in newspaper competition other than provide incentives for new newspaper formation. The area of chain ownership is more sensitive and open to structural changes through direct government action. Newspaper owners cannot hide behind the First Amendment on this issue, and may be susceptible to legislative or judicial rule-making. But as noted in some of the policy questions above, government regulators have options they may first employ to encourage desired behavior (such as the tax incentives not to sell a paper or to invest in start-up situations) before they move into the more ambiguous and dangerous realm of antitrust or other explicit limitations.

FOOTNOTES

1. Bruce M. Owen, *Economics and Freedom of Expression* (Cambridge, Mass.: Ballinger Publishing Co., 1975), p. 47.

2. Quoted by John Tebbel, *The Compact History of the American Newspaper* (New York: Hawthorne Books, Inc., 1963), p. 97.

3. Owen, p. 48.

4. Frank Luther Mott, *American Journalism* (3d ed.; New York: Macmillan, 1962), p. 635.

5. "53 Dailies in 1978 Purchases; 46 of Them Go into Groups," *Editor & Publisher*, January 6, 1979, p. 47.

6. "Number of Dailies in Groups Increased by 100% in 3 Years," *Editor & Publisher*, February 23, 1974, p. 9 and "Half of Daily Circulation in 20 Newspaper Groups," *Editor & Publisher*, September 16, 1978, p. 12.

7. James N. Rosse, Bruce M. Owen and James Dertouzos, *Trends in the Daily Newspaper Industry 1923-1973*, Studies in Industry Economics, No. 57 (Stanford, Calif.: Department of Economics, Stanford University, 1975), p. 28.

8. Raymond B. Nixon and Tae-Youl Hahn, "Concentration of Press Ownership: Comparison of 32 Countries," *Journalism Quarterly* 38:13, Spring 1971.

9. Tebbel, p. 242.

10. Willard G. Bleyer, *Main Currents in the History of American Journalism* (Boston: Houghton-Mifflin, 1927), p. 413.

11. Tebbel, pp. 219-220.

12. 1971 figures computed from Robert L. Bishop, "The Rush to Chain Ownership," *Columbia Journalism Review*, November/December, 1972, p. 14; 1978 figure from Table 13.

13. Oswald Garrison Villard, "The Chain Daily," *The Nation*, CXXX, 1930, pp. 595-597, cited by Gerald L. Grotta, "Changes in the Ownership of Daily

Newspaper and Selected Performance Characteristics, 1950-1968: An Investigation of Some Economic Implications of Concentration of Ownership" (unpublished doctor's dissertation, Southern Illinois University, 1970), p. 5.

14. Denby Fawcett, "What Happens When a Chain Owner Arrives," *Columbia Journalism Review*, November/December, 1972, pp. 29-30.

15. Ibid.

16. Letter to Editor from C. Donald Hatfield, *Columbia Journalism Review*, January/February, 1973, pp. 65-66.

17. Bishop, pp. 14-15.

18. Statement by James H. Ottaway Jr., in an address ("Circulation Growth of Ottaway Newspapers") to the Dirks Forum, New York, May 4, 1976.

19. Bishop, pp. 14-15.

20. "The Big Money Hunts for Independent Newspapers," *Business Week*, February 21, 1977, p. 59.

21. Peter Nichols, "Check it with Bill," rev. of Eric Veblen, *The Manchester Union Leader in New Hampshire Elections* (University Press of New England), *Columbia Journalism Review*, November/December, 1975, p. 53.

22. Address to Conference on the Outlook for the Media, New York, November 30, 1976.

23. Bishop, p. 21.

24. "The Big Money," p. 59.

25. Daniel Wackman, et al., "Chain Newspaper Autonomy as Reflected in Presidential Campaign Endorsements," *Journalism Quarterly* 52:417, Autumn 1975. In this study, a chain or group is defined as "three or more dailies in different cities under the same principal ownership or control," p. 413.

26. Ibid., p. 419.

27. Ibid.

28. Ibid., p. 413.

29. Grotta, p. 79.

30. "The Big Money," p. 58.

31. Robert E. Dallos, "Bidding Sends Prices Higher in Newspaper Acquisition Binge," *Los Angeles Times*, January 9, 1977, Sec. VI, p. 2. He is referring to a statement made by Allen H. Neuharth, president of Gannett.

32. "The Big Money," p. 59.

33. Dallos, p. 5.

34. Times Mirror Co. (Los Angeles, Calif.), Gannett Co. (Rochester, N.Y.), Knight-Ridder Newspapers, Inc. (Miami, Fla.), Annual Reports: 1971 and 1978. It should be noted that acquisitions are also made through the exchange of stock, especially when the acquirers' stock is traded at a high price-earnings multiple.

35. James N. Dertouzos, "Media Conglomerates: Chains, Groups and Cross Ownership," discussion paper prepared for FTC Media Symposium, December 14-15, 1978, p. 11.

36. From corporate annual reports, 1977 and 1978.

37. Warren H. Phillips, president, Dow Jones & Co. Inc., personal interview, April 23, 1973. This policy was reiterated by Mr. Phillips as recently as November 30, 1976, but was reversed in 1978.

38. "The Big Money," p. 58.

39. "Family Paper Faces Problems to Survive as an Independent," *Editor & Publisher*, April 28, 1973, p. 11. Quote is from Robert S. Withers, Publisher, *Rochester* (Minn.) *Post-Bulletin.*

40. "A Bitter Family Squabble Put Oakland's *Tribune* on the Block," *Business Week*, February 21, 1977, p. 60.

41. "The Big Money," p. 58.

42. "Dolly's Last Surprise," *Newsweek*, November 29, 1976, p. 84.

43. "Booth Aims to Thwart a Newhouse Takeover," *Business Week*, March 22, 1976, p. 48. "Newhouse Buys Majority of Outstanding Booth Stock," *Editor & Publisher*, November 13, 1976, p. 14.

44. "The Big Money," p. 62.

45. Ibid.

46. Royal H. Ray, "Competition in the Newspaper Industry," *Journal of Marketing* 15:444, April, 1951.

47. Owen, pp. 17, 34-37.

48. Rosse, "Daily Newspapers," p. 2.

49. Ibid.

50. James N. Rosse, "The Evolution of One Newspaper Cities," discussion paper for the Federal Trade Commission Symposium on Media Concentration; Washington, D.C., December 14-15, 1979, p. 16.

51. Ibid., pp. 50-52. See also James N. Rosse, *Economic Limits of Press Responsibility*, Studies in Industry Economics, No. 56 (Stanford, Calif.: Department of Economics, Stanford University, 1975).

52. "The Big Money," p. 59.

53. Grotta, p. 19.

54. Paul A. Samuelson, *Economics* (6th ed., New York: McGraw-Hill, 1964), p. 498.

55. Grotta, p. 74.

56. Ibid., pp. 77-79.

57. John Henry Langdon, "An Intra Industry Approach to Measuring the Effects of Competition: The Newspaper Industry" (unpublished doctor's dissertation, Cornell University, 1969), p. 159.

58. Ibid., Chapter II.

59. Guide H. Stempel III, "Effects on Performance of a Cross-Media Monopoly," *Journalism Monographs*, No. 29 (June 1973), p. 10-28.

60. George Litwin and W.H. Wroth, "The Effects of Common Ownership of Media Content and Influence," (Washington, D.C.: National Association of Broadcasters, July, 1969); H.J. Levin, *The Policy on Joint Ownership of Newspapers and Television Stations* (New York: Center for Policy Research, 1971); J.A. Anderson, "The Alliance of Broadcast Stations and Newspapers: The Problem of Information Control," *Journal of Broadcasting* 16; all cited by W. Phillips Davison and Frederick T.C. Yu, *Mass Communications Research: Major Issues and Future Directions* (New York: Praeger Publishers, 1974), p. 48.

61. Christopher Sterling, "Trends in Daily Newspaper and Broadcasting Ownership, 1922-1970," *Journalism Quarterly* 52:247-256, Summer 1975.

62. Herbert H. Howard, "Cross-Media Ownership of Newspapers and TV Stations," *Journalism Quarterly* 51:715-718. Winter 1974.

63. Sterling, p. 247. See also U.S., Federal Communication Commission, *Second Report and Order, Docket No. 18110* ("Multiple Ownership of Standard, FM and Television Broadcast Stations," FCC 74-104, Mimeo 29942) January 29, 1975.

64. "Joint Ownership of Media Barred by Appeals Court," *The Wall Street Journal*, March 2, 1977, p. 4. Perhaps anticipating the ruling, Multimedia, Inc. and McClatchy Newspapers announced on March 4 that they would swap stations that were affected by the ruling. Others, including Newhouse, are making adjustments in their broadcasting or newspaper holdings.

65. Sterling, p. 320.

66. Raymond B. Nixon and Robert L. Jones, "The Content of Non-

Competitive vs. Competitive Newspapers," *Journalism Quarterly* 33:299-314, Summer 1956.

67. Raymond B. Nixon, "Changes in Reader Attitudes Toward Daily Newspapers," *Journalism Quarterly* 31:421-433, Fall 1954.

68. Gerald H. Borstell, "Ownership, Competition and Comment in 20 Small Dailies," *Journalism Quarterly* 33:220-222, Spring 1956.

69. John C. Schweitzer and Elaine Goldman, "Does Newspaper Competition Make A Difference to Readers?" *Journalism Quarterly* 52:706-710, Winter 1975. Galen Rarick and Barrie Hartman, "The Effects of Competition on One Daily Newspaper's Content," *Journalism Quarterly* 43:459-463, Fall 1966.

70. David H. Weaver and L.E. Mullins, "Content and Format Characteristics of Competing Daily Newspapers," *Journalism Quarterly* 52:257-264, Summer 1975.

71. Ronald G. Hicks and James S. Featherstone, "Duplication of Newspaper Content in Contrasting Ownership Situations," *Journalism Quarterly* 55:549-554, Autumn 1978.

72. *Associated Press v. United States*, 326 U.S. 1 (1945).

73. Ibid., at 20.

74. *Citizen Publishing Co. v. United States* 394 U.S. 131 (1969).

75. Mike Doogan, "Anchorage Daily News Files Suit to Break Joint Operating Accord with Rival Paper," *The Wall Street Journal*, February 14, 1977, p. 19.

76. H. Celeste Huenergard, "Scripps Hoping for Quick Decision in Cincinnati Case," *Editor & Publisher*, February 6, 1979.

77. *Times-Picayune Publishing Co. v. United States* 345 U.S. 367 (1953).

78. "Monopoly Claimed in U.S. Suit," *Editor & Publisher*, January 22, 1977, p. 40.

79. "Dolly's Last Surprise," p. 84; "Press Lord Captures Gotham," *Newsweek*, January 17, 1977, p. 48-53; Dierdre Carmody and James P. Sterba, "Murdoch About to Take Over Post; Texas Papers Thrive on Violence," *The New York Times*, December 26, 1976, p. 49.

Appendix A2

Newspapers Owned by Largest Groups, 1979

(Current to April 15, 1979)

Cox Enterprises, Inc.

Atlanta (Ga.) Journal and *Constitution*
Austin (Tex.) American-Statesman
Dayton (Ohio) News and *Journal-Herald*
Daytona Beach (Fla.) Journal and *News**
Longview (Tex.) News and *Journal*
Lufkin (Tex.) News
Mesa (Ariz.) Tribune
Miami (Fla.) News
Palm Beach (Fla.) News and *Times*
Port Arthur (Tex.) News
Springfield (Ohio) Sun and *News*
Waco (Tex.) Tribune-Herald
West Palm Beach (Fla.) Post

*47% ownership

Capital Cities Communications, Inc.

General Interest Daily Newspapers:

Belleville (Ill.) News-Democrat
Fort Worth (Tex.) Star-Telegram
Kansas City (Mo.) Star and *Times*
Oakland (Pontiac, Mich.) Press
Wilkes-Barre (Pa.) Times Leader

Other Special Interest Newspapers:

American Metal Market
Daily News Record
Woman's Wear Daily

Dow Jones & Co., Inc.

The Wall Street Journal

Ottaway Newspapers:

Beverly (Mass.) Times
Cape Cod (Mass.) Times
Danbury (Conn.) News-Times
Gloucester (Mass.) Times
Joplin (Mo.) Globe
Mankato (Minn.) Free Press
Medford (Ore.) Mail Tribune
*Middletown (N.Y.) Times
Herald-Record*
*New Bedford (Mass.) Standard-
Times*
Newburyport (Mass.) News
Oneonta (N.Y.) Star
Owatonna (Minn.) Peoples Press
Peabody (Mass.) Times
Port Jervis (N.Y.) Union-Gazette
*Plattsburgh (N.Y.) Press-
Republican*
Sharon (Pa.) Herald
Stroudsburg (Pa.) Pocono Record
Sunbury (Pa.) Daily Item
*Traverse City (Mich.) Record-
Eagle*

Gannett Co., Inc.

Arizona
  Tucson Citizen
California
  Oakland Tribune
  Salinas Californian
  San Bernardino, The Sun
  Stockton Record
  Visalia Times-Delta
Colorado
  Fort Collins Coloradoan
Delaware
  Wilmington, *The Morning News*
    and *Evening Journal*
Florida
  Cocoa, *TODAY*
  Fort Myers News-Press
  The Pensacola Journal and *News*
Guam
  Pacific Daily News

Hawaii
  Honolulu Star-Bulletin
Idaho
  Boise, The Idaho Statesman
Illinois
  Danville, The Commercial-News
  Rockford, Morning Star and
    Register-Republic
Indiana
  Lafayette, Journal and Courier
  Marion, Chronicle-Tribune
  Richmond, The Palladium-Item
Iowa
  Iowa City Press-Citizen
Kansas
  The Coffeyville Journal
Louisiana
  Monroe Morning World and
    News-Star
  The Shreveport Times
Michigan
  Battle Creek, Enquirer and News
  Lansing, The State Journal
  Port Huron, The Times Herald
Minnesota
  Little Falls Daily Transcript
  The St. Cloud Daily Times
Missouri
  Springfield Daily News
  Springfield Leader and Press
Nebraska
  Fremont Tribune
Nevada
  Reno, Nevada State Journal and
    Evening Gazette
New Jersey
  Bridgewater, The Courier-News
  Camden Courier-Post
New Mexico
  Santa Fe, The New Mexican
New York
  Binghamton, The Sun-Bulletin and
    Evening Press
  Elmira Star-Gazette
  The Ithaca Journal
  Niagara Gazette
  Poughkeepsie Journal
  Rochester Democrat and Chronicle and
    The Times-Union
  Saratoga Springs, The Saratogian
  Utica, The Daily Press and

  The Observer-Dispatch
  Westchester Rockland Newspapers:
    Mamaroneck, The Daily Times
    Mount Vernon, The Daily Argus
    New Rochelle, The Standard-Star
    Nyack-Rockland, The Journal-News
    Ossining, The Citizen Register
    Port Chester, The Daily Item
    Tarrytown, The Daily News
    Westchester County, TODAY
    White Plains, The Reporter Dispatch
    Yonkers, The Herald Statesman
Ohio
  Chillicothe Gazette
  Cincinnati Enquirer
  Fremont, The News-Messenger
  The Marietta Times
  Port Clinton, News-Herald
Oklahoma
  Muskogee Daily Phoenix
    and Times-Democrat
Oregon
  Salem, The Oregon Statesman and
    Capital Journal
Pennsylvania
  Chambersburg, Public Opinion
  New Kensington-Tarentum, Valley
    News Dispatch
South Dakota
  Sioux Falls Argus-Leader
Tennessee
  Nashville Banner
Texas
  The El Paso Times
Vermont
  The Burlington Free Press
Virgin Islands
  St. Thomas, The Daily News
Washington
  The Bellingham Herald
  Olympia, The Daily Olympian
West Virginia
  Huntington, The Herald-Dispatch
    and *Advertiser*

Weekly Newspapers:

Connecticut
  Westport Fairpress
Florida
  Melbourne Times
  Titusville Star-Advocate

Minnesota
 Pierz, Royalton, *Royalton Banner*
  and Pierz Journal
New Jersey
 Cherry Hill, *Suburban Newspaper*
  Group (10 weeklies)
New York
 Bronxville Review Press-Reporter
 Saratoga Springs, *Commercial News*
Pennsylvania
 New Kensington, Butler County News,
  North Hills News Record (semi-
  weekly)
 New Kensington, The Herald

Harte-Hanks Communications, Inc.

Texas
 Abilene Reporter-News
 Big Spring Herald
 Bryan-College Station, *The Eagle*
 Corpus Christi Caller and *Times*
 Corsicana Daily Sun
 Denison Herald
 Greenville Herald Banner
 Huntsville Item
 Marshall News Messenger
 Paris News
 San Angelo Standard
 Wichita Falls Record News and *Times*

Other States
 Anderson (S.C.) Independent and
  Daily Mail
 Gloucester County (N.J.) Times
 Hamilton (Ohio) Journal-News
 Russellville (Ark.) Daily Courier-
  Democrat
 Searcy (Ark.) Daily Citizen
 South Middlesex (Mass.) Daily News
 Stuttgart (Ark.) Daily Leader
 Yakima (Wash.) Herald-Republic
 Ypsilanti (Mich.) Press

Other Papers:
 33 weeklies and shoppers

Hearst Corporation

Albany (N.Y.) Times-Union and
 Knickerbocker News

Baltimore (Md.) News American
Boston (Mass.) Herald American
Los Angeles (Calif.) Herald-Examiner
Midland (Tex.) Reporter-Telegram
Plainview (Tex.) Herald
San Antonio (Tex.) Light
San Francisco Examiner
Seattle Post Intelligencer

Knight-Ridder Newspapers, Inc.

Daily Newspapers:

 Aberdeen (S.D.) American News
 Akron (Ohio) Beacon Journal
 Boca Raton (Fla.) News
 Boulder (Colo.) Daily Camera
 Bradenton (Fla.) Herald
 Charlotte (N.C.) Observer and *News*
 Columbus (Ohio) Ledger and *Enquirer*
 Detroit (Mich.) Free Press
 Duluth (Minn.) News-Tribune and
  Herald
 Gary (Ind.) Post-Tribune
 Grand Forks (N.D.) Herald
 Journal of Commerce
 Lexington (N.C.) Herald and *Leader*
 Long Beach (Calif.) Independent and
  Press-Telegram
 Macon (Ga.) Telegraph and *News*
 Miami (Fla.) Herald
 Pasadena (Calif.) Star-News
 Philadelphia (Pa.) Inquirer and
  Daily News
 St. Paul (Minn.) Pioneer Press and
  Dispatch
 San Jose (Calif.) Mercury and *News*
 *Seattle (Wash.) Times
 Tallahassee (Fla.) Democrat
 *Walla Walla (Wash.) Union-Bulletin
 Wichita (Kan.) Eagle and *Beacon*

Less Than Daily Newspapers:

California
 Arcadia Tribune
 Temple City Times
 Monrovia News-Post
 Duartean (Duarte)
 The Buena Park News
 The La Mirada Lamplighter

The Huntington Beach Independent
Anaheim-Fullerton Independent
The Orange County Evening News
Florida
  The Broward Times
  The Florida Keys Keynoter
Georgia
  The Union-Recorder (Milledgeville)

*Knight-Ridder owns 49.5% of the voting stock and 65% of the nonvoting stock.

Lee Enterprises, Inc.

Bad Axe (Mich.) Huron Daily Tribune
Billings (Mont.) Gazette
Bismarck (N.D.) Tribune
Butte (Mont.) Standard
Carbondale (Ill.) The Southern Illinoisan
Corvallis (Ore.) Gazette-Times
Davenport (Iowa) Times-Democrat
Decatur (Ill.) Herald & Review
Edwardsville (Ill.) The Intelligencer
Helena (Mont.) Independent Record
Kansas City (Kan.) Kansan
Kewanee (Ill.) Star-Courier
LaCrosse (Wis.) Tribune
Lincoln (Neb.) Star*
Madison (Wis.) State-Journal
Mason City (Iowa) Globe-Gazette
Midland (Mich.) Daily News
Missoula (Mont.) Missoulian
Muscatine (Iowa) Journal
Ottumwa (Iowa) Courier
Racine (Wis.) Journal-Times

*49% ownership

Media General, Inc.

Richmond (Va.) Times-Dispatch and
  News Leader
Tampa (Fla.) Tribune and *Times*
Winston-Salem (N.C.) Journal and *Sentinel*

Newhouse Newspapers

Birmingham (Ala.) News
Cleveland (Ohio) Plain Dealer
Harrisburg (Pa.) Patriot and News
Huntsville (Ala.) News and Times

Jersey City (N.J.) Jersey Journal
Mobile (Ala.) Register and *Press*
Newark (N.J.) Star-Ledger
New Orleans (La.) Times-Picayune and
  States-Item
Pascagoula (Miss.) Press
Portland (Ore.) Oregonian and
  Oregon Journal
St. Louis (Mo.) Globe-Democrat
Springfield (Mass.) Union and *News*
Syracuse (N.Y.) Post-Standard and
  Herald-Journal

Booth Newspapers (Michigan)

Ann Arbor News
Bay City Times
Flint Journal
Grand Rapids Press
Jackson Citizen Patriot
Kalamazoo Gazette
Muskegon Chronicle
Saginaw News

The New York Times Co.

Gainesville (Fla.) Sun
Henderson (N.C.) Times-News
Lake City (Fla.) Reporter
Lakeland (Fla.) Ledger
Leesburg (Fla.) Daily Commercial
Lexington (N.C.) Dispatch
The New York Times
Ocala (Fla.) Star-Banner
Palatka (Fla.) Daily News
Wilmington (N.C.) Star-News

Four weekly papers

E.W. Scripps Co.
(Scripps-Howard Newspapers)

Birmingham (Ala.) Post-Herald
Fullerton (Calif.) News Tribune
Denver (Colo.) Rocky Mountain News
Evansville (Ill.) Press
Covington Kentucky Post (separate
  edition of Cincinnati Post)
Albuquerque (N.M.) Tribune
Cincinnati (Ohio) Post
Cleveland (Ohio) Press

Columbus (Ohio) Citizen-Journal
Pittsburgh (Pa.) Press
Knoxville (Tenn.) News-Sentinel
Memphis (Tenn.) Press Scimitar and
  Commercial Appeal
El Paso (Tex.) Herald-Post
Hollywood (Fla.) Sun-Tattler
Stuart (Fla.) News
San Juan (P.R.) Star

Thomson Newspapers Limited

Alabama
  The Dothan Eagle
  The Opelika-Auburn News
Arizona
  The Daily Dispatch, Douglas
Arkansas
  Northwest Arkansas Times,
    Fayetteville
California
  The Times-Standard, Eureka
  The Press-Courier, Oxnard
  San Gabriel Valley Daily Tribune,
    West Covina
  El Monte Herald
  La Puente Valley Journal
  Lancaster-Palmdale Antelope
  Valley Ledger Gazette
Connecticut
  The Evening Sentinel, Ansonia
Florida
  Jackson County Floridan,
    Marianna
  Orange Park Daily Clay Today
  The Herald-News, Punta Gorda
  The Key West Citizen
Georgia
  The Daily Citizen-News, Dalton
  The Cordele Dispatch
  The Valdosta Daily Times
Illinois
  Mount Vernon Register-News
Indiana
  The Tribune, New Albany
Iowa
  Council Bluffs Nonpareil
Kansas
  The Leavenworth Times
Louisiana
  The Daily Advertiser, Lafayette

Maryland
  The Daily Times, Salisbury
Massachusetts
  The Daily Sentinel and Leominster
    Enterprise, Fitchburg
  Taunton Daily Gazette
Michigan
  Adrian Daily Telegram
Minnesota
  The Evening Tribune, Albert Lea
  Austin Daily Herald
Mississippi
  Laurel Leader-Call
Missouri
  The Carthage Press
  The Southeast Missourian,
    Cape Girardeau
New Hampshire
  The Portsmouth Herald
New York
  The Palladium-Times, Oswego
  The Evening Telegram, Herkimer
  The Evening News, Newburgh
North Carolina
  The Evening Telegram, Rocky
    Mount
Ohio
  Steubenville Herald-Star
  The Evening Review, East Liverpool
  The Salem News
  The Canton Repository
  The Coshocton Tribune
  The Advocate, Newark
  The Times Recorder,
    Zanesville
  Lancaster Eagle-Gazette
  The Portsmouth Times
  Marion Star
  The Xenia Daily Gazette
  The Franklin Chronicle
  The Middletown Journal
  Greenville Daily Advocate
  Piqua Daily Call
Oklahoma
  Ada Daily News
Pennsylvania
  The Express, Lock Haven
  The Evening Sun, Hanover
  The Meadville Tribune
  The Record-Argus, Greenville
  Leader-Times, Kittanning

The Valley Independent,
   Monessen
The Daily Courier,
   Connellsville
South Dakota
   The Daily Republic, Mitchell
Virginia
   The Progress-Index, Petersburg
West Virginia
   The Fairmont Times-West
     Virginian
   The Weirton Daily Times
Wisconsin
   Fond du Lac Reporter
   Manitowoc Herald-Times-
     Reporter

Times Mirror Co.

Dallas (Tex.) Times Herald
The Greenwich (Conn.) Times
The Los Angeles (Calif.) Times
Newsday (Long Island, N.Y.)
Orange Coast (Calif.) Daily Pilot
Stamford (Conn.) Advocate

Tribune Co.

Chicago (Ill.) Tribune
Escondido (Calif.) Times-Advocate
Fort Lauderdale (Fla.) News
Kissimmee (Fla.) Osceola Sun
New York News
Orlando (Fla.) Sentinel-Star
Palo Alto (Calif.) Times
Pompano Beach (Fla.) Sun-Sentinel
Redwood City (Calif.) Tribune
Van Nuys (Calif.) Valley News and
   Green Sheet (4 times weekly)
Victoriaville (Calif.) Press

The Washington Post Co.

Everett (Wash.) Herald
Trenton (N.J.) Times
Washington (D.C.) Post

3

Television and Radio Broadcasting

INTRODUCTION AND SCOPE

This chapter explores the two major controversial topics in the concentration of radio and television broadcasting: ownership of individual stations, and the more general dominance of the industry by centralized national networks. In each case, information is provided first on the development of the various measures of concentration dealt with (including quantitative information where available), followed by a review of government regulatory moves and industry counter-reactions. The discussion is intended as an introductory primer on the issues, trends, and literature (primarily by means of citation) on broadcast concentration — it does not take sides or espouse specific points of view.

The approach is historical in nature, for an understanding of past trends and regulatory moves is crucial to an assessment of current problem areas. Few controversies in broadcasting are really new — and debates over ownership are nearly as old as the industry itself. In December 1923, for example, the Federal Trade Commission issued its first in-depth analysis of monopoly problems in a communications industry with a report on the radio manufacturing business.[1] Some 55 years later, the FTC held a two day public symposium on the issue of concentration of ownership in all of the mass media.[2] Many of the basic policy questions raised in the two events were similar.

We begin with a short historical overview of the rise and growth of broadcasting to provide background for the longer and more detailed analysis of ownership questions. Any division of history into specific periods is arbitrary, but is necessary to better understand development of important patterns. Here we will deal with but three eras: the formative years of broadcasting (to 1927), the hegemony of AM radio (1928-48), and the rise of the more complicated modern industry (after 1948).

Following this background material is a brief discussion of the major arguments for and against government regulatory action to control concentration in broadcasting. The bulk of this chapter then reviews available information on ownership of individual stations (the special problems of entry in broadcasting, development of ownership concerns and the duopoly issue, multiple station ownership, network station ownership, newspaper broadcasting cross-ownership, conglomerate ownership, and a review of the research evidence on the effects of station ownership on economic and programming functions), as well as issues raised by centralized network operation (affiliate relations, programming practices, sale of advertising time and related issues). The chapter concludes with a brief discussion and comment.

Due to space limitations (for the subject of broadcasting concentration is a big one to which a substantial literature and series of regulatory proceedings have been devoted), several topics are either not dealt with here at all, or only in passing. These include questions of ownership in public or noncommercial broadcasting,[3] the effects television advertising discounts may have on concentration in other industries,[4] cable television, most specific licensing or diversification of ownership case decisions, etc. Because broadcasting is by far the most regulated of all the media, this chapter will deal more with regulatory developments than others in this book. It is not the author's intention to develop new insights as much as it is to provide an overview of what we know now — and still need to know — to develop effective public policy concerning concentration trends in broadcasting.

DEVELOPMENT OF BROADCASTING

Traced briefly in the following pages are the highlight trends of the development first of AM broadcasting, and then (after World War II) of both FM and television. We concentrate here on economic and structural matters (including allocation), for such things are most important to an understanding of the ownership issues raised later. An extensive literature provides information on programming and the audience as well as other historical details too numerous to include here, yet often important as background to ownership decisions.[5]

Radio to 1927: The Formative Years

While many of its roots extended back earlier, radio is commonly accepted to have begun broadcasting operations in 1920,[6] with the slow development of "commercial" or sponsored broadcasting about two years later.[7] For most of this initial period, radio combined a relatively new technology with old content (vaudeville, talks, a little drama and less news). Initially seen as a fad or experimentor's toy, broadcasting after 1922 began to take on signs of a lasting business as the concept of station, network, and sponsorship all developed on parallel paths.

For much of this period, and in some cases even beyond, radio was seen as a secondary occupation at best — it was a sideline activity to a main line of business. Electrical and radio manufacturers and dealers, who early in 1923 controlled nearly 40% of the country's 576 stations, operated broadcast outlets as a means of providing entertainment to attract listeners — and thus purchasers of receivers. Educational institutions (72 stations, or about 13% of the total) flirted with the exciting notion of radio as an extension of the classroom — but educational broadcasting was in decline long before the Depression as costs mounted and results appeared inconclusive. Newspapers and other publishers (69 stations, or 12%) built or bought radio stations out of fear (a new competitor for their audience), prestige (first into a new service), or community-mindedness (the duty of a local paper to boost services to the coverage area). Department stores (5%) sought sale of receivers, or just general advertising of their name by association with a station. Likewise, car and motorcycle dealers (3%), music and jewelry stores (2%) and hardware stores (1%) sought the "advertising" value of radio identification as well as some indirect sales.[8] All shared in common the operation of radio for some reason other than broadcasting itself — i.e., to "sell" an image, a service, or a name in what amounted to a direct forerunner of advertising as we know it now.

Advertising on radio as a modern concept first appeared in August 1922, when WEAF, a New York station owned by American Telephone & Telegraph Co., broadcast a 15 minute real estate message for .$100. But the notion of advertising grew very slowly at first, due partially to strong official concern over such use of the new medium,[9] and partially to a genuine search by many in the industry for other means of support such as subsidies from the wealthy, donations from the public and the like.[10] By the late 1920s, advertising (then akin to what would today be termed "institutional advertising" with little mention of price or hard-sell techniques) was almost reluctantly accepted as the best approach to resolving the ever-increasing technical and programming costs of an increasingly organized, and popular, industry. As radio's audience grew, the interest of potential advertisers followed until in the larger stations the pattern typical today was already at work, i.e., programming was used to attract listeners who were then "sold" to advertisers. The need to appeal to advertiser demands became increasingly paramount in broadcast station operation.

One reason for the increasing audience of radio was experimentation with temporary chains or more lasting networks of stations after 1923, some connecting but two or three stations, and some interconnecting a coast-to-coast chain of outlets for special entertainment or news events. Nearly all of these were special arrangements built around single events, until AT&T, using WEAF in New York and its national web of telephone wires, began regular operation of an interconnected network several hours a week, thus allowing nationally popular individuals and groups to be heard on hinterland stations otherwise unable to afford such entertainment. Thus almost from the start a basic dichotomy in broadcasting was becoming apparent — local stations becoming increasingly dependent on national networks.[11]

The single biggest problem in this formative period was not easily resolved — the chaos on the airwaves brought about by inadequate regulation of spectrum assignments, power use, and hours of operation of the ever-larger number of stations. Radio broadcasting was regulated through this period under the provisions of the Radio Act of 1912 which was designed to control point to point radio transmission, not broadcasting. Unable to get rapid Congressional action, Secretary of Commerce Herbert Hoover called four national radio conferences in 1922-25 to deal with industry control and development inadequately channeled by an obsolete law.[12] Prior to May 1923, all stations shared between one and three selected frequencies, each getting a portion of the day for its own broadcast. Then, working with the fledgling industry, Hoover established the beginnings of a continuous "band" of frequencies for AM broadcasting which was last expanded in 1952.[13] Legally binding regulation of stations was needed as many stations "jumped" to different frequencies, power and hours of operation at will, creating chaos on the air and limiting development of the fad to a legitimate business. By 1925, Hoover had been joined by many listeners and even broadcasters in urging Congressional action.

Hegemony of Radio: 1928-1948

In 1927-28 came a series of seminal developments which transformed the radio business: the coming of effective government regulations as the key to stability, development of permanent national networks to tie stations together, and acceptance of advertising as the prime support for station operation.[14] For the next two decades, the AM industry slowly developed many of the structures and processes still evident in broadcasting today, and did it without competition from either FM or television, which began developing only at the very end of this period.

With the Radio Act of 1927, Congress created the five-member Federal Radio Commission (a temporary body until 1929) which moved quickly to stabilize the industry. In 1928-29, the FRC set up a system of AM radio station classification to reduce interference while providing the most widespread service possible.[15] Specific frequency assignments, hours of operation, and power limits were set up and enforced, and far fewer stations were permitted to broadcast at night (when radio waves travel farther, thus complicating interference problems). In an important series of licensing and renewal decisions over a five-year period, the FRC established important operational definitions for the Radio Act's controlling but otherwise undefined dictum that radio broadcasting must be regulated to best serve in the "public interest, convenience, or necessity." Consistently upheld on court appeal, the FRC undertook initial forays into programming as required by its licensing function.

The FRC gave way to the Federal Communications Commission in mid-1934 as Congress pulled the regulation of all electrical communications together in a new seven-member body with wider regulatory responsibilities. The new commission continued to make important strides in technical and allocation affairs (as FM and then VHF television came out of the laboratory for 1941 commercial operation approval, and then again during World War II in an important series of hearings that led to adjustments in allocations for all three broadcast services),[16] but increasingly turned its attention to the business and programming affairs of broadcasting stations. The FCC developed concerns over network and other ownership patterns in radio (see below), expressing interest in local, live, and public affairs programming (which seemed to be diminishing in quantity if not quality as network and advertiser dominance of the industry developed apace), and expressed specific worries over questionable programming types and practices. It also questioned advertising procedures of stations and networks.[17]

Underlying virtually all of these two decades of developing regulation was an FRC/FCC concern with local station service to local communities. "In the context of broadcasting, localism means three things: local ownership of broadcast facilities, a preference for smaller as opposed to larger service areas for each station, and actual program control and selection being exercised at the station level."[18] Allocation plans for radio and later television were based on this policy (which usually meant less overall choice of service, but did provide one or more locally based services instead), as was rising FCC criticism of centralized programming by networks. The alternative may have been six or seven regional or national stations instead of the two or three local ones in each market.

The other important structural addition to broadcasting was the rise to dominance of national networks. The Radio Corporation of America created NBC as a wholly owned subsidiary in 1926, and it was soon operating two parallel networks in competition with the Columbia

Broadcasting System (CBS) and the weaker Mutual cooperative network, the latter serving mainly smaller stations in more rural areas. The American Broadcasting Company (ABC) appeared only at the very end of this period, its creation due to government action (see below).

By providing a national audience, networks attracted large advertising accounts, and were thus able to provide program variety and quality unavailable to any single station. The key to radio success soon was seen to be affiliation with one or more national networks. In 1927 only 6% of stations were network affiliated, but a decade later this jumped to 46%. Nearly all stations (97%) were network affiliates in the peak year of 1947.[19] Competitive pressures bound stations to networks for up to five years, while networks were bound to their affiliates for but a year at a time. Large chunks of station time were assigned to networks by means of "option time" which effectively gave networks final say on what local stations programmed.

Paced by regulation and the structure provided by networks as well as by increasingly sophisticated methods of audience research ("ratings" were commonplace by the 1930s), radio advertising became more common in the late 1920s, of considerable importance in the 1930s,

Table 3.1   Indicators of Broadcasting's Economic and Structural
Development: 1950-1977

	AM Radio			
	1950	1960	1970	1977
Number commercial stations	2061	3431	4267	4472
Number educational stations	25	25	25	25
Total number of stations	2086	3456	4292	4497
% network affiliates	56%	33%	50%	62%
Number employed	52,000	51,700	65,000	70,500
Total revenues (in millions)	$444.5	$597.7	$1077.4	$1845.9
Total pre-tax earnings (in millions)	$68.2	$45.9	$104.0	$204.4
% total advertising exp.	11%	6%	7%	7%*
% families with receivers	95%	96%	98%	99%
FCC Budget	$6.7	$10.5	$24.5	$46.7*
FCC employees	1285	1396	1537	2136*

* 1976

N.B.   This and other tables compile data from many sources, including FCC reports. Full citations are provided in the two sources listed.

and dominant in many ways by the 1940s. In 1927 about a fifth of radio network time was sponsored, while by 1931 more than 36% was, and by the early war years the majority of network time was sold to advertisers. Advertising agencies moved to a central position in the industry, dominating programming decisions as well as advertising on the network level by the mid-1930s. Given inflation, specific gross billing figures are misleading today — but radio's proportion of the total U.S. advertising dollar climbed from about 7% in 1935 to 15% in 1945, then declined a bit to 12% in 1947 as newspapers rebounded with the end of wartime paper shortages.

The central role played by national networks is shown by the fact that as early as 1937 the networks and their owned and operated stations took in fully half the industry income that year, and still accounted for 25% in the much larger industry of 1947, leaving the remaining hundreds of other stations to share the rest.[20] Naturally, larger stations in bigger markets (especially the 50,000-watt clear channel stations, 10 of which were network owned) made more money — but their profit margins were also substantially larger than those of the average station.

Table 3.1, cont.   Indicators of Broadcasting's Economic and Structural Development: 1950-1977

FM Radio				Television			
1950	1960	1970	1977	1950	1960	1970	1977
733	688	2184	2837	97	515	677	728
48	162	413	839		44	185	256
781	850	2597	3676	98	559	862	984
—	—	—	—	98%	96%	84%	84%
—	1300	6100	15,900	14,000	40,600	58,400	67,200
$2.8	$9.4	$84.9	$428.7	$105.9	$1268.6	$2808.2	$5889.0
—	—	($11.1)	$41.6	($9.2)	$244.1	$453.8	$1401.0
—	—	—	—	3%	13%	18%	20%
—	10%	74%	95%	9%	87%	95%	98%
(See under AM)				(See under AM)			
(See under AM)				(See under AM)			

Sources: Christopher H. Sterling and Timothy R. Haight, *The Mass Media: Aspen Institute Guide to Communications Industry Trends* (New York: Praeger Special Studies, 1978) for all except FCC budget and employee data; Christopher H. Sterling and John M. Kittross, *Stay Tuned: A Concise History of American Broadcasting* (Belmont, Calif.: Wadsworth Publishing Co., 1978) for data on FCC employees and budget.

Regulation, networks, and advertising income contributed to an industry that grew fairly slowly at first (due to regulatory decisions and then Depression economy problems). The number of stations broadcasting declined from 680 just as the FRC began work, through most of the 1930s. There were 831 stations by early 1941, just over 900 by the time the war freeze on most station construction came to an end. But as AM's post-war expansion got underway, the number of stations jumped to more than 1600 at the end of 1947.[21] By the early 1930s, the operation of stations became a full-time occupation and a degree of ownership centralization set in as the economic promise of radio became evident. Although in 1939 networks owned 4% and newspapers about 28% of all stations, their ownership was concentrated such that among the clear channel and higher-powered regional stations, networks and newspapers each had about a fourth and radio-electrical manufacturers about 13% or a combined two-thirds of the total.[22]

Employment in the industry grew from about 6000 in 1930 to over 27,000 by 1941 and some 44,000 in 1947 (including early television workers). Additional thousands were employed in radio equipment manufacture, sales and repair, and allied occupations.[23] Finally, ownership of radio receivers demonstrated the industry's growing importance. While less than a quarter of the nation's households had a radio in 1927, by the time Orson Welles' "War of the Worlds" broadcast scared millions in 1938, 80% of households were radio equipped and more than 93% had at least one radio by 1947.[24] The number of hours spent per day spent listening to radio were up accordingly.

Rise of the Modern Industry

The year 1948 is the dividing line between the essentially prewar AM industry, and the postwar rise of a more complex AM and FM radio and television industry. More specifically, 1948 saw formal establishment of the television networks — and the start of the four year "freeze" on television station applications, both developments demonstrating the rising clout of the new visual medium. Several quantitative measures of broadcast growth from 1950 to 1977 are provided in Table 3.1.

This table only touches on the development of growth patterns in all three media. For example, AM broadcasting grew strongly until the 1960s when a combination of few available frequencies and a determined FCC policy to deflect radio development into FM greatly slowed the pace. While the number of radio communities increased from under 600 in 1945 to over 2200 by the 1970s, many of the new AM outlets were supplementary stations in suburban and urban areas. While virtually all stations (except the 50kw operations) had more power, by the 1970s fully half of all AMs were on the air only in the daytime in an attempt to lessen evening interference patterns. Many others used less power at night and/or directional antennas to limit interference.

Under FCC regulatory care, FM radio initially expanded after World War II, but the limited number of FM receivers — and greater chance for economic gain in expanding AM and TV — turned the medium sour by 1950. Stations went off the air through the 1950s, dropping to just over 500 stations in 1957 before the upturn began again. The decline was speeded by the medium's lack of separate identity, as most programming was duplicated from AM stations. The saturation of AM in major markets, leaving FM the only way to build new stations, and the end of the initial building spree of television stations in the late 1950s helped respark interest in FM. Other factors which have paced its expansion for the past two decades include development of subsidiary communications authorizations (providing specialized services such as Muzak) as a means of income production after 1955, the ongoing high fidelity recording boom, combined with approval of FM stereo standards (1961), a series of FCC decisions which gradually forced FM to program separately from AM stations after the mid-1960s, cheaper and more readily available FM receivers, and thus larger audiences which brought a new flicker of advertiser interest. Only in 1976 did the FM industry break into the black financially, having finally caught up with its rapid expansion and large start-up costs. Advertisers who were happy with AM and did not see what FM could add finally moved to FM with significant portions of their radio budgets.[25]

Television growth was limited to about 100 stations before the FCC's freeze was lifted early in 1952 with its celebrated Sixth Report and Order on TV allocations.[26] That lengthy document, built on the localism doctrine, added the vast UHF spectrum to the already-operating VHF band of channels. Such a divided system would have been bad enough, but the FCC ignored engineering advice and intermixed the new UHF assignments with VHF channels in the same market, thus forcing direct competition of two very unequal services. The UHF problem plagued the commission, Congress, and many hapless broadcasters through the 1950s. Following the FM pattern, television's "second service," after a short initial spurt of growth, went into a decade of decline, only turning the corner in 1965. In this case, the change in fortune was due both to a lack of additional VHF channels for major markets, and to Congressional action in 1962 which required UHF reception capability on receivers shipped in interstate commerce after 1964.[27] Thus, while only 10% of TV sets could receive UHF stations in 1963, well over half could just five years later and virtually all could by the late 1970s.[28] Still, UHF stations generally did poorly economically when compared to VHFs, and networks shunned them as

Table 3.2 Radio and Television Industry Profit Ratios, Selected Years, 1950-1976

COMMERCIAL TV INDUSTRY

Year	Radio Industry Pretax Earnings as % of Revenues	Total Industry Pretax Earnings as % of Revenues	% of Stations Reporting Profit:		% of TV Industry Profit Accruing To:			
			VHF	UHF	Networks	Net O&Os	Total Net	"Other"
1950	15%	(9)%	na	na	—	—	—	—
1955	10	20	63%	27%	—	—	45%	55%
1960	8	19	81	50	7%	42%	39%	61%
1965	10	23	87	66	8	44	36	64
1970	10	16	82	32	4	38	37	63
1972	11	17	86	44	9	31	37	63
1974	7	20	86	47	15	28	45	55
1976	9	24	91	67	14	35	36	64

Source: Sterling and Haight (1978), Table 370-C (for radio) and 380-B, 380-C and 381-A (for TV). Source includes data for all years.

affiliates, forcing them into independent operation, which in television is a grey world of limited profit in most cases. UHF broke into the black economically on a national basis in 1975.

The national networks retained, even strengthened their dominance of the industry in the 1950s, but now it was television as the radio networks declined to mere news and feature services. (Only ABC's split into four formatted networks in 1968 helped to reverse the decline in radio station affiliations by the 1970s). Four networks, including Dumont which had not operated in radio, began networks in the late 1940s, going national when the country was connected by coaxial cable and microwave in 1951. As in radio, advertising agencies dominated network programming in the 1950s until the race for ratings led to the quiz show and payola scandals of the late 1950s, and public pressure to "clean up television." Faced with this, plus pressure from a revitalized FCC as well as rising costs of production and station time, networks took control of their own programming and time sales. Advertising turned from program sponsorship (paying all costs) to "participations," or buying time in television much as advertisers do in print media, with little control over editorial content. Thus the financial risks passed back to the networks and to "package agencies" which produced network series programs on old film lots in Hollywood.

That the networks clearly dominated television is evident in Table 3.2. These profit margins, summarizing vast seas of official FCC annual industry financial data, demonstrate (1) the greater profitability of television over radio, (2) the far greater return to VHF than to UHF stations, and (3) the dominant, though stable, role of networks and their owned and operated (O&O) stations. The latter have nearly always numbered but 15 stations (all VHF, concentrated in the top markets – see Table 3.8), which makes their proportion of total industry profit that much more startling. This apparent economic centralization has led to continued Congressional investigations of "monopoly" in television and to several FCC investigations of the networks.

One overriding trend of the past 30 years has been a clear delineation between broadcast industry "haves" and "have nots."[29] The former are the networks, larger AM stations, and VHF television outlets. The latter are smaller AMs, most FM stations, and all UHF operations. Most of the popular programming, and thus audience and advertising income, accrues to the "haves." The "have nots" in all cases entered the industry after the "haves" were well situated. They have struggled just to break even, often suffering years of declining numbers. As will be discussed later, much of this dichotomy is accentuated by ownership patterns and stems from the FCC's localism guidelines.

RATIONALE FOR REGULATION

Radio and television broadcasting is far more heavily regulated than any of the other media discussed in this book. Under the Communications Act of 1934, the FCC is charged with making effective use of spectrum space by means of allocation to broadcasting and other services. This is performed with "the public interest, convenience, or necessity" as the key, though undefined, guiding principle. In practice, this breaks down into several more specific factors explaining why the FCC regulates broadcasting, and why concern over concentration is a prime aspect of that regulation. The short discussion which follows briefly describes each of the rationales raised, and reviews the key criticisms directed against them, with the broadcasting industry on the threshold of the 1980s.

Spectrum Scarcity

The classic rationale for government's greater role in broadcasting than in other media has long been the technical limitation of usable spectrum space. Potential use of the spectrum depends on priorities and needs at any given time and on technical discoveries impinging on its efficient use. Spectrum which is serviceable for broadcasting is limited in amount as only certain areas have characteristics conducive to broadcasting, and other services compete for, and have been assigned, some of that same space. The result is insufficient space for all who might wish to broadcast, and thus only some may broadcast if any are to be heard (as the confusion of the 1920s demonstrated). This in itself would not imply government regulation. But Congress specifically retained ownership of spectrum as a public resource, and thus services using a portion of the spectrum would have to be licensed for given periods of time while specifically giving up any vested interest in any part of the spectrum. Such a system obviated the normal pricing mechanism as a means of market control, and required some means of objective choosing among applicants to broadcast. Under this approach, a broadcast license is thus a limited privilege — the right to make use of a specific frequency assignment for a specified period (usually three years), subject to renewal if deemed in the public interest.

In reality, however, the number of broadcast stations is not really strictly limited — especially when compared to the far smaller number of daily newspapers in the U.S. The scarcity is government-mandated by allocation systems developed by pitting competing spectrum users and priorities against one another. The scarcity is really the result of compromise. And the compromises in allocation have created at least one type of station with plenty of frequencies and few takers: UHF television in many areas of the country (see discussion below), while cable technology has moved ahead to provide competition which may eliminate the need for more spectrum space. The problem, then, is a forced scarcity brought about by a doctrine of localism. For example, if only UHF frequencies were assigned in a specific market area, far more local channels could be accommodated without any owner having to compete with a superior VHF signal station.

Localism

Though expressed in different ways over the years, the FCC and its predecessors have clearly held that the "best" broadcast station is locally owned and operated. Such ownership was deemed in the public interest as it would presumably be closer to local needs and concerns, and thus the station would more adequately reflect and project that community than some absentee-owned operation or central network. Such a policy strongly affected such basic decisions as AM station classes, e.g., a 1928 ruling for a few national "clear" channels but many more local signals; and television allocaticns, e.g., the 1952 Sixth Report and Order, wherein the need to provide as many local TV channels as possible led directly to the intermixture phenomenon of combining VHF and UHF stations in direct competition. Thus, a fairly consistent public social policy has been developed at as vast an economic cost as has been deemed politically acceptable. But "in practice, localism is futile because it is much more profitable for stations to affiliate with a network (thus giving up most of their practical control over programming) than to produce or select their own programs."[30] Further, because of localism, too few markets have more than three television channels, which limits the formation of additional national networks with the potential benefit of greater diversity.

Public Interest

The FCC regulates broadcasting, beginning with the essential licensing process itself, "in the public interest, convenience, and necessity," the undefined standard on which the Communications Act of 1934 (and its 1927 predecessor) is built. Virtually all FCC decisions and court reviews of those decisions have been decided on varied interpretations of just what the public interest requirement was at any given point in time. As but one example, the FCC's 1965 "Policy Statement on Comparative Broadcast Hearings"[31] declared it in the public interest that seven factors be taken into account when two or more applicants for the same facility were being considered for a license: diversification of control of the media;[32] fulltime participation in station operation by owners; proposed program service; past broadcast record; efficient use of frequency; character; and "other factors."

In the 1943 *NBC* case, Justice Frankfurter specifically noted that the public interest requirement put on the FCC the "burden of determining the composition" of broadcast content as well as supervising it. At the same time, Section 326 of the 1934 Act just as specifically bans the FCC from censorship of programming, going on to say that "no regulation or condition shall be promulgated or fixed by the Commission which shall interfere with the right of free speech by means of radio communication." The horns of this seeming dilemma are manifestly evident in the Fairness Doctrine — and are but one reason why the initial rewrite of the 1934 Communications Act included no mention of a vague public interest standard, but instead called for regulation only "to the extent marketplace forces are deficient."[33] In the meantime, the FCC has been developing a somewhat indirect approach to improve broadcast content.

Structure Affecting Content

Concerned with promoting diversity of content reaching a public with sundry interests, the FCC has followed an unwritten but fairly clear policy of seeking to modify the ownership of broadcasting facilities as a means of effecting changes in content. In the volumes of FCC hearings and reports on questions of ownership, a key and constant element is use of the term "diversity." It is repeatedly asserted that diversity of media control is in the public interest, not just because such diversity presumably prevents undue concentration of media editorial and economic clout, but because such ownership will be more likely to provide a broader variety of content choices to the public. While the economics of commercial broadcasting often mitigate against such a process, the fact remains that the FCC still follows a process of seeking content diversity through ownership diversity. Recent confirmation of this approach by both the FCC and its Appeals Court "watchdog" came early in 1979 when FCC Chairman Ferris and Appeals Court Judge Bazelon specifically noted that the key to diversity in the industry was "structural" regulation of the media.[34] Surely a major rationale for regular investigations of network operations is a recognition of the fact that as networks provide programming for virtually all television stations — even the independents, most of whose re-runs are off-network productions — some degree of control over their operations is essential if government-fostered "improvements" in the level of programming are to have any effect whatever.

Requirement to Regulate Monopoly

Both the 1927 (Section 13) and the 1934 (Section 313 as amended) acts specifically apply antitrust laws to the field of broadcasting, calling for revocation of any station license from an owner accused of monopolistic activities in the industry. If any such license is so revoked, the FCC is further directed to refuse any future construction permits or license applications from that party. Just as these laws constrain the FCC, the Sherman (1890) and Clayton (1910) Acts direct the Antitrust Division of the Department of Justice. As the two governmental agencies most concerned with monopoly in broadcasting, the FCC and Justice have "acted sometimes in tandem, sometimes at cross purposes, and sometimes independently,"[35] partially owing to their differing "triggering" concerns. Whereas the Justice Department looks for undue economic concentration, the FCC is interested in diversifying the public's sources of entertainment and information. In 1978, the Federal Trade Commission joined the fray in its investigation of overall mass media ownership.

The FCC has typically acted either with an overall rule-making or an ad hoc decision on specific situations which may vary considerably on a specific matter of policy over a period of years. Justice has more options: it can and has taken part in FCC rule-making or ad hoc decision-making procedures as an interested party, it can actively petition the FCC to undertake some specific action (either as a rule-making or a specific case decision), or it can file an antitrust suit in the courts. Both agencies have been strongly affected in the past by political aims and pressures of the administration in power as well as by Congress. Both, but especially Justice, can and have acted behind the scenes to pressure business or the other agency to its will without specific action. Justice is somewhat limited in initiating actions by the legal tradition of primary jurisdiction, which simply put says that those seeking redress must first seek action from the regulatory agency in question (here, the FCC) before proceeding directly to the courts.[36] Thus, in several of the discussions which follow, note that the Antitrust division first sought action from the commission, and only after that took more direct action.

Public Investment

While the broadcast industry's investment in tangible property and programming is tremendous, it pales beside that of expenditures by consumers on receivers, both as to purchase and repair. From time to time suggestions appear as to new technological means of providing

Table 3.3   Consumer and Advertiser Expenditures on the U.S. Broadcasting
Industry, 1930-1978

Five Year Period	Average Annual Consumer Expenditures		Average Annual Advertiser Expenditures	
	Receiver Purchase/ Repair (millions)	Percent of Total Expenditures	Radio- Television Advertising (millions)	Percent of Total Expenditures
1935-39	$ 383	72%	$ 150	28%
1940-44	404	59	286	41
1945-49	838	62	517	38
1950-54	1,932	64	1,079	36
1955-59	1,945	51	1,869	49
1960-64	2,278	46	2,628	54
1965-69	4,256	51	4,095	49
1970-74	5,204	48	5,685	52
1975-78	6,057	39	9,586	61

Sources: *Broadcasting Yearbook; Historical Statistics of the United States, Colonial
Times to 1970;* McCann-Erickson.

more stations in the same spectrum space or other technical break-
throughs that could unlock the spectrum stranglehold on industry
expansion. The difficulty is that spectrum assignments to broadcasting
and other services are dictated mainly by the political and technical
realities at the time the assignments were made, i.e., the late 1920s for
AM radio, the mid 1940s for FM and VHF television, and the early
1950s for UHF television. Then millions of receivers are sold, effectively locking in spectrum allocations which may nonetheless become
archaic by later technical standards. But that public investment must be
protected as it is a substantial (though declining) proportion of
combined consumer and advertiser expenditures on radio and television
(Table 3.3). The FCC is assigned this role as protector of the public
investment, in part because the latter represents considerable political
clout if disturbed, as it might be if millions of receivers were made
obsolete by some major allocations change.

OWNERSHIP OF BROADCASTING STATIONS

The core of this chapter is an analysis of ownership patterns of radio
and television stations, and the legal actions which may be taken to
modify those patterns. Assessed first are the factors controlling entry
into broadcasting, which are considerably more complicated than for
other media. Then, the discussion continues with various categories of
ownership concentration. This section can do no more than present a

bare outline of the issue. For greater detail, the reader is directed to the numerous sources provided by the citations.

Entry into Broadcasting[37]

Whereas with most business and industry, including other media, the process of entry is constrained mainly by economic factors, in broadcasting economics and legal requirements combine to create a complex and expensive process, more controlled by government regulation than is the case in any other medium. These basic factors break into two categories: licensee qualifications and public interest qualifications. The first have been consistently upheld over the years, but over the latter, generally more deciding factors, considerably more controversy exists.

License Qualifications Issues: There are essentially three basic categories of qualification, all of which must be satisfied in order to hold a construction permit or license for a broadcast station. First, applicants, officers, and stockholders (all but 20% of the latter) must be U.S. citizens. In addition, other background factors concerning character and legal status must be detailed, including any past problems with the FCC or other legal authorities. Second, basic technical qualifications include availability of a frequency on which to either build or buy a station, antenna and studio location issues, maximum and minimum power and antenna height limitations, signal strength and service area, etc. Finally, financial qualifications center on the applicant's ability to build or buy a station and meet operating expenses for a minimum of one year without depending on income from the station.

These requirements are detailed in the station's application, and are all long-standing and are generally clearly defined.

Public Interest Qualifications: As nearly all applicants for either new or transferred stations meet the requirements noted above, considerable importance falls on the wider-ranging "public interest" qualifications which vary considerably, and on which there is less common ground for agreement. Determining community needs, now a very detailed and specific procedure, is an initial part of this process. Based on that, the station's proposed programming becomes one of the single most important factors, especially in comparative or contested situations. Closely related are the applicant's proposed commercial practices — how much advertising in a given period, etc. The FCC must also consider any economic threats to other existing stations which might develop if the application is granted. Finally, of increasing importance in the past decade or so, are issues of concentration of control. Generally speaking, locally owned and operated stations with no other media ties are preferred by the FCC over applications from sources with other media ties, especially in the same or nearby areas.

Build or Buy: An important trend has been the growth in the transfer of licenses of existing stations as the decline in the number of unused channels makes it more difficult to place new stations on the air. There are no available VHF channels in the top 100 markets for commercial stations — and only 62 remain in all other markets. There are 122 UHF channels in the top 100 markets, but once these are gone there will be no more building of new stations in major markets. Many of the remaining UHF frequencies, however, are not economically viable for one reason or another — which is why the FCC has been considering various proposals for VHF channel drop-ins in some markets by adjusting given co-channel and adjacent-channel spacing rules.* Even if approved, however, such proposals will not substantially change the existing situation.

Similarly for radio, there are few ways to presently squeeze in new AM stations, although in 1979 the FCC was considering the addition of 100 or more stations by breaking down of the last of the clear channels. FM, which like television has a specific table of allocations, is also nearing capacity, ending the chance to build new stations and forcing purchase as the only way to enter the market. This diminishing number of new channels is forcing up prices, and new per-station price records are regularly being set and broken. Prices of $60 million for a top market VHF television station, $17 million for an AM station and more than $6 million for an FM were the top transactions early in 1979. While FCC approval is required for purchase of a broadcast station, in practice the vast majority of such sales are approved.

Minority Groups: A relatively recent wrinkle affecting entry, especially station transfer or assignment of any new channels created in radio and television, is the pressure to assign broadcast licenses to racial and other minority groups. Public policy makers have been aroused by the fact that fewer than 1% of all broadcast properties are under racial minority group control, although such minorities constitute about 20% of the population. The FCC held hearings on the topic early in 1977 and subsequently adopted an industry proposal to defer capital gains taxes for those selling stations to minority groups. In October 1977, the Small Business Administration changed its policy against providing loans for broadcast properties, with minority applicants specifically in mind. Early in 1978, the Carter Administration announced a series of policy initiatives to encourage increased minority ownership in both radio (where 32 AM and 9 FM commercial stations were under

---

* A drop-in is an added VHF channel that rules would not ordinarily allow. Co-channels are the same channel in nearby markets. An adjacent channel is one next to another on the spectrum (although due to the way the spectrum is divided, not all channels are technically adjacent to the number directly behind or ahead).

minority control as of September 1977) and television (minorities were reported to control seven UHF commercial stations, but no VHFs in late 1977). The FCC is being pressured to consider minority ownership a major positive factor in license applications. Industry trade groups, and at least one large group owner, have instituted funding and training programs to encourage and assist minority ownership of stations. Late in 1978, applications were filed for minority (in both cases black) control of two VHF television stations.

The Rise of Ownership Concerns and Duopoly

While considerable concern had been expressed over ownership of broadcast stations as early as the 1920s and 1930s, specific regulatory concern came to a head in the late 1930s, based partially on the New Deal programs which encouraged closer control of business and industry. Arising at about the same time, with investigations of one feeding on the others, were FCC worries over newspaper control of radio stations, network dominance of radio broadcasting (including network ownership of stations), and "duopoly" or ownership of more than one station of the same kind in the same coverage area.

Referred to at the time as multiple ownership (as only AM radio stations then broadcast regularly), FCC action on duopoly came to a head in Genesee Radio Corporation (1938) when the FCC noted:

> It is not in the public interest to grant the facilities for an additional broadcast station to interests already in control of the operation of a station of the same class in the same community, unless there is a compelling showing upon the whole case that public convenience, interest or necessity would be served thereby.[38]

A number of such ownership combinations then existed (they show up in the 1940 column of Table 3.7 where the ratio of voices to outlets refers only to AM stations and the proportions show duopoly control in a few cases). Seeking to avoid an AM situation in the new broadcast media, the FCC in 1940 promulgated a rule against duopoly in FM radio. TV was likewise limited in April 1941. Such a rule controlling AM was proposed in August 1941 but became final only in November 1943.[39] Then, in an unusual action for an agency which more commonly "grandfathers" existing situations when new rules are created, the FCC in April of 1944 issued a rule requiring divestiture of duopoly-controlled AM stations to meet the standard.[40] Divestiture of stations was required in over 40 markets, although the FCC paved the way for tax breaks as the sales were clearly involuntary.[41]

Multiple Station Ownership

Trends: Control of more than one broadcast station in different markets by the same owner is nearly as old as broadcasting. Westinghouse, which placed KDKA on a regular schedule in November of 1920, soon had WBZ near Boston and WJZ outside of New York (fall 1921), followed later by stations in Chicago, Hastings (Neb.) and Cleveland. Though the purpose of these stations initially had been to sell Westinghouse receivers, by the late 1970s, the same groups of stations, now known as "Group W," had expanded to FM and television and was no longer directly related to manufacture as Westinghouse no longer made radio or TV receivers.[42] In similar fashion, and for related reasons, RCA and General Electric, and then other firms, built or bought stations in several different markets. Over the years, as shown in Table 3.4, the proportion of such groups in radio (AM only) began to increase, slowed in the 1950s by expansion into FM and television, but increased again by the 1960s.

The first multiple licensee in television was the Dumont Broadcasting Co. which was building the basis for a television network.[43] The other two groups active by 1948 (see Table 3.4) were Paramount Pictures (which soon sold its stations) and NBC, also building toward a national network. By the end of the Freeze in 1952, CBS and ABC networks

Table 3.4   Group Ownership in Broadcasting, Selected Years, 1929-1976

Year	Total Number of Stations	Number of Group Owners	Number of Group-Owned Stations	Percent of Stations under Group Ownership
Radio				
1929	600	12	20	3.3%
1939	764	39	109	14.3
1951	2232	63	253	11.3
1960	3398	185	765	22.5
1967	4130	373	1297	31.4
Television				
1948	16	3	6	37.5%
1952	108	19	53	49.1
1956	441	60	173	39.2
1960	515	84	252	48.9
1966	585	111	324	55.4
1976	710	119	415	58.0

Source: Sterling and Haight, Tables 260-C and 280-A. Figures are approximations and include newspaper owners. Includes only commercial stations.

Table 3.5 Group Ownership in Television by Market Size: 1956, 1966, 1976

	Markets 1-10	Markets 1-50	Markets 11-50	Markets 51-100	Markets 1-100	Markets 101 and up	Total Stations
1956							
All TV Stations		163		134	297	159	456
Group-Owned Stations		92		48	140	65	205
% Group-Owned		56		36	47	41	45
1966							
All TV Stations		193		164	357	235	592
Group-Owned Stations		134		112	246	150	396
% Group-Owned		69		68	69	64	67
1976							
VHF							
Number of Group-Owned Stations	38		97	71	206	N.A.	N.A.
% of All Stations	95		80	70	78	N.A.	N.A.
UHF							
Number of Group-Owned Stations	16		19	26	61	N.A.	N.A.
% of All Stations	59		46	51	51	N.A.	N.A.
Total Number of Group-Owned Stations	54		116	97	267	N.A.	N.A.
Total % of All Stations	81		73	61	70	N.A.	N.A.

N.A. Not Available.

Source: Sterling and Haight, Table 280-B. Calculation for markets 1-100 for 1976 by Knowledge Industry Publications, Inc.

Table 3.6   Group Ownership in Television: The Top 15 Groups: 1959, 1967, 1975

Ownership Unit	Number of Stations Owned	Net Weekly Circulation (millions)	Percent of Households
1959			
1. CBS	5	11.3	22%
2. RCA (NBC)	5	10.8	21
3. ABC	5	9.6	19
4. RKO General	4	5.4	11
5. Westinghouse	5	4.7	9
6. Tribune Co. (WGN-Continental)	2	4.5	9
7. Metropolitan	4	3.9	8
8. Storer	5	3.3	6
9. Triangle	6	2.8	5
10. Avco	5	1.9	4
11. E.W. Scripps (Scripps-Howard)	3	1.9	4
12. Newhouse	6	1.8	4
13. Hearst	3	1.7	3
14. Times-Mirror	1	1.7	3
15. Time Inc.	4	1.6	3
Total	63		
1967			
1. CBS	5	13.9	23%
2. ABC	5	13.3	22
3. RCA (NBC)	5	13.3	22
4. Metromedia	4	9.1	15
5. RKO	5	7.9	13
6. Westinghouse	5	7.0	12
7. Tribune Co. (WGN-Continental)	4	6.7	11
8. Storer	6	4.5	8
9. Cox	5	3.7	6
10. Triangle	6	3.5	6
11. Chris-Craft	3	3.1	5
12. Taft	6	3.0	5
13. Autry-Golden West	3	2.7	5
14. E.W. Scripps (Scripps-Howard)	4	2.6	4
15. Avco	5	2.6	4
Total	71		

had joined the group owner ranks along with 15 non-network groups including Storer (which had also been in radio group control), RKO General, Avco, Cox Broadcasting, Scripps-Howard, and others. The drop in proportion of group stations by 1956 is due partially to a somewhat successful FCC policy of encouraging non-group applications. Active

Table 3.6, cont.   Group Ownership in Television: The Top 15 Groups: 1959, 1967, 1975

Ownership Unit	Number of Stations Owned 1975	Net Weekly Circulation (millions)	Percent of Households
1. CBS	5	15.1	22%
2. RCA (NBC)	5	14.5	21
3. ABC	5	14.5	21
4. Metromedia	6	11.7	17
5. RKO	4	8.7	13
6. Westinghouse	5	8.6	12
7. Tribune Co. (WGN-Continental)	4	7.3	11
8. Kaiser[a]	7	6.2	9
9. Capital Cities	6	5.1	7
10. Storer	7	5.0	7
11. Cox[b]	5	4.5	6
12. Taft	6	4.3	6
13. WKY Television System[c]	6	3.4	5
14. E.W. Scripps (Scripps-Howard)	5	3.3	5
15. Washington Post Co. (Post-Newsweek)	4	3.3	5
Total	80		

a. Sold to Field Enterprises in 1978.
b. Sale to General Electric pending in 1979.
c. Sold to Gaylord Broadcasting Co.
Source: Sterling and Haight, Table 280-C. "Net weekly circulation" indicates how many millions of households are served by each of the group owners, taking all the markets in which they have stations collectively. "Percent of households" represents the proportion of all U.S. households in the collective markets of each group owner.

buying and selling of stations in the late 1950s and 1960s increased the group proportion of all commercial TV stations. But even more evident in Table 3.5 is the fact that groups sought to improve their station portfolios by concentrating on major market purchases and often "trading up" to get stations in larger markets. At least one such case, between a network and a non-network group owner, led to an important court case and undoing of the "trade" in question (see NBC-Westinghouse trade, p. 91). The proportion of group-owned stations in the top 100 markets increased by nearly 50% between 1956 and 1966, then leveled off through 1976 as more UHF stations (in which few groups are interested or active) came on the air.

As noted by Howard, as broadcast groups approached their saturation in the number of stations they were allowed to control (see below), they often diversified into other fields, as well as began to produce programming for their stations and in other ways acted as mini-networks.[44] The largest group owners (identified in Table 3.6 in terms of the number of television homes reached in a typical week) are the network owned-and-operated stations, which have maintained their lead over two decades. Among the other, non-network groups, changes have been minimal, with some of the changes representing name rather than ownership shifts. Note that in most cases, the total number of stations owned is but five, all of which are VHF. Note also that the overall cumulative proportion of television households reached by these top 15 has increased over the period, demonstrating the effects of "trading up" for stations in the larger markets.

A third of the 120 groups active in the top 100 markets in 1975 had but two stations (the minimal definition of a group) while 25 groups had three stations, 27 had four, 14 had five, nine had six, and only four groups had the full complement of seven television stations.*[45] The pace of group building appeared to pick up in recent years. In mid-1977 Park Broadcasting Inc. became the first group owner to have 21 stations, seven in each service, the largest possible complement of stations. Several other groups have 19 stations and CBS briefly owned 20 in 1958.[46] Two major ownership changes were announced in 1978, with General Electric, owner of 17 stations, offering to purchase Cox Broadcasting, with 11 television and radio stations, for nearly $500 million. If approved by the FCC, this will require divestiture of at least nine stations to stay within FCC limits. Combined Communications, owner of 19 stations, completed a merger in May 1979 with the Gannett chain of newspapers with its three stations in a deal valued at $370 million.[47] Some stations had to be sold to obtain FCC approval.

By the late 1960s a good deal had been written about the pros and cons of group ownership in broadcasting, though much of it was narrowly legal or conjectural in nature. Little research had been done specifically on the actual effects of group ownership on program matter, advertising rates, non-group-owned stations, etc. Much of what research was developed came in direct response to various governmental forays into means of controlling group concentration.

---

* Although seven is the maximum, only five of these may be VHF stations. Few of the largest broadcasters have much interest at present in acquiring UHF facilities.

Broadcasting Revenues of Chains: Among the leading group owners of broadcast properties, American Broadcasting Companies, Inc. derived the most revenue and the greatest portion of total corporate revenue from broadcasting operations. In 1977 it received almost $1.3 billion, compared to $1.2 billion for CBS and $1.1 for RCA. Both of the latter, however, were diversified enough to have nonbroadcast holdings account for more than half of sales.

The three commercial networks clearly owe their lead over other groups that have substantial numbers of broadcast properties not only to their major market owned and operated stations but to their revenue from network operations. Capital Cities Communications, with six television stations and 13 radio stations, in 1977 had only one-eighth the broadcasting revenue of the third ranked network. Metromedia, despite its strength in major market television stations, still had only 14% the broadcast revenue of RCA. Table 3.7 provides revenue data for many of the largest multiple-station broadcasters. Of these, it has already been pointed out that Cox and Combined Communications were engaged to be merged in 1979. Scripps-Howard is publicly owned

Table 3.7   Broadcasting Revenue of Selected Leading Firms, 1976 and 1977

	1977		1976	
	Broadcasting Revenue	As Percent of Total Corporation	Broadcasting Revenue	As Percent of Total Corporation
	(million)		(million)	
ABC	$1,283.7	79	$1,024.2	76
CBS	1,180.3	43	1,043.2	47
RCA	1,097.9	19	955.2	18
Capital Cities	N.A.	N.A.	104.3	49
Cox Broad-casting	186.4	100	168.4	100
Westinghouse Broadcasting	175.8	29	172.3	28
Metromedia	150.8	50	139.5	52
Storer	99.3	81	94.4	84
Taft	68.4	49	59.8	55
Combined Communications[a]	65.9	29	57.5	31
Scripps-Howard Broadcasting (E.W. Scripps Co.)	46.8	94	44.6	94

a. Merger with Gannett approved by stockholders February 1979. FCC approval for broadcast license transfer was still pending.

N.A. Not available.

Source: Annual Reports; calculations by Knowledge Industry Publications, Inc.

but controlled by the parent E.W. Scripps Co., with its substantial newspaper holdings. Only Taft has no other media holdings; Westinghouse and Storer have cable systems, but no print media properties.

Numerical Limits on Multiple Ownership:[48]   As had happened with consideration of duopoly, the FCC moved first to avoid the perceived limitations in AM radio in the new services of FM and television before the latter had time to develop similar ownership patterns. The first numerical limitation on broadcast ownership came in 1940 when ownership was limited to three television stations and up to six FM stations. In 1944, as a compromise to an NBC petition for a limit of seven TV stations to any one owner, the FCC increased the TV limit to five stations. No limit was suggested for AM broadcasting but in rejection of CBS's attempt to acquire KQW in San Jose as its eighth owned and operated station, the FCC created a de facto limit of seven stations to any one AM station owner.

The commission first considered a cohesive policy of multiple broadcasting ownership limitation in 1948. The rules finally adopted in November of 1953 simply used numerical limits of seven AM, seven FM, and five television stations, dropping earlier consideration of such variables as minority control, number of people served, etc. This was the first actual role affecting AM control. Two licensees with greater ownership interest (minority holdings in both cases) were given three years to dispose of those holdings. After further consideration of the problems of UHF television already becoming apparent, the commission modified the limits on television to seven stations, no more than five of which could be VHF. This final (September 1954) adjustment of the rules was upheld in a 1956 Supreme Court decision.[49]   They have never once been waived − a rare thing in FCC ownership controls.

Top 50 Market Policy:[50]   Concerned over group dominance of stations in the top 50 markets (which served about 75% of television homes), in 1965 the FCC issued an outright ban on the acquisition of any further stations in the top 50 markets if the applicant had two VHFs or three television stations of any kind in those markets. At the time the rule was issued, 19 licensees had more stations than the rule would allow for, though divestiture was not required. The next several years saw two developments which eventually killed the policy: (1) an intensive research effort mounted by many of the group owners likely to be affected generally found many positive and few negative points to such ownership and suggested other ways of diversifying ownership and content,[51] and (2) the commission granted waivers in each of the eight cases which arose where the new rule should have dictated a rejection of the application. By February 1968, the policy was formally abandoned to an *ad hoc* consideration of issues on a case by case basis.

Observers at the time suggested that one reason the policy was dropped was the rising number of applications being filed for UHF stations, suggesting infusion of new services and ownerships into the top 50 markets by means other than the proposed rule.

From time to time, other approaches to limiting ownership have been considered by the Commission, but nearly all have suffered from being arbitrary, with little or no specific research data backing them up, and have thus died along the way with little fanfare. One fairly recent example was the 1975 proposed rule to limit ownership to no more than four stations within any one state. No final action was ever taken on the idea.[52]

Minority Holdings by Financial Organizations:[53] The 1953 order establishing overall numerical limits to multiple ownership included a provision whereby licensees with more than 50 stockholders could include financial institutions (banks, investment funds, and the like) owning up to 1% of the total stock without that ownership figuring in or even having to be reported as a part of station ownership. This "one percent rule" recognized the difference between investment in a station as a pure investment and participation in order to have a say in the station management. A decade later several cases came to light where financial groups, especially mutual funds, controlled far more than 1% in a large number of group owners, thus technically violating the group ownership limits. In June 1968, the limit was raised to 3% for mutual funds signing statements specifying their interest in investment rather than station control. Four years later the rate was raised to 5% for bank trusts, a limit extended to insurance firms and other investment organizations in mid-1976.[54]

One to a Customer Policy:[55] Of considerably greater controversy — and having far greater long-term effect on the industry — was a policy first issued by the Commission in March 1968. This had the announced purpose of limiting station ownership to no more than one station of any kind per market. While not calling for divestiture (considering there were some 1600 combinations at the time, including 1200 AM-FM, 212 AM-FM-TV, 124 AM-TV, and 42 FM-TV) the projected rule was to affect any future sales of station combinations, thus forcing them to be broken up and sold to different owners. Furthermore, no future combinations could be built or purchased. The only exception was that daytime AM station owners could have one other station in the same market. The Justice Department agreed with the approach — but called for breakup by divestiture of existing combinations at the time of their first renewal. At about the same time, Justice began a series of antitrust suits in selected markets where it felt combinations were in restraint of competition. Industry reaction, as might be expected, was strongly against the proposed rules.

In March 1970, the FCC moved to formalize, and adjust, its initial proposal. The basic rule as proposed two years earlier was adopted in an expansion of the old duopoly rule, but all existing combinations were permitted to continue until they were sold. Included in the new order was a projected ban on newspaper-broadcast station cross-ownership and controls on ownership of broadcast operations and CATV systems. Newspaper publishers and the broadcast industry rallied against the new rules and many critical research studies were prepared and filed with the FCC. In February 1971, the rules were modified to allow AM-FM combinations and to allow for a case by case decision process on radio-television combinations involving UHF stations. Shortly thereafter, the industry research studies were filed with the commission — and there things sat for some four years. (See pp. 95-97.)

This policy has already had a notable effect on station sales as existing combinations are broken up into two and sometimes three ownerships where only one existed before. Thus, the trend to intra-market concentration, which as Table 3.8 shows had sharply increased in 1950 with the coming of FM and television stations under combined ownership with older AM services, will now slowly decline as combined ownerships break up at the time of sale — a trend which was already

Table 3.8   Measures of Intra-Market Broadcast Station Concentration: 1940-1970

Market Group	1940	1950	1960	1970
Top 10				
Ratio of voices to outlets	.02	.34	.28	.28
Proportion group control	.40	.25	.35	.38
Top 25				
Ratio of voices to outlets	.04	.33	.29	.27
Proportion of group control	.40	.19	.32	.34
Top 50				
Ratio of voices to outlets	.04	.32	.28	.27
Proportion of group control	.45	.17	.31	.34
Top 100				
Ratio of voices to outlets	.06	.28	.27	.28
Proportion of group control	.39	.14	.29	.32

Sources: Sterling and Haight, Tables 200-A and 260-B. Data for 1922 and 1930 is available in that source as well. "Ratio of Voices to Outlets" indicates proportion of stations within the markets indicated which are under the same ownership (such as a radio-TV or an AM-FM-TV combination. Each station is an outlet, but each ownership combination is a "voice"). "Proportion of Group Control" more specifically measures control of stations by groups, chains, or conglomerate owners across markets. In either case, higher proportions indicate greater degrees of ownership concentration. For detailed background and discussion of methods, see Christopher H. Sterling, "Trends in Daily Newspaper and Broadcast Ownership, 1922-1970," *Journalism Quarterly* 52:247-256, 320 (Summer 1975).

evident in comparing the top 100 market situation in 1960 and 1970 before the new rule took effect.

Network Ownership of Broadcast Stations

Occupying a special place among group owners are the national broadcasting networks, both radio and television. While they are under the same controls as other group owners, network owned and operated (O&O) stations have garnered more critical comment over the years due in part to their major market locations (see Table 3.6), their economic performance (see Table 3.2), and the fact that they are the only portion of networks which are directly regulated by the FCC.

Both CBS and NBC began radio operation with owned and operated stations, and over the years expanded their radio holdings. By 1933 (and for the next decade), NBC controlled 10 stations, seven built or purchased in the 1930-33 period. In addition, NBC programmed five stations actually owned by Westinghouse, giving the network complete control of 15 AM outlets.[56] CBS controlled nine stations (one was leased) by 1936.[57] Mutual had no owned and operated stations until 1978.[58] Of these network operations (discounting the Westinghouse stations programmed by NBC), 10 were Class I-A Clear Channel operations with 50,000 watts.[59] Operating two networks, NBC had two stations each in New York, Chicago, Washington, and San Francisco. FCC concern about that ownership and its apparent unfairness helped bring about the first major investigation of the role of networks in broadcasting, the Chain Broadcasting investigation of 1938-41. One result of that investigation, and the Supreme Court decision of 1943[60] which supported the FCC decisions on network radio, was the forced divestiture of the NBC Blue network and its stations, which became ABC in 1945.

The development of network ownership of television O&Os was somewhat more complicated. As shown in Table 3.9, only ABC managed to build all of its O&O stations before the Freeze (and all on channel 7, helping to build a common identity), though the cost of television programming kept the network itself quite weak until a merger partner was found to increase capital. After several other proposals were considered, ABC merged in 1951 with United Paramount Theaters (approved by the FCC early in 1953), but continued as the weakest of the three networks until its success starting in 1975. Only Dumont was weaker until it left the business in 1955 — primarily because of a lack of four station markets where it could obtain sufficient affiliations to compete. CBS was backing its own system of color transmission and receivers and held back on television expansion for that reason; it thus ended up purchasing most of its stations,

Table 3.9   Network Ownership of Television and Radio Stations: 1976

(stations in italics no longer network owned)

Market Ranking and Number of TV Households	% of All U.S. Households	ABC-Owned Stations	CBS-Owned Stations	NBC-Owned Stations
1. New York 6,326,300	8.8%	WABC/7 (1948,C,R)	WCBS/2 (1941,C,R)	WNBC/4 (1941,C,R)
2. Los Angeles 3,814,500	5.3	KABC/7 (1949,C,R)	KNXT/2 (1951,P,R) *KTTV/11 (1948-51,P)*	KNBC/4 (1947,P)
3. Chicago 2,646,500	3.7	WLS/7 (1948,C,R)	WBBM/2 (1953,P,R)	WMAQ/5 (1948,C,R)
4. Philadelphia 2,247,700	3.1	—	WCAU/10 (1958,P,R)	*WRCV/3 (1955-65,P)*
5. San Francisco 1,743,200	2.4	KGO/7 (1949,C,R)	(R only)	(R only)
6. Boston 1,713,200	2.4	—	(R only)	—
7. Detroit 1,554,200	2.2	WXYZ/7 (1948,C,R)	—	—
8. Washington 1,373,200	1.9	(R only)	*WTOP/9 (1950-54,P)*	WRC/4 (1947,C,R)
9. Cleveland 1,297,200	1.8	—	—	WKYC/3 *(1948-55,C)* (1965,P)
12. Houston 944,000	1.3	(R only)	—	—
13. Minneapolis-St. Paul 934,100	1.3	—	*WCCO/4 (1952-54,P)*	—
15. St. Louis 916,300	1.3	—	KMOX/4 (1957,P,R)	—
21. Milwaukee 668,100	.9	—	*WXIX/18 (1954-59,P)*	—
22. Hartford 651,400	.9	—	*WHCT/18 (1956-58,P)*	*WNBC/30 (1956-58,P)*
28. Buffalo 617,600	.9	—	—	*WBUF/17 (1955-58,P)*

Source: Sterling and Haight, Table 262-A citing Sterling-Kittross (1978), p. 266.

Note: Listings show the television station call letters and channel number on first line, and in parentheses below the year the station began operations for that network. The symbol C indicates the station was constructed by the network; P indicates purchased by the network from a previous owner; R indicates a combination AM-FM radio station owned by the network in that market. Those stations in italics are no longer network-owned. The end date, if any, indicates the year the network relinquished control of the station.

including several minority ownerships and two UHF stations in the 1950s. NBC also experimented briefly with UHF ownership in the 1950s.

An important cause celebre in network O&O stations is represented by NBC's operations in Cleveland and Philadelphia. In the normal group owner policy of attempting to "trade up," NBC pressured Westinghouse, another group owner, and an NBC affiliate in several markets, into "trading" its Philadelphia station for the NBC outlet in Cleveland plus several million dollars to sweeten the deal. Westinghouse was pressured by the threat of losing its all-important network affiliations. The trade was approved by the FCC in 1955, but a year later the Justice Department brought suit in Philadelphia to undo the trade, charging parent RCA with antitrust violations by use of the network affiliation threat to force Westinghouse to give in. The case went to the Supreme Court which found against RCA,[61] but attempts by the network to modify the result dragged on for six more years. Not until 1965 was the trade actually undone. As important as the events and court case themselves was the adverse publicity and Congressional attention directed to network station ownership and general operating tactics. Early in 1979, NBC announced it planned to expand its radio holdings by purchase of an additional three AM and three FM outlets, though specific target markets or stations were not named (earlier in the decade, NBC had tried to sell off its radio holdings entirely).[62]

At no time has the FCC seriously considered a policy of network O&O divestiture, though on several occasions the commission has suggested that if the issue were being approached for the first time, it might well have been better to separate network operation from station ownership. The prime concern expressed by critics is the excessive economic clout the networks have with their own operations plus the stations — which as Table 3.6 shows have always been the three top groups in number of homes reached (and in per station profits as well). For a number of years, the networks argued that the O&Os were their prime source of income, as network operation otherwise lost money. Table 3.2 shows that network margins were indeed low for many years but that by the mid-1970s, the networks were making substantial profits even without their O&Os, which continued to make substantial profits as well.

In the late 1970s, as investigations of network concentration mounted, one target was again the network O&O. The FCC's network investigation, begun in 1977, includes this issue although the Justice Department's antitrust suits do not. One factor recently discussed is the limitation on effective competition from a fourth network, given the O&O base of the existing three in the major markets, and the difficulty any new network would face in being able to build a similar stable of stations in major markets both as an economic base and as a core around which to sign up affiliates among independent stations. There is something of a conflict of interest for networks which on one hand are concerned with network operations and their stations as outlets for that programming and advertising, and on the other hand with the stations as individual outlets in their markets and the latitude they should have in selecting other programming. The outlook, however, is for little or no change in status of network O&Os in the foreseeable future.

Newspaper-Broadcasting Cross-ownership

Certainly one of the oldest ownership regulatory concerns, one of the most controversial, and the one most recently definitively resolved is cross-ownership of newspapers and broadcast facilities, especially when the print and broadcast properties are in the same market. Newspaper-owned stations is one of the oldest patterns in broadcasting and was once of considerable importance in each of the broadcast services.

Trends:[63]   One of the first stations on the air, WWJ in Detroit, was owned by a local daily newspaper. Initially, newspapers entered radio to increase circulation through mention on the air, for prestige reasons and good will, and to protect themselves against a fad which might become a competitor in news delivery. Press ownership in the 1920s seldom exceeded 10% of all stations on the air, and was often but half that level. But in the 1930s, newspaper control of the industry grew substantially — from about 6% of all stations in 1930 to nearly a third of all stations a decade later. Clearly radio was no longer a fad, but was becoming an obvious competitive threat to newspapers. Control of one or more radio stations was seen as one way of protecting newspaper investments, both against radio and against other newspaper-radio combinations. Late in the decade combined newspaper-broadcasting chains controlled about 11% of both newspapers and broadcast stations. With the coming of FM and television, newspapers moved rapidly into the new services, getting a quarter of FM authorizations in 1941, thereby prompting FCC action.

Table 3.10 provides a summary of the cross-ownership situation since 1945. For radio the pattern is a clear one of diminishing proportions of control in both relative and (though only marginally with FM) absolute terms. With television, however, newspaper ownership has been increasing, although the proportion of newspaper control of the industry has declined from its peak as other ownership interests have entered the business. Initial entry into FM and television paralleled the entry into AM in that the press sought to protect both its newspaper and older

Table 3.10 Newspaper/Broadcasting Cross-Ownership, Selected Years, 1945-1977

Year	AM Radio			FM Radio			Television		
	Total Stations	Newspaper-Owned Number	Percent	Total Stations	Newspaper-Owned Number	Percent	Total Stations	Newspaper-Owned Number	Percent
1945	919	260	28.4%	46	17	36.9%	8	1	12.5%
1950	2086	472	22.6	733	273	37.2	98	41	41.8
1955	2669	465	17.4	552	170	30.8	411	149	36.3
1960	3456	429	12.4	688	145	21.1	515	175	33.9
1965	4044	383	9.5	1270	159	12.5	569	181	31.8
1970	4292	384	9.2	2184	245	11.2	677	189	27.9
1975	4432	321	7.2	2636	236	9.0	711	193	27.1
1977	4497	322	7.2	2837	238	8.4	728	209	28.7

Sources: Sterling and Haight, Table 261-A. 1977 data from an unpublished paper by Richard Vincent, p. 15. All data as of January 1 of each year and figured on stations actually on-air, with these exceptions: 1965 is actually as of October 31, 1964; 1970 is actually December 1, 1969; 1975 is actually December 1, 1974; and 1977 is actually December 1, 1976. "Total" column includes only commercial stations, except for AM where educational stations (about 25 in each case) are included.

(AM) broadcast interests. Initial television purchases were primarily in the same market as the newspaper (over 80% of the cross-ownerships were local in 1955), but under regulatory pressures and competition from other buyers, the local proportion of cross-ownerships declined to 72% in 1960, and only 46% in 1974.[64] This proportion declined still further late in the decade as newspaper owners, under increasing FCC and court pressure over local cross-ownership, began to discuss and in a few cases carry out plans to exchange stations, thus breaking up local combinations, while maintaining interests in both media.

One landmark switch came in late 1977 when the Washington Post Co. and the Detroit News Co. exchanged television stations.[65] With final Supreme Court action requiring divestiture in only a few markets, the future ownership situation is likely to parallel the past — a continued slow decline in newspaper ownership of local stations due to an upheld FCC ban on formation of any such new combinations.

Regulation: Long Search for an Answer: Until the past decade, the government's stance on newspaper ownership of broadcast stations has had little consistency. While cited in a few licensing decisions of the 1930s, and argued on occasion in Congress, the newspaper ownership issue came to a head only after the substantial increase in press control of radio in the 1930s more or less forced FCC action. In 1941 the FCC froze newspaper-owned construction of or application for FM stations and began what was to be a three year investigation into the entire press-radio interconnection. Three years later the commission closed the proceeding and continued on its *ad hoc* basis of a case by case consideration of ownership diversification.

Many newspaper-owned licenses were routinely renewed in the 1940s and 1950s, though in a very few cases, ownership diversification or some bad business practice of a newspaper appeared to play a part in an application denial.[66] In 1956 something of a landmark was struck when, on appeal, the U.S. Court of Appeals for the District of Columbia upheld the FCC's right to consider diversification as a deciding factor in the awarding of broadcast licenses.[67] In the 1960s the situation was somewhat fuzzy:

As a comparative factor, newspaper ownership: 1) is a discrediting, not a disqualifying factor; 2) will be decisive only where all other comparative criteria have been equally met by all the applicants; 3) will depend for its importance upon the nature and extent of newspaper interests of the applicant; and 4) where a non-comparative proceeding is involved, there will be no hearing save where collateral public interest matters, such as suppression of competition, are material.[68]

The focus of action turned from the case by case approach of the FCC to the Justice Department, which began in 1968-69 to both contest FCC license decisions and to file actual suits to undo some ownership combinations. Further, Justice urged on the FCC a policy of breaking up existing newspaper-broadcast combinations and not allowing new ones to form. The focus switched rapidly back to the FCC early in 1969 when it voted to deny renewal of the license for Boston's channel 5 to the *Herald-Traveler*, turning it over instead to an independent local owner with no other media ties. While many other factors entered into the case, the clear cross-media aspects of the decision shocked the industry.[69] Prior to this decision, diversification of control had been taken into account for new applicants, but not renewals. Action was initiated in Congress to somewhat nullify the precedent value of this FCC decision, and the commission itself adopted a position statement reiterating the primacy of incumbent licensees. It was nullified on appeal.[70]

In 1970, still under pressure from Justice, the FCC issued a proposed rule to require divestiture within five years of either newspaper or broadcast stations in local markets where there was cross-ownership.[71] Massive filings against the proposal came to the FCC from industry trade groups, all protesting that no effective case had been made against newspaper ownerships — and that in any case such ownership was on the decline. The FCC's ability to act on the issue was questioned in that the commission had no clear Congressional mandate to take such drastic action. While the debate in the trade press and among researchers continued,[72] the FCC took no action in the 1971-74 period. Once again, the Justice Department entered with formal opposition to renewals of cross-owned media in several different markets.

Finally, in January 1975, the FCC issued a second report and order in the cross-ownership proceeding, considerably toning down its original divestiture proposal to cover but 16 smaller markets where the only newspaper owned either the only radio or only television station in the same coverage area. Future local cross-ownerships were also barred. Other existing cross-ownerships were exempted until sold, in which case they would have to be broken up as well.[73] The new rules were appealed by Justice and many others, and the case was thus taken up by the Court of Appeals for the District of Columbia, which rendered its decision March 1, 1977. The three-judge panel remanded the rules back to the FCC, saying that full divestiture was required, given the arguments the FCC had used to limit future combinations while calling for only limited divestiture. Only if such combinations could be found specifically in the public interest did the court suggest exceptions should be made.[74] The court-ordered change could have affected some

153 broadcast-newspaper combinations involving nearly 300 stations.[75]
On further appeal the Supreme Court agreed to hear the case. In June 1978, the high court upheld the FCC — agreeing to a ban on future cross-ownerships, as well as to limiting divestiture to the 16 markets the FCC originally selected. Amidst all the verbiage was the important finding that the FCC was fully within its rights in limiting future cross-ownerships as a means of promoting the public interest in diversified mass communications media; that such action did not violate the First Amendment rights of those denied broadcast licenses.[76] Thus this longest-lasting of the ownership questions appears finally laid to rest. The FCC is now mandated to disallow any further local cross-ownerships, and existing combinations will be broken up if sold. A likely trend appears to be continued swapping of local cross-owned facilities for those in other markets.

Conglomerate Ownership of Broadcasting

Of somewhat more recent vintage as an ownership category in broadcasting is the conglomerate firm. Loosely defined, this is a business organization with control of a wide variety of manufacturing and/or service divisions, which may include media interests. Often such conglomerates are also group owners of broadcast stations and may have one or more chains of newspapers or other media holdings. As shown in Table 3.11, they vary tremendously in size and depend to widely varying degrees on media supported by advertising as one contributor to total annual revenues. Among the highlights found in this selection of media-involved conglomerates are:

1) All but one have some broadcast station ownership, five of them only in television, nine in both radio and TV.

2) The three networks are included (RCA owning NBC).

3) Among these large revenue earners, holdings in broadcasting are more common than of any other media.

4) With one exception, all have shunned UHF television, preferring the more profitable VHF stations (only nine UHF stations are owned by the top 39 firms while the same firms control 112 VHF operations).

Another recent analysis of media conglomerates also shows the pervasiveness of broadcast station ownership among firms of this type. Of 10 firms controlling holdings in six or more different media

Table 3.11 Major Broadcast Holdings of Conglomerate Firms

Revenue Rank	Corporation	Rank in Fortune 1000 Mfg. Companies	1977 Revenues (millions)	Percent Revenues from Advertising	Broadcast Holdings AM	FM	TV	Other Media Holdings Books	Mags	Newsps	Film	Cable
1.	General Electric	9	$17,518.6	N.A.	6	2	3	—	—	—	—	—
2.	Westinghouse	26	6,137.6	3%	7	2	5	—	—	—	—	—
3.	RCA	30	5,923.4	19	4	4	5	×	—	—	—	—
4.	CBS	91	2,776.3	57	7	7	5	×	×	—	—	—
5.	General Tire/Rubber	122	2,110.1	5	6	5	4	—	—	—	—	—
6.	Fuqua Industries	—	1,629.5	7	2	—	3	—	—	—	—	—
7.	ABC	152	1,616.9	83	7	7	5	—	×	—	×	×
8.	Time Inc.	198	1,249.8	43	—	—	1	×	×	—	×	×
9.	Warner Comms.	214	1,143.8	5	—	—	—	×	×	×	×	×
10.	Times Mirror	219	1,143.7	55	—	—	2	×	×	×	—	×
11.	Schering-Plough	—	950.7	3	6	6	3/1*	—	—	—	—	—
12.	Knight-Ridder	293	751.7	98	—	—	2	—	×	×	—	—
13.	Jefferson-Pilot	—	669.3	8	5	4	2	—	—	×	—	—
14.	McGraw-Hill	314	659.0	35	—	—	4	×	×	—	—	—
15.	Dun & Bradstreet	—	636.9	42	—	—	5	×	×	—	—	—

* Three VHF and one UHF station.
N.A. Not Available.
Source: *Media Decisions* (October 1978), p. 64.

industries, all but one had broadcasting properties; of eight firms with holdings in five media industries, five included broadcasting; of 13 firms with holdings in four different media industries, 10 included broadcast holdings; of 38 firms with holdings in three media, 31 had at least one radio or television station; and of 18 additional firms with holdings in two media industries, only one lacked broadcast stations.[77]

Further, merger activity in firms of this type is continuous. In 1978, General Electric announced plans to merge with the 33rd-ranked firm (Cox Broadcasting).[78] American Express attempted to take over No. 14-ranked McGraw-Hill,[79] although eventually it was rebuffed by an opposed McGraw-Hill Board. Firms ranked 16 and 28 (Gannett and Combined Communications) announced merger plans in mid-1978, which if approved by the FCC, would make Gannett 12th in annual revenues.[80] Many of these mergers are of sufficient scope as to require large divestitures of broadcast stations to stay within overall ownership limits of seven stations in each service.[81]

Some of the sales and transfers were prompted by what the sellers termed government pressure over such issues as cross-media controls. For example, Newhouse Broadcasting, part of the multi-media conglomerate built mainly on newspapers and magazines, late in 1978 announced plans to sell its five television stations (while holding on to five radio stations) to Times Mirror, giving the latter its full complement of seven television stations. Newhouse executives claimed they "were not happy" over the $82 million sale but did it to eliminate the pressures on them from the FCC and elsewhere over their broadcast properties amidst their larger print holdings.[82]

It has been suggested that there are at least three kinds of conglomerate media owners:

- the media conglomerate with holdings in several different media but not much else;

- the concentric conglomerate with one or more major media industry holdings plus substantial revenues from non-media business or manufacturing industry; and

- the diversified conglomerate which includes media holdings in an otherwise patternless combination of many unrelated business and industry holdings.[83]

Author Kevin Phillips suggests three major approaches to the control of such organizations:

- treating the media as semi-governmental bodies due to their key role as information conduits both to and from government;

• regulation of content; or

• using antitrust to break the conglomerates into smaller media business units which would obviate the need for the first two somewhat more odious regulatory options.[84]

A good example of the issues, and problems facing the issues, arose in the 1965-67 attempted takeover of ABC by the ITT conglomerate. Several issues were raised as the FCC considered the merger (because title to ABC's O&O stations was involved): whether money would be put into ABC or siphoned off from the network; the effect on ABC news of all ITT's other (including extensive defense) interests; excessive concentration in communication (broadcasting, recordings, filmmaking and distribution/exhibition); the effect on ABC of ITT's extensive overseas business (about 60% of its income at that time).

The Commission's consideration of the merger began in September 1966, and despite a request from the Justice Department to hold off on a final decision, it approved the merger on a 4-3 vote in late December. Acting a few days before the order became final, Justice petitioned the FCC to reconsider the whole affair. By this time, the pressures on the merger partners had risen to the level where both were seeking favorable press comment on the issues. Despite Justice's argument concerning anti-competitive aspects of the case, the Commission again approved the merger in May 1967, feeling that ABC needed the greater financial security ITT backing would provide − so that the then weakest network could more effectively deal with RCA-owned NBC and the highly diversified CBS. The Justice Department then appealed the decision to the Court of Appeals for the District of Columbia, not on antitrust grounds (where the Department felt its case was too speculative), but rather because the FCC had not adequately considered the public interest. Faced with further delays, and a change in stock values which would have cost ITT nearly $300 million more for the merger than when it had been proposed late in 1965, ITT withdrew its offer the first day of 1968.[85] Ironically, some of the same arguments had been raised in the two years of FCC consideration before finally approving ABC's merger with United Paramount Theaters in 1953.

Prompted both by the ABC-ITT spectacle as well as by a perceived trend to more merger activity generally, the FCC initiated a broad investigation into conglomerate owners of broadcast stations in 1969. That year, and again in 1971, the commission sent out detailed survey questionnaires to elicit information on which firm really owned what. While the study group continued its work, no specific rule-makings resulted. Various hearings in both houses of Congress on conglomerate trends had one specific related result − the ownership limit suggested in the initial rewrite of the 1934 Communications Act. Only five radio or five television stations were to be allowed — a policy which if carried through in subsequent work on the bill would require substantial industry divestiture.[86]

Evidence on the Effects of Station Ownership

Most of the research done on media concentration issues has served to provide various descriptive measures of how extensive that ownership trend is — but comparatively little work has analyzed the effects of such concentration. Many of the FCC and court decisions on various ownership cases have spoken out about this dearth of reliable and valid information on what really is the most important policy-related question of all — just what effect on programming and advertising does ownership appear to have? If there are substantial differences, do owners of multiple broadcast stations do a "better" or "worse" job of serving the public interest? Or, on the other hand, if there are no discernable differences, is there really any point in making clearly arbitrary rules concerning ownership?

In 1974 the Rand Corporation published the best single integrated analysis of research literature to that date on the effects of concentrated ownership.[87] Massive problems with published studies were found in both methodology and in simply defining the criteria for determining "good" or "bad" broadcast station performance in the context of serving the public interest, convenience or necessity. The Rand researchers found that most studies dealt with economic effects of ownership, as these, while less important to the public in many ways, were clearly easier to quantify than content measures — especially when the problem of policy (let alone operational) definitions was raised. Assessing many studies of both economic and content variety, they concluded:

> ... The results of assessing the state of current knowledge about the effects of media ownership concentration can be expressed in the well-known Scotch verdict: "Not proved." ... The form of media ownership generally seems to have a small impact on economic or content performance. ... Most statistical studies simply show no significant differences among media ownership classes. Differences reported in certain studies have not been reproduced in other situations. And many of the prior studies seem flawed by inadequate data or by methodological problems, such as failure to control for other important variables.[88]

More specifically, the Rand researchers concluded:

- "... There is little evidence of a statistically significant relationship between cross-ownership and newspaper flat line advertising rate or the price of an hour of prime time television. . . ."[89]

• ". . . Findings of no significant cross-ownership effects on individual station audience ratings. . . ."[90]

• ". . . Any effects of cross-ownership are not strong enough to distort an entire market's behavior in competing for national advertising."[91]

• "The question of cross-ownership's effects on local advertising rates at the individual station and newspaper level is the one most pertinent to the cross-ownership debate, but it remains unresolved on the basis of presently available research."[92]

• ". . . Group ownership does raise the average time sales, revenue, and income of television stations in a market. . . ." (but the study did not control for market competition, UHF-VHF status, market demographics, etc.).[93]

• ". . . Studies . . . do not provide evidence of any significant differences [in televised news and public affairs programming, or hours with excessive advertising] among group owners, cross-media owners, and other broadcast station owners . . . ."[94]

• In none of these program types — news, public affairs, instructional or local programs generally — do the newspaper owners systematically outclass the non-newspaper licensees" when measuring quantity (not quality) of these programming types.[95]

• ". . . Network affiliation variables seem to be the most consistently significant. The group ownership variable is insignificant . . ." in assessing amounts of news, local programming, feature films, high and low brow entertainment, and public affairs programming.[96]

• "There is case evidence showing abuses by media owners with both concentrated and nonconcentrated holdings. But taken individually or collectively, the body of case evidence has not shown that group or cross-media owners influence their media outlets or otherwise behave differently from other media owners."[97]

These Rand results are important because, first, they represent the best unbiased and detailed assessment of all the literature, regardless of who supported it (and many of the studies, if not most of them, have received support from one or more interested parties in the regulatory proceedings discussed earlier). Second, they are quite consistent in their findings of little or no difference between concentrated and non-concentrated ownership across a number of variables in many different situations. Third, they clearly pinpoint the difference between broad statistical surveys and specific case studies; most of the regulatory proceedings are studded with the latter, which, while useful in adversary proceedings, are not clear indicators necessarily of industry-wide practice. Finally, very little has appeared in the nearly five years since the Rand overview to change any of the judgments summarized above.

A later study assessing the amount of news and public affairs programming by television stations in the top 75 markets concluded that ". . . Deficiencies in the communication flow . . . cannot then be blamed on the preponderance of group owners in the business structure. The local owner, like the group owner, is most likely to avoid that programming which is most likely to approximate a forum function . . . his allocations [of] air time do not differ from that of the group owner."[98] When controlled for VHF affiliates only, the results are the same.

Another analysis of FCC quantitative data on news and public affairs programming of 677 commercial TV stations in 1973 concluded that "multimedia-owned television stations perform at least as well, and sometimes significantly better, than all other stations. In particular, multimedia-owned stations are likely to provide significantly more news."[99] The authors also found, as have other studies, that network affiliated stations do better on similar program measures than independents, and VHFs do better than UHFs. As most group-owned stations are VHF affiliates, that factor may well be of more importance than any ownership difference. On the other hand, a detailed content analysis of newspaper and television news stories in cross-owned and independent operations "found that common ownership of a newspaper and a television station in the same city does tend to restrict the variety of news available to the public — and further, that the homogenizing effects of cross-ownership are most noticeable in smaller cities." [100]

Clearly, there is no strong research underpinning for breaking up various kinds of combined ownership situations. There are a number of negative case findings,[101] but overall studies (done mainly in the cross-ownership area) can generally be summed up as reporting "no significant difference" in either economic or quantity-of-programming effects. More basic is the problem that much of the needed research has yet to be done.[102]

THE DOMINANT ROLE OF NETWORKS

National networks exist to interconnect stations for common and simultaneous distribution of programs and advertising. Put another way, networks sell access to audiences, the buyers being national advertisers. The "bait" to attract the audiences is programming. The network thus acts as something of a broker between the local station (and its viewers or listeners), program producers, and advertisers. This central role developed in the late 1920s in radio, and has remained essential to broadcasting in the U.S. since, though radio networks offer few concerns for policy-makers today, given the localization of that medium in the face of network television after the late 1940s.

From those radio days until the present, basic issues of public policy concern have remained, generally speaking, those of excessive domination of advertising, programming, and local affiliate stations. These may be translated into four policy objectives which have guided government regulation:

1) to make available the highest quality programming, especially in news and public affairs;

2) to provide for diversity in the sources of those programs, and control over selection of programs by industry gatekeepers;

3) to minimize economic market power by any industry institution (or centralization of that power by a few groups); and

4) to encourage minority and specialized program content rather than wasteful duplication of the usual lowest common denominator broadcast content.[103] Clearly, these issues go beyond networks, but given the generally acknowledged dominant role of the networks over the past half century, most concerns have begun there.

Development of Network Regulation

Both the Radio Act of 1927 (Section 4h) and the Communications Act of 1934 (Section 303i) gave the FRC/FCC authority to make special regulations applicable to stations engaged in chain (or network) broadcasting. Few such regulations emerged until the FCC undertook the first detailed analysis of the role and impact of networks in the chain broadcasting investigation of 1938-41. An initial report in 1940[104] and a final published report in May 1941[105] examined the rise of the radio networks, the predominance of NBC and CBS in radio, contractual arrangements between the networks and their affiliate stations, network option time and "clearance" policies, and the commission's jurisdiction to consider and act upon such matters. The report's conclusion called for a limitation on the network's power to force affiliates to clear time for network programs; a shorter, one year affiliation contract period; limits on network control over station advertising rates; and an end to NBC's operation of two national networks.[106] As the FCC cannot directly regulate network companies, all regulations were couched in terms of station licensees — in other words, no station license would be granted to any station affiliated with a network that violated specified regulations. The 1941 report led directly to the network case of 1943,[107] and the eventual formation of what became the American Broadcasting Company.

The expansion of television in the 1950s led to various Congressional investigations, especially into the potential monopoly role of networks. Catalysts for the probes included the decline of the Dumont television network, the weakness of ABC as a distant third in television networking, the merger of ABC with Paramount Theaters Inc. in 1951 (approved by the FCC early in 1953), and the general problems of UHF, including the clear lack of network interest in affiliating with such stations. Frustration was widely expressed over the changes occurring in broadcasting and the dominant role of networks, which to many observers seemed to make allocations and other issues difficult to resolve.[108]

A second FCC investigation of networks was sparked by the Congressional concerns, and occupied a special staff under Roscoe L. Barrow from 1955 to 1957. Its massive *Network Broadcasting* report focused on television networking, with detailed information on the measurement of network concentration and control, affiliation practices, option time, advertising rates, station compensation arrangements, "must buy" program practices, station ownership, etc.[109] Among the report's recommendations were a ban on option time, a curb on station ownership, separating networks from station representation, and a general loosening of network control over talent.[110]

While the FCC considered the recommendations of the network study, another staff began a detailed analysis of network programming methods, problems, and trends which had not been dealt with in the "Barrow" report. Reports from this investigation appeared in 1960, 1963, and finally in 1965.[111] At the same time, the quiz show and payola scandals rocked the industry and brought forth further pressure on the FCC and on Congress to "clean up" television and to investigate still further the role of networks in program content. Partially based on these events, the FCC began to consider specific rules to limit network control of evening programming.

Eventually, the Prime Time Access Rule (PTAR) was unveiled in 1970 to take effect at the beginning of the Fall 1971 season. Networks were limited to three hours nightly of prime-time programming (effectively a half hour reduction in the existing pattern), and their role in ownership and distribution of independently produced programs was also reduced. The FCC hoped thereby to increase local program production at best, but to diversify program production sources at the very least.[112] The basic result was a glut of syndicated game shows (which cost about 40% of any other entertainment formats). On several subsequent occasions, the FCC modified PTAR to allow for various exemptions, but the basic rule remains in effect, despite court appeals.[113]

In April 1972, the Justice Department's Antitrust Division entered the fray with antitrust suits against all three national networks, aimed at further divorcing them from control, ownership, and syndication rights to prime-time programming.[114] Apparently based on research activities going back to the early 1960s, but thought by others to be blatantly political given the then Nixon administration's views toward television,[115] the suits were dismissed late in 1974 – and immediately reintroduced. The networks were unable to get a summary dismissal of the refiled suits on political grounds,[116] and thus filings and counter-filings leading up to a potential trial continued through the 1970s. The suit against NBC was settled out of court late in 1976 (and approved by the presiding judge in 1977), placing a number of programming restrictions on the senior networks, most to come into effect only if the ABC and CBS cases come to fruition for the Justice Department along similar lines.[117]

The suits, and settlement of one of the three, provided the background to an increasingly complex play of events concerning the networks in the 1970s. The Office of Telecommunications Policy, under considerable political pressure from several quarters, conducted several years of investigation into network policy on expanding the number of reruns each season. No specific regulations came from the study.[118] In September 1976, Westinghouse Broadcasting brought a petition to the FCC calling for a major commission investigation of the economic and programming domination of the television networks, charging that affiliate stations had become under-compensated pawns in the network race for supremacy.[119] Justice filed a supporting petition with the commission, suggesting such a process would not interfere with the suits.[120] Only the networks opposed the study. Early in 1977, the FCC formally announced commencement of its third major study of the role of networks.[121] A funding hassle held up the study, but a staff was appointed and work begun in mid-1978, with a final report expected in 1979 or 1980. Focus of the study was to be the fundamental changes in advertising and program patterns in the years since the Barrow report. Almost lost in the shuffle was the FCC's action lifting the radio network regulations of 1941 (based on the first FCC study of networks), due to the totally changed role of radio in the 1970s.[122]

Table 3.12 Comparative Indexes of Network-Affiliate Economic Relations, 1964-1977
(Index: 1964=100)

Year	Consumer Price Index	Network Sales	Network Income	Index	Payments by Networks to Stations: as % of Network Income	as % of Station Income	Station Income
1964	100	100	100	100	23.1%	19.8%	100
1965	102	109	99	107	24.0	19.6	109
1966	105	125	131	114	21.2	18.8	117
1966	108	130	93	115	20.6	18.7	101
1968	112	136	94	115	19.5	16.3	123
1969	118	150	154	118	18.6	15.4	130
1970	125	148	83	112	17.3	14.4	114
1971	131	143	89	107	17.4	13.9	94
1972	135	161	184	105	15.0	12.0	124
1973	143	180	307	109	14.2	11.3	132
1974	159	191	374	116	13.8	11.1	144
1975	174	206	346	120	13.4	10.7	161
1976	184	256	491	124	11.3	8.8	269
1977	196	310	675	134	10.0	8.7	280

Sources: 1964-1973: "Petition for Inquiry, Rule Making and Immediate Temporary Relief," filed before the Federal Communications Commission on September 3, 1976 by Westinghouse Broadcasting Company, Inc. Based on official FCC financial figures for the television industry.
1974-1977: Westinghouse Reply Comments (December 1, 1978), as reprinted in *The Foreseeable Future of Television Networks* (Los Angeles: UCLA School of Law, 1979) pp. 82-83.

Domination of Affiliates

Central to the investigation of networks over the years has been the degree of freedom accorded to local station network affiliates. In television, the controlling factor here has been the commission's spectrum allocation decisions to provide local stations to as many communities as possible — thus creating about 70 of the top 100 markets with three commercial VHF channels, and only about 15 with more than three. There are many smaller markets with but one or two VHF channels. More than anything else, this has limited the number of networks to three, as affiliation with UHF channels is still avoided given the latter's smaller coverage area and related limitations. Entry to network affiliation status is thus limited as there can be but one per network in a given market area, and except for markets with more than three VHF channels, a "bilateral oligopoly" exists where neither networks nor stations have much flexibility (changing affiliations, etc.). Markets with fewer than three VHF channels, the smaller markets, actually have the upper hand in network relations as one of the networks must take a secondary affiliation with but few of its programs being carried. Only in the largest markets, few in number but important economically because of the proportion of audience reached, do the networks have the upper hand by holding the threat to remove an affiliation by giving it to an independent VHF outlet.[123]

The length of affiliation contracts now generally runs for two years, though in fact they run until cancelled by network or station, a fairly rare occurrence. Recently, with the staying power ABC has demonstrated as the top-ranked network in prime-time popularity, a number of traditional CBS and NBC affiliates have switched over to ABC, giving that network true coverage parity with the others for the first time.

A prime factor behind the Westinghouse petition of 1966 was the level of affiliate compensation by the networks. As shown in Table 3.12, network income increased 575% between 1964 and 1976, while network payment to affiliates was up only 34%. This is reflected in the declining proportion of network revenue going to affiliates and the decline in network payments as a percent of station income. The networks retorted that the dramatically increased risks of program costs in a period of true three-network competition had to be covered in some fashion, and that stations did not share in the increased risk, so why should they share unduly in the "spoils" of success? But the Westinghouse figures clearly show a declining economic role of network payments in individual affiliate financial return over a 13 year period. To Group W, this suggested increased network economic power at the expense of local stations. The FCC agreed sufficiently to eventually call for its third major investigation of network practices.

Several factors enter into affiliate compensation. Where at one time there was a direct connection between station compensation and advertising sales rates, that is no longer the case — partially due to the end of program sponsorship on television. Instead, stations are compensated for network advertising only, not program time or public service announcements, on a contract basis; the contract details, on a station by station basis, are not made public, so that great differences in what various stations are able to negotiate from the network may exist. Furthermore, for all three networks, there is a basic 21 to 24 hour per week base for programs for which compensation is relatively low. Then, a higher rate of compensation is calculated for program time taken over that base. This naturally encourages higher levels of program "clearance" by the station.[124] An example of network clout came in 1969 when AT&T raised its interconnection charges, and that rise came out of compensation payments rather than overall network income.[125] Previous FCC action on compensation came with its rejection of a CBS plan in 1963 which called for a graduated increase in compensation depending on how many hours were taken ("cleared") from the network.[126]

A final matter of contention for many years has been the network practice of demanding options on large chunks of affiliate time — a right of first refusal to make use of such time. The chain broadcasting report of 1941 called for an end to this practice, saying it effectively removed the local station from responsibility for what it broadcast. But only in 1963, long after the Barrow report urged the same thing, did the commission end the practice. The issue is now one of how much time stations "clear" for network shows.[127]

Network Control of Advertising

An important factor underlying the FCC's undertaking yet another investigation of networks, as well as increasing FTC interest in network operation, is the radical change which has taken place in television network advertising in the past 15 years or so. As summarized in Table 3.13, sponsored programs have given way to programming in which many different advertisers "participate," buying time in much the same way as space is purchased in print media. Another change is that the standard television commercial has shrunk in length from 60 to 30 seconds. Moreover, while the total number of commercial minutes has increased about 15%, the number of different commercials aired (due to the shorter length) has almost doubled, bringing on viewer and advertiser complaints about clutter and over-commercialization on television. This network TV advertising represents about 9% of total advertising expenditures in the country, and about 15% of the national advertising dollar.[128]

Table 3.13 Network TV Commercials: Number, Length and Sponsorship, Selected Years, 1965-1975

Year	3 Network Total Commercial Minutes Per Year	Percent of Commercials by Length		3 Network Total Number of Commercials		Number of Prime-Time Programs by Type of Advertising Support	
		30 Secs	60 Secs	Number	Index	Sponsored	Participating
1965	N.A.	N.A.	N.A.	N.A.	N.A.	32	51
1967	100,000	6%	94%	103,000	100	20	60
1969	100,424	15	85	108,600	105	6	67
1971	99,867	49	51	132,300	128	3	63
1973	101,955	71	29	158,000	153	0	70
1975	109,135	79	21	180,400	175	N.A.	N.A.
1977	114,656	82	18	194,342	189	N.A.	N.A.

N.A. Not Available.

Sources: 1965-1973: Sterling and Haight, Table 381-B, citing information in all but last two columns from Westinghouse petition to the FCC (1976). Last two columns from unpublished information of L.W. Lichty, University of Wisconsin, Madison. 1975-1977: *The Foreseeable Future of Television Networks*, p. 80.

The prime cause for the decline of sponsorship and 60-second ads was the increasing cost of television. Given the fairly static amounts of time available, increased revenue, as seen in Table 3.11, grows only through increasing the rates charged. Advertisers, who sponsored and provided perhaps half the network programming in the 1950s, provided only 3% of the programming by 1968. As costs increased, advertisers preferred to spread their risk by placing messages in different programs rather than banking heavily on but one or a few. By the late 1960s, network rates for two 30-second ads added up to a good deal more than one 60 — thus easily recovering the added costs of selling more different advertisements.

The effects of this change in support have been widespread, and the cause for affiliate concern. For one thing, networks now compete directly with stations for national spot advertising income as they did not when sponsorship was the rule. As a result of economies of scale and lower selling costs (a whole network of stations is sold rather than individual sales to separate stations), networks can and have often undercut local cost per thousand viewer rates, pulling national spot accounts to network coffers. This role has been strengthened as advertising agencies have gotten out of the programming business with the end of sponsorship, and now merely buy time. The higher resultant network income has not been passed on to the affiliate stations.

The effects of advertising rates on other businesses is also of concern, though too involved to detail here. Briefly, this issue concerns network volume discounts which encourage mergers of industries using television advertising extensively. The volume discounts not only save money, but research has shown that repeated ads sell better. When a special kind of programming (such as national sports, given a unique status under Congressional action in 1962) is combined with the network oligopoly, only a few can afford the advertising rates charged. Roger Noll points to the increasing concentration trend in the beer industry, stemming from the network advertising cost structure of sports telecast.[129] This is an extreme example of a concentration problem: limited entry into television advertising due to the high minimum fixed costs incurred limits effective use of the medium to large, usually consumer goods, firms. A substantial literature further explores these issues.[130]

Network Control of Programming and its Distribution

Of special concern to regulators is the control networks exercise over the form and structure of the TV programming industry. Prime-time viewing options for the majority of the national audience are provided by networks. Other viewing hours are also heavily indebted to network choices in that (1) affiliates use network programs about 65% of their total broadcast time, and (2) independent stations make heavy use of syndicated off-network material originally programmed by a network. Several issues are involved.

First, the decline of advertiser-supplied programming noted above was due mainly to cost factors — but also to the quiz show scandals of the late 1950s. That brought forth pressures for the networks to clean up their operation — and coincided with increased network concern for audience flow, requiring network control of which programs got on the air and when. At the same time, the impact of television on the film industry had created vast unused production facilities in Hollywood suitable for telefilm (series program) production. By the early 1960s, the program production company, or "package agency" (so named as it presents a finished program package to the network), was producing a majority of network programming, and today produces at least 80% of prime-time programming under contract to the networks. No longer are networks merely conduits for advertiser-supplied programming; now networks control the programs and sell participating time to advertisers.

Second, the number of network hours broadcast has increased at a steady rate over the past 15 or so years. Table 3.14 notes that much of the increase has been from ABC's finally filling in its schedule to really compete with the offerings of CBS and NBC. Most of the increase has come in fringe time as prime was already fully occupied by the late 1950s. The decline evident in 1972 is due to imposition of the Prime Time Access Rule (PTAR) in September of 1971, whereby the FCC limited network prime-time programming to three hours. The Westinghouse petition suggests this expansion makes local station programming even more unlikely as there is some network programming available nearly all hours. The economics of syndicated programs to fill the PTA slot is much more favorable to local stations than trying to produce its own programming.

Table 3.14 Weekly Half-Hours of Regularly Scheduled Network Programming, Selected Years, 1960-1976

Year	ABC	CBS	NBC	Total	Index (1960=100)
1960	115.5	165.5	173.5	454.5	—
1965	143.0	161.0	171.5	475.5	105
1970	145.0	179.0	172.0	496.0	109
1972	144.0	171.0	162.0	477.0*	105
1974	145.0	175.0	180.0	516.0	114
1976	169.0	179.5	180.0	528.5	116

*Prime Time Access Rule effective Sept. 1, 1971.

Source: "ABC Opposition to Westinghouse Petition," before the Federal Communications Commission, November 22, 1976. Attachment A. Index calculated by Knowledge Industry Publications, Inc.

Third, while special *ad hoc* networks have often appeared in the past several seasons built around either single programs or multi-part dramatic serials, such approaches face a difficult time because of network O&Os, which almost always take all network shows – and are thus effectively removed from the independent "network" market. The O&Os are important because of their large market locations (see Table 3.6) and thus hold a pivotal position when trying to reach sufficient audience to sell advertisers on such special hook-ups. But even reaching affiliates rather than O&Os is made difficult by the fact that most affiliates clear 95% of network programs offered, which make up about 65% of their programming time. Only if an affiliate can be persuaded that a non-network offering is financially beneficial will the outside offering have a chance.

In the final analysis, that is the key question: networks succeed in this system because given the constraints of allocation, stations simply find it more profitable to affiliate than to go independent. As long as that is true, it will be extremely difficult to let market pressures create substantial change in the dominating role of networks. Pressures for change will have to come from the outside.

One such source has been the independent production community in Hollywood, generally divided into the "majors," which are part of theatrical film firms, and the independents, which usually rent facilities for production from others. Although producers have been accused of being a rather tight group, there is in fact easy entry to the production circle. Pricing is affected by the ability of the networks to produce their own programming if costs become too high, and the combined program share of the top producers is under 60% of the total (and varies considerably from year to year). Moreover, the power of the producers is limited because they do not control first-run distribution, which is handled by the networks.[131]

Despite their lack of monopoly status, various package firms have tended to work most closely with one or two networks. In the 1970s, for example, CBS made heavier use of the independent firms than did the other networks. The packagers have felt constrained in having but three markets for their product. But with the rise of more "independent network" operations and a slowly increasing market of stations for syndicated products (both off-network and first-run), the packagers are finding less reason to complain. The rerun issue remains, however, since the networks have increased their proportion of reruns per season simply because they cost only 25% of an original program. Increased emphasis on reruns mean less work for the Hollywood craft unions, and became a political issue in the early 1970s.[132] Further, network decisions on how long a series plays on a network are important to the potential syndication life of that series off-network, for with too few episodes, syndicators can't sell the material to local stations for typical "stripping" (running five days a week) for a minimum of several months at a time. Few series break even, let alone make money on network runs, as network payments do not usually cover the cost of production, so syndication is an important source of profits for producers. Network decisions on series length thus have a direct impact on the profits of program packagers.

Policy Options on Network Power

Examining all of the issues, Willard Manning and Bruce Owen conclude in an article in *Public Policy:*

> . . . Network power is not based in the advertising and television program supply markets, which are nearly competitive. Instead the major sources of network dominance are the technological economies of scale in simultaneous networking and the networks' bargaining position relative to stations in the largest television markets. However, the networks cannot realize all of the potential monopoly profits because they are locked into a dynamic noncooperative rivalry, in terms of program quality, which is only partly offset by their ability to cooperate on the level of reruns. The policy options to reduce the remaining network power and to increase the diversity of program content and control tend to be ineffective or so radical that they are politically unfeasible.[133]

Summarizing the literature, the economists conclude that two types of option exist: behavioral approaches which serve to limit power in specific ways, but do little to change the underlying source of that power; and structural approaches which include antitrust and other approaches and are usually more effective over time.[134] Either category must be measured against gains and losses in freedom of expression generally, viewer welfare, the economic health of related industries (such as major advertisers), and the FCC's policy of localism. Theories expressed over the past 25 years or so to explain broadcast and specifically network behavior suggest that, given our present system of allocation and networks, similar common denominator programming will result. Therefore, economists have examined various kinds of "controlled monopolies" as effective ways to seek real change in both economic and programming concentration.

A commonly posed question concerns the likelihood of a fourth or even more commercial networks to compete with the three operating at present. For the reasons already noted above, especially the limited number of markets with more than three commercial VHF channels, a

Rand study in 1973 concluded a permanent new network was extremely unlikely. No less than 17 specific options, many including combinations of television stations and cable systems, were considered and rejected for the same basic reason: the inability of any such new network, however based, to economically compete with the established system.[135] Temporary additional networks built around a special program or series have worked in recent years, but they do not, of course, face the problem of broad programming requirements or overhead a regular network must deal with.

A variety of other options have been considered by economic theorists and policy makers. As a rule, the theorists have concentrated more on the structural remedies, given their greater effectiveness, often purposely ignoring political/technical realities in their search for some new approach to the issues. A recent analysis by Owen,[136] for example, considers in detail such things as deintermixture (making UHF stations a more viable base for network expansion by limiting a given market to either all VHF or *all* UHF stations), divestiture of network O&O stations to even up chances for new network entrants, common carrier access to network facilities (though many critics fear this would throw television back to the hands of advertisers as in the 1950s, with little positive benefit for viewers), promotion of cable and pay television as competitors, geographic disintegration (limiting the number of affiliates for any network which would force either more national networks, or a series of regional networks, the latter somewhat paralleling German practice), and even outright nationalization. All of these have benefits but the drawbacks are often severe.

In one well-known economic model to which much attention has been devoted over the past quarter century, monopoly is given serious consideration as possibly better serving the public interest than the present oligopolistic network structure.[137] Theoretically, a monopolist might program a greater real diversity of materials on two or three network channels (in an attempt to reach more of the total audience) than three competing network owners all trying to reach the same general audience. Since absolute monopoly is clearly a political impossibility, the suggestion of some kind of temporal (time-based) monopoly has been put forth. Here, one owner might control all network channels for a given part of the day (morning, afternoon, part of prime time, late evening, etc.) across the week, or for all of a given day in the week (firm A on Monday, firm B on Tuesday, etc.).

Something of an operating model of such an approach exists today in the way that Great Britain's commercial Independent Broadcasting Authority has divided the lucrative London market. One company telecasts the commercial channel during the week (Thames Television), while a separate firm provides service on Saturdays and Sundays

(London Weekend). Thus there are two gatekeepers through which program access may be achieved rather than the more normal one (indeed, only one operates in the other IBA market areas). One important caveat to such an approach is that viewers would still have the same number of viewing options at any one time (three network choices) despite the actual number of temporal monopoly networks (seven if one a day, many more if the day-part approach is taken). But theoretically, at least, this could lead to greater segmentation of the market and hence to greater diversity of actual program types than is the case now.

To some degree, the Prime Time Access Rule is the leading edge of such a temporal monopoly option. Clearly the amount of time in question is too limited to promote formation of an agency to serve the half hour period. But an extension of that rule might pave the way for such an expansion of network voices, the number being quite variable depending on the specific choices made. The antitrust approach of the Justice Department is another way of creating substantial structural change, but it has already taken seven years and only one network has tentatively settled out of court. The most likely option may be new competition from the outside — cable, satellite transmissions from independent syndicators, video cassettes and the like.

DISCUSSION

Is the commercial broadcasting industry, and more specifically television, monopolistic? Noll suggests not:

> Television is not among the most concentrated industries, such as automobiles, aluminum, tobacco, or copper. Nevertheless, in relatively few industries do three firms [in this case the networks and their O&O stations] account for over half the sales. The proportion of the market accounted for by the three largest firms is greater in television than in such industries as steel, farm machinery, and electric motors and generators, all of which are generally regarded as imperfectly competitive.[138]

It can be said that commercial television is by some criteria the most concentrated of all mass media with the exception, perhaps, of pay cable distribution, though the trend to increased concentration appears to affect most media. Indeed, such a pattern of concentration extends to the "support" industries manufacturing equipment for broadcasting.[139]

Ironically, concentration of power in broadcasting has its basis in the Federal Communication Commission's continuing doctrine of localism.

This chapter identified the close connection between localism as a policy and radio and television allocations as an outcome — and those allocations have decided the shape of the semi-competitive industry we have today. The concentrated ownership of stations is merely an accentuating overlay on this basic allocation — without the enforced scarcity of channels, ownership concentration would not be as likely. The operation of networks is quite clearly all but dictated by the large number of markets with three commercial VHF channels brought about by an allocation scheme whose first priority was to provide as much local service as possible — even if, as has proven to be the case, resultant programming is all very much alike. The division of the industry into economic haves and have-nots is a direct outgrowth of the FCC's attempts to broaden the number of stations in order to make localism work.[140]

Clearly localism does not work in achieving the FCC's intended objectives — and has not worked as it was supposed to for several decades. This fact must be recognized if future regulatory options are to deal realistically with a relatively limited number of choices remaining to substantially modify the structure, operation, and product of broadcasting.

In the end, much of the controversy analyzed in this chapter may become moot — if competition from cable television, pay cable, and home cassette or disc video systems (which places scheduling options in the hands of the viewer) continues to expand as it appears to be doing in 1979. FCC attempts to limit some of these competitors in order to preserve a localism-based system of broadcasting have been systematically thrown aside on court appeal in the late 1970s.[141] It is most probable that more television users will get a broader variety of viewing options from cable systems using pay channels and satellite distribution than they ever could from traditional broadcasting. The television networks may well heed the lessons that should have been learned when television itself displaced the entrenched radio networks. An important policy question here is whether owners of the "old" business of broadcasting will become dominant in the "new" competing technologies, which at least have the potential to open up electronic communications to new communicators and types of content.[142]

Appendix A3*

Public Television

The primary broadcast alternative to commercial station programming is provided by the public television and radio stations. By 1979, more than one-fourth of all television stations (but only 17% of VHF channels) were licensed for noncommercial use. Among the nearly 8500 radio stations, only 950, all but 25 on the FM band, were noncommercial.[143]

Public television is noncommercial broadcast television supported by funds from the federal and state governments, voluntary viewer contributions, and foundation and corporate grants. The nation's 286 public television stations are linked by the Public Broadcasting Service, established in 1969 by the Corporation for Public Broadcasting. Programming on public television is designed to offer viewers a mix of quality cultural, dramatic, public affairs and educational shows.

Background

The Public Broadcasting Service evolved from an effort on the part of educators during the late 1940s and early 1950s to secure some noncommercial television channels to be used for educational purposes. In 1952, the FCC acted to reserve 242 channels throughout the United States for noncommercial television — 80 were VHF channels, 162 were UHF. Later, the FCC increased the channel allotments to 116 VHF and 516 UHF. They received some financial support from the Ford Foundation, which created the Educational Television and Radio Center to provide the educational channels with programming. Eventually the Center became National Educational Television (NET) but still derived most of its support from the Ford Foundation. In 1962 educational television got a boost from Congress, which authorized the Department of Health, Education and Welfare to aid stations through a five-year, $32 million grant program. The next significant development was the creation in 1965 by the Carnegie Corporation of a commission to study educational television and make recommendations designed to further its development. The report, issued in 1967, formed the basis for the Public Broadcasting Act of 1967 which created the Corporation for Public Broadcasting charged with administering federal funds for the public television system, promoting its growth, and protecting it from political influence.

---

*Added by editor.

Funding

In 1977, public broadcasting had total revenue of $482.1 million, 6% of the revenue of commercial broadcasting.[144] The Public Broadcasting System spent $67.5 million on national programming, compared to an average of $506 million for each of the commercial national networks. The budget of the average public television station was two-thirds that of an average commercial station.[145]

Between 1975 and 1980 public television was authorized a total of $452 million in federal funds to be made available through annual appropriations by Congress. The federal funds are distributed on a matching basis — $1.00 in federal money for every $2.50 raised from alternate sources, i.e., state governments, viewer contributions and corporate and/or foundation grants. Public television stations solicit contributions from viewers via mailings and on-the-air fund-raising drives. They acknowledge corporate and foundation support by announcing the source of funding at the beginning of each program.

Programming

In setting forth its recommendations for the development of the Public Broadcasting Service, the Carnegie Commission called upon public television to "broaden its scope" from its original education mandate and include in its programming "all that is of human interest and public importance." It also stressed the need for local service programming. However, many of the stations have continued to provide the same type of programming they offered initially. Many see themselves as primarily educational; 73 public television stations are licensed to colleges and universities, 19 to municipal boards of education, school districts or agencies serving elementary and secondary education, 99 to state authorities, commissions or boards of education, and 73 to nonprofit civic corporations.

On a national level programming has ranged from such dramatic and cultural presentations as *Masterpiece Theater, Great Performances* and *Live from Lincoln Center*, children's programs such as *Sesame Street* and *The Electric Company,* and documentaries such as *Nova.* PBS has carried such public affairs programming as the Senate Watergate hearings in 1973, Presidential news conferences, a variety of Congressional hearings, and United Nations events.

Despite some notable programming successes, audiences still tend to shun the Public Broadcasting System's offerings. Whereas the average prime-time network rating in March 1978 was 18.8 (18.8% of all television households tuned in to a particular program), the rating for public television was 1.5. Of all households watching television at a given prime-time minute, an average of 30.0% were tuned in to a commercial network show, while 2.4% watched a public television offering.[146]

Programming Sources

For its national programming PBS has turned to a variety of sources both domestic and foreign. It has relied heavily on imports of dramatic programs from Britain, including the widely popular *Masterpiece Theater* presentation "Upstairs, Downstairs," produced by London Weekend Television; *The Forsyte Saga,* produced by the British Broadcasting Co. (BBC); and *Monty Python's Flying Circus,* also from the BBC.

To a great extent PBS has relied for domestic production on a handful of active stations, such as Boston's public television station, WGBH, which also acquires and assembles programming for *Masterpiece Theater.* Among WGBH's domestic productions are *The French Chef,* the long-running cooking lessons by Julia Child, distributed on 1/2-inch cassette by the Video Tape Network; *The Advocates; Nova;* and *Zoom.* Another big city public television station, New York's WNET, produced the $5.2 million 13-part series, *The Adams Chronicles,* and produces most of the programming for the *Great Performances* series including *Theater in America, Dance in America,* and *Live from Lincoln Center.* WNET is co-producer with WETA in Washington of *The MacNeil-Lehrer Report,* a nightly news program. WETA is the source of *Washington Week in Review,* another PBS public affairs presentation. *Wall Street Week* is produced by Baltimore's WMPB.

Its heavy reliance on British imports for dramatic programming is necessitated by public television's limited funding. In 1977, PBS spent $3.3 million on foreign acquisitions, 103 hours of programming that would have cost an estimated $36.9 million to produce in the United States. Funding problems also force PBS to rely heavily on repeat presentations in its national programming. The system disclosed in 1977 that three out of every four programs carried nationally are repeats.

The Future

In a report issued in 1967, the Carnegie Commission on Educational Television set forth recommendations that resulted in the development of the Public Broadcasting Service. It also provided the impetus for public television to expand from being merely educational to a broader perspective stressing programming of public importance and general enrichment.

A second Carnegie Commission on the Future of Public Broadcasting issued its report in early 1979, less than a dozen years later. It found that the Corporation for Public Broadcasting was not fulfilling its intended role as the "national leadership organization."[147] The commission recommended its replacement with a Public Telecommunications Trust to act as the agent for disbursing funds to local stations and overseeing overall system activities. It also urged that the overall budget of public broadcasting be expanded so that by 1985, federal government expenditures will be $630 million, compared to the $200-210 authorized for 1983.[148]

Clearly, however, the commission sees a continued need for public television to improve its standing as an alternative to commercial broadcasting. The report recommended giving "the highest priority" to the improvement of "programs of excellence, diversity and substance,"[149] with the emphasis on producing its own programming, rather than continued purchases from outside sources.

FOOTNOTES

1. *Report of the Federal Trade Commission on the Radio Industry* (Washington: Government Printing Office, 1924; reprinted by Arno Press, 1974).

2. See reports of this two-day seminar in *The Wall Street Journal* (November 2, 1978), p. 10; *The New York Times* (December 15, 1978), p. A-18; *Broadcasting* (December 18, 1978), pp. 24-5; and *Publishers Weekly* (December 25, 1978), pp. 25-26.

3. For some information on this, see Christopher H. Sterling and Timothy R. Haight, *The Mass Media: Aspen Institute Guide to Communication Industry Trends* (New York: Praeger Special Studies, 1978), unit 281; and Robert K. Avery, "Public Broadcasting and the Duopoly Rule," *Public Telecommunications Review* 5:1:29-37 (January/February 1977).

4. U.S. Senate, Committee on the Judiciary. *Possible Anticompetitive Effects of Sale of Network TV Advertising*, Hearings . . . 89th Cong., 2nd Sess. (two parts, 1966).

5. The literature on broadcasting is best analyzed in Christopher H. Sterling, "A Selective Guide to the Literature of Broadcasting," in Sydney W. Head, *Broadcasting in America* (Boston: Houghton-Mifflin, 1976, 3rd ed.), pp. 511-550.

6. See Joseph E. Baudino and John M. Kittross, "Broadcasting's Oldest Stations: An Examination of Four Claimants," *Journal of Broadcasting* 21:61-83 (Winter 1977).

7. The definitive analysis is in William Peck Banning, *Commercial Broadcasting Pioneer: The WEAF Experiment 1922-1926* (Cambridge, Mass.: Harvard University Press, 1946).

8. Ibid., pp. 132-3 citing Department of Commerce figures. ruary 1st.

9. Herbert Hoover's famous phrase, "I believe that the quickest way to kill broadcasting would be to use it for direct advertising," came in his comments to the Third National Radio Conference, as reprinted in *Recommendations for Regulation of Radio* (Washington: Government Printing Office, 1924), p. 4 (reissued in John M. Kittross, ed. *Documents in American Telecommunications Policy* (New York: Arno Press, 1977, Volume I).

10. See, for example, Gleason L. Archer, *History of Radio to 1926* (New York: American Historical Society, 1938), pp. 342-3 (reissued by Arno Press, 1971).

11. See Christopher H. Sterling and John M. Kittross, *Stay Tuned: A Concise History of American Broadcasting* (Belmont, Calif.: Wadsworth Publishing, 1978), pp. 68-69.

12. Edward F. Sarno, Jr. "The National Radio Conferences," *Journal of Broadcasting* 13:189-202 (Spring 1969).

13. See allocation development chart in Sterling and Kittross, op cit, p. 86.

14. John W. Spalding, "1928: Radio Becomes a Mass Advertising Medium," *Journal of Broadcasting* 8:31-44 (Winter 1963-64).

15. See Sterling and Kittross, pp. 128-130; and Walter B. Emery, *Broadcasting and Government: Responsibilities and Regulations* (East Lansing: Michigan State University Press, 1971, 2nd ed.), especially chapter 7.

16. Sterling and Kittross, pp. 228-234.

17. Federal Communications Commission. *Public Service Responsibility of Broadcast Licensees* (Washington: Government Printing Office, 1946; reprinted by Arno Press, 1974).

18. Bruce M. Owen, *Economics and Freedom of Expression: Media Structure and the First Amendment* (Cambridge, Mass.: Ballinger, 1975), p. 111.

19. Sterling and Haight; table 171-A provides a fully detailed listing of radio network affiliates, 1927-77.

20. Ibid., table 303-C; Sterling and Kittross, p. 114; and *Broadcasting Yearbook 1951*, p. 12, table V.

21. Sterling and Haight, table 170-A.

22. Sterling and Kittross, p. 156

23. Sterling and Haight, table 460-A.

24. Ibid., table 670-A.

25. See Sterling and Kittross, pp. 254-5, 322-3, and 379-381.

26. Federal Communications Commission, "Sixth Report and Order on Dockets 8736, 8975, 9175, and 8976," April 14, 1952. FCC 52-294.

27. See especially Sterling and Kittross, pp. 356-359, 381 and 417.

28. Sterling and Haight, table 680-A.

29. Sterling and Kittross, p. 452.

30. Owen, p. 112.

31. Federal Communications Commission, "Policy Statement on Comparative Broadcast Hearings," 1 FCC2d 393 (reprinted in Frank J. Kahn, ed. *Documents of American Broadcasting* [Englewood Cliffs, N.J.: Prentice-Hall, 1978, 3rd ed.] pp. 329-338).

32. For one analysis see John C. Busterna, "Diversity of Ownership as a Criterion in FCC Licensing since 1965," *Journal of Broadcasting* 20:101-110 (Winter 1976).

33. H.R. 13015, Section 101, 95th Cong., 2nd Sess. (1978).

34. *Broadcasting* (February 5, 1979), p. 29. Both men were speaking at a UCLA-sponsored symposium on the future of the networks.

35. Walter S. Baer, et al. *Concentration of Mass Media Ownership: Assessing the State of Current Knowledge* (Santa Monica, Calif.: Rand Corp. R-1584-NSF, September 1974), p. 10.

36. Owen, p. 139.

37. For general background, see Emery (op cit, note 15), and Douglas H. Ginsburg, *Regulation of Broadcasting: Law and Policy Towards Radio/Television and Cable Communications* (St. Paul, Minn.: West Publishing, 1979), especially chapter 3.

38. *Genesee Radio Corporation* 51FCC 186 as quoted in Robert R. Smith, "Duopoly and ETV," *NAEB Journal* (May-June 1966), p. 42.

39. See Avery (op cit, note 3), and Herbert H. Howard, "Mutliple Broadcast Ownership: Regulatory History," *Federal Communications Bar Journal* 27:1:1-70 (1974).

40. 11 FCC 12 (1945).

41. Ibid., and Baer et al, p. 17.

42. Sterling and Kittross, p. 61.

43. Herbert H. Howard, "The Contemporary Status of Television Group Ownership," *Journalism Quarterly* 53:399-405 (Autumn 1976), at p. 399.

44. Ibid., p. 401.

45. Ibid., p. 403, table 3.

46. *Broadcasting* (June 27, 1977), p. 24.

47. *Broadcasting* (October 9, 1978), p. 21.

48. Howard, "Multiple Broadcast Ownership" pp. 8-18 provides the basis for what follows.

49. *United States v. Storer Broadcasting Corp.* 351 US 192 (1956).

50. Howard, "Multiple Broadcast Ownership" pp. 46-55 is the basis for what follows.

51. A massive research study first issued in two volumes in 1966 was later commercially published in Paul W. Cherington, et al. *Television Station Ownership: A Case Study of Federal Agency Regulation* (New York: Hastings House, 1971).

52. Michael Botein, *Legal Restrictions on Ownership of the Mass Media* (New York: Advanced Media Publishing Associates, 1977), p. 97.

53. Howard, "Multiple Broadcast Ownership," pp. 14, 42-45 is the basis for the following discussion.

54. Federal Communications Commission, "Report and Order on Docket No. 20520," June 18, 1976. FCC 76-540.

55. What follows relies heavily on Howard, "Multiple Broadcast Ownership," pp. 57-63.

56. Federal Communications Commission, *Report on Chain Broadcasting* (Washington: Government Printing Office, 1941, reissued by Arno Press, 1974), p. 16.

57. Ibid., p. 23.

58. See *Broadcasting* (January 1, 1979), p. 60 — Mutual got its first O&O with the purchase of WCFL in Chicago late in 1978.

59. FCC, *Report on Chain Broadcasting*, p. 67.

60. *National Broadcasting Co. Inc., et al. v. United States et al.* 319 U.S. 190 (1943).

61. *United States v. Radio Corporation of America* 358 U.S. 334 (1959).

62. *Broadcasting* (January 24, 1979), pp. 54-55.

63. This discussion mainly from Christopher H. Sterling, "Newspaper Ownership of Broadcast Stations, 1920-68," *Journalism Quarterly* 46: 227-236, 254 (Summer 1969), as updated in Sterling and Haight, table 261-A.

64. Richard Bunce, *Television in the Corporate Interest* (New York: Praeger Special Studies, 1976), p. 45, table 5.

65. *The New York Times* (December 13, 1977), p. 17; and *Broadcasting* (December 12, 1977), p. 19.

66. As in *Mansfield Journal Co. v. Federal Communications Commission*, 180 Fed 2d 28 (1948).

67. *McClatchy Broadcasting Co. v. Federal Communications Commission*, 299 Fed 2d 15 (1956).

68. Daniel W. Toohey, "Newspaper Ownership of Broadcast Facilities," *Federal Communications Bar Journal* 21:1:44-57 (1966), at p. 52.

69. For the background of this case, see Robert R. Smith and Paul T. Prince, "WHDH: The Unconscionable Delay," *Journal of Broadcasting* 18:85-96 (Winter (1974), while a popular treatment is in Sterling Quinlan, *The Hundred Million Dollar Lunch* (Chicago: J. Philip O'Hara Inc., 1974).

70. *Citizen's Communications Center et al.* v. *Federal Communications Commission* 477 F 2d 1201 (1970).

71. Howard, "Multiple Broadcast Ownership," p. 63.

72. Walter S. Baer, et al. *Newspaper-Television Station Cross-Ownership: Options for Federal Action* (Santa Monica, Calif.: Rand Corp. R-1585-MF, September 1974).

73. Federal Communications Commission, "Second Report and Order on Docket 18110," January 31, 1975. FCC 75-104.

74. *National Citizens Committee for Broadcasting* v. *Federal Communications Commission et al.* 555 F. 2d 938 (1977).

75. *Broadcasting* (March 7, 1977), pp. 22-23.

76. *Federal Communications Commission* v. *National Citizens Committee for Broadcasting, et al.* 98 S. Ct. 2096, 56 L. Ed. 2d 697 (1978).

77. Sterling and Haight, tables 201-A and 201-B citing 1977 data.

78. *Broadcasting* (October 9, 1978), pp. 21-22.

79. *Broadcasting* (January 15, 1979), p. 30.

80. *Media Decisions* (October 1978), p. 64.

81. See, for example, the divestiture requirements in the GE-Cox merger detailed in *Broadcasting* (October 9, 1978), p. 21, which reported that at least nine outlets would have to be sold. The total price was later set at over $76 million (*Broadcasting* [January 15, 1979], p. 30).

82. *Broadcasting* (December 11, 1978), p. 29.

83. Bunce, chapter 6.

84. Kevin Phillips, "Busting the Media Trusts," *Harper's* (July 1977), pp. 23-34.

85. *Broadcasting* (January 8, 1968), pp. 34-36, 41-42.

86. H.R. 13015, Section 440, 95th Cong., 2nd Sess. (1978).

87. Baer, et al. *Concentration of . . .*, especially chapters 4 and 5.

88. Ibid., p. 79.

89. Ibid., p. 92

90. Ibid., p. 95.

91. Ibid., p. 100.

92. Ibid., p. 101.

93. Ibid., pp. 106-107.

94. Ibid., p. 127.

95. Ibid., p. 132.

96. Ibid., p. 133.

97. Ibid., p. 143.

98. Bunce, p. 34.

99. Michael O. Wirth and James A. Wollert, "Public Interest Program Performance of Multimedia-Owned TV Stations," *Journalism Quarterly* 53:223-230 (Summer 1976), at p. 230.

100. William T. Gormley, Jr. "How Cross-Ownership Affects News-Gathering," *Columbia Journalism Review* (May/June 1977), pp. 38-46.

101. See especially Stephen R. Barnett, "Cross-Ownership of Mass Media in the Same City: A Report to the John and Mary R. Markle Foundation," (Santa

Monica, Calif.: Rand Corp., September 1974); and Peter M. Sandman, "Cross-Ownership on the Scales," *More* (October 1977), pp. 21-24.

102. See Baer et al., *Concentration of . . .*, pp. 143-165.

103. Willard G. Manning and Bruce M. Owen, "Television Rivalry and Network Power," *Public Policy* 24:33-57 (Winter 1976), at pp. 55-56.

104. "Report of the Committee Appointed by the Commission to Supervise the Investigation of Chain Broadcasting, Commission Order No. 37, Docket No. 5060," June 12, 1940 (Washington: FCC, 1940).

105. FCC, op cit (note 55).

106. Ibid., pp. 91-92.

107. See note 59.

108. See, for example, the following reports all based on extensive hearings: all of these are U.S. Senate, Committee on Interstate and Foreign Commerce. Robert F. Jones, "Investigation of Television Networks and the UHF-VHF Problem," Committee Print, 84th Cong., 1st Sess. (1955). Harry M. Plotkin, "Television Network Regulation and the UHF Problem," Committee Print, 84th Cong., 1st Sess. (1955). "The Television Inquiry: Television Network Practices," Committee Print No. 2, 85th Cong., 1st Sess. (1957).

109. U.S. House of Representatives, Committee on Interstate and Foreign Commerce, *Network Broadcasting*, Report . . . 85th Cong., 2d Sess., House Report 1297 (January 27, 1958).

110. *Broadcasting* (September 30, 1957), p. 31.

111. U.S. House of Representatives, Committee on Interstate and Foreign Commerce, *Television Network Program Procurement*, Report . . . 88th Cong., 1st Sess., House Report 281 (May 8, 1963). This includes "Responsibility for Broadcast Matter" (June 1960), as well as the title report of 1963. See also Federal Communications Commission, *Second Interim Report by the Office of Network Study: Television Network Program Procurement, Part II* (Washington: Government Printing Office, 1965).

112. *Broadcasting* (May 11, 1970), pp. 22-24, 26.

113. *The Wall Street Journal* (April 29, 1975), p. 22.

114. *Broadcasting* (April 17, 1972), pp. 8, 21.

115. *The New York Times* (December 11, 1974), p. 83.

116. *Washington Post* (April 23, 1976), p. D-9, and *Broadcasting* (March 6, 1978), p. 102.

117. *New York Times* (November 18, 1976), pp. D-1 and D-5, and *Broadcasting* (November 22, 1976), pp. 21-23.

118. Office of Telecommunications Policy (Executive Office of the President). *Analysis of the Causes and Effects of Increases in Same-Year Rerun Programming and Related Issues in Prime-Time Network Television* (Washington: OTP, March 1973).

119. Westinghouse Broadcasting Co., Inc. "Petition for Inquiry, Rule Making and Immediate Temporary Relief," filed before the Federal Communications Commission, September 3, 1976.

120. *The New York Times* (November 24, 1976), p. 43, and *The Wall Street Journal* (November 24, 1976), p. 40.

121. 42 *Federal Register* 4992 (January 26, 1977).

122. 40 RR 2d 80 (1977).

123. Manning and Owen, p. 43.

124. Roger G. Noll, "Television and Competition," unpublished paper prepared for the Federal Trade Commission Symposium on the Media, December 1978, p. 11.

125. Roger G. Noll, et al. *Economic Aspects of Television Regulation* (Washington: Brookings Institution, 1973), pp. 62-63.

126. 1 RR 2d 696 (1963).

127. Current Developments in CATV, TV, and Pay Television (New York: Practicing Law Institute, 1978), p. 547.

128. Manning and Owen, p. 35.

129. Noll, "Television and Competition," p. 8.

130. See note 4, and also Noll, et al., *Economic Aspects*, p. 37, note 15; p. 62, notes 5-6.

131. Bruce M. Owen, et al. *Television Economics* (Lexington, Mass.: Lexington Books, 1974), p. 19.

132. OTP, 1973; see also Dennis B. McAlpine, *The Television Programming Industry* (New York: Tucker Anthony & R.L. Day, January 1975).

133. Manning and Owen, pp. 34-35.

134. Bruce M. Owen, "Structural Approaches to the Problem of TV Network Economic Dominance," (Durham, N.C.: Duke University Graduate School of Business Administration, Center for the Study of Business Regulation Paper No. 27, 1978). Note: this paper is not paginated, so references are made to the text by means of the footnote numbers which appear throughout; in this case, text at notes 127-129.

135. R.E. Park, *New Television Networks.* (Santa Monica, Calif.: Rand Corp. R-1408-MF, December 1973), especially pp. 27-30 which summarize the options and weigh them.

136. See Owen, "Structural Approaches . . ." generally.

137. Manning and Owen, pp. 43-53 reviews the models and their applications; see also the Owen paper (note 132) and Noll, et al. *Economic Aspects. . .* , pp. 49-53.

138. Noll, "Television and Competition," p. 14.

139. Sterling and Haight, table 260-D summarizes Census data on three important related manufacturing industries.

140. For an excellent discussion of the limits and relatively few benefits of localism, see Noll, et al. *Economic Aspects . . .* , pp. 108-120.

141. See Chapter 7, Cable and Pay Television.

142. See, for example, Cliff Christians, "Home Video Systems: A Revolution?" *Journal of Broadcasting* 17:223-234 (Spring 1973).

143. *A Public Trust: The Landmark Report of the Carnegie Commission on the Future of Public Broadcasting* (New York: Bantam Books, 1979). Table C-1, p. 329.

144. Ibid., Table C-3, p. 331.

145. Ibid., Table C-4, p. 331.

146. Ibid., Table C-2, p. 330.

147. Ibid., p. 13.

148. Ibid., p. 15.

149. Ibid., p. 16.

Magazines

The threshold of the 1980s finds the magazine industry having substantially completed a fundamental change. As a modern publishing form, the magazine is barely a hundred years old. For much of their life, magazines served as the mass medium in American society. Now that other media, principally television, serve that purpose, magazine publishers are justifying their existence by serving either portions of the entire literate audience, or small groups of readers with intense interest in a particular subject. This change does not mean, as has been reported, that the mass circulation, general interest magazine is dead. It does mean that an increasing proportion of magazines published – and probably of total magazine circulation – will be accounted for by special interest or limited audience publications.

The terms *magazine* and *periodical* are used interchangeably in this section. Moreover, a magazine is defined as a publication that appears – or at least is intended to appear – on a regular basis with a minimum frequency of four times annually under a common title. This definition excludes from discussion many of the annual publications that are listed by magazine publishers in *Standard Rate & Data Service*'s consumer magazine and business magazine directories. Publications with frequency less than quarterly are not counted in determining size of publishing groups.

EVOLUTION OF MAGAZINES

Magazines evolved because of two unique characteristics that differentiated them from newspapers. First, since they did not have to carry up-to-the minute news, they could rely on more leisurely delivery systems than newspapers, especially to spread-out rural areas. More importantly, in an age before television and radio, they were able to offer an advertiser national coverage. As Americans spent increasing amounts of money on raising their material standard of living, magazines benefited from the expanding market for the goods and services advertisers offered.

Throughout the 20th century, the magazine responded to the dynamics of several factors:

1) more people with more money for discretionary spending;
2) the spread of popular education;
3) the increase in the amount of leisure time.

The magazine has always faced competition in taking advantage of these changes. In the early years of the century, newspapers were the primary competition and, to a lesser extent, books. Soon movies became an important form of entertainment. In the twenties, radio swept the nation, unmatched in speed of penetration until television came along beginning in the late 1940s. And the inexpensive paperback books, getting under way just before World War II, have become a major form of mass media in the past two decades.

Under this barrage of competition, magazines nonetheless continued to expand, for in many ways each new medium helped the older ones. As book publishers have learned that a successful movie spurred rather than harmed book sales, so magazine publishers have been able to take advantage of television. Popularity of televised spectator sports has stimulated sales of sports magazines, and fast breaking news on TV has created opportunities for deeper analysis and perspective in the news weeklies (since 1946 the combined circulation of the newsweeklies has about quadrupled).

MAGAZINES BECOMING MORE SPECIALIZED

But perhaps the most significant reason for the magazine's survival has been its ability to adapt to a changing role in society. It is no longer needed as a national advertising tool for mass-oriented products. Television can supply far-flung regions with the same advertisement seen in New York at the same time. Nor is it needed purely for entertainment, as television and the movies satisfy those needs. Magazines have changed — out of necessity as much as through foresight — into a medium for serving discrete interests within the mass population. Whereas most magazines used to be published for a mass readership, today even most of the so-called mass consumer magazines have narrowed their audiences down to definable proportions.

This specialization covers not just consumer magazines but the diverse information needs of business and the professions through a steadily increasing number of trade magazines, both paid and controlled (sent free to an eligible population) circulation. As with consumer magazines, business magazines serve the need of advertisers who wish to reach a well-defined audience for their product or service.

Number of Magazines Increasing

One indication of this specialization is that the number of magazines has been growing, even though total magazine circulation is fairly level. In 1950 there were 6960 periodicals in the *Ayer Directory*.[1] By 1979 the number had increased by almost 40%, although with deaths and births, the actual number of different titles is no doubt much greater. Most of these have been small circulation, specialized publications serving alumni groups, industry associations, clubs, professional societies and the numerous consumer interests that have emerged. But growth in total circulation has been less, since it takes many 25,000 and 150,000 circulation magazines to replace the mass circulation versions of *Life, Look, Saturday Evening Post* and *Colliers.* (Although the first three have reappeared they are all structured to survive on less circulation than the six or eight million of their predecessors).

Publishers have always been quick in sensing new interests within the public and then establishing new publications to cater to them. When the movies made Hollywood the center of attention for those curious about the private lives of the stars, *Photoplay* appeared and grew into a fat fan magazine. In 1934, with model railroad hobbyists numbered in the hundreds, an entrepreneur put out *Model Railroader,* a magazine whose circulation is now near 175,000. And when, in 1951, the aqualung made underwater adventure available to skilled swimmers, an enthusiast launched *Skin Diver,* now selling 166,000 copies a month.

Whole categories have sprung up to meet new interests and imitators join the successful innovators. By 1979 there were magazines for gamblers, private pilots, brides-to-be, horse breeders, home decorators and fixer-uppers, antique collectors, followers of politics, sports, news, hair styles and psychology. Business periodicals exist for food engineers, automotive mechanics, consumer electronics, retailers and even for magazine publishers.

The Fragmenting Society[2]

To elaborate on the earlier list of factors that have contributed to the general climate of magazine readership, it is necessary to comment on those causes that have forced the magazine industry, more than the other media, to diversify:

• Job specialization. A more complex society creates a need for specialized subgroups of managers, engineers, researchers, financiers. To meet the needs of these subgroups, many of which don't understand the language of the other, there are the special publications tailored to their needs – the business and professional press.

• The assertion of new freedoms and tastes. American society is becoming more permissive, resulting in magazines that have responded to different groups asserting their potential of becoming new markets. This includes the "new" women's magazines like *Ms.*, the city magazines like *Philadelphia,* or the sex books beginning from *Playboy* to the more explicit *Penthouse.* Youth is served as *Rolling Stone* moves beyond rock music to youth culture, while blacks are finding a continually widening range of magazines directed at them.

• Spread of education. In the past two decades, higher education has become mass education in the U.S. Half of all high school graduates now go on to college. In the past 10 years more than 12 million individuals have received a bachelor's degree (millions more attended but did not receive a diploma), and the number receiving degrees in the next 10 years will be even greater. The result has been the creation of a vast college-educated, literate audience with a multiplicity of personal and intellectual interests.

• A consumer haven. With a market as vast and wealthy as that of the U.S., almost any well-presented idea can create a highly lucrative, if limited, submarket for itself.

• Increased opportunities to pursue interests. More than just leisure time, Americans have the discretionary income to embrace a wide variety of pursuits, from bowling to camping, furniture building to wine-making. People with similar interests join together, identifying with one another. Advertisers have adpated to new consumer trends by seeking out publications that will reach like groups of consumers. Among other things, they've learned that an individual will not react to a liquor ad found in *TV Guide* as he would to one in *Gourmet.*

ROLE OF MAGAZINES

Throughout their history – and because of it – magazines have made substantial contributions to society and popular culture.

First, by their very diversity, they have provided the populace with an inexpensive and open marketplace for an exchange of ideas, opinions and information, as well as a forum for debate. Among the nearly 10,000 periodicals there are magazines devoted to subjects from Ukranian culture to the problems of retirement. This diversity has come at something of a price to the publisher: the high level of failure among the seemingly secure and established as well as the new. It has been calculated that of the 40 magazines with a circulation of over one million in 1951, fully 30% were dead by 1974.

Second, magazines play a role in the public enlightenment. Magazines have often taken the initiative in delving into national issues and problems, going back at least to the muckraking days of Ida Tarbell and Lincoln Steffens at *McClure's*. They have dealt with such concerns as the problems of black equality, poverty in the midst of affluence, the decay of the cities, the administration of justice, the war in Vietnam, the corruption of politicians. In many cases, these issues were first brought up by the small, limited audience magazines and were then picked up for mass attention by the big magazines, sometimes years later. Consumer education has been a major topic for the *Journal of Home Economics* since the 1930s; the *New Republic* headlined "Consumers United!" back in November 1933.

Third, the magazine has long been the communicator and sometimes initiator of popular culture. The comic book heroes are an obvious example. But magazines also help create fads, in language as well as form. Often a scholarly journal will use certain words, such as "rubric." These words are picked up by the small circulation, high-brow periodicals like *New York Review of Books*, then make their way to an *Esquire*, and finally are adopted for ultimate diffusion by *Time* or *Newsweek*. Skipping the intermediate steps, *Time* picked up a Susan Sontag essay in *Partisan Review* about something she called "camp." Within weeks after *Time*'s article the term was cropping up in the other mass media.

Fourth, magazines have provided a wide range of diversion — from sexual escapism to informative pieces on the space program.

Finally, they are instructors that help with daily living: they tell how to prepare food better, or to cope with the rigors of living in New York, how to order wine, how to build a radio receiver, or where to go for a quiet vacation. *Better Homes & Gardens* once estimated that 2.2 million readers clip something for future reference from an average issue. *Hot Rod* has been found to be very popular in school libraries and is ordered in bulk by teachers who have found that issues hold great appeal for slow readers.

DEVELOPMENT OF THE INDUSTRY

The American magazine dates back to February 1741, when Andrew Bradford brought out *American Magazine, or a Monthly View of the Political State of the British Colonies*. His first issue beat Benjamin Franklin's *General Magazine* by three days.[3]

For the next 150 years, magazines existed on a small scale and with limited life — Bradford's effort died in three months, Franklin's lasted only twice as long. Most magazines were for a small set of the educated and had limited circulations, 2000 to 3000 being good-sized. The modern magazine can find its origins in two events of the late 19th century. In 1879 Congress decided to provide low-cost mailing privileges for periodicals. This helped fuel the boom in publishing, already being fed by the growth in secondary education, as the number of magazines leaped from 700 in 1865 to 3300 in 1885. Still, a large circulation was 100,000. Then, in October 1893, Frank A. Munsey announced a reduction in his *Munsey's Magazine* subscription price from $3 to $1 per year and his single copy price from 25 cents to a dime. Munsey was putting into practice what was then just an emerging concept, that by selling his magazine for less than its cost of production, he could achieve a large circulation. His profits would come from the large volume of advertising a hefty circulation would attract. For the first time, publishers such as Cyrus Curtis, Edward Bok, S. S. McClure and others began to provide magazines for the masses, filling the gap between the "class" books such as *Harper's* and *Scribner's* and inexpensive pulp readers like the *People's Literary Companion.*

Munsey's idea worked. Circulation of his first 10-cent issue was 40,000. By April 1895 it was up to 500,000. At the beginning of the 20th century, the characteristics of the modern magazine had begun to emerge.

• Magazines had become low in price, typically 10 cents, sometimes five cents.

• As a result of this low price, mass production and mass distribution, they had achieved previously undreamed-of circulations. By 1900 the *Ladies' Home Journal* was near one million.

• The role of advertising became paramount. Publishers needed it to make their low circulation prices work, while advertisers were attracted to magazines for the first time as a means of reaching a national market.

• In attempting to serve wider audiences, magazine content was reaching out to appeal to new and diverse interests.

By the early years of the 20th century, the magazine industry was dominated by giant publishers. In 1918, Curtis Publishing Co.'s three big magazines, *Saturday Evening Post, Ladies' Home Journal,* and *Country Gentleman*, accounted for 43% of all national advertising dollars spent in consumer and farm publications. In 1920 the five leading magazines in advertising revenues grossed $41.9 million, or 56% of the total. By 1977 such dominance had waned somewhat. Time Inc., the largest publisher in advertising revenue, even without *Life*, accounted for 12.7% of the total, while the five leading magazines (*TV Guide, Time, Newsweek, Parade* and *Sports Illustrated*) together brought in about 28% of all magazine ad revenue, down from about 31% in 1973.[4]

If any single characteristic dominates the history of the magazine it is its constant state of flux. Since 1900 thousands of publications have come and gone. In 1930, 25 consumer and farm magazines had circulations in excess of one million. Thirty years later, 15 were dead. Yet others keep trying. Many of today's top magazines did not even exist 30 years ago: *Sports Illustrated, TV Guide, Playboy, People* to name a few.

COMPETITIVE NATURE OF MAGAZINE BUSINESS

Magazine publishing has been a vigorous, highly competitive business primarily because of its economic structure. It has traditionally been an easy field to enter. With a month or two credit from a printer, one or two people can put out a first issue with almost no capital. Multi-million-dollar full-blown national distribution explosions from a Time Inc. notwithstanding, magazine publishing is still possible for low rollers. Hugh Hefner reportedly assembled the first issue of *Playboy*, appropriately enough, from his bedroom, while *Rolling Stone* began in a loft.

Besides its dynamic nature, a second pervasive feature of the industry is the central role of the entrepreneur: the individual with a concept. Time and again the history of periodical publishing shows the role of the idea paramount. Money and initial execution are secondary. Hadden and Luce initiated the news summary magazine concept and got an edge that *Newsweek* is still trying to overcome. DeWitt Wallace didn't do a mammoth marketing study before launching *Reader's Digest*, he just "felt" that it could sell and used his intuition to guide him. Publishing histories are dominated by the names of men, rarely organizations. It was Edward Bok who made the *Ladies' Home Journal* the largest circulation magazine in the world for a time and Cyrus Curtis who made the *Saturday Evening Post* into the most successful weekly of its time. Curtis could somehow sense a market for a new publication: business associates and advertising people had advised him against starting the *Journal* and later the *Post*.

Theodore Peterson, author of *Magazines in the Twentieth Century*, divides publishers into two rough groups: the missionaries and the merchants. Their behavior is often similar, but their motivation differs.

Those in the former group are publishers devoted to their cause, some "secular gospel." *Reader's Digest*'s Wallace preached optimism; Luce believed in the efficacy of photographs as vehicles for information and education; Harold Ross of the *New Yorker* strived for perfection; and Bernarr Macfadden of *True Story* and *True Romances* used his publications to either directly promote his cause of bringing "health and joy through exercise, diet and the simple life" or to amass profits to further such ends through his foundation.

The merchants are not particularly champions of some cause. They regard magazine publishing strictly as a business enterprise to be operated for little else than profit. Nonetheless, in pursuit of this, they often put out superior publications, such as S.S. McClure's *McClure's Magazine* in its muckraking days. Condé Nast saw a niche for fashion publications catering to luxury-loving readers who would be attracted by slick, elegant publications, and the result was *Vogue, Glamour* and *Mademoiselle*. Wilford Fawcett and George T. Delacorte Jr. found profits in magazines edited for a lower level of sophistication. Fawcett's *Captain Billy's Whiz Bang* was followed by his copy of the confession magazines, then *Mecahnix Illustrated,* working on the formula made successful by *Popular Mechanics. Men* copied *Esquire, Spot* followed *Life* and not even Superman was immune from an imitation in Captain Marvel. A more recent merchant is Bob Guccione, whose *Penthouse* is the first serious threat to *Playboy.*

Magazine history is littered with a sense of *déja vu.* Time Inc.'s *People* was preceded by Newsweek's *People Today*, introduced in 1950 as a 10-cent magazine "to portray ... in words and pictures people in all their facets — at work, asleep, or very much alive." In 1900 outdoorsmen could subscribe to *Shooting and Fishing, American Golf* or *Bird-Lore.* Today publishers are complaining about the hardships being imposed by the increase in second-class postage rates. Rate hearings in 1949 and 1962 produced the same complaints, but the resulting increases came and there has been little change in the string of new magazines started, nor can any publications trace their demise to the postal burden alone.

The industry is highly fragmented, so much so that no one company or group of companies dominates it. While *TV Guide* accounts for 5.5% of the combined per issue sales for 375 audited magazines, the great diversity of magazine editorial matter, combined with the considerable segmentation of interests within the population, insures the existence of a large number of differentiated publications.

The great diversity of publishers and publications has its counterpart in a paucity of detailed information about the industry. Publishers are extremely close-mouthed about the economics of their operations; only a small minority report to the Publishers Information Bureau, an industry clearing house for advertising and circulation data. Most small publishing houses and many of the largest are privately owned and therefore need not release any of the details of their operation. Even many publicly owned firms, such as Times Mirror Co. and CBS, lump operating figures of various enterprises together, making an analysis of magazine finances difficult.

SIZE OF THE INDUSTRY

The periodical publishing industry is a relatively small segment of the total industrial milieu and accounts for 25% of shipments of the print media industry. Value of shipments in 1978 was an estimated $6.6 billion, up 210% since 1960 and an increase of 107% from 1970. During the same periods, the overall economy, as measured by current dollar GNP, showed increases of 316% and 114%, respectively. Thus, as

Table 4.1   Value of Periodical Shipments Compared to Gross National Product, Selected Years, 1960-1978

	GNP (billions)	Industry Value of Shipments (millions)
1960	$ 506.0	$2,133.0
1965	688.1	2,626.0
1970	982.4	3,195.0
1975	1,528.8	4,380.0
1976	1,706.5	5,044.0
1977	1,889.6	5,800.0[a]
1978	2,106.6	6,612.0[a]
% Change		
1960-78	316%	210%
1970-78	114	107

a. Estimate.

Sources: U.S. Bureau of the Census, as published in the *U.S. Industrial Outlook, 1979* and previous editions. GNP: U.S. Bureau of Economic Analysis.

seen in Table 4.1, the relatively sluggish growth of magazines of the 1960s has given way to a decade of near-average expansion. Industry employment in 1978 reached 77,400,[5] 19% of the number of employees in the newspaper industry, although periodicals had shipments equal to 45% of newspapers.

Circulation

There are no current complete tabulations of magazine circulation, in part owing to the large number of magazines and the fact that many do not belong to an auditing agency. In 1975, when the Magazine Publishers Association (MPA) last tabulated total annual copies of all general and farm magazines, annual sales had reached 5.7 billion copies, an increase of 34% from 1960. The average circulation per issue was 334,000, compared to 250,034 in 1960.

Table 4.2 provides a less than complete picture of circulation trends because it covers only 375 consumer magazines audited by the Audit Bureau of Circulation (ABC). It indicates that 266.8 million copies

Table 4.2   Magazine Circulation and Adult Population, 1914-1978

	Number of Magazines	Circulation[a] (millions)	Average Annual Change	Avg. Circulation per Magazine per Issue (thousands)	Circulation per 100 Adults
1914	54	17.9	—	331	26.5
1920	146	44.1	24.4	302	60.7
1930	232	78.8	7.7	340	90.5
1940	224	94.8	2.0	423	123.8
1950	250	147.3	5.5	589	133.3
1955[b]	272	180.0	4.4	662	155.8
1960	273	190.4	1.2	697	153.7
1965	275	215.5	2.6	784	160.9
1970	300	244.2	2.7	814	168.1
1975	327	250.8	0.5	767	170.9
1976	336	255.4	1.8	760	170.9
1977	373	263.9	3.3	708	173.5
1978[c]	375	266.8	1.1	711	172.4
% Change					
1914-1978	594	1391.0	4.3[d]	115	551.0
1970-1978	25	9.0	1.1[d]	−13	2.6

a. A.B.C. audited circulation for second six months of each year.
b. *Reader's Digest* first counted as A.B.C. member.
c. First six months average circulation.
d. Compounded annual change.

Source: Magazine Publishers Association, Inc.

were sold for an average issue of the 375 audited magazines in 1978. Perhaps more significantly, it shows that circulation per adult has risen steadily over the years, standing at about 1.7 per adult in 1978. Table 4.2 also tabulates the average circulation per magazine per issue. This actually peaked in 1971 at about 827,000 (not shown in the table) and declined to slightly over 700,000 by the late 1970s. This is no doubt due in part to the demise of some of the largest mass circulation magazines in that period. The slight increase from 1977 to 1978 cannot yet be viewed as part of a trend.

In recent years magazine publishers have been concentrating more on "quality" circulation rather than numbers. Rapidly increasing postal costs — second-class rates alone were up 413% between 1971 and 1979 — as well as significant increases in paper costs have forced publishers to look to the consumer to carry a greater share of the expense. Some publications have built their distribution around greater emphasis on newsstand sales as a result: *Playboy* has long concentrated in this area, while some women's magazines — CBS' *Woman's Day* and The New York Times Co.'s *Family Circle* — are virtually all single copy sales. Time Inc. has sold its new and successful *People* through newsstands and supermarkets, offering subscriptions only through offers in the magazine itself and then only at a price relatively close to the single copy price.

It should be no surprise, therefore, that magazine prices have advanced substantially faster than consumer prices in general during the 1970s. The average subscription cost of general interest magazines in 1970 was reported to be $8.47. This was up 104% to $17.26 by 1978. During this period, consumer prices rose 78%. All periodicals, including academic journals and technical, professional and business periodicals, advanced even more, 165%, from $10.41 to $27.58.[6] Single copy prices have risen commensurately.

Number of Magazines

The number of periodicals increased almost 40% between 1950 and 1979, with 9719 magazines published in 1979. The number peaked at 9872 in 1976. Among the most common frequencies of publication listed in Table 4.3, the bimonthly format showed the greatest increase in popularity, with 607 more titles, 139%, in 1979 than in 1950. Monthly publication remains the most common interval, with 40% of periodicals appearing at that frequency. Quarterly publication — popular for many scholarly journals — showed a strong jump in use, with much of the growth coming in the 1960 to 1970 period, coinciding with the boom in educational funding and enrollments.

Advertising

Magazine advertising revenue, although strong in recent years, has nonetheless fallen precipitously as a proportion of total advertising expenditures. Consumer magazines accounted for 13% of advertising expenditures in 1945, before television and about 5.9% in 1978, a small rebound from 1977. Business publications accounted for an additional 3.3% of advertising.

Table 4.3   Number of Periodicals, by Frequency, Selected Years, 1950-1979

	1950	1960	1970	1979	Percent Change 1950-1979
Weekly	1,443	1,580	1,856	1,764	22.2%
Semimonthly[a]	416	527	589	594	42.8
Monthly	3,694	4,113	4,314	3,850	4.2
Bimonthly	436	743	957	1,043	139.2
Quarterly	604	895	1,108	1,261	108.6
Other	367	564	749	1,207	228.9
Total	6,960	8,422	9,573	9,719	39.6

(peaked at 9,872 in 1976)

a. Includes bi-weeklies (every other week).

Source: *Ayer Directory of Publications,* annual (Bala Cynwd, Pa.: Ayer Press). Some portion of the increase over the years may be due to better reporting on the part of the *Ayer Directory.* Figures refer to year of completion of Directory, usually that preceding year shown.

In 1978 about $2.7 billion was spent by advertisers in magazines, up 20% from a year earlier. Business publications did not fare quite as well, with a 16% increase. Both, however, outperformed overall advertising growth, which was up about 15% in 1978. Table 4.4 traces advertising

Table 4.4   Advertising Expenditures in Magazines, Selected Years, 1935-1978

	Total	Magazines (millions)	Business Publications (millions)	Percent of All Advertising Expenditures
1935	187	$ 136	$ 51	11.1%
1945	569	365	204	19.8
1950	766	515	251	13.4
1955	1,175	729	446	12.8
1960	1,550	941	609	13.0
1965	1,870	1,199	671	12.3
1970	2,063	1,323	740	10.5
1975	2,458	1,539	919	8.7
1976	2,910	1,875	1,035	7.3
1977	3,473	2,252	1,221	9.1
1978[a]	4,120	2,700	1,420	9.4

a. Preliminary.

Sources: 1935-1970: *Historical Statistics of the U.S.: Colonial Times to 1970.*
1975-1978: *Advertising Age,* compiled by McCann-Erickson, New York.

expenditure trends in magazines and business publications since 1935 and shows that periodicals regained some market share in 1977 and 1978.

A tabluation of advertising revenue and pages in those general magazines that report to the Publishers Information Bureau arm of the MPA shows that magazine revenue gains since 1970 have performed close to the overall economy, although since 1929 magazines have lost considerable ground to GNP. Moreover, Table 4.5 shows revenue has advanced at more than twice the rate of advertising pages since 1970. Even more dramatically, since 1950 the 71% growth in annual adver- tising pages spawned a 498% hike in advertising revenue. This has been the result of a rapid escalation in average per page cost for magazines, from $5886 for this group in 1950 to $20,597 in 1978. (However, magazine ad rates have gone up less than any other mass medium since 1967 on an absolute dollar basis and only radio advertising has increased less on a cost per thousand basis).[7]

Table 4.5   General Magazine Advertising Revenue and Pages and GNP, Selected Years, 1929-1978

Year	Number of Magazines	Adv. Revenue (millions)	Adv. Pages	Average Rev./Page	GNP (billions)
1929	61	$ 185.7	N.A.	–	$ 103.4
1933	106	92.6	N.A.	–	55.8
1945	97	286.7	N.A.	–	212.3
1950	85	396.7	67,392	$ 5,886	286.2
1960	79	380.0	74,861	11,087	506.0
1965	91	1,055.3	80,147	13,167	688.1
1970	89	1,168.7	76,924	15,193	982.4
1971	91	1,235.2	77,008	16,040	982.4
1972	83	1,297.7	82,007	15,824	1,063.4
1973	85	1,309.2	85,665	15,283	1,171.1
1974	93	1,366.3	86,305	15,831	1,306.6
1975	94	1,336.3	80,735	16,552	1,412.9
1976	93	1,622.0	93,253	17,394	1,528.8
1977	96	1,965.4	103,307	19,025	1,889.6
1978	102	2,374.2	115,266	20,597	2,106.6
% Change:					
1929-1978	67	1,179.0	–	–	1,937.0
1950-1978	20	498.0	71	250	636.0
1970-1978	15	103.0	50	36	114.0

N.A.   Not available.

Sources: Advertising: Publishers Information Bureau (does not include Sunday supplements).
         GNP: U.S. Bureau of Economic Analysis.

Table 4.6 Concentration in the Periodical Publishing Industry, Selected Years, 1947-1977

	1947	1958	1963	1967	1972	1977[a]	Median for Large Industrial Firms, 1972
Number of companies	2106	2246	2562	2430	2451	N.A.	
Value of shipments (billions)	$1.1	1.7	2.3	3.1	3.5	4.8	
Percentage accounted for by:							
4 largest	34	31	28	24	26	20	38
8 largest	43	41	42	37	38	30	53
20 largest	50	55	59	56	54	37[b]	72
50 largest	N.A.	69	73	72	69	N.A.	86

a. Percentages estimated by Knowledge Industry Publications, Inc.
b. 12 largest.
N.A. Not available.

Sources: U.S. Bureau of the Census, Census of Manufacturers, 1972.
Median calculated by Knowledge Industry Publications, Inc.

INDUSTRY STRUCTURE

There were 2451 periodical publishing companies in 1972, according to the 1972 Census of Manufacture. The 9700 periodicals they publish can be roughly divided into three categories: consumer, farm and business. By far the largest segment is the general consumer magazines, accounting for almost 60% of magazine revenue. Farm publications make up only 2% of the market, with business, trade, organization and professional magazines accounting for the remainder.[8]

Revenue Structure

Traditionally, magazines derived the bulk of their revenue from advertising. Although still a primary component of sales, circulation income has been providing an increasing share in recent years, especially for consumer magazines. Most business magazines are still supported almost exclusively by advertisers, since they tend to be sent free to their audience.

In the late 1960s advertising accounted for 60% of total receipts for general consumer magazines. But by 1976 it accounted for only 45% of revenue,[9] as publishers pushed up subscription and newsstand prices and accepted lower circulation and slower growth rather than offer the discount subscriptions of the past. While farm publication advertising revenue has held steady at about 80% of the total, even business publications have experienced an increase in circulation revenue, dropping the advertising proportion from 78% in 1967 to 69% in 1976.[10] (This may be somewhat misleading when viewed as an average, in that business publications tend to be either mostly free or mostly paid. The change may be the product of both: 1) paid-for business magazines sharing a trend similar to consumer magazines while the controlled circulation publications continue being 100% advertiser supported; and 2) paid-for business magazines simply increasing in number.)

CONCENTRATION

Besides the considerable number and diversity of magazines, the periodical publishing industry shows relatively less concentration of ownership than large industries overall and a decline in concentration between 1947 and 1972 (Table 4.6). Compared to newspaper and book publishing, periodical publishing is somewhat more concentrated at the four and eight largest firm level, but the trend to 1972 was toward a slight lessening in concentration for periodicals, while the others showed slight increases. (See Chapters 2 and 6.)

Knowledge Industry Publications further estimates that the degree of concentration in 1977 was no higher and perhaps lower than in 1972. Based on magazine revenues for the leading publishers in Table 4.7 and industry receipts, the top four publishers in 1977 accounted for 20% of industry receipts, the eight largest publishers for 30% and the 12 largest for 37%. Although these figures are not directly compatible with Census Bureau calculations, they should provide an early indication of direction.

Table 4.6 also indicates that the number of periodical publishing companies, while lower in 1972 than in 1963, was nonetheless greater than in any other year of the census.

It will be shown below that many of the largest circulation magazines are independent − that is, published by firms that publish no other magazines (Table 4.8). Of the leading magazine publishers in revenue, two (Reader's Digest and Washington Post Co.), have only one title, although both are dominant forces in other mass media. Triangle owns only two major titles, although it announced a new title, *Panorama*, for 1980.

There are 285 multiple title publishers of consumer, farm and business periodicals identified by Standard Rate & Data Service in November 1978. (SR&DS itself does not provide the tally). There is some double counting, in that some groups, such as Ziff-Davis and Harcourt Brace Jovanovich, are included in both business and consumer/farm sectors. On the other hand, SR&DS lists only those publishers that accept advertising for their magazines. It is also incomplete, since Triangle (*TV Guide* and *Seventeen*) is not included

Table 4.7   Selected Characteristics of Group-Owned and Independently Published Magazines, 1978

	Group-Owned	Non-Group
Consumer		
Average circulation	466,000	247,000
Subscription cost	10.95	11.17
Cost per thousand		
1 time black and white ad	14.98	20.44
Business		
Average circulation	33,000	34,000
% Paid	29	43

Source: Knowledge Industry Publications, Inc. Non-group figures from sample of magazines listed in SR&DS, Nov. 1978. Group owned from tabulation of actual circulation and subscription prices of all such magazines listed in SR&DS, Nov. 1978. CPM for groups taken from sample of group-owned magazines.

and others may not be. Furthermore, many publications, such as academic journals, are not listed in any SR&DS publication, yet many of these journals do accept advertising and are published by groups. (John Wiley and Elsevier are among the many book publishers with a stable of journals. Pergamon Press alone publishes 226 journals.)[11]

For all these reasons, it is difficult to accurately measure the proportion of magazines that are published as part of multi-title firms. It can be calculated that 281 identifiable business and consumer/farm magazine groups published 1308 titles of quarterly or greater annual frequency in 1978, which accounts for 13.5% of the 9719 periodicals identified by the *'79 Ayer Directory*.

Difference Between Groups and Non-Group Magazines

As might be reasonably expected, there are some overall differences between magazines published as part of a group and those that are independent. Table 4.7 summarizes selected characteristics of the two types of ownership. The average circulation of group-owned consumer periodicals is about 89% greater than independently owned titles. It would be expected that as an independent magazine becomes larger, more visible and presumably gains greater revenue and profit potential, it becomes a more promising prospect for either being purchased by a group publisher or gaining the financial wherewithal to start or purchase additional publications itself, thus becoming part of a group.

Subscription price of both types of magazines are quite similar, reflecting in part the common competition they face for the consumer's magazine budget and price expectations. They also must factor in the same postal rates. Single copy sales tend to be insignificant for most small magazines and were not calculated here.

On the other hand, basic cost per thousand (cpm) advertising rates are substantially higher for the sample of independent magazines, again a likely outcome of the tendency of this group to include a greater proportion of small, highly selective special interest magazines with their commensurately higher cpm than general interest periodicals.[12]

Among business periodicals, which tend to have small circulations because they are almost all limited audience, special interest publications, there is virtually no difference in average circulation between the group and non-group publishers. The sample of non-group publishers, however, appears to have a somewhat higher percentage of paid subscribers.

Largest Magazines

Table 4.8 lists the 50 leading A.B.C. magazines in 1978 by circulation per issue. *TV Guide* passed long-time leader *Reader's Digest* in the

Table 4.8   50 Largest Circulation A.B.C.-audited Consumer and Farm Magazines and Their Owners, 1978

Rank		Publisher	Circulation
1	TV Guide	Triangle Publications, Inc.	19,881,726
2	Reader's Digest	Reader's Digest Association, Inc.*	18,300,843
3	National Geographic	National Geographic Society*	9,960,287
4	Family Circle	New York Times Co.	8,277,077
5	Better Homes & Gardens	Meredith Corporation	8,032,920
6	Woman's Day	CBS Inc.	8,002,758
7	McCall's	McCall Publishing Co.	6,503,187
8	Ladies' Home Journal	Charter Co.	6,001,578
9	National Enquirer	National Enquirer, Inc.*	5,719,918
10	Good Housekeeping	Hearst Corp.	5,198,082
11	Playboy	Playboy Enterprises, Inc.	4,824,789
12	Penthouse	Penthouse International Ltd.	4,510,824
13	Redbook	Charter Co.	4,431,266
14	Time	Time Inc.	4,311,084
15	Star, The	World News Corp.	3,008,948
16	Newsweek	Washington Post Co.	2,958,851
17	Cosmopolitan	Hearst Corp.	2,658,571
18	American Legion	The American Legion*	2,597,816
19	Sports Illustrated	Time Inc.	2,336,344
20	People	Time Inc.	2,319,097
21	U.S. News & World Report	U.S. News & World Report, Inc.*	2,100,796
22	Field & Stream	CBS Inc.	2,042,764
23	True Story	Macfadden Group Inc.	2,000,791
24	Popular Science	Times Mirror Co.	1,862,418
25	Workbasket	Modern Handicrafts Publications	1,814,486
26	Glamour	Condé Nast Publishing Co.	1,795,596
27	Outdoor Life	Times Mirror Co.	1,746,025
28	Midnight Globe	Midnight Publishing Corp.*	1,736,886
29	Mechanix Illustrated	CBS Inc.	1,704,774

30	Smithsonian	Smithsonian Institution National Associates*	1,682,831
31	V.F.W. Magazine	Veterans of Foreign Wars of the United States, Inc.*	1,681,561
32	Popular Mechanics	Hearst Corp.	1,670,832
33	Today's Education	National Education Assn. of the U.S.*	1,667,888
34	Boy's Life	Boy Scouts of America	1,620,673
35	Elks	Benevolent and Protective Order of Elks of the U.S.*	1,613,266
36	Southern Living	Progressive Farmer	1,594,117
37	Parents' Magazine	Parents' Magazine Enterprises, Inc. (Gruner & Jahr)	1,516,333
38	Hustler	Flynt Publications	1,507,901
39	Seventeen	Triangle Publications, Inc.	1,457,871
40	Farm Journal	Farm Journal, Inc.*	1,417,030
41	Sunset	Lane Publishing Co.	1,391,140
42	Sport	Charter Co.	1,305,219
43	Ebony	Johnson Publishing Co.	1,264,718
44	Psychology Today	Ziff-Davis Publishing Co.	1,172,440
45	Nation's Business	Chamber of Commerce of the U.S.*	1,165,411
46	Grit	Grit Publishing Co.*	1,096,234
47	Moneysworth	Avant-Garde Media, Inc.*	1,094,193
48	House & Garden	Condé Nast Publishing Co. (Newhouse)	1,031,324
49	Scouting	Boy Scouts of America	1,018,126
50	Vogue	Condé Nast Publishing Co. (Newhouse)	975,487
	Total — 50 Magazines		175,585,097

*Independent (non-group) publisher.

Source: Magazine Publishers Association, A.B.C. circulation, first six months, 1978.

early 1970s and has slowly been widening the gap. The 18.3 million for *Reader's Digest*, however, represents domestic circulation only, with another 11.7 million in 14 languages sold abroad. The top 10 magazines alone account for 36% of the total average per issue circulation of the 375 A.B.C. member magazines.

Of the top 10, seven have long been among the leaders. The demise of the old *Life, Look* and the *Saturday Evening Post*, long in the top ranks, opened the way for *National Geographic, National Enquirer* and *Good Housekeeping*, the junior members of the top ten.

Although 72% of the leading circulation magazines are part of magazine publishing groups, ironically two of the top three are nominally independent. *TV Guide* is controlled by Walter Annenberg's Triangle Publications, which also owns 39th ranked *Seventeen*. *Reader's Digest* is part of a $1 billion firm that derives a substantial portion of its income from books and other audio-visual media materials, but the company publishes no other magazines. *National Geographic* is published by the society and subscribers are technically "members." Number nine in circulation, *National Enquirer*, a weekly supermarket-distributed gossipy tabloid, is currently the firm's only periodical.

Of the remaining top 50, Hearst runs three with 9.5 million circulation, Time Inc. has three with 9.0 million circulation (but all weeklies, to Hearst's monthlies), CBS three with 11.6 million per issue and Chartcom (division of Charter Co.) three circulating 11.7 million. Times Mirror, Condé Nast (Newhouse) and the Boy Scouts of America are other organizations with more than one periodical in the list.

Leading Publishers

By Revenue. With its three profitable weeklies, a bi-weekly and two monthly magazines, Time Inc. is by far the largest magazine publisher in the United States. Table 4.9 identifies the largest publishers by revenue derived from periodical publication. *Reader's Digest*'s revenue includes foreign edition sales and Triangle is primarily *TV Guide*. With the exception of *Business Week*, McGraw-Hill's revenues are from business publications, the only predominately business publisher on the list. The Washington Post Co.'s only magazine is *Newsweek* and revenue includes the international edition. Ziff-Davis publishes mostly special interest magazines, but has four business periodicals as well. The only publisher that would not have been on a similar listing for 1973 is CBS, which took over Fawcett's spot when it acquired the publisher of *Woman's Day* in 1977.

Number of Magazines. At the end of 1978 there were 92 identifiable firms publishing more than one consumer or farm magazine. Among them they published 383 periodicals. With little overlap in membership,

ERRATUM: Table 4.9, page 147, should read as follows:

Table 4.9   Largest Magazine Publishers in the U.S., by Revenue, 1978

	Revenue from Magazine Publishing (millions)	Number of Domestic Magazines [b]
1. Time Inc.	$572	6
2. Reader's Digest Assn. Inc.	312[a]	1
3. Triangle Publications, Inc.	310[a]	2
4. Washington Post Co.	242	1
5. McGraw-Hill, Inc.	232	29
6. Charter Co.	196	4
7. CBS Inc.	150[a]	8
8. Hearst Corp.	145[a]	14
9. Ziff-Davis Publishing Co.	140[a]	15
10. New York Times Co.	131	4
11. Meredith Corp.	120[a]	5
12. Playboy Enterprises	113	3

a. Estimate.
b. Current to Feb. 28, 1979.

Source: Knowledge Industry Publications, Inc., and annual reports.

Table 4.9   Largest Magazine Publishers in the U.S., by Revenue, 1978

	Revenue from Magazine Publishing (millions)	Number of Domestic Magazines[b]
1. Time Inc.	$ 572	6
2. Reader's Digest Assn. Inc.	312[a]	1
3. Triangle Publications, Inc.	310[a]	2
4. Washington Post Co.	242	29
5. McGraw-Hill, Inc.	232	1
6. Charter Co.	196	13
7. CBS Inc.	150[a]	12
8. Hearst Corp.	145[a]	5
9. Ziff-Davis Publishing Co.	140[a]	4
10. New York Times Co.	131	3
11. Meredith Corp.	120[a]	4
12. Playboy Enterprises	113	8

a. Estimate.
b. Current to Feb. 28, 1979.

Source: Knowledge Industry Publications, Inc., and annual reports.

193 firms publish two or more domestic business publications, accounting for 925 titles. The average size of the business magazine group is almost five titles per company, while consumer publishers owned an average of 4.2 periodicals each. The most significant difference in the two categories is in average circulation per magazine. As seen already in Table 4.7, the typical group-owned business magazine had a 1978 circulation of 33,000, about 29% paid, the remainder free. The consumer magazines owned by chains averaged a paid circulation of 466,000.

Tables 4.10 and 4.11 identify the largest publishers in the consumer and business areas, respectively, by number of magazines. Broadcasting giant American Broadcasting Companies has moved determinedly into the magazine business in recent years, having purchased *Los Angeles* magazines, several special interest periodicals, two groups of farm publications and controlling interest in business magazine and book publisher Chilton, the latter acquisition announced in February 1979. Hearst is one of the oldest groups with many long running titles. *Cosmopolitan* was founded in 1836, *Harper's Bazaar* in 1867.

There is great diversity among the magazines published by these groups. Harcourt Brace Jovanovich, best known as a book publisher, owns farm and business publications and the average combined circulation of an issue of its magazines is only 609,000. On the other hand,

Table 4.10 Largest Consumer and Farm Magazine Publishers, by Number of Magazines in Group, 1978

	Number of Magazines in Group	Total Annual Average Circulation (thousands)	Total Average Circulation per Issue (thousands)
1. Hearst Corp.	12	145,016	12,085
2. American Broadcasting Companies Inc.	11	27,795	1,815
2. Petersen Publishing Co.	11	49,628	4,136
4. Challenge Publications, Inc.	10	5,492	493
4. Harcourt Brace Jovanovich, Inc.	10	2,952	609
4. Scholastic Magazines, Inc.	10	94,846	6,066
4. Webb Company	10	23,081	2,445
4. Ziff-Davis Publishing Co., Inc.	10	59,030	5,135
9. East/West Network, Inc.	9	14,443	1,204
9. The Laufer Company[a]	9	31,431	2,619
9. Lopez Publications, Inc.	9	13,175	1,155
12. CBS Inc.	8	112,261	13,392
12. Davis Publications, Inc.	8	12,794	1,156
12. Macfadden Group, Inc.	8	50,626	4,219
Total	134	641,828	56,619
Total consumer groups	92		
Total titles for groups	383		

a. Acquired by Harlequin Enterprises, 1978.

Source: Tabulated from *Standard Rate & Data Service Consumer Magazine and Farm Publication,* Nov. 27, 1978.

CBS has a stable of mass circulation and special interest magazines, with an average total circulation per issue of each publication of 13.4 million. Scholastic magazines are sold almost exclusively through subscriptions in school, while the East/West Network produces magazines for airlines to put in the seat pockets and none are paid for by readers. The total list accounts for 15% of the groups and 35% of the number of titles published by groups.

The magazines in each group are included in Appendix A4. The breadth of magazine coverage is evident by examining the titles for each group.

Harcourt Brace Jovanovich is the leading business periodical publisher in number of titles with 49, well ahead of McGraw-Hill. The total circulation of the HBJ publications, however, is substantially below that of McGraw-Hill. The publishers of business periodicals tend to be less well known than their consumer magazine counterparts. Business publications are a decidedly less glamorous side of the business for most journalists. Again, it can be seen that there is little cross-over between the consumer and business publications list.

Table 4.11 Largest Business Magazine Publishers, by Number of Magazines in Group, 1978

	Number of Business Periodicals
1. Harcourt Brace Jovanovich Publications, Inc.	49
2. McGraw-Hill, Inc.	29
3. Penton/IPC (subsidiary of Pittway Corp.)	23
4. Reed Publishing Corp. (Cahners)	21
5. Williams & Wilkins Co.	20
6. Technical Publishing Co. (subsidiary of Dun & Bradstreet)	20
7. Chilton[a]	19
8. Harper & Row Publishers, Inc. (with Lippincott)	17
9. American Chemical Society	15
9. North American Publishing Co.	15
	228
Total business groups	229
Total titles	925
Leading 10 group-owned titles as % of all group titles	25%

a. Acquired by American Broadcasting Companies, 1979.

Source: Tabulated from *Standard Rate & Data Service Business Publication Data,* Nov. 24, 1978. Table includes only those periodicals that solicit advertising through SR&DS listing. Thus, journal publishers such as John Wiley and Pergamon Press are not covered.

Magazine Circulation. The most common method for calculating total circulation for all magazines or for any group is to sum up the average circulation for one issue of each magazine. By this reckoning, which is the basis for the MPA's computations in Table 4.2, Triangle Publications, with *TV Guide* and *Seventeen*, would be the largest, followed by Reader's Digest (though not a group publisher), CBS, Hearst and Charter Co. (*Redbook, Ladies' Home Journal*). However, since the revenue and the impact of a magazine is based on how many copies it sells annually, it is more valid to factor in frequency per issue, so that a weekly carries 4.3 times the weight as a monthly of the same circulation per issue.

Table 4.12 has ranked the consumer magazine publishers by total copies circulated, based on first six month 1978 average circulation per issue. By this accounting, Triangle is still the largest magazine publisher, but Time Inc., with its group of weeklies, calculates to be twice the size of Reader's Digest. Newsweek, owned by the Washington Post Co., is fourth and The New York Times Co.'s periodicals are fifth. (In all cases, foreign editions have been omitted). Technically, neither Reader's

Table 4.12 Largest Consumer Magazine Publishers, by Total Annual Circulation, 1978

	Total Annual Circulation[a] (thousands)	Total Combined Circulation per Issue	Number of Magazines Published[b]
1. Triangle Publications, Inc.	1,051,360	21,299	2
2. Time Inc.[c]	492,623	10,377	6
3. Reader's Digest Assn.	220,452	18,371	1
4. New York Times Co.	157,349	10,890	5
5. Washington Post Co. (Newsweek)	153,868	2,959	1
6. Hearst Corp.	145,016	12,085	12
7. Charter Co.	143,645	11,970	4
8. Meredith Corp.	121,788	10,618	5
9. CBS Inc.	112,261	13,392	8
10. Scholastic Magazines	94,846	6,066	10
11. McCall Publishing Co.	80,482	6,707	2
12. Times Mirror Co.	75,496	5,446	6
13. Playboy Enterprises	69,730	5,811	3
14. Ziff-Davis Publishing Co.	59,030	5,135	10
15. Macfadden Group, Inc.	50,626	4,219	8
16. Newhouse (Condé Nast)	49,747	4,303	9
17. Petersen Publishing Co.	49,628	4,136	11
Total	3,185,890	159,117	102

a. Average circulation per issue x frequency.
b. Includes those started or acquired through February 1979. May not be in circulation totals.
c. Does not include *Life.*

Source: Knowledge Industry Publications, Inc. from ABC circulation figures, first 6 months 1978.

Digest nor Newsweek are group publishers, unless separate foreign editions are included.

For purposes of comparison, the table also calculates circulation on a straight per issue basis. These 17 magazine publishers produce 102 titles, or 26% of the periodicals totaled in Table 4.2. Their combined circulation per issue of 159 million represents 60% of the circulation of the magazines in Table 4.2.

The largest business publications groups are shown in Table 4.13. The calculation is based on a strict sum of the circulation of one issue of each title. Only McGraw-Hill has a significant number of weeklies with sizeable circulation (although the largest, *Business Week*, is sometimes considered a consumer publication). Reed Publishing is essentially the Cahners Publishing Co.'s list. While there are far more business magazine groups than consumer publishing groups (193 compared to 92), the number of titles per group was seen to be greater, but

Table 4.13 Largest Business Groups by Total Circulations, 1978

		Total Circulation (thousands)	Number in Group
1.	McGraw-Hill Inc.	2,419	29
2.	Penton/IPC	1,693	23
3.	Technical Publishing Co. (Dun-Donnelly Publishing Corp.)	1,215	20
4.	Harcourt Brace Jovanovich Publications	1,143	49
5.	Reed Publishing Corporation (Cahners)	1,122	21
6.	Chilton Company (A.B.C. Inc.)	1,076	19
7.	American Medical Association	755	11
8.	Medical Economics Company	729	7
9.	Irving-Cloud Publishing Company	537	8
10.	Fairchild Publications, Inc. (Capital Cities Communications Inc.)	507	14
	Total	11,196	201

Source: Tabulated from *Standard Rate and Data Service Business Publications Data*, Nov. 24, 1978.

the circulation per group is dramatically lower. Business publications, by their very nature, tend to be highly specialized (*Southern Pulp & Paper Manufacturer* and *Kitchen Business* are typical titles) and thus have strictly limited possible audience. That, of course, is their attraction to advertisers — the very selective market they deliver.

The total circulation of these groups, 11.2 million, represents 36% of the per issue circulation of the 31.2 million circulation of the 925 magazines published by groups. They also account for 22% of the magazines, though they are only 5% of the number of groups.

Relative Group Size

Most group publishers are relatively small in aggregate circulation. Of the 92 consumer groups, Table 4.14 tabulates that 37, or 40%, have aggregate circulation for all their magazines of under 300,000. At the other extreme, only seven group owners have total per issue circulation in excess of 10 million.

Among business magazine publishers, 41% of the groups have only two periodicals, while over three-fourths own five or fewer publications. As seen in Table 4.15, more than a third of these groups have aggregate circulation exceeding 50,000, and 95% send out fewer than 500,000 per issue of all titles. This again confirms the specialized and extremely diverse nature of the business periodicals end of the industry.

Table 4.14 Circulation Size of Consumer Magazine Groups, 1978

Total per Issue Circulation:	Number	Percent	Cumulative Percent
Under 300,000	37	40%	40%
300,000 to 999,999	15	16	56
1 million to 3 million	12	13	69
3 million to 10 million	13	14	83
Over 10 million	7	8	91
Not reported or unpaid	8	9	100
	92	100%	

Source: Calculated from circulation reported in *Standard Rate & Data Service, Consumer and Farm Magazines,* November 27, 1978.

Table 4.15 Circulation Size of Business Magazine Groups, 1978

Total per Issue Circulation	Number	Percent	Cumulative Percent
Under 50,000	68	35%	35%
50,000 to 99,999	44	23	58
100,000 to 199,999	34	18	76
200,000 to 499,999	36	19	95
500,000 to 1 million	4	2	97
Over 1 million	5	3	100
Not reported	2	1	101
	193	101%[a]	

a. Total exceeds 100% due to rounding.

Source: Calculated from circulation reported in *Standard Rate & Data Service Business Publications Data,* November 24, 1978.

TRENDS IN NEW PUBLICATIONS

In 1973 about 127 new consumer magazines were announced or made their first appearance. Some of them are major, well financed operations, such as George Hirsch's *New Times* or Bob Guccione's *Viva.* Others are obscure and of uncertain origins, like *New Awareness* and *Alaska Geographic.* Of these four, by the beginning of 1979 only *Alaska Geographic* was still a going concern.

Premature Obituaries

Five times in this century the doubters have written off the magazine's future.

1) After World War I, when the automobile became established as a legitimate business and pleasure vehicle for the masses, observers felt that people would no longer have time to read magazines.

2) In the mid-twenties, the radio was the source of dire predictions — who needs to read when you can just listen to the box?

3) Still later in that decade, the addition of "talkies" to the movie world added more cause for doom.

4) Then, of course, came television after World War II, the medium that did knock the others for a loop and which, more than any single factor, has changed the nature of the other media.

5) Finally, in the late 1960s and early 1970s, the demise of such icons as the *Saturday Evening Post, Look,* then *Life,* convinced many that magazines had finally had it.

But they have not gone away. True, evidence points to a different role for the magazine, but its survival seems assured.

Turnover, New Title and Interests

In 1977, 272 new magazine start-ups were announced, following 334 launchings in 1976 and 254 in 1975.[13] Most were consumer magazines:

	1975	1976	1977
Total new magazines	254	334	272
Consumer	N.A.	191	161
Business	N.A.	130	97
Other	N.A.	13	9

As is frequently the case, many do not last long, often but not always because they are undercapitalized. Among the major launchings of 1973, *New Times* entered the world having to turn away venture capital. It was sold in 1978 to entertainment conglomerate MCA Inc., which nonetheless let it fold before the year was over. Its place in the magazine lineup was taken by *The Runner,* from the same firm.

Also in 1973 *Penthouse,* flush with success, added a woman's magazine, *Viva.* That too was allowed to expire in 1978, as the company also brought out a replacement, *Omni.* McCall's gave *Your Place* a big build up, being its first new publication in 102 years. Introduced in February 1978, it too quit publishing before it celebrated its first birthday. McCall's, however, had a replacement waiting with *Working Mother.*

Harcourt Brace Jovanovich, which spent $4 million on *Human Nature*, a slick consumer magazine started in November 1977, folded the magazine in March 1979.

Clearly magazine publishing is high risk, yet it brings a constant stream of hopefuls into the marketplace each year. Among the start-ups announced in 1977 were *Kosher Home, Skateboard World, Ohio, Violent World, California Arts* and *Death Education.*

This profusion of new titles, added to the constantly changing titles over the years, has been the reason that magazines as an industry have been able to survive as well as they have. As leisure time for most Americans has increased, they have discovered a great assortment of hobbies, cults and pursuits. Interests have become more diversified and publishers have always been quick to establish new magazines catering to them. Titles such as *Shooting and Fishing, American Golf, Bird-Lore* and *Snap-Shots* are not of today — these were the special interest publications of 1900. One can scarcely name a specialized subject that does not have its own publication. Moreover, it has already been shown that as a title in a new category becomes successful, it is copied by others.

Even television may have given a boost to some magazines. Although TV is blamed for the demise of the entertainment value of magazines, TV as another medium of information often whets the appetite of its viewers for more information. Thus, *Time*'s newsstands sales jumped 34% in the last six months of 1973, the period of great television coverage of the Watergate hearings, drastically reversing the steady decline in single copy sales that had been occurring since 1964. The growth of *TV Guide* is of course linked closely to the penetration of television, and a book such as *Sports Illustrated* can look to television's expanding coverage of sports as a factor in its success.

ROLE OF THE ENTREPRENEUR

Quite possibly more than in any other industry the success or failure, the mediocrity or acclaim, of a general interest magazine can be traced to a specific individual: a Hugh Hefner, DeWitt Wallace, Henry Luce, Cyrus Curtis, a Bok, Gingrich, McClure or Ross. Magazines — the best magazines — have long been closely associated with a personality. And although it doesn't have to happen, all too frequently when that individual passes from the scene, the magazine begins to fade also. It may survive, but as a different book, reflecting the personality of another.

It is this observation that has led Clay Felker, among others, to postulate the life cycle hypothesis of magazine longevity. "There appears to be an almost inexorable life-cycle of American magazines that follows the pattern of humans," wrote Felker, former editor of *Esquire* and *New York Magazine*, in the Spring 1969 issue of *The Antioch Review*. That pattern is "a clamorous youth eager to be noticed; vigorous, productive middle-age marked by an easy-to-define editorial line; and a long, slow decline, in which efforts at revival are sporadic and tragically doomed."

This hypothesis strikes a logical note because magazines are so intensely personal. A successful editorial policy is more than just the assembling of data by a committee or an analysis of a market — the fall of the *Saturday Review* under Nicholas Charney and John Veronis demonstrates that. "A key fact about magazines," notes Felker, is that unlike any other mass medium, "one man can influence every idea, every layout, every word that appears in print." Yet a basic problem that faces the successful magazine is that both the publishers and their formulas become obsolete. And a corollary of this hypothesis is that the bigger the book is, the more reluctant it is to change.

One of the significant trends in 1977 and 1978 has been the increased willingness of chains to undertake start-ups. Traditionally, the large firms have acquired existing publications: the survivors from the many start-ups undertaken by individuals and small publishers. The attitude of many large publishers was summed up by John Purcell, president of CBS/Publishing Group. Asked why CBS did not engage in more start-ups, he noted that some were being considered but added: "Bear in mind that the equivalent of starting a new magazine the size of *Road & Track*, with all its success, is just about the same as adding another issue of *Woman's Day*, which has a lot less risk."[14]

Nonetheless, the high prices being paid for successful publications by acquisition-minded firms has made start-ups relatively more attractive. Staid Condé Nast introduced *Self* in 1978. As noted, McCall's has started two new publications recently. Hearst is investigating a start-up and New York Times came out with *Us*. Time Inc., of course, has long been the exception of the giant willing (and rich enough) to engage in start-ups on a regular basis. They have also been known to stick with a publication, while today even well financed magazines seem to be given a year or two to make it. Henry Luce kept *Sports Illustrated* alive for seven years before it made money.

Starting a New Magazine

For the most part, however, magazines are still started by independent entrepreneurs. Starting a new magazine takes a set of skills that are very different from successfully managing ongoing magazines. The entrepreneurial type personality is often absent in large firms and compensation for the initiators of new projects is difficult to determine. Existing publicly owned businesses also tend to shy away from high risk ventures that might dilute earnings on the income statement. Thus, the strategy of established publishers seems to involve letting the independent operator take the risks and raise the financing, then buying him out when things look successful, using the corporate strengths to expand a going concern. CBS has followed this line, as have Ziff-Davis, Times Mirror, and Hearst, among many.

GROUP PUBLISHING

There is a good reason why most magazines are published by multi-magazine groups: a single book, especially one of limited audience circulation, must carry too great a burden of overhead to make economic sense. The economies of scale are not great in magazine publishing, but the natural limits to the size of the consumer and business special interest books make acquisitions and start-ups a necessity if a company wishes to keep growing. Once a periodical reaches a saturation point, ad revenue growth becomes limited to cost per thousand increases or total pages. Take *New York* magazine, for example. From a start-up circulation of 50,000 in 1968, circulation grew rapidly to 171,000 by 1969, 292,000 in 1971, 342,000 in 1973 and 391,000 in 1978. The rate of circulation growth was 35% from 1969 to 1970, 26% the next year, down to 10% in 1972 and slowed to 6% in 1973. Between 1973 and 1978, circulation grew an average of 2.7% annually. So after some heady growth, *New York* logically turned to the outside for further revenue increases, first by its acquisition of the *Village Voice* and then the *New West* start-up. Yet there are few notable economies that can result from having these three publications under the same corporate banner.

In a few areas, it's true, group publishers do gain some synergistic advantages over a one-magazine publisher:

• A publisher of well established magazines has greater leverage in getting distribution of a new book and may be able to negotiate a more favorable deal with a national distributor.

• Bulk acquisition of paper may be slightly less expensive and easier.

• Printing contracts can be negotiated en masse.

• Subscription fulfillment contracts for a small circulation book can be combined with other books for a more economical rate.

• In-house circulation staffs can be centralized.

• A good publishing group can also provide corporate research and management expertise adding to this economic leverage.

On the other hand, most magazine operations must be run as separate entities and their costs vary little from independent to group status. Editorial staffs for each book are generally strictly segregated, often because of the disparate subject matter of the books: CBS' *World Tennis* has little in common editorially with *Rudder* or *Woman's Day*. Similarly, advertising staffs are separate, although regional offices can be combined in a single facility and many groups of small magazines sell insertions on a package basis. Macfadden's Women's Group, for example, sells for all eight books in combination. Postage on subscription mailings is strictly per unit, and mailing cost for the magazines is figured separately for each title.

There are then minimal economies of scale: some small cost savings in printing, paper and production, some helpful leverage in distribution, and little else. The quest for a chain then lies in the fact that magazine publishing is an industry with good margins, but on a small scale. Time Inc., for example, had a 12% pretax profit for publishing operations in 1978. In its heyday (1974), Playboy had earnings before taxes on its magazine of 21%. (By 1978 it was barely 10%.) McGraw-Hill had a 1978 operating margin of 18.8%. The *New Yorker* magazine, the only major publicly owned firm with income almost exclusively from a single magazine, had an after tax profit of 5.9% in 1978. Although the magazine industry as a whole reports 3% to 6% pretax earnings, there are many profitable magazines making 15% pretax, according to an official of an acquisitions-minded firm.

While starting a new magazine has a certain excitement, buying an existing one is quicker, easier and not necessarily more expensive. The key is buying at the right price. Profitable books either aren't for sale or are only at a high price, while unprofitable books are usually in bad straits for a reason.

"What you're buying is good will," notes an analyst at one of the most highly regarded special interest publication groups. This firm looks for a 30% to 50% return on its investment — and never less than 25%. It boasts of this because it does with the property what the seller is not doing, and that's more than just cutting costs. It may mean that the book is underpriced or that its cpm is too low for its category. The New York Times paid $8 million for *Family Circle* and claims that the investment was paid for in two years. Ziff-Davis expected a similar payback on *Psychology Today*. Once a title saturates its market, opportunity for growth of circulation and ad revenue become tied to higher rates rather than more purchasers and ad pages. A publisher thus tends to seek another magazine.

As in any make or buy decision, there are cost tradeoffs in acquiring or starting a book. The first question is, "Do we want a title in this marketplace?" If yes, then the field of available publications can be scouted. The cost of available books must be compared to the cost of starting fresh. An important factor in the equation is the management that comes with a new publication. In developing a publication internally, a company must include the cost of the management time used in developing the new publication, an expense that would be far greater in most cases than in acquiring an existing book.

In many ways it is surprising that a giant like CBS would even bother with books like *Pickup, Van & 4WD* or *Sea*, which it purchased. This latter was a 55,000 circulation book for boating enthusiasts in the West. CBS claimed that it was "very profitable" with its 1400 ad pages in 1973. By 1978 it was national, with 177,000 circulation, while *Pickup, Van & 4WD*, which was of similar size and just starting to make money in 1973, had a 211,000 circulation in 1978. With just about the same amount of time and investigation needed in buying a book that has a potential of 100,000 circulation as 500,000 circulation, the usual scenario would be for the smaller groups or independents to take over the limited audience books, while the bigger companies use their earnings to buy magazines with more substantial cash flows. But clearly potential for growth must be a major factor in the decision.

MAGAZINE NETWORKS FOR SPECIAL PUBLISHERS

A general interest magazine is in molecular form many different specialized topics combined within one cover. Conversely, the special interest and limited audience books taken together reach a general audience. It is this second point that provides a unique marketing device for some special interest publishing groups. By offering advertisers in several highly specialized books a discount over single title insertions, the network makes general advertising more attractive. For instance, it is difficult to convince a cigarette manufacturer to promote its brand in *Stereo Review*, with a possible cpm of $22.84 on a circulation base of 525,000. However, by selling a package with *Boating* and *Skiing*, Ziff-Davis offers over one million circulation and a cpm of $14.49. A black and white page in *Boating, Car and Driver, Cycle, Flying* and *Skiing*, offering the equivalent of a 2.2 million circulation magazine, yields a cpm which begins to be competitive with *Playboy*.

In addition to Ziff-Davis, Petersen Publishing has its "Action Group" network; Condé Nast offers a four book combination; Dell, Ideal,

Macfadden Sterling Women's Group, Times Mirror, CBS and many other group publishers offer such arrangements. For those groups that do not embrace diverse special interest books, however, the advantage is not as profound for the advertiser. For example, the Ideal Fan Group of *Screen Stories, Movie Stars, Movie Life*, et al, contains magazines that are far more likely to have overlapping readership than Ziff-Davis's span of special interest books. In these situations, the group buy is justified purely on the economics of the discounts.

THE TREND TOWARD GROUPS

One group publishing several magazines is not an innovation. Curtis, Hearst, Time, Fawcett and Macfadden operations are among the many that have long been group publishers. The increased desirability of special interest consumer and business publications, however, makes multi-magazine houses all the more necessary for the future. When giant CBS decided to get into magazines, it did not launch or buy up mass circulation magazines but chose to accumulate a stable of smaller special interest books. With the exception of *Field and Stream*, none of them until *Woman's Day* was significant by itself, but as a group they provide substantial revenue and potentially strong profits. The New York Times Co., while purchasing *Family Circle,* has also taken over *Tennis* and *Golf Digest.* Time Inc., accustomed to circulation figures in the millions, has added *Money*, with its modest potential, to its house as well as *People* and the new *Life,* which have circulation ambitions more in keeping with Time Inc.'s tradition.

ABC got into the magazine business by acquiring *High Fidelity* and *Modern Photography,* and has expanded its presence in the industry through the purchase of additional limited audience consumer, farm and business magazines.

With the re-emergence of *Life* and *Look*, the success of *People* and the staying power of *Us*, it may seem that mass circulation magazines are making a comeback. But even at two or three million circulation, these are a shadow of the eight and nine million of the old mass circulation periodicals. And these popular magazines tend to get the publicity, while the scores of small business and special interest magazines, independent and group owned, make up the bulk of the industry.

With the risk still high and the entry cost great, new mass circulation books will be a rarity in the field. Publishers will thus have to rely on good profits from relatively small revenues from several publications for company or division viability.

FOREIGN PUBLISHERS IN U.S. MARKET

The strength of many foreign currencies vis-à-vis the dollar is only a small part of the increased interest on the part of foreign publishers in entering the U.S. market. European publishers see the U.S. as a vast market, with a far greater potential for a title than the magazines they publish in their home bases. Although the entry of the foreigners has involved buying up some going magazines, they have also committed funds to the start-up of new publications.

Among the ventures:

• Gruner & Jahr, Germany's largest publisher (*Stern, Brigitte*), has set up a U.S. subsidiary to publish *Geo,* a slick picture magazine not unlike *National Geographic.* In April 1978, the company also purchased Parents' Magazine Enterprises, publisher of the 1.6 million circulation monthly *Parents',* as well as *Children's Digest, Humpty Dumpty* and others. Gruner & Jahr is itself 75% owned by German publishing giant Bertelsmann Gütersloh, which directly owns a majority interest in leading U.S. mass market paperback publisher Bantam Books (the rest is owned by Italy's Agnelli family, of Fiat fame).

• Daniel Filipacchi has made good on his promise to revive *Look,* killed by Cowles Communications in 1971. He is aiming at a one million circulation biweekly, with primarily newsstand distribution. This follows up his acquisition of Popular Publications, Inc., a group that includes *Argosy, Camera 35* and *Railroad.* Filipacchi's French publishing base includes *Paris-Match* (which sells nearly 800,000 weekly) and the sex-oriented *Lui.*

• Britain's Associated Newspapers Group Ltd., the owner of 45 publications, has bought a minority interest in the *Soho Weekly News* (a competitor of New York's *Village Voice*) and financed Clay Felker in his take-over of *Esquire* in 1977. (In April 1978 Associated sold most of its interest in *Esquire* to a U.S. firm 50% owned by Sweden's Bonnier Magazine group.)

• *The Economist,* Britain's respected financial weekly, is looking for expanded circulation in the U.S. with added coverage of U.S. events and a beefed-up U.S. editorial operation.

• Harlequin Enterprises, the Canadian publisher best known for its romance novels, has announced its intention to build a magazine publishing empire in the U.S. Its first step in that direction was the acquisition of the Laufer Company, which publishes *Tiger Beat* and associated periodicals for teenagers and a series of Rona Barrett gossip magazines. Total group circulation is 2.6 million.

• In the business publications area, Britain's Reed acquired the large Cahners groups in the U.S. The Reed International Group had a pretax profit in 1977 of almost $76 million.

So far the presence of the foreign publishers is rather small. The total circulation of their consumer magazines (not counting *Geo* and *Look*) is 7.0 million and business publications, 2.8 million. Their interest in the market can only add to the competition for the acquisition of existing publications, driving their prices higher. But their willingness to start up new ventures can also add to the diversity of magazines for the consumer. And, if they follow the form of most publishers, profits will be kept in the country to add further publications.

DISCUSSION

Magazines are like no other media. They do not essentially compete with each other. The nearly 10,000 different titles are misleading, since the essence of almost every title is to create a monopoly for itself with a distinct audience. *Motorcycle Product News* does not compete with *Time* or *College and Research Libraries. Ski* and *Skiing* magazines do battle for the same audience, but are not in direct competition with *Prairie Farmer* or *Teen.* Magazines are perhaps the best example of monopolistic competition − many similar products, but each one perceived as being different enough from the others to create its own unique market. The distinction may be by geography (*Philadelphia, Southern Living, Wisconsin Agriculturalist*), specialized content (*Popular Photography, Insurance Marketing*), demographics (*Town & Country, Modern Romances, Seventeen*), intellectual level (*Harper's, Marvel* comics, *New Yorker*), generalized content (*People, TV Guide, Better Homes & Garden*) or other designations.

Although it may be argued that newspapers do not compete with one another in different cities, daily newspapers all tend to provide the same function for a single mass audience each day. Although a fire in Cincinnati and a budget hearing in San Jose are reported only locally, any given paper across the country on a given day will have much the same national and international news, similar types of local stories and advertising. Magazines have no such similarities.

It is for this reason, perhaps, that group ownership of magazines is seldom raised when discussion turns to media concentration. It is not easy to support the hypothesis that the purchase by ABC of Chilton's *Hardware Age* gives that magazine an unfair advantage over other magazines. Nor should the fact that Times Mirror publishes *Popular Science* and *Outdoor Life* have any impact on the free flow of ideas through these or other magazines.

Moreover, many magazines also face competition from thousands of newsletters, such as "Old House Journal" or "Kipplinger's." While many cost far more than magazines and are thus directed to special business audiences, they serve as an even less expensive format than magazines for a publisher to provide information for a market. Newsletters tend to be supported 100% by circulation revenue and thus can serve many diverse audiences that are too small to support an advertising-backed publication.

The nature of the market is such that competition is restricted to a great extent by the limited audience for most publications. The first publisher to discover a market niche, either in a trade or the consumer area, has an edge in reaching those interested in that subject. Sometimes there is room for a second or third publication. In the case of fads, such as the sudden discovery of running, several magazines may hit the market at once, but the size of the market — both the limited advertising base and the potential universe of subscribers — may not economically be able to support all the entries. In this case, the better financed publication may be able to survive best and the strength of being part of a large publishing entity may be an advantage over an independent entrepreneur.

But in most cases, magazines are started to fill a niche that no one else has noticed or was felt to be too small to deal with. While an individual may not consider it worthwhile to run a business publication with a potential free circulation of 5000, a group that specializes in such periodicals may start or acquire at an early stage such a magazine and use its management and marketing skills to make it a profitable operation.

A recent example of an individual magazine finding and filling a void is the 1978 introduction of *American Photographer*. The dominant magazines for amateur photographers are *Popular Photography* (Ziff-Davis) and *Modern Photography* (ABC). *Petersen's Photographic* (Petersen) is a distant third. Entrepreneur Alan Bennett saw all these magazines as being editorially oriented to the technical and engineering aspects of photography and thus created a magazine that concentrated on the creative side. As a result he was able to attract a different type of subscriber, thus offering new reach to advertisers. After a year of publishing Bennett felt confident enough of success to have no need for additional capital.[15]

Except for the largest mass circulation magazines, publishers must also be aware of the limited resources of their advertisers. Bobit Publishing Co.'s *School Bus Fleet* may be the only vehicle for advertisers that wish to reach that market. But the many small suppliers who advertise in the periodical would have to cut down on their space or stop advertising altogether if the publisher exercised its "monopoly" position to raise rates with abandon. At the same time, most special interest publishers have a limited universe of potential advertisers and cannot afford to lose too many.

The magazine industry is diverse and dynamic. Like book publishing, it is an easy entry field and this brings into it a profusion of new products each year. Also like book publishing, the tendency is for successful publications to be purchased by multiple title publishers, or for the success of one title to provide the resources for the publisher to start or acquire additional publications and thus become a group. Despite the high mortality rate and the competition from other media, the growth in additional magazine titles shows no sign of letting up. In addition, a single magazine with a wide circulation, such as *TV Guide, Newsweek* or *Reader's Digest*, can be a very effective voice, even when published by a company that owns no other magazines. Along with books, magazines provide society with a broad range of information, education and entertainment.

FOOTNOTES

1. *Ayer Directory of Publications*, annual (Philadelphia: Ayer Press).
2. See Jean-Louis Servan-Schreiber, *The Power to Inform* (New York: McGraw-Hill, 1974), pp. 36-38.
3. Among the better histories of magazines are James L. C. Ford, *Magazines for Millions* (Carbondale, Ill.: Southern Illinois University Press, 1969); Frank Luther Mott, *A History of American Magazines*, 5 volumes (Cambridge, Mass.: Harvard University Press, 1968); Theodore Peterson, *Magazines in the Twentieth Century* (Urbana, Ill.: University of Illinois Press, 1964); and John W. Tebbel, *The American Magazine: A Compact History* (New York: Hawthorn Books, 1969).
4. Calculated from Publishers Information Bureau gross advertising revenue with estimates from Knowledge Industry Publications, Inc.
5. *U.S. Industrial Outlook, 1979*, U.S. Dept. of Commerce (Washington, D.C.: Government Printing Office, 1979), p. 94.
6. *Bowker Annual of Library and Book Trade Information* (New York: R. R. Bowker Co.) 1971 and 1979 editions.
7. *Advertising Age*, Sept. 26, 1977, p. 87.
8. Rose Marie Zummo, "Periodical Publishing," *U.S. Industrial Outlook, 1979*, p. 93.
9. Ibid.
10. Ibid., p. 74
11. Dantia Quirk, *The Library Market for Publications and Systems, 1979-83* (White Plains, N.Y.: Knowledge Industry Publications, Inc., 1978), p. 81.
12. Benjamin M. Compaine, *Consumer Magazines at the Crossroads: A Study of General and Special Interest Magazines* (White Plains, N.Y.: Knowledge Industry Publications, Inc., 1974), pp. 89-105.
13. *Folio*, December 1977, p. 16 and January 1977, p. 14.
14. *Media Decisions*, June 1978, p. 46.
15. *Media Industry Newsletter*, February 12, 1979, p. 5.

Appendix A4

Magazines Published by Major Groups*

American Broadcasting Companies – 17

Consumer:

High Fidelity (M)
Stereo (Q)
Modern Photography (M)
Schwann Record & Tape Guide (M)
Los Angeles (M)

subtotal 1,208,494 paid

Farm:

Prairie Farmer (BW)
Wallaces Farmer (BW)
Wisconsin Agriculturist (SM)
Dairy Herd Management (M)
Feedlot Management (M)
Hog Farm Management (M)
Miller Agriculturist (M)

subtotal   714,777 paid/unpaid

Business/Trade:

Quality (M)
Assembly Engineering (M)
Industrial Finishing (M)
Infosystems (M)
Office Products (M)

subtotal   302,381 unpaid
Total   2,225,652

(Agreement has been reached for ABC to acquire a majority interest in Chilton Co.)

*Notes: Circulation for groups most current available to November 1978.
Titles in group current, where changes known, to March 1979.

Key: (M) monthly; (BM) bi-monthly; (SM) semi-monthly; (W) weekly;
(Q) quarterly; (10x, etc. – 10 times annually).

American Chemical Society – 15

Business/Trade:

Biochemistry (BW)
Chemical Reviews (BM)
Inorganic Chemistry (M)
Journal of Agriculture & Food Chemistry (BM)
Journal of the American Chemical Society (BW)
Journal of Chemical Information & Information Science (Q)
Journal of Medicinal Chemistry (M)
Journal of Organic Chemistry (BW)
Journal of Physical Chemistry (BW)
Macromolecules (BM)
Chemical & Engineering News (W)
Chemical Technology (Chemtech) (M)
Chemistry (M)
Environmental Science & Technology (M)
Analytical Chemistry (M)

Total   279,057 paid

CBS Inc. – 8

Consumer:

Mechanix Illustrated (M)
Woman's Day (15x)
Cycle World (M)
Pickup, Van & 4WD (M)
Road & Track (M)
Field & Stream (M)
World Tennis (M)
Sea (M)

Total   13,344,557 paid

Challenge Publications, Inc. – 10

Consumer:

Air Classics (M)
Air Progress (M)
Military Modeler (M)
Minicycle/BMX Action (M)
Modern Cycle (M)
Popular Off Roading (M)
Rod Action (M)
Scale Modeler (M)
Sport Flying (BM)
Street Machine (BM)

Total   485,470 paid

Charlton Publications, Inc. – 8

Consumer:

CB Times (BM)
Charlton Comics Group (BM)
    (17 titles)
Charlton Crossword Group (BM)
    (7 titles)
Country Song Roundup (M)
Hit Parader Combination (M)
Official Karate (8x)
Real West (BM)
Your Astrology (Q)

Total   4,314,200 paid

Charter Co. – 4

Consumer:

Ladies' Home Journal (M)
Redbook (M)
Sport (M)
American Home Crafts (Q)

Total   11,970,428 paid

Chilton Company – 20

(American Broadcasting Companies Inc. reached agreement in February 1979 to acquire a majority interest in Chilton.)

Consumer:

Tennis U.S.A. (M)
Going Places (BM)

subtotal   278,641 paid

Business/Trade:

Accent (M)
Automotive Industries (M)
Automotive Industries/International (M)
Automotive Marketing (M)
Commercial Car Journal (M)
Distribution Worldwide (M)
Electronic Component News (M)
Fleet Specialist (BM)

Food Engineering/International (BM)
Hardware Age (M)
Instruments & Control Systems
Instrument & Apparatus News (M)
Iron Age (W)
Jewelers Circular – Keystone (M)
Motor/Age (M)
Product Design and Development (M)
Review of Optometry (M)
Iron Age Metalworking International (M)

subtotal 1,075,942 paid/unpaid

Condé Nast Publications Inc. (Newhouse) – 9

Consumer:

Analog (M)
Brides (BM)
Glamour (M)
House & Garden (M)
House & Garden Building Guide (Q)
House & Garden Decorating Guide (Q)
Mademoiselle
Self (M)
Vogue (M)

Total   4,213,312 paid

(*Self* started publication January 1979. Condé Nast acquired *Gentleman's Quarterly* (10x annually, 348,000 circulation) in February 1979.)

Davis Publications, Inc. – 9

Consumer:

Backpacking Journal (5x)
Camping Journal (9x)
Elementary Electronics (BM)
Ellery Queen's Mystery Magazine (M)
Hi-Fi/Stereo Buyers' Guide (BM)
Income Opportunities (M)
Isaac Asimov's Science Fiction Magazine (M)
Science & Mechanics (Q)
Today's Homes – Plans & Ideas (Q)

Total   1,130,931 paid

Fairchild Publications, Inc. (Capital Cities Communications, Inc.) — 15

Business/Trade:

> *Clinical Psychiatry News* (M)
> *Electronic News* (W)
> *Energy Users News* (W)
> *Family Practice News* (M)
> *Footwear News* (SM)
> *HFD Retailing Home Furnishings* (W)
> *Internal Medicine News* (SM)
> *Men's Wear* (BM)
> *Metal/Center News* (M)
> *Metalworking News* (W)
> *OB Gyn News* (SM)
> *Pediatric News* (M)
> *Skin & Allergy News* (M)
> *Supermarket News* (W)

subtotal   507,490   paid/unpaid

Consumer:

> *W* (BW)

subtotal   193,153   paid
Total   700,643

Harper & Row Inc. (includes J.B. Lippincott Co.) — 18

Business & Trade:

> *American Journal of Pathology* (M)
> *Journal of Obstetrics, Gynecologic & Neonatal Nursing* (BM)
> *Obstetrics & Gynecology* (M)
> *American Journal of Clinical Pathology* (M)
> *American Surgeon* (M)
> *Annals of Surgery* (M)
> *Cancer* (M)
> *Clinical Nuclear Medicine* (M)
> *Clinical Pediatrics* (M)
> *Diseases of the Colon & Rectum* (8x)
> *Hospital Pharmacy* (M)
> *Investigative Radiology* (BM)
> *Journal of Preventive Dentistry* (BM)
> *Laboratory Medicine* (M)
> *NITA* (BM)
> *Respiratory Care* (M)
> *Review of Surgery (Current Surgery)* (BM)
> *Transfusion* (BM)

Total   366,291   paid/unpaid

Harcourt Brace Jovanovich, Inc. — 59

Farm:

Kansas Farmer (SM)
Michigan Farmer (SM)
Missouri Realist (SM)
Ohio Farmer (SM)
Pennsylvania Farmer (SM)
Nebraska Farmer (SM)
Colorado Rancher & Farmer (M)
Florida Grower & Rancher (M)
Flue Cured Tobacco Farmer (8x)
Peanut Farmer (7x)

subtotal   608,739   paid/unpaid

Business/Trade:

Body Fashions/Intimate Apparel (M)
Body Fashions/Intimate Apparel Market Maker (7x)
Communications News (M)
Dental Industry News (M)
Dental Laboratory Review (M)
Dental Survey (M)
Drug & Cosmetic Industry (M)
Electronic Technician/Dealer (M)
Fast Service (M)
Food Management (M)
Hearing Instruments (M)
Home & Auto (BW)
Hosiery & Underwear (M)
Housewares (18x)
Kitchen Planning (6x)
LP-Gas (M)
Paper Sales (M)
Pets/Supplies/Marketing (M)
Professional Remodeling (M)
Quick Frozen Foods (M)
Rent All (M)
RSI (M)
RTW (M)
Snack Food (M)
Telephone Engineer & Management (BM)
Toys Trade News (5x)
Geriatrics (M)
Hospital
Modern Medicine (21x)
Neurology (M)
Physicians Management (M)

Energy Management Report (M)
Ocean Resources Engineering (M)
Petroleum Engineer International (12x)
Pipeline & Gas Journal (14x)
Alcoholism (Q)
Blood (M)
Journal of Pediatric Surgery (BM)
Progress in Cardiovascular Diseases (BM)
Seminar in Arthritis & Rheumatism (Q)
Seminar in Hematology (Q)
Seminar in Nuclear Medicine (Q)
Seminar in Oncology (Q)
Seminar in Perinatology (Q)
Seminar in Roentgenology (Q)
Golf Business (M)
Lawn Care Industry (M)
Pest Control (M)
Weeds Trees and Turf (M)

subtotal 1,142,964 paid/unpaid
Total   1,751,703

Hearst Corp. – 14

Consumer:

Cosmopolitan (M)
Good Housekeeping (M)
Sports Afield (M)
Connoisseur (M)
Motor Boating & Sailing (M)
Popular Mechanics (M)
Science Digest (M)
Harper's Bazaar (M)
House Beautiful (M)
House Beautiful's Colonial Homes (BM)
House Beautiful's Home Decorating (Q)
Town & Country

subtotal 11,943,633 paid

Business/Trade:

American Druggist (M)
Motor (M)

subtotal   198,614 unpaid
Total   12,142,247

Ideal Publishing Corp. — 9

Consumer:

Intimate Story (M)
Movie Life (M)
Movie Stars (M)
Personal Romances (M)
Screen Stories (M)
Teen Beat (M)
TV Dawn to Dusk (M)
TV Radio Talk (M)
TV Star Parade (M)

Total   1,131,765 paid

Macfadden Group Inc. — 8

Consumer:

True Story (M)
Photoplay/TV Mirror (M)
True Confessions (M)
Secrets (M)
True Romance (M)
True Experience (M)
True Love (M)
Modern Romances (M)

Total   4,181,598 paid

McGraw-Hill, Inc. — 29

Business/Trade:

American Machinist (M)
Architectural Record (M)
Aviation Week & Space Technology (W)
Business Week (W)
Chemical Engineering (BW)
Chemical Week (W)
Coal Age (M)
Construction Contracting (M)
Data Communications (M)
Electrical Construction & Maintenance (M)
Electrical Wholesaling (6x)
Electrical World (SM)
Electronics (BW)

Engineering and Mining Journal (M)
Engineering News-Record (W)
Fleet Owner (M)
Housing (M)
Industry Mart (9x)
Medical World News (SM)
Modern Plastics (M)
Modern Plastics International (in English) (M)
National Petroleum News (M)
Physician and Sportsmedicine (M)
Power (M)
Textile World (M)
33 Metal Producing (M)
Technical Education News (BM)
American Industrial Report (6x)
International Management (M) (English edition)

Total   2,419,095 paid/unpaid

Meredith Corporation – 5

Consumer:

Apartment Life (M)
Better Homes and Gardens (M)
Better Homes and Gardens Building Ideas (Q)
Better Homes and Gardens Remodeling Ideas (Q)

subtotal 9,656,133 paid

Farm:

Successful Farming

subtotal   775,235 paid
Total   10,431,367

Mosby, C.V. Company (Times Mirror Co.) – 14

Business/Trade:

American Heart Journal (M)
American Journal of Obstetrics & Gynecology (SM)
American Journal of Orthodontics (M)
Chemical Pharmacology (M)
EMT Journal (Q)
Heart & Lung (BM)
Investigative Opthalmology (M)
Journal of Allergy & Clinical Medicine (M)
Journal of Hand Surgery (BM)
Journal of Pediatrics (M)

Journal of Prosthetic Dentistry (M)
Journal of Thoracic & Cardiovascular Surgery (M)
Oral Surgery (M)
Surgery (M)

Total 214,169 paid/unpaid

The New York Times Co. — 4

Consumer:

Us (BW)
Family Circle (M)
Golf Digest (M)
Tennis (M)

Total 10,375,464 paid

North American Publishing Co. — 20

Consumer:

Pickin' (M)
Audio (M)
Cue (BW)
New Dawn (BM)
Yacht Racing/Cruising (10x)

subtotal 585,190 paid

Business/Trade:

American Import & Export Bulletin (M)
American School & University Magazine (M)
Bestsellers (Marketing Bestsellers) (M)
Business Forms Reporter (M)
Executive Housekeeper (M)
Food Trade News (BW)
Lab World (M)
Media & Methods (M)
Package Printing (M)
Plant Facilities (10x)
Printing Impressions (M)
Reproduction Review & Methods (M)
Web Newspaper and Magazine Production (BM)
World-Wide Printer (6x)
Zip (9x)

subtotal 463,506 paid/unpaid
Total 1,048,696

Parents Magazine Enterprises, Inc. (Gruener & Jahr, U.S.A.) — 6

Consumer:

    Baby Care (Q)
    Expecting (Q)
    Parents' Magazine (M)
    Young Miss (M)
    Children's Digest (10x)
    Humpty Dumpty (10x)

                            Total   4,078,098 paid/unpaid

Penton/IPC — 23

Business/Trade:

    Airconditioning & Refrigeration Business (M)
    Government Product News (M)
    Hospitality-Lodging (M)
    Hospitality-Restaurant (M)
    Hydraulics & Pneumatics (M)
    Material Handling Engineering (M)
    Occupational Hazards (M)
    Power Transmission Design (M)
    Precision Metal (M)
    School Product News (M)
    Welding Design & Fabrication (M)
    Welding Distributor (BM)
    Handling & Shipping Management (M)
    Modern Office Procedures (M)
    Foundry (M)
    Industry Week (BW)
    Machine Design (28x)
    New Equipment Digest (M)
    Production Engineering (M)
    Airtransport World (M)
    Heating/Piping/Air Conditioning (M)
    Materials Engineering (M)
    Progressive Architecture (M)

                            Total   1,692,676 unpaid/paid

Petersen Publishing Co. — 11

Consumer:

    Car Craft (M)
    4 Wheel & Off-Road (M)

Guns & Ammo (M)
Hot Rod Magazine (M)
Hunting (Petersen's) (M)
Motorcyclist Magazine (M)
Motor Trend (M)
Petersen's Photographic Magazine (M)
Skin Diver (M)
Vans & Pickups (M)
'Teen (M)

Total   4,071,097 paid

Reed Publishing Corporation (includes Cahners Publishing) — 21

Business/Trade:

Appliance Manufacturer (M)
Brick & Clay Record (M)
Building Design & Construction (M)
Building Supply News (M)
Ceramic Industry (M)
Construction Equipment (13x)
Design News (SM)
EDN (SM)
Electronic Business (M)
Foodservice Distributor Salesman (M)
Foodservice Equipment Specialist (M)
Mini-Micro Systems (M)
Institutions (SM)
Modern Materials Handling (M)
Modern Railroads/Rail Transit (M)
Package Engineering (M)
Professional Builder & Apartment Business (M)
Purchasing Magazine (M)
Service World International (BM)
Specifying Engineer (M)
Traffic Management (M)

Total   1,111,685 unpaid

Playboy Enterprises Inc. — 3

Consumer:

Games (BM)
Playboy (M)
Oui (M)

Total   6,200,747 paid

Scholastic Magazines, Inc. — 10

Consumer:

Co-ed (10x)
Scholastic Coach (10x)
Scholastic Newstime (W)
Scholastic Wheels (Q)
Scholastic Magazines Groups (10x):
   Senior Scholastic
   Scholastic Voice
   Scholastic Search
   Scholastic Scope
   Science World
   Junior Scholastic

Business/Trade:

Forecast for Home Economics (M)

Total   5,597,803   paid

Technical Publishing Co. — 20

Business/Trade:

Consulting Engineer (M)
Datamation (13x)
Electric Light & Power (M)
Plant Engineering (BW)
Pollution Engineering (M)
Power Engineering (M)
Purchasing World (M)
American Journal of Cardiology (M)
American Journal of Medicine (M)
American Journal of Surgery (M)
Cutis (M)
Dun's Review (M)
Firm Engineering (M)
Mining Equipment International (9x)
Water & Wastes Engineering (M)
World Construction (M)
Control Engineering (M)
Graphic Arts Monthly (M)
Highway & Heavy Construction (M)
Industrial Research/Development (M)

Total   1,098,375   unpaid

Time Inc. — 6

Consumer:

Fortune (BW)
Life (M)
Money (M)
People Weekly (W)
Sports Illustrated (W)
Time (W)

Total 16,005,855 paid
(does not include *Life*)

Times Mirror Magazines, Inc. — 7

Consumer:

How to (BM)
Golf Magazine (M)
Outdoor Life (M)
Popular Science (M)
Sporting News (W)
Ski (7x)

subtotal 5,446,477 paid

Business/Trade:

Sporting Goods Dealer (M)

subtotal 16,000 paid/unpaid
Total 5,462,477

Webb Company — 10

Consumer/Farm:

Beef (M)
Consumer Life (Q)
Family Handyman (10x)
Farm Industry News (9x)
  Farm Industry News/South
  Farm Industry News/West
Irrigation Age (9x)
National Hog Farmer (M)
Passages (M)
Snow Goer (5x)
Snow Week (17x)
TWA Ambassador

Total 2,445,200 paid/unpaid

Williams & Wilkins Company — 21

Business/Trade:

Acta Cytologica (BM)
American Journal of Physical Medicine (BM)
Endocrinology (M)
Gastroenterology (M)
Investigative Urology (BM)
Journal of Biological Chemistry (SM)
Journal of Clinical Endocrinology (M)
Journal of Histochemistry (M)
Journal of Immunology (M)
Journal of Investigative Dermatology (M)
Journal of Nervous & Mental Disease
Journal of Pharmacology & Experimental Therapeutics (M)
Journal of Trauma (M)
Journal of Urology (M)
Laboratory Investigation (M)
Microbiological Reviews (Q)
Neurosurgery (BM)
Obstetrical & Gynecological Survey (M)
Plastic & Reconstructive Surgery (M)
Stain Technology (BM)
Urological Survey (BM)

Total   130,776 paid

Ziff-Davis Publishing Company, Inc. — 15

Consumer:

Boating (M)
Car and Driver (M)
Flying (M)
Modern Bride (BM)
Popular Electronics (M)
Popular Photography (M)
Psychology Today (M)
Skiing (7x)
Stereo Review (M)
Fly Fisherman (7x)

subtotal 5,134,806 paid

Business/Trade:

Business & Commercial Aviation (M)
Meetings & Conventions (M)
Photomethods (M)
Travel Weekly (SW)

subtotal   203,861 paid/unpaid
Total   5,338,667

5

Theatrical Film

The long term propensity toward concentration of ownership, endemic to the capitalistic system, is exemplified by the motion picture industry. Its history and present status show as well the recurrent waves that propel this business to market concentration and the inevitable rise of giant concerns that not only dominate the film business, but also spread to allied communications sectors and other industrial and service fields. In some respects, it is no longer sufficient to talk just about a film industry, as if it were comprised of a set of discrete companies operating exclusively in that business. Expansion and diversification have spawned entertainment conglomerates operating globally that are major sources of mass amusement for us and the rest of the world.

HISTORICAL OVERVIEW

From its beginning, the film industry has been characterized by repeated attempts at domination by a small number of firms that customarily tried either to exclude others from the business or to deprive competitors of resources. The industry developed from the monopoly position conferred upon Edison by the patent he received for a motion picture camera invented in 1889. A peephole machine, patented in 1891, was introduced to the public in the Kinetoscope parlor that opened in New York City in 1894. Although it attracted clientele because of its novelty, the Kinetoscope was limited commercially. A significant advance in scale was achieved when the film projector was introduced in 1896 by Edison. It was followed immediately by devices from other companies. These made their debuts in vaudeville houses where their short, 50-foot reels of plotless occurrences allowed films to become one of the string of acts that entertained audiences.

By the turn of the century, Edison, Biograph, and Vitagraph were the three principal companies that produced films and marketed equipment. Their pictures, sold outright to users, probably were of less financial importance than the projecting apparatus they sold, not unlike the soon-to-develop broadcasting business in which set manufacturers operated stations so as to encourage public demand for radio receivers. Although the three companies tried to control the industry by refusing to sell cameras to others, the obstacle was overcome by enthusiastic businessmen who imported cameras from Europe or found ways to obtain them in North America. Little capital was needed to produce the short films of the day, and the possibility of quick profits undoubtedly appealed to speculators. Necessarily, there was extensive patent litigation similar to periods in the telegraph and telephone industries when suits alleged broader plaintiff control of apparatus than defendants were willing to concede. In this way, litigation was used as a weapon to cripple competitors and assert spheres of monopolistic control.

Short films gradually gave way to longer productions offering development of story lines. Theatres were opened specifically to show films, thereby legitimizing the new medium and establishing a path away from the vaudeville stage that the medium began to take. The possibility for quick profit from little investment enticed entrepreneurs to enter exhibition, and probably 10,000 theatres of varying quality and comfort existed by 1910. That film already had become a commodity by this time, and had been staked out by the private sector, necessarily dictated what was being done with the medium. This was evident as amusement dominated − if not excluded − other ways in which the medium could have been employed.

To increase spectators and earnings, exhibitors realized they needed frequent program changes. This was made possible, first by exhibitors trading films among themselves, and then by the establishment of exchanges, beginning in 1902. Within a few years, well over 100 exchanges existed, institutionalizing the producer-wholesaler-retailer chain in the film industry. Indeed, by 1905, industrial and occupational specialization and differentiation already had been established.

Rise and Fall of MPPC

To control an increasingly fluid industry, the seven largest American producers, the leading importer-distributor, and two French producers established the Motion Picture Patents Company in 1908. In addition to pooling their patents and acknowledging Edison's claim, the MPPC licensed only its members to manufacture cameras and produce pictures. Eastman Kodak, moreover, agreed to sell raw stock only to licensees of the Trust. To further control the industry, the MPPC granted licenses to 116 distributors who were to deal only with exhibitors licensed by the Patents Company. The exchanges also agreed to handle only films from MPPC members, who pledged to channel their films only through these distributors.

By restraining trade, the MPPC achieved almost complete control of the market and reaped the largest profits ever made in the industry up to that time.[1] To further tighten control, the MPPC in 1910 established its own distribution subsidiary, General Film Company, and forced other exchanges out of business. In 1915, however, federal courts dissolved General Film because it restrained commerce. Two years later, the Supreme Court, attempting to stimulate competition in the industry, held that the MPPC had monopolized the film business and that its exclusive licensing procedures were illegal. Other suits effectively killed the MPPC, and it was not until the innovation and diffusion of sound motion pictures that patents were used again to thwart competition and assert oligopolistic control.

With the power of the MPPC broken, independent companies were allowed to develop, and with them came the star system and the feature film. The foundation also was prepared for the rise of new firms that eventually dominated the industry. Whereas previous control had centered on patent supremacy, the 1920s saw a battle for theatres, because large holdings conveyed bargaining power and market strength. Vertical integration became a primary business objective. "The industry had already passed from one of many small independent companies to one controlled by a few relatively powerful organizations. . . . By 1927, the industry was launched in a period of reckless spending and extravagance which would have meant the inevitable wreck of enterprises in more settled lines. Of necessity, financial dependence on Wall Street increased enormously."[2]

The industry quickly conformed to the classic model of internationalization. World War I and its aftermath allowed America to assert its economic and political interests abroad, and the nation swung from being a debtor to an international creditor. The war had disrupted European film industries, whereas the productive capacity of American companies was burgeoning, and this in turn prompted the development of new markets in which investments could be amortized. In the decade up to 1923, the volume of America's film exportation quadrupled and by 1925 it stood at 235 million feet. During these dozen years, film exports to Europe increased five times and exports to the rest of the world 10 times, as the industry staked out markets in the Far East, Latin America, and elsewhere. It was possible for American films to achieve this dominance because, in part, investments in them were recouped in the home market, which had about half the world's theatres, and thus films could be rented abroad at rates often undercutting those of foreign competitors. The maintenance of overseas markets for American films eventually became an important aspect of the industry's foreign policy and set the tone for the later exportation of television programs, part of what has been called America's "media imperialism."[3]

The 1920s and 1930s

During the 1920s, several technically different sound-on-film and sound-on-disc systems emerged, and corporations exploiting key patents asserted as much control as they could, hoping to keep competitors out of the field. Subsidiaries of the American Telephone & Telegraph Company entered into agreements with Hollywood producers for the use of sound recording equipment. Battles from the radio broadcasting industry carried over into the film business as the Radio Corporation of America innovated its sound film system, cracking the industrial control that had been created by AT&T. To enter the film field, RCA was instrumental in organizing the Radio-Keith-Orpheum Corporation in 1928, which became an instant vertically integrated major producer. Almost all the rest of the industry, however, was tied to AT&T through exclusive contracts not unlike those instituted earlier by the MPPC. RCA filed a complaint charging AT&T and its affiliates with unlawful restraint of trade, but an out-of-court settlement in 1935 conceded RCA's place in the sound film industry.

As it entered the 1930s, the industry was dominated by five vertically integrated companies that exercised control through important holdings and trade practices. Together they produced about half the total number of motion pictures, but a much larger share of the grade A features. Although they controlled or owned only about an eighth of all theatres, most were key first run houses that gave the majors influence far beyond their numerical share. Nonetheless, the industry was not spared from the general economic crisis. In 1933, Paramount was judged bankrupt, while RKO and Universal went into receivership. The Fox Film Corporation was reorganized and emerged as Twentieth Century-Fox.

Restraints of Trade

Constant maneuvers by companies to control their markets and to avoid competition not only prompted suits by others that felt deprived of reasonable attempts to compete, but also stimulated governmental efforts to destroy restraints of trade. Antitrust cases since the late 1920s probably had made the major distributors "well aware that their system of control violated the Sherman Act,"[4] but they persisted in attempts to maintain their positions. In 1938, the Justice Department filed a complaint against the five major companies and three minor companies, accusing them of combining and conspiring to restrain trade in the production, distribution, and exhibition of films, and of attempting to monopolize motion picture trade. The five majors accepted a consent decree in 1940. The government reopened the case in 1944 and demanded that the five majors divorce their exhibition circuits and that certain trade practices engaged in by them and the three other defendants be ruled illegal.

The case was fought to the Supreme Court, which in 1948 upheld a lower court's decision that, among other things, "two-price-fixing conspiracies existed — a horizontal one between all the defendants [and] a vertical one between each distributor-defendant and its licensees." Block booking, the practice in which distributors would only rent entire packages of films to theatres, forcing them to accept poorer films in order to get the ones they really desired, was held to be illegal. In its place competitive bidding arose with exhibition licenses "to be offered and taken theatre by theatre and picture by picture."[5] Exhibition circuits were divorced from the major production-distribution companies and some theatre chains were dissolved. In 1948, RKO, Warner, Twentieth Century-Fox and National Theaters agreed to consent decrees, and Paramount followed the next year. In 1951, further decrees were entered with Warner, Twentieth Century-Fox and National Theaters. Loew's finally agreed to a decree in 1952.

Although the rise of television makes it difficult to determine the precise impact of the *Paramount* decision, several points are clear. Columbia, Universal, United Artists and some smaller companies were able to obtain larger shares of the market. Theatre operators gained greater control over their business, especially in the selection of films, while independent producers and foreign filmmakers had better opportunities to have their films exhibited. Moreover, the majors were cut loose from large investments in theatres at precisely the moment when theatrical attendance tumbled. Enforcement of the industry's censorship system, embodied in the Production Code, became more difficult because the major studios no longer owned theatres, whereas exhibitors as well as producers were willing to expand the screen's version of morality in order to compete with television.

Developments since 1950

In the 1950s and 1960s the foreign market assumed added significance, as the major companies were deriving about half of their theatrical revenue from it. They began investing in foreign filmmaking on a large scale in order to deplete their accounts of blocked earnings abroad and to take advantage of European subsidization programs designed to stimulate national film production. At home, the major studios gradually began offering their libraries for television exhibition and found this to be a new source of badly needed revenue. The growth of video abroad created another market for American companies. Further cooperation with television developed as the studios began producing series and made-for-TV movies. .

Motion picture production dropped considerably as studios were no longer interested in filling the screens of their own theatres. Double features became a thing of the past, as did matinees in many communities. Admissions to theatres fell from about $1.7 billion in 1946 to only $.9 billion in 1962, and this paralleled a decline in the number of theatres, from about 18,600 in 1948 to fewer than 12,700 in 1962. Studios diminished the number of contract workers and also took other means to reduce overhead, including sale of property. Nonetheless, several motion picture companies had deficit years and assumed the burdens of significant long term debt. Production costs skyrocketed, and massive advertising and marketing campaigns became common to ensure that the public would become an audience. Some companies, Paramount and United Artists for example, became small parts of massive conglomerates, while others such as Disney and Warner became diversified entertainment corporations.

Although there were annual fluctuations, it was not until the early 1970s that the production-distribution sector began to turn itself around financially. Exhibitors, on the other hand, constantly pointed to a product shortage and claimed they were not participating proportionally in the box office successes of the mid-1970s. Blind bidding, advances and guarantees emerged as common distributor trade practices. Nonetheless, large national and regional theatre circuits expanded in this decade, and multi-screen theatre complexes became the rule. By 1978, "the movies" were having their best year ever, although the wealth was not spread evenly around the industry.

PREVIOUS STUDIES AND INVESTIGATIONS

The literature about film runs an extreme range from the most obscurantist academic study of cinema theory to the parochial reportage of the trades. In the latter category, periodicals such as *Variety, The Hollywood Reporter, Boxoffice,* and *The Independent Film Journal* provide a chronicle of events, but without benefit of context or framework. As one would expect, their writings, although occasionally critical of some specific practice, are supportive of the industry as a whole and raise no questions about its role and function in capitalist society.

The bulk of non-trade writing about film deals with theoretical or aesthetic matters, and a smaller share concerns itself with historical aspects. It is curious that although film is a multi-billion dollar business and firmly entrenched in the cultural industry sector of capitalism, relatively little has been written about its commercial structures and policies.[6]

Government Investigations and Activities

Literature (in the broadest sense) about the industrial aspects of the medium has come from private and government sources. Aside from material developed for litigation, one of the earliest comprehensive studies was *The Motion Picture Industry — A Pattern of Control* (1941), prepared for the Temporary National Economic Committee's monograph series about concentration of economic power in America. The study explained the economic development of the film industry and, as the document's Letter of Transmittal pointed out, how the "struggle for dominance [by a few large companies] goes forward ruthlessly, with ofttimes little regard for the ... industry's social responsibilities."[7] The monograph argued that it would be a "mistake to assume that any such cure-all as 'divorcement of exhibition from production' or 'restoration of competition in the production field' " would resolve the film business's problems because they "are part of the large problem of the development and direction of American industry."[8]

In the *Paramount* decision, the Supreme Court formally outlawed certain business practices, but the Senate Select Committee on Small Business held hearings in 1953 and 1956 on film industry trade practices,[9] charging that the Justice Department had been reluctant to monitor the industry and enforce the decrees. According to the Committee's 1953 report, "Spokesmen for the Department of Justice ... admitted tacitly that they are ill-equipped to discharge their responsibilities under the court decrees [because of] the heavy volume of complaints from exhibitors" and understaffing. The Committee recommended "a more forceful and more vigilant policy on the part of the Antitrust Division of the Department of Justice in assuring compliance with the decrees...."[10] Three years later, the Committee took note of the declining number of independent exhibitors and again reviewed distributor-exhibitor relations. Reluctant to recommend any federal intervention, the Committee could only call upon "responsible leaders on both sides [of the industry to] put a stop to the constant fratricidal warfare which does nothing but worsen a difficult situation."[11]

In 1965, the Federal Trade Commission concluded an investigation of industry performance since the consent decrees and forwarded its report to the Department of Justice. The FTC recommended that

Justice "consider the feasibility of instituting contempt or other appropriate action" against Paramount Pictures and Universal for alleged violation of consent decrees to which they had agreed in 1949 and 1950.[12] The FTC pointed out, however, that the alleged violations apparently had ceased in 1962. Perhaps the Department of Justice saw this as sufficient justification for not instituting a formal complaint against the two companies.

More recently, the Washington Task Force on the Motion Picture Industry in a 1978 report argued that the "major producers/distributors are effectively limiting competition by maintaining tight control over the distribution of films, both by their failure to produce more films and by their failure to distribute more films produced by others."[13] The study's authors, while discounting any "invidious or criminal intent" on the part of film company managers, charged nonetheless that major companies "tacitly limit production among themselves and ... create sufficient barriers to entry to effectively squash new competition."[14]

Unemployment in the film industry was reviewed during Congressional hearings in 1961-62 and 1971. The first investigation included motion pictures as one of many domestic industries affected by exports and imports.[15] Runaway production policies of American film producers were singled out for criticism, although the blame ultimately was thrown on foreign governments that prohibited American film companies from exporting earnings, thereby enticing them to make pictures abroad to spend that revenue. Film subsidization programs in foreign countries and lower labor costs also were shown to have drawn production away from Hollywood. Hearings in 1971 were prompted by publicity about extraordinarily high unemployment levels among Hollywood craft and artistic personnel.[16] Although importation of foreign-made television programs occasionally was pointed to, testimony was diffuse, inconclusive, and lacking perspective because it failed to relate film industry unemployment to the context of general unemployment and the dynamics of a private enterprise economy.

As a partial response to unemployment, a federal tax shelter program was developed to stimulate film production, but this indirect subsidization of business was stopped when the 1976 Tax Reform Act became law. In its place, the Small Business Administration launched a program in 1978 to finance production by independent companies, a move that could be criticized as being away from the private enterprise doctrine, and one that preserves private ownership at public expense.

The position of the production-distribution companies favoring unfettered growth of pay television was presented in testimony in 1975 and 1976.[17]

Other federal government hearings inquired into the role of film and the film industry as international propaganda vehicles in the Cold War and inevitably touched on the development and structure of Hollywood's overseas market.[18] The Informational Media Guaranty Program was reviewed in 1967,[19] and the U.S. film industry's global status was considered in 1977 hearings[20] that stressed the importance to this country's balance of payments of Hollywood's film exports.

The Federal Trade Commission in 1967 published a 50-year review of the Webb-Pomerene Export Trade Act that permits companies supposedly competitive in the domestic market to combine in order to form export cartels. One of these is the Motion Picture Export Association of America (MPEAA), to which the major film production-distribution companies belong. The FTC declared that the "kind of firms which have gained advantages from the act has not been the smaller firms in our economy, but rather those which are large in an absolute sense and which simultaneously have major positions in the markets they serve."[21] "More often than not those exercising the right [to form export cartels] were least in need of it," the Commission concluded.[22]

The long and involved history of industry litigation and consent judgments was not touched by the House Committee on the Judiciary when it investigated in 1958 and reported in 1959 on the *Consent Decree Program of the Department of Justice*.[23] The film industry also escaped specific attention when the Senate Committee on the Judiciary examined economic concentration between 1964 and 1970.[24] The Senate Committee on Finance similarly overlooked the international operations of the production-distribution companies in its 1973 study of multinational corporations.[25] However, the House Committee on the Judiciary, in its investigation of conglomerate corporations in 1969 and 1970, and in its report published in 1971, did review Gulf + Western Industries (Paramount's parent) as well as the now defunct National General Corporation (which started from the divorced Fox theatre circuit). But the study of each company touched film industry matters only incidentally.[26]

The industry's censorship system was considered in 1960 by the House Committee on Post Office and Civil Service.[27] Hearings in 1977 by the House Committee on Small Business, and its report the following year, dealt with independent producers' charges that they were treated unfairly by the Classification and Rating Administration, which the major Hollywood production-distribution companies helped to establish. The Committee found no evidence of discrimination, but avoided studying the adequacy of the rating system and the secrecy in which rating decisions are made.[28]

Private Studies and Articles

Among non-governmental studies of the industry, one of the earliest to explain institutional matters, albeit from the industry's point of view, was *The Story of the Films* (1927) edited by Joseph Kennedy, who at the time was president of FBO Pictures Corporation and soon was to be involved with RKO. An unusual aspect of the volume was its recognition of the impact American films were having overseas, even at that time, "as silent salesmen for other products of American industry"[29] — and obviously for American ideology as well. Other early industry studies were done by Hampton[30] and Lewis.[31]

A landmark was Huettig's *Economic Control of the Motion Picture Industry* (1944),[32] highlighting industrial organization and trade practices at the moment they were under litigation by the Department of Justice. The author declared that "concentration of control exists in the pervasive influence exercised by the five theatre-owning companies (Paramount, Loew's, Warner Brothers, Twentieth Century-Fox, and RKO) over the production, distribution, and exhibition of films. The nature and extent of the influence varies in each branch of the industry, but its existence is indisputable."[33] The possibility for new competition was felt to be slight. "Only by springing forth as a fully integrated unit, equipped for production, distribution, and exhibition simultaneously, could a new company secure a substantial share of the market. The costs and risks currently attached to any such venture make it unlikely."[34]

Economic aspects of the industry occasionally have been treated in journal articles, and more rarely as chapters in collections, but only Conant has offered a book-length treatment of antitrust problems. This careful and detailed study, published in 1960, warned that monopoly power in the industry "can be offset only to the extent of continuous vigilance by the Department of Justice to insure free entry of rivals into the market."[35] Conant found that although the Paramount decrees had destroyed some restraints of trade, they did not go far enough to generate competition in all sectors of the industry.

Another side was dealt with by Guback in *The International Film Industry* (1969),[36] which explained the trans-Atlantic trade in films since 1945. The author demonstrated how the major companies, allied in the Motion Picture Export Association of America, had regained and enlarged their position in Europe after World War II, not only through the export of films, but also through production abroad that took advantage of foreign subsidy programs. The study identified cultural dangers that flowed from the economic structure and foreign policy of the American majors.

Foreign Studies

Several studies written abroad also have considered, in varying degrees, the economic status of the film business in America, frequently relating it to problems in foreign countries. In *Money Behind the Screen* (1937),[37] Klingender and Legg outlined the domination of the British cinema by a handful of American companies and sketched the banking and financial interests behind them. A few years later, Bächlin also explored economic aspects of the American film industry, analyzed its oligopolistic structure, and showed its impact on the prewar film business in Europe.[38] The study built upon the concept of film as commodity in capitalist society, and although factual material is now dated, the basic premises retain their validity. Mercillon in 1953[39] examined the monopolistic structure of the American industry, and Batz[40] a decade later devoted part of his study to showing how American film companies were related to the economic and cultural crisis of European film industries. In 1972, Degand[41] drew upon new material and pointed out how the American majors, by integrating themselves with national film industries in Europe, were therefore integrated with the film and cultural policies of the European Economic Community. He argued that a European cinema could not exist as long as it was tied to American finance and distribution. Bonnell in 1978[42] examined the problems and economics of the French industry primarily from the standpoint of consumption, and his findings necessarily are relevant to understanding the consequences of American companies' operations in that country.

Postwar studies in the United Kingdom were done by Political and Economic Planning,[43] a private research organization, in 1952 and 1958. These described the status of the British industry after decades of American supremacy and demonstrated how the American majors, by extending their control to Britain, had stunted the growth of an indigenous production industry there. Spraos in 1962[44] analyzed the erosion of the exhibition sector in the United Kingdom, and Kelly in 1966[45] again considered, in part, the operation of American subsidiaries in that country. The same year, the Monopolies Commission[46] issued its report on the supply of films in the United Kingdom and pointed to the role played by American production and distribution subsidiaries. The Association of Cinematograph, Television and Allied Technicians published a report in 1973 calling for nationalization of the film industry, from raw stock manufacture through exhibition.[47] Again, it identified the dominant position of the American majors and the influence they exerted over industry policy, trade practices, and labor relations. The Prime Minister's Working Party, in its 1976 report on the *Future of the British Film Industry*, briefly mentioned that the supply of finance for British film production depended partially on the changing policies of the major American distribution companies.[48]

Elsewhere, the massive study of the German film industry by Roeber and Jacoby (1973)[49] gave some attention to the operations of American companies. They receive only passing notice from Giannelli,[50] even though Italy was (and continues to be) a major market for American films and draws considerable American production investment. Berton's examination of Canada in part described how American companies and the MPEAA operated there, particularly in the 1940s and 1950s. Canada's failure to develop a domestic feature film industry can be explained largely by American companies' control of the market, the study argued.[51]

A general assessment of governmental and non-governmental studies of economic aspects shows the continuous proclivity in the industry for collusion, parallel action to restrain trade, anti-competitive practices, and oligopolistic control. Patterns of dominance in the American market are carried abroad by the major companies, which cannot escape blame for the inability of many foreign countries to develop indigenous film production industries. The worldwide operation of American companies necessarily has cultural and social consequences as well that are now being clarified and understood.

ROLE OF FILM

In the United States — as in other countries in which film is dominated by the private sector — the medium has grown almost entirely as a means of mass amusement, built predominantly around fictionalized portrayals. People have become accustomed to identifying film as a form of entertainment, and exposure to the medium customarily is for the purpose of diversion. As a recording medium and a vehicle for communication, film naturally can be employed in a variety of ways, and the theatrical film business is only part of a larger industry that embraces non-theatrical film uses as well, including educational and instructional films. All of us routinely see television commercials as well as news and public affairs on film. Instructional motion pictures are used commonly in the educational system and by the military; scientific work often is photographed for later reference, and films made by religious groups openly convey their norms and values.

However, the distinguishing characteristic of film in the private enterprise economy is that a large and powerful business has developed for the purpose of manufacturing and selling access to motion pictures as *commodities,* with regard neither for the medium's instructive capacity, its ability to be used for social transformation, nor its potential for contributing to solutions of society's problems.

It is true, of course, that not all films are frivolous escapist fare, and that many are dreadfully serious. However, what they have in common is an identity primarily as a commodity, and their production, distribution, and exhibition have been prompted by the anticipation of financial returns on investments. Marketplace considerations dictate that popular interests take precedence over significance, and this is embodied in the slogan "giving the public what it wants," which means, in reality, "selling profitably what the public is willing to buy." Sales validate what is sold, according to this system of logic, and what is sold is entertainment, occasionally of the most violent kind.

Naturally, not every entertainment film is profitable. But this does not deny that the basic thrust of the industry is centered on amusement, and usually within so well-defined parameters that even culturally similar entertainment films from other English-speaking lands or western Europe hardly are distributed in the United States. Moreover, the feature-length documentary is virtually a lost art in America, with distribution and exhibition limited to the non-commercial sector of the industry.

Although films overtly entertain, they covertly teach. More than a half century ago, the previously mentioned Kennedy collection pointed out how desire abroad for American goods was created by the exportation of American films. Their propaganda value certainly was the reason why the industry and the government worked together to have them broadly distributed overseas in the years after World War II. It also was the rationale behind the Informational Media Guaranty program that allowed film companies to sell some of their soft currency earnings to the American government for dollars, just to make sure that our films would be exhibited in critical foreign areas. Inasmuch as the social and cultural role of film has always been acknowledged, it is not surprising that many countries are now beginning to rebel against the cultural invasion by American media. Nor is it surprising that American media struggle to maintain their foreign markets.

Self-Censorship and Industry Codes

The impact of film on society, especially on supposedly impressionable young minds, has been a subject of concern for as long as films have existed. Censorship by government and pressure from religious and other groups have plagued the business from its earliest days. Indeed, one of the chief tasks of the industry's trade associations over the years has been to deflate external censorship by creating a system of industrial self-censorship. Until the late 1960s, the dominant themes in self-censorship were the elimination of nudity and sexual innuendo, the preservation of family life and its roles, reinforcement of the crime-doesn't-pay dictum, and general support for the ideology of the American way of life. Violence and brutality were treated more leniently. Industry codes of various dates spelled out these guidelines, and the Production Code Administration enforced them, a task made all the easier because the major producers, who supported the Code, owned major first run theatre circuits. State and municipal censorship boards oversaw film content as well. Inasmuch as the Supreme Court in 1915 had declared that exhibition of films was a business, and not properly to be considered as part of the nation's press, this medium of communication was not seen as deserving the shield of the First Amendment.[52] In 1952, however, the Supreme Court found that motion pictures did warrant constitutional protection,[53] and that decision led to two decades of litigation that by and large struck down censorship laws across the country.

In the 1950s and 1960s, films produced by independent companies and others imported from abroad began to stretch the restraints of the Production Code, and some ignored them altogether. Hollywood's version of morality was becoming quickly antiquated, while competitive pressures pushed producers toward themes, language, and sexual content that were not then offered on television. Consequently, the old Code was replaced in 1966 with a more liberal, streamlined version, and two years later a system of classification was introduced so that the young and the adolescent would not be admitted to films with content unsuitable for them. Previously, every film exhibited had to be potentially suitable for a child's eyes and ears, but the new system recognized that not every film had to be made on that level. In the late 1970s, the Code and Rating Administration was subtly renamed the Classification and Rating Administration, a change interpreted by some groups as the death of production content guidelines. The U.S. Catholic Conference was not alone in criticizing the classification system for rating some films PG (Parental Guidance) that should have been awarded an R (Restricted).

Since the mid-1960s, Hollywood's "new freedom" has been exercised largely by more explicit violence and sexual portrayals, but little should be anticipated as far as rigorous analysis or critique of social and economic problems. After all, no formal code has ever prohibited their treatment on the screen, yet their depiction has been limited by the emphasis upon entertainment and diversion that sells to the mass market and yields the necessary returns on the substantial production investments.

MEANS OF DISTRIBUTION

The flow of films from producer to public involves three chief commercial markets that, for the most part, are analogous to those normally found in industrial organizations. The producer (manufacturer) employs a distributor (wholesaler) to handle the finished product. The distributor licenses the film to an exhibitor (retailer), who in turn deals with the public (consumer). But the film business is not quite as simple as this because theatre companies occasionally finance production. Moreover, major companies, which are both producer and distributor, often finance the production of so-called independent companies, and also pick up for distribution films already completed by others.

The distribution company charges a fee for its service, often about 35% of film rental payable by theatres, and this covers the basic overhead of the organization. In addition, a distribution company deducts from film rental payable to producers the costs of promotion and advertising directly associated with the film. If the distributor has advanced production money (or guaranteed the advance of production money), it charges for that service as well. Necessarily, this description is very schematic; endless complications and refinements exist in particular cases.[54]

The motion picture theatre held a monopoly of sorts during the first four decades of the film industry's life. If you wanted to see a movie, you had to see it there. But since the 1950s, other ways have been innovated to distribute filmed entertainment to the public, and the theatre can no longer take its audience for granted. Although major production-distribution companies initially withheld their film libraries from television exhibition, they have long since admitted that it is an important source of revenue, and have cooperated with it. Their enthusiastic encouragement of unregulated pay television has been apparent as well.

The public consumes its filmed entertainment in several ways. Traditionally, it has dealt with exhibitors as retail outlets. A spectator buys a ticket that admits him/her to a hall in which a film is shown. The transaction in this case consists of renting a portion of a theatre's space to view shadows projected on a screen. A spectator also can view a film through the intermediary of television. Rather than involving money, this transaction is based upon the television station selling to advertisers the collective attention of the thousands of viewers who have been assembled to watch the film. The viewer trades his/her presence before the screen for a free-of-charge look at the motion picture. The advertiser who buys this attention includes the cost in the price of the product or service that is offered for sale. This deviates from the pattern of non-commercial television in which the broadcast becomes more a public service and less a commodity involving exchange of money or attention. It also deviates from the pay television model in which a viewer normally subscribes to an entire month's programming, including films, sports, and other entertainment. In any of these cases, however, the consumer takes part in a service transaction and no physical product changes hands. Video cassette and video disc change this relationship because the recording medium is sold as a good to which the buyer acquires ownership and viewing rights. This is an extension of direct sales to consumers of 8mm and 16mm films, which have been available for decades. Figure 5.1 diagrams the distribution channels of theatrical films.

When ordered differently, these transactions identify the ways in which theatrical motion pictures can be delivered to consumers. The major or mass markets are theatres and television, and sub-markets include the 16mm college circuit, military bases, commercial aircraft (and ocean liners), penal institutions, and 8mm home movie purchasers. Video disc and video cassette are potential mass markets as well. Distributors earn between $30 million and $40 million annually from sub-markets, excluding airlines and military installations.[55]

Figure 5.1   Distribution Channels for Theatrical Film

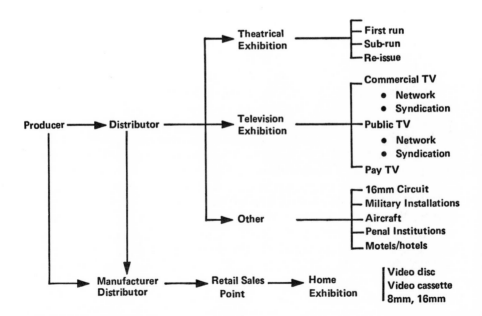

The major markets are themselves composites of smaller ones. Theatrical exhibition can be described by the kind of theatre — drive-in or hard-top — and by where a particular house stands in line, waiting its turn to rent a film. In most communities, there are first run houses that show major films as soon as they are released, and behind them are subsequent run houses that play majors' reissues as well as newly-released films from minor producers and distributors. Very large cities normally have a few theatres that play showcase or flagship runs, before films go into broader distribution in first run theatres. Depending upon the film, three months or so may elapse between its big city premiere and its initial run in a small community, with a corresponding drop in rental rates and length of run.

Within theatrical exhibition, there also is a division of houses according to the type of film played. Throughout the country, there are some theatres that show only X-rated films, and in very large cities it is common to find a few houses exhibiting only foreign pictures. In addition, there are about 500 theatres showing Spanish language films,[56] and other houses present pictures oriented to black audiences.

On television, theatrical films are exhibited by national networks, each having about 200 affiliated stations that can broadcast a film simultaneously. Beyond that is the syndication market, consisting of individual stations to which distributors lease packages of films. Separate from the advertiser-supported medium are pay television networks, with local cable TV affiliates to which households subscribe, and over-the-air pay television stations.

General Patterns of Release

A general domestic sequential release pattern describes how a typical film flows through the primary motion picture markets. Initially, the film is released by the distributor to flagship and first run theatres, and three to four months later it may complete its opening run in theatres in small communities. Perhaps six months to a year after its initial theatrical release, the film may appear on pay television. This can be simultaneous with, or even before, its re-release to theatres — an aggravating point that causes opposition to pay television from some exhibitors, especially neighborhood houses that depend upon reissues.

The film may have its first network telecast three years or so after its theatrical release, with a second network telecast two or more years behind the first. At that point, the film is likely to be released by the distributor for syndication to individual stations. Large city stations can afford to pay premium prices for films just entering syndication, and it is not uncommon for smaller communities to have to wait. Within this general sequential release pattern fall the sub-markets. The limited audiences of military bases, airborne exhibition and the college circuit normally are served before television networks. Foreign theatrical release can follow domestic release by several months or more, which gives the distributor proof of a film's drawing power and reason to demand certain rental terms.

Particular films deviate from this model for several reasons. An exceptional box office attraction may be re-released for theatrical exhibition before being licensed for television because the distribution company management believes a subsequent nationwide theatrical run will generate further revenue without diminishing the price a TV network would likely bid for the film. For example, Twentieth Century-Fox initially released *Star Wars* on May 25, 1977 and re-released it in about 1700 theatres on July 21, 1978, asking exhibitors to take the film for seven-week engagements. Its reissue produced about $35 million in rentals.[57] By late 1978, the film had not been licensed for television exhibition, and it was clear Fox management was in no rush to dispose of this highly valuable property. The ratings war among the three networks could be counted on to generate a substantial price for network broadcast of the picture. *Silver Streak*, released by Fox during the 1976 Christmas season, was part of a $40.5 million package licensed to the CBS network for telecast during the 1979-1981 period, when the theatrical play-off is completed.

Other patterns exist for films that do poorly at the box office and demonstrate no chance for theatrical re-release. If such is the case, a film may be pulled from distribution before additional overhead and promotional expenses are incurred. If the film has any potential at all, it may be offered to pay television shortly after the initial, and abbreviated, theatrical run is completed, but television networks may ignore it altogether because it has no ability to draw an audience. In that case, the distributor may decide to syndicate it, or simply to forget about the picture.

Occasionally new, longer versions of films are made especially for television by the insertion of material not included in the original theatrical release. This allows a network to show a film in two parts, hopefully with audience carry over, and to add more commercial minutes. The television versions of *Airport '77* and *King Kong* are longer than originally cut for theatres.

A recent trend in film financing involves the presale of television rights — that is, a network may guarantee to buy a film based on its script and stars, before the picture goes into production. This allows the producing company to take into account the special needs of material presented on television and to shoot two versions of scenes involving nudity or violence. The network gambles, hoping that the film will be a winner, and that its presale price will be a bargain compared to what the producer could demand later, after the popularity of the film is demonstrated.

Role of the Theatres

The mechanics of theatrical distribution revolve around the three heavy theatre-going periods of the year — summer, Christmas, Easter — and major distributors usually hold their best films for release at those times. The rest of the year may be the doldrums, to be filled by exhibitors with products from minor distributors or with other films offered by the majors. Most films now released by the major companies are on a blind bid basis that requires the exhibitor to offer terms for a film before having seen it. Indeed, the film may not even be near completion. Pictures are put out for bid to first run theatres often six months before the anticipated release date, although this has been stretched lately. Paramount, for example, announced on September 29, 1978 that it was accepting bids no later than October 12, 1978 for the June 15, 1979 release of *Prophecy*. American International Pictures announced on July 28, 1978 that it was accepting bids for a June 15, 1979 release of *Meteor*.

Some companies occasionally offer a cancellation clause that gives an exhibitor who won a blind bid the right to reject the film within 48 hours after having seen it. Often this is cosmetic because a film may not be available for screening until just shortly before its release, and an exhibitor who rejects it must try to book, at very short notice, another picture in its place. Moreover, a distributor may be obliged at the last moment to postpone release because the film has not been completed. Originally, *Superman* was to have been Warner's summer 1978 release, but it was delayed until Christmas.

A distribution company that solicits bids on a film in a market may decide to reject all bids and to negotiate terms with exhibitors. Indeed, the bidding process itself may be illusory because in many markets some or all of the exhibitors may be involved in a product split. In this case, the distributor's bid solicitation letter to all the market's exhibitors is a *pro forma* ritual, inasmuch as supposedly competitive exhibitors already have agreed among themselves that all but one will refrain from seeking a license for the picture. Exhibitors not party to the split generally find it difficult to rent quality first run films. Bidding also may be by-passed because a distributor and a particular theatre are "married" — meaning that the distributor first will offer its pictures to that theatre, and the theatre will give preference to films from that distributor. Additionally, a company such as United Artists had its preferred customers in many markets and did not put films up for bid until the late 1970s.

Splits and marriages exist in the gray area between what are and what are not attempts to restrain trade and competition. Since the early 1950s, the Department of Justice had held that splitting, for example, was an acceptable practice, but on April 1, 1977 it revised its opinion and declared splitting to be illegal. Under the auspices of the National Association of Theatre Owners, a case has been brought in the Federal District Court in Charlottesville, Va., seeking a declaratory judgment as to the legality of non-predatory splitting. Meanwhile, some independent exhibitors in several markets across the country are suing competitors who have split product, alleging restraint of trade and conspiracy to deprive them of suitable first run films.

Bid solicitation letters suggest terms that guide an exhibitor in making an offer. If a split is not operating, an exhibitor often will try to exceed these in order to keep a picture from falling into the hands of a competitor, and this becomes particularly risky when a film is blind bid. The distributor's appraisal of the exhibitor's offer is highly subjective because many variables are involved, not all of which are stated on paper.

A bidding exhibitor identifies the name, location, and capacity of the theatre in which the film is to be played. The bid also sets an opening date, which normally is the release date specified by the distributor, and states whether the run is to be exclusive or one leg of a multiple release in a market. The length of run in weeks is specified and occasionally conditions are offered for a holdover. The most important part of the bid is the terms. On a major release, a distributor will request 90% of the gross admissions after deduction of an agreed figure for house overhead, versus a straight 70% of the gross, whichever is greater. In addition, a distributor can require a minimum guaranteed rental and advance payment. The percentage terms normally change every second or third week toward the exhibitor's favor, but then attendance also falls throughout the run.[58] It is entirely possible, of course, for an exhibitor to guarantee, say, $25,000 on a run and not take in that much at the box office, but the theatre is still liable for the entire amount.

Blind bidding customarily is practiced only by the major distributors. Exhibitors consider it so onerous that they have persuaded legislatures in five states to declare it illegal, and anti-blind bidding bills are to be introduced in 27 other states during 1979.* Why have exhibitors engaged in blind bidding? For one thing, they feel there is a shortage of good commercial product and in order to obtain what is available, they must resort to buying it sight unseen. They also feel that the majors are in a

---

*By mid-June 1979, 15 states had already passed such statutes.

position to spend on lavish advertising and promotion campaigns that stimulate business. Furthermore, major company products frequently boast name stars who have proven box office appeal. Exhibitors also believe they have a better chance of acquiring a box office smash from the majors because of the majors' previous track records.

Although many films from the majors do not live up to these expectations — and blind bidding can be a way of hiding disasters — it takes only a couple of substantial hits each year for a theatre (and a distributor) to do well. Minor companies do not offer films for blind bid because they cannot command the same prestige or expectations, and in many cases contractual terms for films are not bid at all, but negotiated. Regardless, majors tie up theatres months in advance, for lengthy runs, at peak theatre-going periods, a practice that works against the exhibition of other films.

The release of a film by a major frequently demands capital reserves to which a smaller company does not have access. While "hype" cannot guarantee the success of any picture, it is unusual to find smash hits that have not been heavily promoted. Part of this involves the orchestration of a release campaign with publicity and advertising for weeks and months prior to the actual opening, so that a "want-to-see" is developed in the public and an audience is created. The strategy of a media blitz requires the simultaneous nationwide release of the film in hundreds of theatres, and sometimes over 1000.[59] Although the negative cost of a picture may be, say, $5 million, at least that amount may have to be invested to launch a major film coast-to-coast. The entire industry is reported to have spent $200 million on advertising and promotion in 1977.[60] Norman Levy, president of distribution for Columbia Pictures, claims that it costs a minimum of $2 million to market a film domestically, and estimates that Columbia will spend about $70 million to push about 20 releases during 1979.[61]

Foreign Films

This can be contrasted with the procedures for distributing foreign films in the United States. American distribution companies share overseas markets with foreign competitors (who frequently are dominated by the majors), but the United States market is essentially monopolized by American companies. Thus, a foreign language film, to be released in this country, must be picked up by an American distributor, and the majors rarely do that. Consequently, the distribution of imported pictures is handled by much smaller companies, some of which specialize in this aspect of the business.

Although the United States has been a world power for years, it is still a curiously provincial nation when it comes to motion pictures.

Public taste in films has been formed and cultivated for decades by the vertically integrated industry in which majors showed their films in their own theatres, and these acquired patterns of preference persist. Aside from theatres in a few major metropolitan areas and in a handful of university-oriented communities, foreign films simply are not exhibited in the commercial sector. During the year ending in September 1977, 54 imported pictures opened in New York City, the foreign film capital of America. In any recent year, only a few will earn more than $1 million in rentals nationwide. During 1977 for example, *Cousin Cousine* earned about $3.3 million and *Black and White in Color* about $1.4 million, and those were leaders.[62] In 1978, the foreign film with the most prospects, *Madame Rosa*, had less than $1.7 million in rentals, which even the reissue of *Blazing Saddles* was able to beat.[63]

In the late 1970s, a small distributor may have had to invest $100,000 to market an imported film in the United States, and a good portion of that would have been spent in New York City for advertising, promotion, and prints. Some foreign films start life in America with two dozen prints, and only a few eventually have over 200 in circulation. To break even, an imported film may need a box office gross of at least $400,000. A picture's reviews and track record in New York largely determine whether it will be distributed nationally and selected by exhibitors in other markets.

Dominance of the Major Firms

A pattern of circularity that has become a closed ring persists in the film industry. The major distribution companies have roots going back more than a half century. During that time, their trade practices, structure, and horizontal cooperation were successful in excluding new entrants from the field and stunting the growth of already existing competitors. Indeed, the companies that have been established in the last 30 years or so have had to hang on to ledges around the mountain of the majors. Typically this has meant specializing in some species of film and catering to a specific market that the majors have not elected to stake out. In practice, this yields G-rated films for the children's market, exploitation and sexploitation films for drive-ins, X-rated films for adult theatres, or motorcycle/trucking films and the like for some regional audiences. Even some independent production, which the *Paramount* decrees were supposed to have encouraged, depends upon the majors' financing and distribution.

The scale on which the core of the industry operates has been made so substantial that entrants and challengers must arrive on the scene, not only fully grown, but also with considerable capital or ways of obtaining it. In this respect, things have changed little since Huettig found that to be the case almost 40 years ago. It is not so much that good films are extraordinarily expensive, at least by the standard of the majors. Arthur Krim, now chairman of Orion Pictures Corporation, has pointed out that when he was with United Artists, "eight of our 10 Academy Award-winning pictures were little pictures. Their average cost was only slightly over $2 million."[64] But awards do not pay bills, and films must cover not only their own production and distribution costs, but also general company expenses. For example, a global distribution organization and sales force may require $20 million a year to operate.

Money is not invested in production without reasonable assurances that the resulting pictures will be exhibited broadly enough to cover expenses and yield profit, at least commensurate with risk. The larger the size of the actual (or perceived) market, the greater the investment can be. A distributor, therefore, must get a film into theatres, and many hundreds of them, at the right time of year. The majors have the power to do that because they have resources accumulated and built over decades that have carried them through bad years and bad decisions. Major distributors know they can get the bulk of their films booked — and booked widely — because there are exhibitors who need them, and large national and regional circuits with centralized decision-making are the guaranteed customers with thousands of important screens. The rules of the system dictate that an exhibitor try to book the most commercial film, and this means that pictures with little perceived commercial value stand in line far behind the blockbusters. The majors are often the ones with well-performing commercial films, but they are well-performing sometimes because they are booked widely.[65]

INDICATORS OF STRUCTURE AND GROWTH

A basic problem in providing a statistical profile of the film industry is that important data often are published in less than complete form and some figures are not available publicly at all. Companies and trade associations in the industry dispense information when it serves their interests. The industry exercises a monopoly of knowledge and therefore is in a position to impose selective ignorance. The federal government collects and publishes data, but that is done less to give an investigator a view of the industry's structure and operation, and more to show how the industry fits in the general economy on the national, state, and local levels. Furthermore, the privacy of private enterprise is preserved because no single-company data are published by the government, and no companies ever are identified by name.

The United States is the world's largest film market, and for more than half a century has been the world's leading exporter of filmed entertainment. Specific organizational and financial information on these points fill in the otherwise colorful and glamorous aspects of the industry that draw attention away from basic and determinative economic concerns. Companies in the industry are important because they are merchants of culture, dealing not only in theatrical films, but also television programs, and frequently recorded music, books, and magazines. Their empires, often spreading beyond the media to other service and manufacturing sectors, are integrated with the nation's centers of economic power. Production and distribution companies have global influence as well.

Size

The social significance of the film industry is far greater than the revenue of its companies would indicate. Although many familiar names fall within *Fortune*'s top 500 industrial firms (Table 5.1), it is mostly by virtue of their diversified, conglomerate activities. When only revenue from filmed entertainment is concerned (Table 5.2), companies appear appreciably smaller, overshadowed by hosts of corporations in

Table 5.1   Selected Motion Picture Industry Companies Ranked According to Revenue in *Fortune*'s 500 Largest American Industrial Firms, 1977

Rank	Company
29	Eastman Kodak Company
59	Gulf + Western Industries Inc.
[77] [a]	Loews Corporation
[164] [b]	Avco Corporation
214	Warner Communications Inc.
266	MCA Inc.
[332] [c]	Fuqua Industries Inc.
[333] [c]	Walt Disney Productions
391	Twentieth Century-Fox Film Corporation
[409] [d]	United Artists Corporation
417	General Cinema Corporation
463	Columbia Pictures Industries Inc.

a. If ranked as "industrial." As a "diversified-financial" company, Loews is ranked by *Fortune* in 9th place according to assets.

b. If ranked as "industrial." As a "diversified-financial" company, Avco is ranked by *Fortune* in 17th place according to assets.

c. If ranked as "industrial."

d. If ranked as "industrial." The parent of United Artists Corporation, Transamerica Corporation, is ranked by *Fortune* in 11th place according to assets among "diversified-financial" companies.

Source: *Fortune*, May 8, 1978; company annual reports for fiscal year 1977.

Table 5.2   Filmed Entertainment Revenue of Publicly Owned Companies with Interests in the Motion Picture Industry, 1977[a]

	Total Revenue (millions)	Filmed Entertainment	
		Revenue (millions)	Percent of Total Revenue
MCA Inc.	$ 877.6	512.2	58.4%
Twentieth Century-Fox Film Corp.	506.8	438.0	86.4
United Artists Corporation	474.1	378.2b	79.8
Warner Communications Inc.	1,143.8	353.2	30.9
Gulf + Western Industries Inc.	3,643.0	334.0c	9.2
Columbia Pictures Industries Inc.	390.5	298.3	76.4
General Cinema Corporation	465.1	213.8	46.0
United Artists Theatre Circuit	147.0	139.2	94.7
Metro-Goldwyn-Mayer Inc.	293.0	139.2	47.5
Walt Disney Productions	629.8	118.1	18.8
Technicolor Inc.	126.9	104.7	82.5
Fuqua Industries Inc.	631.7	56.8d	9.0
American International Pictures Inc.	51.1	49.2	96.3
Loews Corporation	3,237.9	41.5	1.3
Wometco Enterprises Inc.	225.1	39.3e	17.5
Cinerama Inc.	57.5	36.9	64.2
Commonwealth Theatres Inc.	33.9	32.1	94.7
Movielab Inc.	27.6	27.6	100.0
Filmways Inc.	125.3	26.7f	21.3
Inflight Services Inc.	22.6	22.3	98.7
Avco Corporation	1,537.9	19.0g	1.2
Allied Artists Industries Inc.	53.2	12.5	23.5
Cablecom-General Inc.	29.2	11.4	39.0
First Artists Production Co. Inc.	41.9	10.0h	23.9
Cinema 5 Ltd.	8.3	8.3	100.0
Cox Broadcasting Corporation	186.4	4.7	2.5

a. Includes revenue derived from theatrical motion pictures, material produced for television, and the operation of theatres and film processing plants. It is likely that revenue is included as well from the licensing of trademarks and characterizations.

b. United Artists Corporation revenue is equal to 11.8% of total revenue for its parent company, Transamerica Corporation.

c. Paramount Pictures Corporation and its subsidiaries.

d. Includes broadcasting station operation.

e. Includes tourist attractions.

f. Includes revenue from recording studios, audio design and sales, syndication of radio programs, music publishing, and a race track.

g. Avco Embassy Pictures Corporation.

h. Includes production and consulting fees.

Source: Company annual reports and Form 10-K reports for 1977.

Table 5.3　Selected Publicly Owned Companies with Interests in the Motion Picture Industry or other Mass Media, 1977

	Revenue (millions)	Net Income (millions)	Assets (millions)
Eastman Kodak Company	$5,967.0	$643.4	$5,904.2
RCA Inc.	5,880.9	247.0	4,351.7
Gulf + Western Industries Inc. [1]	3,643.0	150.3	4,159.1
Loews Corporation	3,237.9	177.4	6,983.4
CBS Inc.	2,776.3	182.0	1,518.1
American Broadcasting Cos. Inc.	1,616.9	109.8	963.1
Avco Corporation [2]	1,537.9	116.6	4,125.6
Time Inc.	1,249.8	90.5	1,053.3
Warner Communications Inc.	1,143.8	70.8	1,071.1
Times Mirror Co.	1,143.7	96.1	843.3
MCA Inc. [3]	877.6	95.1	876.8
Knight-Ridder Newspapers Inc.	751.7	61.2	563.2
McGraw-Hill Inc.	659.0	51.4	549.8
Fuqua Industries Inc.	631.7	18.1	422.8
Walt Disney Productions	629.8	81.9	964.5
Gannett Co.	557.9	69.4	529.0
The New York Times Co.	509.5	26.1	297.0
Twentieth Century-Fox Film Corp.	501.5	50.8	433.2
United Artists Corporation [4]	474.1	26.6	441.0
General Cinema Corporation	465.1	20.2	258.4
Washington Post Co.	436.1	35.5	278.6
Columbia Pictures Industries Inc.	390.5	34.6	336.0
Dow Jones & Co.	317.3	39.0	221.9
Metromedia Inc.	300.6	32.1	337.7
Metro-Goldwyn-Mayer Inc.	288.5	33.2	426.7
Wometco Enterprises Inc.	225.1	12.7	203.6
Cox Broadcasting Corporation	186.4	25.5	284.5
United Artists Theatre Circuit Inc.	147.0	4.2	110.9
Technicolor Inc.	126.9	3.9	82.7
Filmways Inc.	125.3	2.7	68.0
Viacom International Inc.	58.5	5.6	117.2
Cinerama Inc.	57.5	.2	67.8
Allied Artists Industries Inc.	53.2	(2.1)	28.6
American International Pictures Inc.	51.2	3.3	50.9
First Artists Production Co. Inc.	41.9	3.0	12.6
Commonwealth Theatres Inc.	33.9	1.6	21.9
Cablecom-General Inc.	29.2	4.0	45.3
Inflight Services Inc.	22.6	(2.0)	21.0
Movielab Inc.	22.6	.9	15.8
Cinema 5 Ltd.	8.3	(.7)	8.1

1. Parent of Paramount Pictures Corporation.
2. Parent of Avco-Embassy Pictures Corporation.
3. Parent of Universal.
4. Subsidiary of Transamerica Corporation.

( ) deficit

Source: Company annual reports for fiscal year 1977.

all industrial sectors customarily thought of as dominating the economy. Even within the domain of the mass media, as Table 5.3 demonstrates, many broadcasting and publishing companies have far greater revenue, income, and assets than film industry counterparts. The New York Times Company, for example, is larger in these categories than General Cinema Corporation, which owns the world's biggest theatre circuit and is a major soft drink bottler. CBS Inc. has revenue greater than the combined figure for Warner Communications, Walt Disney, Twentieth Century-Fox, and United Artists.

The "film industry" consists of establishments in the production, distribution and exhibition sectors as well as those that provide allied services. Within the economy at large, the film industry accounts for about 0.4% of the Gross National Product.[66] As Table 5.4 shows, for 1976 there were over 4300 establishments with payrolls in production,

Table 5.4   Indicators of Size of the Motion Picture Industry, 1963-1976 (dollars in millions)

	1963	1967	1972	1976
Motion picture, distribution and allied services				
Number of establishments	3,729	4,565	8,555	N.A.
Receipts	$ 1,520	$ 2,183	$ 2,920	N.A.
Establishments with payroll	2,829	3,375	4,704	4,346
Receipts	$ 1,510	$ 2,169	$ 2,857	N.A.
Payroll	$ 479	$ 699	$ 795	N.A.
Paid Employees	48,806	64,581	64,660	N.A.
Motion picture theatres				
Number of establishments	12,652	12,187	12,699	N.A.
Receipts	$ 1,063	$ 1,293	$ 1,833	N.A.
Establishments with payroll	12,040	11,478	11,670	10,289
Receipts	$ 1,057	$ 1,283	$ 1,816	N.A.
Payroll	$ 250	$ 281	$ 381	N.A.
Paid Employees	112,521	112,109	127,435	N.A.
Total				
Number of establishments	16,381	16,752	21,254	N.A.
Receipts	$ 2,583	$ 3,476	$ 4,753	N.A.
Establishments with payroll	14,869	14,853	16,374	14,748
Receipts	$ 2,567	$ 3,452	$ 4,673	$ 6,100
Payroll	$ 729	$ 980	$ 1,176	$ 1,549
Paid employees	161,327	176,690	192,095	184,607

N.A.   Not available.

Source: U.S. Department of Commerce, Bureau of the Census: 1963, 1967, 1972: *Census of Selected Service Industries, Motion Pictures.* 1976: *County Business Patterns,* and *U.S. Service Industries in World Markets* (December 1976).

Table 5.5   Motion Picture Industry: Establishments, Employees, Payroll, 1976

	Establishments	Employees	Payroll (millions)
Film production except TV	1,299	15,998	$ 243.6
Film production for TV	978	22,150	396.4
Services allied to production	740	14,315	200.
Film production and services	3,220	52,963	857.1
Film exchanges	719	8,958	145.5
Film or tape distribution for TV	145	2,918	49.5
Services allied to distribution	226	3,228	30.9
Film distribution and services	1,126	15,358	228.2
Theatres, except drive-in	7,519	94,720	370.3
Drive-in theatres	2,680	20,118	83.2
Motion picture theatres	10,289	115,752	457.0
Film industry total	14,748	184,607	1,549.1

Source: U.S. Department of Commerce, Bureau of the Census, *County Business Patterns,* 1976.

distribution, and allied services, and close to 10,300 theatrical establishments. (A multi-screen theatre complex counts as one establishment.)
Together, their receipts were estimated to be $6.1 billion in 1976.
According to the 1972 benchmark census, theatrical establishments
accounted for 39% of film industry receipts. Table 5.5 indicates that
whereas more than six out of 10 industry employees worked in the
theatrical sector, they earned only $3 out of every $10 paid as wages.
More than half of all wages were paid to employees in production and
allied services.

Compared to other mass media (Table 5.6), the film industry has
more establishments than newspapers and broadcasting combined, but
this is due solely to the number of theatres. The film industry payroll
ranks behind that of newspapers and broadcasting.

In 1977 the public spent about $4.075 billion for admission to film
theatres, or about 0.3% of all personal consumption expenditures

Table 5.6   Establishments, Employees, Payroll of Mass Media Industries, 1976

	Establishments	Employees	Payroll (millions)
Motion pictures	14,748	184,607	$1,549
Newspapers	7,871	360,264	4,098
Radio & TV broadcasting	5,743	147,577	1,914
Periodicals	2,503	69,047	926
Book publishing	1,283	57,739	728
Phonograph records	540	20,440	210

Source: U.S. Department of Commerce, Bureau of the Census, *County Business Patterns, 1976.*

Table 5.7 Selected Personal Consumption Expenditures, 1977

	Expenditures (millions)
Personal consumption expenditures	$ 1,206,507
Admission to film theatres	4,075a
Admission to legitimate theatres, opera, etc.	1,078
Admission to spectator sports	1,936
Funeral and burial expenses	3,534
Flowers, seeds, potted plants	4,059
Cleaning, laundering, dyeing, pressing, alteration, storage, repair of garments	4,138
Books and maps	4,338
Magazines, newspapers, sheet music	9,037
Foreign travel by U.S. residents	10,493
Tobacco products	16,530
Radio and TV receivers, records and musical instruments	18,005
Physicians	29,068
Gasoline and oil	46,457

a. Préliminary.

Source: U.S. Department of Commerce, Bureau of Economic Analysis, *Survey of Current Business,* July 1978.

Table 5.8 Admissions to Film Theatres, Selected Years, 1930-1977

	Admission to film theatres (millions)	Admission to spectator amusements[1] (millions)	Personal consumption expenditures (millions)
1930	$ 732	$ 892	$ 69,916
1935	556	672	55,764
1940	735	904	70,979
1965	1,067	2,123	430,154
1966	1,119	2,310	464,793
1967	1,128	2,404	490,358
1968	1,294	2,653	535,932
1969	1,400	2,903	579,711
1970	1,521	3,141	618,796
1971	1,626	3,359	668,171
1972	1,644	3,487	733,034
1973	1,965	3,870	809,885
1974	2,495	4,621	889,603
1975	2,538	4,775	979,070
1976	2,987	5,577	1,090,244
1977	3,490	7,089	1,206,507

[1] Includes motion picture theatres, legitimate theatres, opera, spectator sports, and entertainments of non-profit institutions.

Source: U.S. Department of Commerce, Bureau of Economic Analysis.

(Table 5.7). This was double the sum spent to see spectator sports, and just about as much as the amount spent for flowers, seeds, and potted plants. Although paid admission to motion picture theatres was more than five times greater in 1977 than in 1930, total personal consumption expenditure had increased 17 times and admission to all spectator amusements was eight times larger (Table 5.8). In 1930, about $8 of every $10 spent on spectator amusements went for theatre tickets, but by 1977 the share was less than $6 out of $10. Moreover, in 1930, admission to motion pictures accounted for about 1% of total personal consumption. It is clear that "going to the movies" — even with sensational box office receipts in recent years and higher ticket prices — is not the dominant form of out-of-home entertainment it once was, and that there has been a significant reallocation of personal expenditures that has affected theatrical admissions.

Although ticket prices have risen constantly, it was only in the 1970s that they increased rapidly enough to catch the general rise in consumer prices behind which they usually have lagged. But even during 1977, when the overall consumer price index rose 6.9%, ticket prices increased only 3.5% in indoor theatres and 5.8% at drive-ins.[67] Table 5.9 covers average admission prices over the last three decades, with figures apparently taking into account adult, senior citizen, and children's ticket prices.

Globally, the United States has been a dominant cinematic power, at least in commercial terms, for more than 60 years. American companies have the only international distribution claims, and this has given them the ability to place their films in theatres around the world, while

Table 5.9   Average Motion Picture Admission Prices, Selected Years, 1948-1978

	Admission Price	Index (1967=100)	Consumer Price Index (1967=100)
1948	$ 0.36	29.5	72.1
1954	0.49	40.2	80.5
1958	0.68	55.7	86.6
1963	0.86	70.5	91.7
1967	1.22	100.0	100.0
1971	1.65	135.2	121.3
1974	1.89	154.9	147.7
1975	2.03	166.4	161.2
1976	2.13	174.6	170.5
1977	2.23	190.2	181.5
1978	2.32	190.2	195.4

Sources: National Association of Theatre Owners: *Encyclopedia of Exhibition*, 1978.
Consumer prices: U.S. Bureau of Labor Statistics, Monthly Labor Review.

Table 5.10 Estimated Rental Revenue of Major Film Companies, 1963-1977

	Foreign (millions)	Domestic (millions)	Worldwide (millions)
1963	$ 293.0	$ 239.4	$ 532.4
1964	319.9	263.2	583.1
1965	343.5	287.2	630.7
1966	361.5	319.5	680.9
1967	357.8	355.9	713.7
1968	339.0	372.3	711.3
1969	348.4	317.4	665.8
1970	360.4	381.3	741.7
1971	347.0	336.7	683.7
1972	388.6	426.4	815.1
1973	428.9	390.5	819.4
1974	494.8	545.9	1,040.7
1975	604.0	628.0	1,232.0
1976	571.0	576.6	1,147.5
1977	563.0	802.7	1,365.7

Source: Motion Picture Association of America data as published in *Variety,* June 25, 1975;
September 1, 1976; June 14, 1978. Includes revenue of MPAA members only.

maintaining a virtual monopoly of their home market. In most
countries, American films take the largest share of all rentals, but in a
few markets they trail the domestic industry, although they out-
distance all other competitors. For the last three decades or so,
American distributors have received just about half of their theatrical
rentals from abroad, although this fluctuates annually depending upon

Table 5.11 Estimated Foreign Rentals of American Film Companies, 1971-1976

	Total Foreign Rentals (millions)	Source	
		Motion Pictures (millions)	Television (millions)
1971	$ 305	$ 230	$ 75
1972	342	258	84
1973	390	275	115
1974	460	350	110
1975	514	N.A.	N.A.
1976	531	379	152

N.A. Not available.

Source: Motion Picture Export Association of America data as reported to the U.S. Department
of Commerce and published annually in *U.S. Industrial Outlook.*

the tides of box office smashes. American films exhibited in overseas markets naturally deprive foreign producers of the chance to amortize their own films, but the sum lost to them cannot be estimated in any practical way. Table 5.10 discloses that worldwide rentals for the American majors have exceeded the $1 billion mark during the last four years.

These data can be compared with others in Table 5.11 that show the division in foreign rentals between motion pictures and television. Theatrical sources provide about 75% of total rentals. The major companies — that is, members of the Motion Picture Export Association of America — generally account for about 85 to 88% of all foreign rentals, with their share of television rentals being slightly less and theatrical rentals slightly more.

Table 5.12 Motion Picture Industry Corporate Profits and Dividend Payments, Selected Years, 1930-1977

	Corporate Profits		Net Dividend Payments
	Pre-Tax (millions)	Post-Tax (millions)	
1930	$ 51	$ 42	$ 33
1931	2	(2)	26
1932	(82)	(86)	10
1933	(40)	(43)	5
1934	2	(2)	7
1935	13	8	6
1940	51	37	18
1945	238	99	35
1950	112	60	38
1955	124	61	26
1960	49	1	22
1965	104	39	3
1970	93	8	10
1971	15	(29)	24
1972	1	(50)	17
1973	94	46	13
1974	190	116	31
1975	226	131	30
1976	426	311	53
1977	514	377	57

( ) deficit

Source: U.S. Department of Commerce, Bureau of Economic Analysis, as reprinted in National Association of Theatre Owners: *Encyclopedia of Exhibition, 1978.*

Table 5.13 Employment, Compensation and Wages in the Motion Picture Industry

	Employees	Compensation	Wages and Salaries
	(thousands)	(millions)	(millions)
1930	160	$ 313	$ 311
1935	159	282	280
1940	192	353	339
1945	238	573	552
1950,	249	688	658
1955	231	805	774
1960	187	810	772
1965	181	1,027	966
1970	201	1,386	1,274
1971	200	1,437	1,277
1972	199	1,480	1,343
1973	204	1,595	1,429
1974	203	1,763	1,575
1975	204	1,873	1,662
1976	205	2,140	1,887
1977	211	2,429	2,133

Source: U.S. Department of Commerce, Bureau of Economic Analysis, as reprinted in National Association of Theatre Owners: *Encyclopedia of Exhibition, 1978.*

The overall economic health of the film industry can be judged from Table 5.12, which shows the sector's ability to operate profitably and reward private investors.

Employment

Data for industry employment, compensation, and wages are displayed in Table 5.13. The peak years for employment were 1946 and 1947, but the industry has rebounded in the 1970s after two decades of decline. Table 5.14 shows that most film industry companies do not rank within the nation's 500 largest employers, and when they do it is because they have diversified interests beyond motion pictures. Data presented in Table 5.6 indicated that the film industry had close to 185,000 employees in 1976, slightly more than the broadcasting industry but only about half as much as the newspaper industry. Of those employed in the motion picture industry (Table 5.5), about 8% were in film distribution and services, 29% in production and services, and 63% in exhibition. For July 1978, the Bureau of Labor Statistics reported that the industry had 234,100 employees, of which

**Table 5.14 Selected Companies Ranked According to Employees in *Forbes*
Magazine's List of 500 Largest Employers, 1977**

Rank		Employees
		(thousands)
21	Eastman Kodak	123.7
22	Gulf + Western Industries	116.6
26	RCA Inc.	110.0
170	CBS Inc.	33.9
223	Transamerica Corp.	26.4
247	Avco Corp.	24.0
263	Loews Corp.	23.0
305	Times Mirror Co.	19.4
317	MCA	18.1
319	Walt Disney Productions	18.0
340	Macmillan	16.9
359	Time Inc.	15.9
393	Gannett Newspapers	14.4
399	Knight-Ridder Newspapers	14.0
419	Fuqua Industries	13.4
468	McGraw-Hill	11.9
496	General Cinema	11.0

Source: *Forbes,* May 15, 1978.

60% worked for theatrical establishments.[68] Overall, women accounted
for 37% of all employees, but in the exhibition sector the figure is 42%.

Number of Firms

The actual number of motion picture production and distribution
companies is elusive. The Bureau of the Census publishes data per-
taining to establishments, but that term is not synonymous with
company. An establishment is a single physical location at which
business is carried out, and so a company may consist of one or a dozen
establishments. Table 5.15 shows that as of 1976 there were almost
1300 establishments engaged in non-TV motion picture production and
that films from them flowed through more than 700 exchanges to
theatres and other points of exhibition.

There probably are several hundred active and inactive motion
picture production companies in the United States. The output of
operating companies consists not only of theatrical films, but also
non-theatrical films in religious, educational, industrial, and documentary forms. Similarly, there are several hundred film distributors,
but somewhat less than 200 offer pictures to the commercial theatres.

One measure of distributors is the number of companies that submit feature films to the Classification and Rating Administration (formerly Code and Rating Administration), but this may underestimate distributors of adult films. In any case, in 1975, 1976, and 1977, there were, respectively, about 190, 200, and 170 companies identified, and usually a shade more than 10% are cited as "production company" rather than releasing company.[69] Based upon these data, it would seem that there are about 175 distribution companies, but more than half of them submitted only one film for rating, and about three-quarters submitted no more than two films. These proportions vary from year to year, of course, but the rule is unmistakable.

Table 5.15 Motion Picture Production and Distribution Establishments with Payroll, 1967, 1972 and 1976

	1967	1972	1976
Film production, other than TV	909	1392	1299
Film or tape production for TV	686	1138	978
Film exchanges	710	877	719
Film or tape distribution for TV	147	151	145

Source: U.S. Department of Commerce, Bureau of the Census, *1967 Census of Business, Selected Services, Motion Pictures; 1972 Census of Selected Service Industries, Motion Picture Industry; 1976 County Business Patterns.*

Another estimate is based upon data from the Motion Picture Association of America. Table 5.16 shows that "national distributors" peaked in the early 1970s, and that there were about as many national companies in 1977 as there were a decade before.

Annual Releases

The number of annual releases is not any easier to establish than the number of production and distribution companies. Part of the problem is due to faulty data gathering by the industry and the government, and this is complicated by definitional problems, if not by the nature of the business itself. Each year, there are hundreds of projects started that never reach the filming stage. Of those that do, an unidentifiable number are never completed. Some of the finished pictures may never be released by their producers, for one reason or another, and not all films put into distribution are selected by theatre owners for exhibition. Among those that do reach screens, some will have so few playdates that it is hardly worth counting them as released features. Occasionally, made-for-TV pictures are released theatrically outside the United States, and some television programs have been re-edited as well for foreign release. Moreover, it is impossible to state with precision the

Table 5.16 National Distributors of Motion Pictures, Selected Years, 1930-1977

	Distributors
1930	9
1935	10
1940	11
1945	11
1950	15
1955	12
1960	12
1965	14
1966	16
1967	18
1968	19
1969	19
1970	22
1971	22
1972	25
1973	23
1974	25
1975	23
1976	21
1977	16

Source: Based upon data from the Motion Picture Association of America.

number of foreign pictures that are released in the United States because of the extensive overseas production and financing activities of American companies, which raise questions about how a "foreign" film can be defined.

With these limitations considered, Table 5.17 shows that the annual number of features released by national distributors has been decreasing consistently since 1940, with the number of new releases in the late 1970s about a third the level of the early years of the 1940s. The number of features submitted to the Classification and Rating Administration shown in Table 5.18 demonstrates a similar trend. Although submission is not mandatory, these data are more comprehensive than those in Table 5.17 because the latter excludes pictures offered by non-national distribution companies.

Theatres

The number of motion picture theatres also is a problematic statistic that has been complicated in recent years by the rise of multi-screen

Table 5.17 Motion Pictures Released by National Distributors, 1930-1977

Year	New	Re-issues	Total
1930	—	—	355
1935	388	3	391
1940	472	3	475
1941	497	7	504
1942	484	8	492
1943	426	6	432
1944	409	6	415
1945	367	8	375
1946	383	17	400
1947	371	55	426
1948	398	50	448
1949	406	85	491
Average, 1940-49	421	25	446
1950	425	48	473
1951	411	28	439
1952	353	33	386
1953	378	36	414
1954	294	75	369
1955	281	38	319
1956	311	35	346
1957	363	19	382
1958	327	25	352
1959	236	18	254
Average, 1950-59	338	36	374
1960	233	15	248
1961	225	15	240
1962	213	24	237
1963	203	20	223
1964	227	15	242
1965	257	22	279
1966	231	26	257
1967	229	35	264
1968	241	17	258
1969	241	10	251
Average, 1960-69	230	20	250
1970	267	39	306
1971	281	32	313
1972	279	39	318
1973	237	38	275
1974	229	45	274
1975	190	40	230
1976	187	30	217
1977	154	32	186
Average, 1970-77	228	37	265

Source: Motion Picture Association of America.

Table 5.18 Motion Pictures Rated by the Classification and Rating Administration, 1965-1977

	Total	MPAA Companies[a]
1965	191	175
1966	168	149
1967	215	206
1968	230	201
1969	325	171
1970	431	181
1971	513	177
1972	540	208
1973	584	185
1974	523	151
1975	459	123
1976	486	119
1977	378	95

a. Allied Artists, Avco-Embassy, Columbia, Metro-Goldwyn-Mayer, Paramount, Twentieth Century-Fox, United Artists (distributing MGM films after 1973), Universal, Warner.

Source: Motion Picture Association of America, Classification and Rating Administration.

theatre complexes, either newly constructed or resulting from the remodeling of single-screen houses. Other difficulties appear because estimates by the Motion Picture Association of America do not necessarily match those provided for recent years by the National Association of Theatre Owners, which cites "various sources" as the basis for its own figures.[70] The Bureau of the Census counts establishments, not screens, and makes a division between those with and without payrolls. The Department of Commerce admitted in a 1976 publication that precise figures "are lacking since chain operators are reluctant to release such information."[71] Personal queries to circuit operators across the nation routinely go unanswered as if they fear disclosure, and one can only conclude, as a writer for *Variety* did in 1975, that for some obscure reason exhibitors want to keep secret the number of their houses.[72] (But secrecy pervades other sectors of the industry as well.) Table 5.19 is thus reviewed as only an approximation. But, there is no doubt that the number of multi-screen indoor houses has risen dramatically in the 1970s, and that the number of drive-ins has been relatively stable, with slight decline, due to urban sprawl and the increase of real estate values on community peripheries.

Company Finances

A review of company revenue by business segment (Appendix A5) provides another indicator of structure and shows some of the dramatic financial changes that have taken place in the industry during the 1970s. The major production-distribution companies are publicly owned and their yearly reports provide important data, but several of the important exhibition circuits are not publicly owned and no financial data about them are available. Nonetheless, problems exist even with information that is reported to the public by all companies. For one thing, company accounts — which constitute the financial history of corporations — are forever being reclassified and restated, making the construction of time series exasperating. Furthermore, all companies do not cut the revenue pie in the same way, and while one may list revenue according to the buyer (i.e., network television, syndication, theatres, etc.), another may list it according to the item marketed (theatrical features, television series, made-for-TV films, etc.). Some companies lump two business segments, recorded music and music publishing for example, while others may make no distinction in financial reports between theatrical revenue from the United States and overseas, and may include revenue from pay television in the theatrical category rather than under television. Furthermore, Canada is considered a domestic market by most companies although it actually provides the most revenue of any foreign country. Other problems exist because a distributor may decide not to break out revenue from, say,

Table 5.19 Number of Motion Picture Theatres, Selected Years, 1948-1977

	Indoor	Drive-In	Total
1948	—	—	18,532
1954	—	—	18,491
1958	—	—	16,354
1963	—	—	12,652
1964	9,200	3,540	12,740
1965	9,240	3,585	12,825
1970	10,000	3,750	13,750
1971	10,300	3,770	14,070
1972	10,580	3,790	14,370
1973	10,850	3,800	14,650
1974	11,612	3,772	15,384
1975	12,175	3,822	15,997
1976	12,996	3,833	16,829
1977	12,990	3,564	16,554

N.B.   1. Census figures do not agree with private tabulation. Census total for 1967 is 12,187, compared to 13,000 for MPAA; for 1972, Census shows 12,699.

      2. Figures for 1974 through 1977 refer to screens.

Sources: 1948-1963 — U.S. Dept. of Commerce, Census of Business.
          1964-1976 — Motion Picture Association of America.
          1977 — National Association of Theatre Owners.

syndication sales, after having done so in previous years. Operating income by product segment may not always be reported by some companies, and if it is, a comparison with that for competitors may be difficult because of assignment of general overhead and administrative expenses. Even unsuspected and unspecified items may creep into revenue columns and therefore into income (and loss) figures. Finally, the business done by production-distribution companies, or theatre circuits, may be swallowed in the accounts of a much larger parent, leaving significant holes in an industry-wise tabulation.

DEGREE OF INDUSTRY CONCENTRATION

Conditions of industrial structure necessarily intersect with ownership and markets, and in the motion picture business this becomes all the more crucial because as a medium of communication, film sets before us images and ideas that influence us and our cultures. In this respect, patterns of concentration and control in film are of more concern than, for example, machine screw manufacturing, plastics, saw mills, or laundries. The extent of centralized control affects entry and the ability of new and smaller competitors to thrive. Inasmuch as the American film industry is a global enterprise, consequences of this kind are multiplied throughout other countries.

Power is conveyed by the ownership of resources, whether they be in the form of cash, studios, films, distribution companies, theatres, etc. Power is translated into the ability to decide how those resources will be used, and by whom. In the film industry, it can mean, for example, the authority to select who will make what kinds of films, or which films will be accepted for national and global distribution, or which films will be exhibited. Concentration renders that power all the more influential and awesome. Indeed, the film business can be understood as several pyramids of concentration in which the business and cultural decisions of a few companies predominate. There remain instances, however, where small firms have achieved some measure of success supplementing limited financial resources with ingenuity, creativity and persistence.

Distribution and Production

The superficial aspects of concentration should be disposed of first. It is common knowledge that three periods — summer, Christmas, Easter - generate the bulk of film rentals. MGM has declared that 17 weeks provide 40% to 50% of its theatrical rentals.[73] Furthermore, the bulk of rental for most films is earned within a few months of release,[74] and amortization increasingly is helped by advances from theatre owners and presale to television. Films are pushed into distribution, and after their relatively short life in theatres, are moved aside to make room for others that must be amortized. Declining production and longer theatrical runs operate in unison. When a film is booked into a first run theatre for seven or eight weeks — a few films longer, others less — the house needs only 10 or so a year to operate, although exhibitors would like to have blockbuster audiences every day. About a third of national admissions comes from nine major metropolitan areas, but these account for less than a quarter of promotional expenditures.[75] The territories served by film exchanges in four cities typically generate a third of all rentals.[76] In terms of indoor theatres, the 1972 census found that those going into operation between 1964 and 1972 represented less than 30% of all establishments, but that they took in 43% of all receipts.[77]

Overseas, the top five markets for American companies in 1977 yielded about 45% of all foreign rentals ($563 million) and the top 10 contributed 68% — a pattern that seems to be solidifying into a law.[78] In any recent year, there probably are about 3600 feature films made throughout the world, but American production, routinely less than 10% of that amount, occupies about half of world screen time and probably captures close to that share of the world box office. This is all the more startling because the bulk of this revenue abroad is earned by just a small number of films, as it is in the United States.

In 1978 for example, the top 10 films had gross box office receipts of $1.2 billion in the United States-Canadian market, while the total U.S. box office was estimated to be $2.7 billion.[79] Over 40 films had rentals of more than $8 million each. Indeed, a half dozen films each year generate perhaps a third or more of the American box office, and the top 10 or dozen can garner a half or two-thirds. Throughout the 1970s, the MPAA's Classification and Rating Administration reviewed an average of considerably more than 400 films each year. It is clear then that at the top of the box office pyramid is a handful of films that earn half the rentals, while what is left is shared by several hundred other pictures.

But these figures really do not identify the extent of concentration in the industry. The mega-hits, as a rule, are from the major distributors — Columbia, Paramount, Twentieth Century-Fox, United Artists (through which MGM distributes in the United States), Universal, and Warner. In 1978, they handled the 10 highest rental films in the North American market and received $434.5 million for them. In the preceding year, they distributed nine of the top 10 and received $344.8 million in rentals. Of the 27 films earning $10 million or more in rentals in North America in 1978, the above companies distributed 25 and received $642.9 million; Buena Vista (Disney) distributed the other two, which earned $26.1 million. In 1977, there were 28 pictures that had rentals of $10 million or more in North America. The majors handled 23 of them ($622.6 million), Buena Vista distributed four ($52.8 million), and an independent had one ($23 million). The highest rental independent film in 1978 returned $9.7 million to its distributor. Of 82 new releases earning more than $2 million in rentals in 1978, the majors distributed 66, Buena Vista handled five, Avco Embassy and Allied Artists two each, and American International one. Independent companies distributed only six films with at least $2 million in rentals. In 1977, there were 78 new releases that earned at least $2 million, and the majors distributed 53 of them. American International handled eight, Buena Vista five, and Avco Embassy and Allied Artists two each. Independents had only 10 films among those earning $2 million or more in rentals. Table 5.20 summarizes the dominant position of the six leading distributors.

Overall, the majors handle a small portion of films on the market and themselves constitute probably 6-7% of all distribution companies. Table 5.21 shows that during the 1970s, MPAA companies accounted for only a third of all films rated by the Classification and Rating Administration. Looking at only national distributors, Table 5.22 indicates that MPAA companies distributed 60% of all new releases. The addition of Buena Vista and American International increases the figure to 70%. Including reissues has no appreciable effect on the percentages.

The share of domestic rentals accounted for by each of the major companies is identified in Table 5.23, with Paramount in 1978 being the clear leader, followed by Universal. The division of foreign receipts for American companies is presented in Table 5.24, showing Warner as the leading distributor in 1974. During the 1970s in North America, the

Table 5.20 Market Domination by Six Leading Distributors of Theatrical Films[a]

	1978	1977
Number of:		
Top 10 grossing films handled	10	9
Rental revenue (million)	$434.5	$344.8
Films with $10 million or more in North American rentals	25 of 27	23 of 28
Rental revenue (million)	642.9	622.6
Films with $2 million or more in North American rentals	66 of 82	53 of 78

a. They are Columbia, Paramount, Twentieth Century-Fox, United Artists, Universal, Warner.

Source: *Variety*, January 4, 1978; January 3, 1979; January 10, 1979. Does not include reissues.

Table 5.21 Films Distributed by MPAA Companies as Percent of all Films Rated by the Classification and Rating Administration, 1970-1977[a]

	Percent
1970	42.0%
1971	34.5
1972	38.5
1973	31.7
1974	28.9
1975	26.8
1976	24.5
1977	25.1

a. Allied Artists, Avco Embassy, Columbia, Metro-Goldwyn-Mayer, Paramount, Twentieth Century-Fox, United Artists, Universal, Warner.

Source: MPAA, Classification and Rating Administration.

majors captured between 70% and 89% of the revenue accruing to films earning more than $1 million in rentals (Table 5.23). Adding receipts for Buena Vista and American International pushed the upper limit to 95% in 1978 for the eight top distributors. Throughout the 1970s, the top three distribution companies accounted for about 50% of the domestic rentals. Inasmuch as the majors are the only companies with international distribution chains, they do not have to share the foreign market with minor or independent American distributors. In foreign areas, the top three American companies accounted for somewhat more than 50% of the rentals earned by all U.S. distributors for the years presented. If television programs are added to American films shown abroad, then about 88% of all rentals are earned by the eight leading companies.

Agreements among the major distributors have decreased the number of companies operating abroad. Paramount and Universal formed Cinema International Corporation in 1970, with each owning 49%. Since then, CIC has handled distribution of Paramount and Universal films in most foreign territories, in addition to operating theatres in Europe, South America, and South Africa. CIC also began foreign distribution of MGM films in December 1973, after MGM shut down its global organization. CIC is reported to be the world's largest distributor of films, and in fiscal 1977 accounted for a third of American films' foreign rentals. Its revenue was about $133 million in 1977 and was expected to be about $145 million in 1978.[80] In addition, CIC produced *The Sorcerer*, which was distributed in the western United States by Universal and in the east by Paramount.

Other American distribution companies frequently engage in joint ventures abroad. As of 1977, for example, Columbia shared about a dozen foreign offices each with Fox and Warner, and in late 1978

Table 5.22 Major Company Share of New Releases Handled by National Distributors

	1970	1971	1972	1973	1974	1975	1976	1977	Total Number	Total Percent
New Releases Total	267	281	279	237	229	190	187	154	1,824	100.0%
Allied Artists	7	8	8	1	3	7	6	4	44	2.4
Avco Embassy	11	6	13	11	10	15	8	5	79	4.3
Columbia	28	37	27	16	21	15	15	10	169	9.3
Metro-Goldwyn-Mayer	21	20	22	16	a	a	a	a	79	4.3
Paramount	16	21	14	26	23	11	18	14	143	7.8
Twentieth Century-Fox	14	16	25	14	18	19	19	14	139	7.6
United Artists	40	26	20	18	21	21	22	14	182	9.9
Universal	17	16	16	19	11	10	13	16	118	6.5
Warner	15	17	18	22	15	19	11	14	131	7.2
Total MPAA companies	169	167	163	143	122	117	112	91	1,084	
Percent of new releases	63.3	59.4	58.4	60.3	53.3	61.6	59.9	59.1	–	59.4
Buena Vista (Disney)	4	5	4	4	5	6	5	5	38	2.1
Amer. International	25	24	28	19	18	17	17	18	166	9.1
*Percent of new releases MPAA companies, Buena Vista and Amer. International	74.2	69.8	69.9	70.0	63.3	73.7	71.7	74.0	–	70.6

a. Distributed by United Artists since 1974.

Source: Motion Picture Association of America.

Table 5.23 Major Company Percent of U.S.-Canadian Market Receipts for Films Earning Rentals of $1 Million or More, 1970-1978

	1970	1971	1972	1973	1974	1975	1976	1977	1978
Columbia	14.1%	10.2%	9.1%	7.0%	7.0%	13.1%	8.3%	11.5%	11.6%
Metro-Goldwyn-Mayer	3.4	9.3	6.0	4.6	a	a	a	a	a
Paramount	11.8	17.0	21.6	8.6	10.0	11.3	9.6	10.0	23.8
Twentieth Century-Fox	19.4	11.5	9.1	18.8	10.9	14.0	13.4	19.5	13.4
United Artists	8.7	7.4	15.0	10.7	8.5	10.7	16.2	17.8	10.3
Universal	13.1	5.2	5.0	10.0	18.6	25.1	13.0	11.5	16.8
Warner	5.3	9.3	17.6	16.4	23.2	9.1	18.0	13.7	13.2
Total, seven largest, 1978	75.8	69.9	83.4	76.1	78.2	83.3	78.5	84.0	89.1
Buena Vista	9.1	8.0	5.0	6.5	7.0	6.0	6.7	5.6	4.8
Amer. International					3.8	3.4	3.8	3.4	1.4
Total, nine largest, 1978	84.9	77.9	88.4	82.6	89.0	92.7	89.0	93.0	95.3

a. Distributed by United Artists since 1974.

Source: *Variety,* January 15, 1975; February 11, 1976; January 18, 1978; January 10, 1979.

announced the merger of its Australian distribution facility with Fox.

In the domestic market, the major companies interlock in several ways. Since late 1973, MGM films have been distributed by United Artists, with the two companies agreeing on how pictures will be handled and on what terms.[81] *Towering Inferno*, a blockbuster of a few years ago, was jointly produced and jointly distributed by Warner and Twentieth Century-Fox, which would be analogous to Ford and General Motors manufacturing and marketing a new automobile. A sequel to *Gone With the Wind* is to be co-produced by Universal and MGM, with Universal to distribute the film in the United States and Canada, while CIC will handle foreign distribution. MGM also collaborated with Columbia on *The Wind and the Lion*, each sharing the production costs as well as working out a common advertising approach that would serve both domestic and foreign markets. Columbia and Universal will co-produce *1941* and *The Electric Horseman*, and Universal will cooperate with Paramount to produce *Havana*. MGM and Warner shared the financing of *The Goodbye Girl* and *Grand Hotel*, and United Artists joined Allied Artists to produce *The Betsy*. United Artists also co-financed *Network* with MGM. Other jointly-produced films could be cited as well.

Table 5.24 Major Company Percent of Foreign Rentals Earned by American Companies

	1972	1973	1974
Columbia	12.0%	10.5%	14.0%
Metro-Goldwyn-Mayer	14.0	14.0	8.5
Paramount	14.5	14.0	10.0
Twentieth Century-Fox	16.5	16.0	12.0
United Artists	21.0	22.5	16.0
Universal	9.0	10.5	17.0
Warner	13.0	12.5	22.5
Total	100.0	100.0	100.0

Source: *Variety*, August 6, 1975.

In terms of properties, Warner and Columbia established The Burbank Studios in January 1972 in order to operate the studio and production facilities owned by each of them. On another level, when two companies have films on very similar subjects, they might attempt to avoid excessive duplication. This happened with Universal's *Two Minute Warning* and Paramount's *Black Sunday* (both distributed abroad by CIC). Officials of Universal and Paramount met to discuss how to minimize similarity, and Universal eventually agreed to make certain edits in its picture.[82]

Concerning trade practices, United Artists had a long standing policy against blind bidding, but this was abandoned in 1977, allegedly because other majors prevailed upon U.A. management to bring the company into line with the majors' policy.[83] The majors, moreover, are members of the Motion Picture Association of America at whose meetings industry problems are considered. Such was the case when company representatives agreed to a common policy of vigorous opposition to anti-blind bidding legislation introduced in state legislatures. The majors also belong to the Motion Picture Export Association of America and other film export organizations that allow them to operate in concert in foreign markets. There are, therefore, a variety of ways in which companies interact at home and overseas.

Of course, the motion picture is no longer the sole line of filmed entertainment. Major and independent producers provide most of the non-public affairs and non-sports programming on commercial television, and suits directed against the networks seek to open this market even more.[84] A few of the majors have strong television production subsidiaries that contribute important revenue. As Table A5.6 in Appendix A5 shows, MCA (Universal) derived more revenue from television than from theatres during the 1970s; Paramount and Columbia also drew considerable revenue from licensing material to television. Prime time schedules now are chaotic compared to what they were just as recently as the early 1970s. One series after another becomes a casualty in the ratings war, while specials, mini-series and frequent reshuffling of program schedules are the rule. At the beginning of the 1978-79 season, it seemed that seven companies (Columbia, Disney, MGM, Paramount, Twentieth Century-Fox, Universal, and Warner) provided 20.5 hours of regular prime time programming, not counting theatrical films and made-for-TV films. Of this amount, Universal supplied about half, a good portion of which went to NBC. Seventeen independent producers supplied 25.5 hours and the networks themselves provided five hours.[85] Compared to several previous seasons, the majors' share of *regular* series was down slightly in 1978.[86]

Major Hollywood production-distribution companies have found a growing market in pay television, which now might spend from $.6 million to $1 million for each film licensed to it.[87] The MPAA companies generally account for about 58% of the films exhibited on pay television systems in a typical month.[88]

Film Theatres

On the retail level of the industry, there are literally thousands of companies in exhibition, from Mom and Pop operations to multi-million dollar enterprises. A few of these companies, however, have such substantial holdings and revenue-generating ability that they are set apart from the rest just as is the case for firms in production and distribution. Although the latter exercise their power in a national and international sphere, exhibition companies can assert their dominance on other levels. Several large chains, such as General Cinema and United Artists Theatre Circuit, have national importance. Others, such as Commonwealth and Fuqua's Martin Theatres, have significant regional holdings. Some, including Pacific Theatres, Georgia Theatre Co., and Kerasotes are major state-wide groups. Chains exist as well that are important in specific cities, such as Wehrenberg in St. Louis or Cinemette in Pittsburgh. Although Wometco has holdings in the Caribbean, American exhibitors as a rule confine their business to the domestic market. This is not so for production-distribution companies because Paramount, Fox, and CIC have circuits overseas.

In the domestic market, small towns frequently constitute monopoly situations for some exhibitors, but the possibility of competition increases with the size of the community. It is not uncommon, therefore, to find three or four major national and regional chains, plus

Table 5.25 Screens in Selected Theatre Chains

	Screens	Date
General Cinema	739	October 31, 1977[a]
United Artists Theatre Circuit	661	August 31, 1977[a]
American Multi Cinema	462	October 1978[d]
Plitt	412	November 1, 1978[c]
Commonwealth	347	October 3, 1978[a]
Mann	310	End of 1978[g]
Fuqua (Martin Theatres)	283	December 31, 1977[a]
Kerasotes	180	October 1978[f]
Cinemette	160	February 22, 1978[c]
Stewart & Everett	138	December 31, 1978[e]
Cablecom-General	125	November 30, 1977[b]
Pacific Theatres	125	1978[h]
Cobb	125	July 26, 1978[c]
Gulf States	120	December 31, 1978[e]
Loews	117	December 31, 1977[a]
Cooperative Theatres of Michigan	105	1978[h]
Total	4409	

Source: a. Annual report for year indicated.
b. Form 10-K report for year indicated.
c. *Variety* for date indicated.
d. Company newsletter for month indicated.
e. Letter to author.
f. Interview.
g. Projection by *Variety*, January 18, 1978.
h. *International Motion Picture Almanac*, 1978.

smaller companies, in moderate-size metropolitan areas. Although all are in the exhibition business, they might not be directly competitive because of market segmentation among first run, second run, drive-in, ethnic, and adult theatres. Consequently, apparent competition may be effectively reduced, as it also is when each of the few companies owns several theatres in the same town, and when rival firms agree to split first run product among themselves.

Table 5.25 presents the holdings of several large theatre chains, although the list is by no means all-inclusive. The location of the theatres is of considerable importance because that can generate substantially different revenue for chains with the same number of screens. If one assumes 16,500 screens in the nation, then the top three chains account for about 11% and the top five almost 16%. But this understates the position of the large chains because drive-ins are included in the national figure, and the major chains consist almost exclusively of conventional theatres. Furthermore, as *Paramount* and other cases have taught, holdings amounting to a small proportion of all theatres can convey considerable market leverage. For example, at the time the Justice Department brought its case to force the five major distributors to sell off their theatres in 1945, the majors wholly or partially owned only about 17% of all theatres.

The *Paramount* decision made circuit-wide booking and package leasing illegal. Although there is competition for spectators in most communities and large chains face each other regionally and nationally, the major producer-distributors know that at the retail end of the industry they have but a handful of best customers who together control a substantial share of first run theatres. The establishment and financing of major chains, moreover, is predicated on the assumption that they will be able to rent a substantial share of the major first run films from the big companies. Similarly, the studios and distributors assume as a basis for their own operations that they will be able to place their films in enough of the important houses so as to have adequate play-off. The congruence of interests, multiplied market-by-market to a national scale, demonstrates that the industry, from manufacturer to retailer, moves on the basis of decisions made in a dozen or so of the largest companies. Other firms that elect to do business on that level have to conform, or else they try to carve niches elsewhere in which they will be more secure.

Major theatre groups and distributors do the most business with each other. In the five years up to 1978, General Cinema was the largest customer for each of the major distributors, with the exception of United Artists distribution company.[89] In fiscal 1978, for example, General Cinema contributed about $12 million in film rental to Columbia, or about 8.5% of the distributor's total domestic rentals.

Probably in second and third places were United Artists Theatre Circuit and ABC Theatres (subsequently sold to Plitt), each contributing about $6 million in rentals.[90] Consequently, three chains provided, perhaps, 17% of Columbia's domestic theatrical revenue. Similarly, a blockbuster or two running in a significant number of a chain's theatres can have an explosive effect on an exhibition company's annual admission revenue as well as on concession stand receipts, which might amount to $.20 for each dollar spent at the box office of a conventional theatre. *Jaws* grossed over $20 million in General Cinema's houses, and represented $13 million in extra business for the company.[91]

Concentration in the industry, however, is comparable to other communications industries. Table 5.26 reveals that for production, distribution and allied services, the four largest firms accounted for over 29% of all receipts, and the eight largest firms accounted for over 44%. In exhibition, the four largest companies had 19% of all receipts, and the eight largest had over 26%, but they had, respectively, only 10% and 14% of all establishments. Concentration in the film industry as a whole also is significantly greater than in automobile rental and leasing, computer and data processing services, and advertising.[92] Among manufacturing fields, the four largest newspaper publishing companies accounted for 17% of the value of shipments, and the eight largest accounted for 28%. Figures for periodicals were 26% and 38%; radio and TV communications equipment, 19% and 33%; and photographic equipment and supplies, 74% and 85%.[93]

Another indicator of concentration is that in film production, distribution and allied services, 10 firms captured 48% of all 1972 revenue, as shown in Table 5.27. The top 15 firms constituted only 0.2% of all firms, yet they received 53% of all receipts. In the

Table 5.26 Concentration of Revenue in the Motion Picture Industry, 1972

	Production, Distribution and Services		Motion Picture Theatres	
	Receipts (millions)	Percent of Total	Receipts (millions)	Percent of Total
All firms	$2,920.4	100.0%	$1,833.0	100.0%
4 largest firms	852.4	29.2	350.4	19.1
8 largest firms	1,295.6	44.4	482.2	26.3
20 largest firms	1,628.9	55.8	639.1	34.9
50 largest firms	1,882.2	66.4	819.3	44.7

Source: U.S. Department of Commerce, Bureau of the Census, *Census of Selected Service Industries,* 1972; Volume 1, Summary and Subject Statistics.

theatre-owning sector, four firms accounted for 19% of all receipts. The top seven theatre firms constituted only 0.1% of all firms, but they generated 25% of all receipts.

Table 5.27 Concentration of Firms by Annual Receipts, 1972

	Production, Distribution and Services			Motion Picture Theatres		
	Firms	Receipts (millions)	Percent of Receipts	Firms	Receipts (millions)	Percent of Receipts
All firms	7,898	$2,920.4	100.0%	6,938	$1,833.0	100.0%
Annual receipts of:						
$50 million or more	10	1,413.2	48.4	4	350.4	19.1
$20 million or more	15	1,542.3	52.8	7	462.6	25.2
$10 million or more	27	1,711.9	58.6	19	630.3	34.4

Source: U.S. Department of Commerce, Bureau of the Census, *Census of Selected Service Industries, 1972; Volume 1, Summary and Subject Statistics.*

Ownership of Individual Firms

Information about market concentration is significant in its own right, as is evidence of cooperation among rival companies in the industry. However, an important aspect customarily overlooked is the narrow structure of ownership behind the companies that dominate the business. In firms whose stock is not available for public purchase, the proprietors might be a family, or several business associates, or just one person. Stock offerings to investors at large somewhat widen this circle of ownership, but in contrast to political democracy in which "one person, one vote" is the theoretical rule, "one share, one vote" is the principle in corporate democracy. Even so, large minority holdings can convey enormous power and allow an important stockholder representation on the board of directors. Moreover, "Control of a small block of stock in a widely held company by a single or few like-minded financial institutions," according to one government report, "provides them with disproportionately large powers within the company."[94]

There are no public studies disclosing ownership of stock specifically in the motion picture industry. However, the findings of government investigations of companies owning broadcasting properties are suggestive because several film companies are station licensees. An inquiry into the holdings of the 25 largest bank trust departments[95] revealed that as of mid-1972 the Bank of New York had voting rights to 6.6% of the common stock of Columbia Pictures and 4.2% of Twentieth Century-Fox, as well as 3.7% of Cox Broadcasting and 1.3% of Wometco, two companies that have co-produced a number of films

with Fuqua Industries. Bankers Trust Company of New York voted
1.1% of Columbia, 1.6% of Wometco and 2.0% of Cox. Old Colony
Trust of Boston held 2.1% of Columbia and 1.9% of Twentieth
Century-Fox. The Chase Manhattan Bank held 2.4% of Fox's common
stock and 7.4% of Fuqua Industries' stock, while Chemical Bank of
New York held 1.5% of Columbia's stock. In sum, over 11% of
Columbia's stock was voted by four bank trust departments, and 8.5%
of Fox's stock was voted by three. Four banks voted 5.9% of
Wometco's common stock and two banks voted 5.7% of Cox Broad-
casting. Film companies without broadcasting properties escaped attention.

There is considerable range in the dispersion of stock from companies with interests in the film business, as Table 5.28 demonstrates,
and the number of shareholders tends to increase with the diversification of the company. Hidden, however, are important concentrations of
holdings that render dispersion figures somewhat irrelevant. Indeed, a
concentration of holdings becomes all the more significant when the
remainder of stock is widely held.

Although Fox has more than 14,000 stockholders, a bit more than
51% of the stock is owned and voted by Cede & Co., a depository for
certain brokers, dealers, banks, and other nominees. Cablecom-General
has more than 655 stockholders, but RKO General owns about 98% of
the shares. Charles Bluhdorn, board chairman of Gulf + Western
Industries — of which Paramount is a subsidiary — owns slightly more
than 6% of the parent company's common stock. The board of

**Table 5.28 Number of Shareholders of Principal Companies in the Motion
Picture Business**

Firm (film subsidiary in parenthesis)	Shareholders	As of:
Commonwealth Theatres, Inc.	650	January 13, 1978
Cablecom-General, Inc.	655	November 30, 1977
American International Pictures, Inc.	801	May 16, 1978
United Artists Theatre Circuit	820	November 1, 1977
General Cinema Corporation	3,128	October 31, 1977
MCA Inc. (Universal)	6,000	December 31, 1977
Allied Artists Industries, Inc.	7,912	March 31, 1978
Warner Communications, Inc.	9,859	January 31, 1978
Columbia Pictures Industries, Inc.	10,740	June 25, 1977
Metro-Goldwyn-Mayer, Inc.	14,000	August 31, 1977
Twentieth Century-Fox Film Corp.	14,673	December 31, 1977
Avco Corporation (Avco Embassy)	47,755	November 30, 1977
Gulf + Western Industries, Inc. (Paramount)	56,681	July 31, 1978
Walt Disney Productions	65,000	December 6, 1977
Transamerica Corporation (United Artists)	157,192	December 31, 1977

Source: From 10-K reports and announcements of annual meeting of shareholders.

directors of MCA owns 28% of the company's voting stock. As a group, three officers and board members of American International own more than 53% of AIP's shares. More than 8% of Allied Artists Industries' stock is owned by its board chairman, Emanuel Wolf, and all directors and officers of the company own over 11%. As of late 1978, Kirk Kerkorian owned almost 48% of MGM's common stock as well as about 5.5% of Columbia's shares. Tracinda, an investment corporation he also owns, announced it was seeking to acquire an additional 20% of Columbia's shares, prompting speculation that Kerkorian would try to merge the two film companies. The tender offer was supported by a bank that reportedly was loaning $38 million to Tracinda. Shortly after, General Cinema, which itself owns 4.6% of Columbia shares, announced it would seek to buy a further 20%, but Columbia's board of directors refused to endorse this offer. Richard Smith, board chairman of General Cinema, sits as well on the board of the First National Bank of Boston, which has a representative on the General Cinema board. First National is a prominent lender to film industry companies, and also led a consortium of banks that assisted the Teleprompter Corporation in arranging early in 1979 an $80 million loan from five insurance companies. This is the single largest insurance company loan ever made to the cable TV industry.

Film Industry Conglomerates

Oligopolistic market structures and concentration of ownership are only parts of a pattern that includes as well cross-media holdings and diversification into spheres beyond communications. A quick survey reveals an elaborate array of ever-developing connections in which film companies are either parts of considerably larger concerns or conglomerates in their own right.

Allied Artists Industries was formed early in 1976 from a merger of Allied Artists Pictures Corporation, Kalvex Inc., and PSP Inc. Its business now consists of motor home manufacture and distribution, importation of consumer products, cosmetic and drug distribution, and film financing, production, and distribution. Theatrical and television rentals provided about 30% of the company's revenue in fiscal 1978. By contrast, about 96% of American International's fiscal 1978 revenue came from rentals. AIP was considering a merger with Filmways, but this was cancelled in late 1978. Avco Embassy provides a little more than 1% of its parent's revenue, which is derived from fields such as consumer finance, insurance, credit cards, space research, aircraft and farm machinery manufacture, medical products, and real estate development. In addition to filmed entertainment, Columbia Pictures Industries produces and distributes recorded music, is a broadcast licensee, and in 1976 acquired for $50 million the world's largest manufacturer of non-gambling, coin-operated pinball machines. Columbia also produces television commercials for sponsors and advertising agencies.

Disney, associated mostly with children's films, drew only 20% of its fiscal 1978 revenue from that source. The largest share of the company's revenue was derived from its amusement parks. Similarly, the majority of MGM's 1978 revenue came from non-cinematic sources. Hotels and gaming contributed about 55%, and filmed entertainment the rest. In addition to production and distribution for theatres and television, MCA is active in music publishing and recorded music, book publishing, video disc development, retail and mail order sales, financial services, real estate, tourist services, and data processing. Paramount Pictures is part of Gulf + Western's leisure time group that includes book publishing, ownership of sporting teams and a sports center, as well as 400 theatre screens in Canada and more than 60 in France. This group contributed less than 19% of G+W's 1978 revenues, which came from such diverse activities as financial services, consumer and agricultural products, apparel, paper and building products, automotive replacement parts, and natural resource development.

Twentieth Century-Fox, aside from financing, producing, and distributing filmed entertainment, is engaged in film processing and the operation of an international theatre chain. It derives revenue as well from its television stations, recorded music and music publishing subsidiaries, its soft drink bottling business, and a recently acquired ski recreation company in Aspen, Colorado. Entertainment services provided 15% of Transamerica's 1977 revenue. One of its subsidiaries, United Artists Corporation, is engaged in film distribution, music publishing and recording, and broadcasting. Transamerica's business interests range from consumer lending and insurance to manufacturing, aircraft operation, data processing, real estate, and moving and storage. Warner Communications operates the world's third largest music business, behind CBS and EMI. Beside financing, producing and distributing filmed entertainment, Warner manufactures and leases optical equipment, publishes books and magazines, designs and sells home electronic video games, owns a professional soccer team, and operates numerous cable television systems, one of which, QUBE, offers two-way communication. Warner also owns a portfolio of stock worth over $100 million.

In exhibition, General Cinema is the nation's largest independent bottler of soft drinks, in addition to owning a television station, financing film production, and operating the world's largest theatre chain. Fuqua Industries' entertainment group includes the Martin Theatre circuit and five broadcasting stations. Other Fuque interests are in sporting goods, transportation, photo-finishing, food and beverage distribution, metals, home construction and garden equipment.

RECENT ANTITRUST ACTIONS

Federal antitrust activity has been greater in the film industry than in any of the other mass media industries covered in this book. Recent Federal suits, for example, drew a "no contest" from Fox on black booking,[96] a consent order from Warner on four-walling,*[97] and a consent decree from United Artists Theatre Circuit to divest itself of certain theatrical holdings in the New York metropolitan area.[98] Although these and a few others have some importance, their significance pales when seen in the context of the entire industry's structure and behavior. On the other hand, private suits have been more outspoken, some projecting conduct to national levels, as a few citations demonstrate.

In Syufy Enterprises v. Columbia Pictures Industries *et al.,* the plaintiff alleged that several major distributors engaged in a "horizontal combination or conspiracy to fix prices and to institute blind bidding."[99] In United Artists Theatre Circuit Inc. *et al.* v. Twentieth Century-Fox Film Corporation, RKO-Stanley Warner Theatres Inc. and Mann Theatres Corporation of California,[100] the plaintiff charged among other points that the defendants "have combined, conspired and agreed that Fox would not offer licenses to the New York plaintiffs for first-run feature length motion pictures distributed by Fox on a picture by picture, theatre by theatre basis solely on the merits and without discrimination, but rather that Fox would arbitrarily license such pictures to theatres operated by RKO, Mann and co-conspirators in the New York Metropolitan Area." Similar conduct was alleged in the Milwaukee metropolitan area. UATC also charged that "Fox agreed to unconditionally guarantee repayment of the principal and interest on the indebtedness incurred by RKO to the [First National] Bank [of Boston] under [a] Credit Agreement" that allowed RKO to renovate and construct theatres. "Fox agreed to give RKO preferential license terms and conditions for Fox-distributed first-run feature length motion pictures exhibited at the RKO theatres to enable RKO to repay the indebtedness to the Bank under the Credit Agreement and to limit Fox's exposure under its guarantee of such indebtedness." This case was settled out of court.

In National Amusements Inc. v. Columbia Pictures Industries Inc. and ITC Entertainment,[101] the plaintiff declared that "Columbia has

---

*Four-walling describes the rental by a distributor of a fully staffed theatre for a short period of time, for exhibition of a particular film. The distributor often sets the admission price. The theatre operator receives a fixed compensation from the distributor during the rental period, rather than the usual percentage of gross receipts. This approach is often used by a small distributor that otherwise has trouble getting films booked into movie theatres.

combined, contracted and conspired ... with the competitors of National in cities throughout the United States in which National owns and operates theatres, to restrain the trade of National and to limit and to exclude National in and from the right to compete in the licensing and exhibition of motion pictures."

In Balmoral Cinema Inc. v. Allied Artists Pictures Corporation *et al.*,[102] defendant distribution and exhibition companies were said to be part of a "national conspiracy" to restrain trade and competition in the film business. Members and employees of the Motion Picture Association of America and the law firm of Sargoy, Stein & Hanft were identified as co-conspirators.

DISCUSSION

The film world is a business world and companies' similarity of interest is considerably more profound than mere market concentration data would indicate. The pinnacles of the various pyramids of concentration are linked to the country's centers of financial power, as even rudimentary data reveal. Within this context, it is somewhat myopic to debate ease of entry because entrance is only a ritualistic fig leaf confirming oligopolistic control. Access to a film camera can make one a director, and a bit of capital can make one a producer as well. But those resources give one about as much power as the owner of a mimeograph machine when confronting Time Inc. or the Gannett newspaper chain. In broadcasting and cable, there are formal barriers to entry: the license and the franchise. Neither exists in the film industry. Anyone can call himself or herself a producer or director. Anyone can rent a hall, install a screen, a projector, some seats, call it a theatre, and request distributors to send bid invitation letters and announcements of availabilities. Although this is part of the American myth, realities demonstrate that the business does not operate like that, as suits throughout the industry's history have argued and current ones seek to prove.

Market concentration and anti-competitive behavior are not unique to the motion picture business, although its history demonstrates how those resources give one about as much power as the owner of in the inherent features of the private enterprise system, of which the film industry is only part. After all, no economic law makes the competitive process automatically self-perpetuating, especially in industries of great capital requirements. If anything, there is a compelling propensity toward oligopoly and oligopsony. The job of antitrust laws and enforcement is to maintain sufficiently competitive market structure and conduct so that private enterprise performs in an acceptable manner. On this basis, the theory of antitrust is not an adversary of the institution of business; to the contrary, it seeks, against an evident tide, to make the system perform according to the principles of competition in an idealized world. Although symbolic progress toward that goal can be made sporadically, such action is a palliative at best, and a placebo at worst. The problem of concentration in the film industry cannot be separated from the entire economic system. Antitrust enforcement, even if vigorously pursued, cannot be expected to have more than limited impact, and certainly is not a cure.

However, the response need not — and should not — be thought of as government control of the industry within the present context of society. Other alternatives, among them worker control and democratic public trusts, need to be explored, as they have been in other countries. But a change of this magnitude could not be isolated in the film industry, for it really suggests a complete remodeling of our economic system away from capitalism and an upheaval of the class structure. Because this prospect has great political and cultural, as well as economic, implications, it is resisted by supporters of the present system, whatever their opinions about the antitrust program, concentration of ownership, or trade practices. Consequently, the bulk of debate is not about how to change monopoly tendencies in capitalism, but about how to manage it. As this appears to be the acceptable arena for debate, discussions about media ownership necessarily will remain on the technical level until fundamental problems are confronted.

FOOTNOTES

1. Michael Conant, *Antitrust in the Motion Picture Industry* (Berkeley: University of California Press, 1960), p. 19.

2. Temporary National Economic Committee, *Investigation of Concentration of Economic Power;* Monograph 43, *The Motion Picture Industry — A Pattern of Control* (Washington: Government Printing Office, 1941), p. 6.

3. The concept of media imperialism has been discussed by several writers. See, for example, Herbert Schiller, *Mass Communications and American Empire* (New York: Augustus M. Kelley, 1969); Herbert Schiller, *Communication and Cultural Domination* (White Plains: M.E. Sharpe, Inc., 1976); Cees Hamelink (editor), *The Corporate Village* (Rome: International Documentation and Communication Centre, 1977); Armand Mattelart, *Multinationales et Systèmes de Communication* (Paris: Editions Anthropos, 1976).

4. Conant, p. 84.

5. *United States v. Paramount Pictures*, 334 U.S. 131, 142, 161.

6. Thomas Guback, "Are We Looking at the Right Things in Film?", paper presented at the 1978 convention of the Society for Cinema Studies.

7. Temporary National Economic Committee, p. ix.

8. Temporary National Economic Committee, p. 56.

9. *Motion Picture Distribution Trade Practices*, hearings before a subcommittee of the Select Committee on Small Business, U.S. Senate, 83rd Congress, 1st Session (Washington: Government Printing Office, 1953); and *Motion-Picture Distribution Trade Practices – 1956*, hearings before a subcommittee of the Select Committee on Small Business, U.S. Senate, 84th Congress, 2nd Session (Washington: Government Printing Office, 1956).

10. *Problems of Independent Motion-Picture Exhibitors*, report of the Select Committee on Small Business, U.S. Senate, 83rd Congress, 1st Session, August 3, 1953 (Washington: Government Printing Office, 1953), p. 18.

11. *Motion-Picture Distribution Trade Practices – 1956*, report of the Select Committee on Small Business, U.S. Senate, 84th Congress, 2nd Session, July 27, 1956 (Washington: Government Printing Office, 1956), p. 54.

12. Paramount Pictures Inc., et al. Consent Judgments and Decrees Investigation. Report of the Federal Trade Commission, February 25, 1965.

13. *Analysis and Conclusions of the Washington Task Force on the Motion Picture Industry* [1978], p. 15.

14. Washington Task Force, p. 15.

15. *Impact of Imports and Exports on Employment, Part 8*, hearings before the Subcommittee on the Impact of Imports and Exports on American Employment of the Committee on Education and Labor, U.S. House of Representatives, 87th Congress, 1st and 2nd Sessions (Washington: Government Printing Office, 1962).

16. *Unemployment Problems in American Film Industry*, hearings before the General Subcommittee on Labor of the Committee on Education and Labor, U.S. House of Representatives, 92nd Congress. 1st Session (Washington: Government Printing Office, 1972).

17. *Communications – Pay Cable Television Industry*, hearings before the Subcommittee on Antitrust and Monopoly of the Committee on the Judiciary, U.S. Senate, 94th Congress, 1st Session (Washington: Government Printing Office, 1975); and *Cable Television Regulation Oversight, Parts 1 and 2*, hearings before the Subcommittee on Communications of the Committee on Interstate and Foreign Commerce, U.S. House of Representatives, 94th Congress, 2nd Session (Washington: Government Printing Office, 1977).

18. For example, see *Overseas Information Programs of the United States, Part 2*, hearings before a subcommittee of the Committee on Foreign Relations, U.S. Senate, 83rd Congress, 1st Session (Washington: Government Printing Office, 1953).

19. *U.S. Informational Media Guaranty Program*, hearings before the Committee on Foreign Relations, U.S. Senate, 90th Congress, 1st Session (Washington: Government Printing Office, 1967).

20. *International Communications and Information*, hearings before the Subcommittee on International Operations of the Committee on Foreign Relations, U.S. Senate, 95th Congress, 1st Session (Washington: Government Printing Office, 1977).

21. Federal Trade Commission, *Webb-Pomerene Associations: A 50-Year Review* (Washington: Government Printing Office, 1967), p. 34.

22. Federal Trade Commission, *Webb-Pomerene*, p. 59.

23. *Consent Decree Program of the Department of Justice*, report of the Antitrust Subcommittee (Subcommittee No. 5) of the Committee on the Judiciary, U.S. House of Representatives, 86th Congress, 1st Session (Washington: Government Printing Office, 1959).

24. *Economic Concentration, Parts 1 to 8*, hearings before the Subcommittee on Antitrust and Monopoly of the Committee on the Judiciary, U.S. Senate, 88th

Congress, 2nd Session to 91st Congress, 2nd Session (Washington: Government Printing Office, 1964-1970).

25. *Multinational Corporations*, hearings before the Subcommittee on International Trade of the Committee on Finance, U.S. Senate, 93rd Congress, 1st Session (Washington: Government Printing Office, 1973).

26. *Investigation of Conglomerate Corporations, Parts 1 to 4*, hearings before the Antitrust Subcommittee (Subcommittee No. 5) of the Committee on the Judiciary, U.S. House of Representatives, 91st Congress (Washington: Government Printing Office, 1970); and *Investigation of Conglomerate Corporations*, report by the staff of the Antitrust Subcommittee (Subcommittee No. 5) of the Committee on the Judiciary, U.S. House of Representatives, 92nd Congress, 1st Session (Washington: Government Printing Office, 1971).

27. *Self-Policing of the Movie and Publishing Industry*, hearings before the Subcommittee on Postal Operations of the Committee on Post Office and Civil Service, U.S. House of Representatives, 86th Congress, 2nd Session (Washington: Government Printing Office, 1960).

28. *Movie Ratings and the Independent Producer*, hearings before the Subcommittee on Special Small Business Problems of the Committee on Small Business, U.S. House of Representatives, 95th Congress, 1st Session (Washington: Government Printing Office, 1977); and *Movie Ratings and the Independent Producer*, report of the Subcommittee on Special Small Business Problems of the Committee on Small Business, U.S. House of Representatives, 95th Congress, 2nd Session (Washington: Government Printing Office, 1978).

29. Joseph P. Kennedy, ed., *The Story of the Films* (Chicago: A.W. Shaw Company, 1927), p. 6.

30. Benjamin B. Hampton, *History of the American Film Industry* (New York: Dover Publications Inc., 1970), previously published as *A History of the Movies* (New York: Covici, Friede, 1931).

31. Howard T. Lewis, *The Motion Picture Industry* (New York: Van Nostrand Co., 1933).

32. Mae D. Huettig, *Economic Control of the Motion Picture Industry* (Philadelphia: University of Pennsylvania Press, 1944).

33. Huettig, p. 143.

34. Huettig, pp. 149-150.

35. Conant, p. 220. See as well Robert W. Crandall, "The Postwar Performance of the Motion-Picture Industry," *The Antitrust Bulletin*, 20:1, Spring 1975.

36. Thomas H. Guback, *The International Film Industry* (Bloomington: Indiana University Press, 1969).

37. F.D. Klingender and Stuart Legg, *Money Behind the Screen* (London: Lawrence and Wishart, 1937).

38. Peter Bächlin, *Der Film als Ware* (Basel: Burg Verlag, 1947); also published with very slight changes as *Histoire Economique du Cinéma* (Paris: La Nouvelle Edition, 1947). See as well Georg Schmidt, Werner Schmalenbach, and Peter Bächlin, *The Film – Its Economic, Social and Artistic Problems* (London: The Falcon Press, 1948).

39. Henry Mercillon, *Cinéma et Monopoles* (Paris: Librarie Armand Colin, 1953).

40. Jean-Claude Batz, *A Propos de la Crise de l'Industrie du Cinéma* (Bruxelles: Université Libre de Bruxelles, 1963).

41. Claude Degand, *Le Cinéma, Cette Industrie* (Paris: Editions Techniques et Economiques, 1972).

42. René Bonnell, *Le Cinéma Exploité* (Paris, Editions du Seuil, 1978).

43. Political and Economic Planning, *The British Film Industry* (London: P.E.P., 1952), and *The British Film Industry 1958*, 24:424, June 1958.

44. John Spraos, *The Decline of the Cinema* (London: George Allen and Unwin Ltd., 1962).

45. Terence Kelly, *A Competitive Cinema* (London: Institute of Economic Affairs, 1966).

46. *Films, A Report on the Supply of Films for Exhibition in Cinemas*, The Monopolies Commission (London: Her Majesty's Stationery Office, 1966).

47. Association of Cinematograph, Television and Allied Technicians, *Nationalising the Film Industry* (London: ACTT, 1973).

48. *Future of the British Film Industry*, report of the Prime Minister's Working Party (London: Her Majesty's Stationery Office, 1976).

49. Georg Roeber and Gerhard Jacoby, *Handbuch der Filmwirtschaftlichen Medienbereiche* (Pullach bei München: Verlag Dokumentation, 1973).

50. Enrico Giannelli, *Economia Cinematografica* (Rome: Reanda Editore, 1956).

51. Pierre Berton, *Hollywood's Canada, The Americanization of our National Image* (Toronto: McClelland and Stewart Ltd., 1975).

52. *Mutual Film Corp. v. Ohio*, 236 U.S. 230.

53. *Burstyn v. Wilson*, 343 U.S. 495.

54. For example, see Judith Adler Hennessee, "Gross Behavior: How to Get Your Percentage Back," *Action*, 2:4, January-February 1978.

55. U.S. Department of Commerce, *U.S. Industrial Outlook, 1978* (Washington: Government Printing Office, 1978), p. 458. In 1977, Inflight Services Inc. received about $18.5 million from airlines for airborne exhibition of films, and a portion of this sum is passed on to principal distributors. Inflight Services Inc., Form 10-K Report for 1977.

56. Jack Valenti, president, Motion Picture Association of America, quoted in *Variety*, September 6, 1978.

57. Twentieth Century-Fox Film Corporation, 1978 First Quarter Report and 1978 Second Quarter Report.

58. As one example, on September 30, 1975, Warner Bros. Distributing Corporation announced it was accepting bids no later than October 9, 1975 for the April 9, 1976 release in Washington, D.C., of *All the President's Men*. Naturally, this was a blind bid. Warner's suggested terms included a minimum of 12 weeks playtime, a guarantee of $175,000 payable no later than seven days prior to opening, an advance of $175,000, and rental terms of 90/10% over house expenses versus 70% of the gross for the first three weeks, sliding to 40% for the last three weeks. Warner proposed a run in a maximum of four theatres, and therefore sought to have guaranteed at least $700,000 in rentals from Washington, D.C. alone.

59. In December 1978, Warner launched *Superman* with about 800 prints and *Every Which Way But Loose* with 1,275 prints in the United States and Canada.

60. Standard & Poor's Industry Surveys, *Leisure Time, Basic Analysis*, August 31, 1978.

61. *Variety*, December 6, 1978.

62. *Variety*, May 17, 1978.

63. *Variety*, January 3, 1979.

64. Aljean Harmetz, "Orion's Star Rises in Hollywood," *Warner World*, No. 2, 1978.

65. For 1978, *Variety* listed 104 new releases as having earned rentals of $1 million or more in the U.S.-Canadian market. Ten of these films were distributed by independent companies, with the biggest rental being $9.7 million. Five of the films

earned $2 million or less in rentals. *Variety*, January 3, 1979, and January 10, 1979.

66. U.S. Department of Commerce, *U.S. Service Industries in World Markets*, December 1976, p. A-211.

67. U.S. Department of Commerce, *U.S. Industrial Outlook, 1978* (Washington: Government Printing Office, 1978), p. 458.

68. Bureau of Labor Statistics, *Employment and Earnings,* 25:10, October 1978.

69. Classification and Rating Administration, annual reports for years cited.

70. National Association of Theatre Owners, *Encyclopedia of Exhibition, 1978*, p. 28.

71. U.S. Department of Commerce, *U.S. Service Industries in World Markets*, December 1976, p. A-213.

72. Richard Albarino, *Variety*, January 8, 1975.

73. Metro-Goldwyn-Mayer Inc., preliminary prospectus, September 25, 1975.

74. American International Pictures uses a table of production costs amortization based on the rate at which theatrical revenue is earned. The first 13 weeks of release contribute 49% of rentals, and the next 13 weeks, 26%. The rest of the first year yields another 13%. American International Pictures, Form 10-K Report for 1978.

75. U.S. Department of Commerce, Bureau of the Census, *1972 Census of Selected Service Industries, Motion Picture Industry* (Washington: Government Printing Office, 1975).

76. National Association of Theatre Owners, *Encyclopedia of Exhibition, 1978.*

77. U.S. Department of Commerce, Bureau of the Census, *1972 Census of Selected Service Industries, Motion Picture Industry* (Washington: Government Printing Office, 1975).

78. *Variety*, June 21, 1978.

79. Frank Rosenfelt, president, Metro-Goldwyn-Mayer, *The Hollywood Reporter*, January 8, 1979; and Jack Valenti, president, Motion Picture Association of America, *The Hollywood Reporter*, January 5, 1979.

80. *Variety*, February 15, 1978.

81. *Syufy Enterprises v. Columbia Pictures Industries Inc., et al.*, U.S. District Court for the District of Utah, Civil No. C-77-0181. *Supplemental Memorandum in Support of Motion for Preliminary Injunction*, p. 10.

82. *Syufy Enterprises v. Columbia Pictures Industries Inc., et al.*, p. 23.

83. *Syufy Enterprises v. Columbia Pictures Industries Inc., et al., Memorandum of Points and Authorities for Motion for Preliminary Injunction*, pp. 15, 20.

84. Several members of the Motion Picture Association of America filed suit in 1970 against ABC and CBS, charging the networks with monopoly and conspiracy to deprive plaintiffs of access to television markets. At that time, both networks were engaged in the production, distribution and exhibition (via television) of feature length motion pictures, and ABC also owned a circuit of motion pictures theatres. In 1972, the Department of Justice filed suits against ABC, CBS, and NBC. The suits were refiled in 1974 after the original ones were dismissed without prejudice. The government suits charged that each of the networks had used and continued to use its control over access to network air time to restrain and to monopolize prime time television entertainment programming. NBC agreed to a consent stipulation in 1976, but parts of it could not be put into effect until the other defendants approved, something which they declared they had no intention of doing. In 1978, a group of 20 independent film producers filed an antitrust suit

against ABC, CBS, and NBC alleging the networks and their owned and operated stations in New York City restrained trade and monopolized news and public affairs programming. The plaintiffs contended that the networks refused to purchase or broadcast independently produced news or public affairs programs.

85. Data for 1978 were computed and made available by Dennis Dombkowski, Department of Speech Communication and Theatre, Wayne State University.

86. See Thomas Guback and Dennis Dombkowski, "Television and Hollywood — Economic Relations in the 1970s," *Journal of Broadcasting*, Fall 1976, 20:4; and Thomas Guback, "Les Relations Cinéma-TV aux Etats-Unis Aujourd' hui," *Film Echange*, No. 2. Spring 1978.

87. According to Frank Rosenfelt, president, Metro-Goldwyn-Mayer Inc., *The Hollywood Reporter*, January 8, 1979.

88. *The Pay-TV Newsletter*, Paul Kagan Associates, November 17, 1978; October 19, 1978; November 22, 1977; November 8, 1977; November 30, 1976. Member companies of the Motion Picture Association of America had the following shares of feature films exhibited on pay television: 1976 — October 58.6%, November 58.6%, 1977 — October 67.5%, November 58.2%, 1978 — October 57.8%, November 57.7%.

89. Richard Smith, president and chief executive officer, General Cinema Corporation, deposition, November 17, 1978; *Balmoral Cinema Inc. v. Allied Artists Pictures Corporation et al.*, U.S. District Court for the Western District of Tennessee, Civil No. 77-2101.

90. Norman Levy, president of distribution for Columbia Pictures, deposition, August 8, 1978; *Balmoral Cinema Inc. v. Allied Artists Pictures Corporation et al.*, U.S. District Court for the Western District of Tennessee, Civil No. 77-2101. Also see *The Hollywood Reporter*, January 4, 1979.

91. General Cinema Corporation, annual report for 1975.

92. U.S. Department of Commerce, Bureau of the Census, *Census of Selected Service Industries, 1972*, volume 1, *Summary and Subject Statistics*. Comparable figures for the eight largest firms are automotive rental and leasing, 32.9%; computer and data processing services, 26.9%; advertising, 23%.

93. U.S. Department of Commerce, Bureau of the Census, *Statistical Abstracts of the United States, 1977* (Washington: Government Printing Office, 977).

94. *Disclosure of Corporate Ownership*, prepared by the Subcommittee on Intergovernmental Relations and the Subcommittee on Budgeting, Management and Expenditures of the Committee on Government Operations, U.S. Senate, 93rd Congress, 1st Session (Washington: Government Printing Office, 1973), p. 9.

95. *Disclosure of Corporate Ownership*, pp. 163-182.

96. *United States v. Twentieth Century-Fox Film Corporation*, U.S. District Court for the Southern District of New York, September 12, 1978. Fox was fined $25,000 and ordered to pay court costs of $18,171.67.

97. *United States v. Warner Bros. Pictures Inc.*, U.S. District Court for the Southern District of New York, Equity No. 87-273; consent order filed April 2, 1976.

98. *United States v. United Artists Theatre Circuit Inc.*, U.S. District Court for the Eastern District of New York, Civil No. 71-C-609; consent decree filed July 26, 1976.

99. *Syufy Enterprises v. Columbia Pictures Industries Inc., et al., Memorandum of Points*, p. 29.

100. *United Artists Theatre Circuit Inc. et al. v. Twentieth Century-Fox Film Corporation, RKO-Stanley Warner Theatres Inc. and Mann Theatres Corporation of California*, U.S. District Court for the Southern District of New York, Civil No. 77-3489, *Complaint.*

101. *National Amusements Inc. v. Columbia Pictures Industries Inc. and ITC Entertainment*, an ATV Company, U.S. District Court for the District of Massachusetts, Civil No. 77-155-5, *Complaint*.

102. *Balmoral Cinema Inc. v. Allied Artists Pictures Corporation et al.*, U.S. District Court for the Western District of Tennessee, Civil No. 77-2101, *Complaint*.

Appendix A5

Revenue and Income of Selected Publicly Owned Companies in the Motion Picture Industry
(dollars in millions)

Table A5.1 ALLIED ARTISTS INDUSTRIES INC.

			Motion Pictures	
Fiscal Year[a]	Revenue	Net Income	Revenue	Operating Income
1978	$63.7	$ 4.2	$19.8	$ 1.8
1977	53.2	(2.1)	12.5	(2.7)
1976	55.8	(3.4)	17.4	(2.5)
1975[b]	11.7	(1.1)	11.1	
1974	23.4	1.3	23.0	
1973	15.3	1.5	14.6	
1972	8.3	.1	7.9	
1971	2.7	(3.3)	2.5	
1970	6.8	.05	6.6	

a. Year ending June 30 through 1974; ending April 1 since 1975.
b. 39 weeks.

Table A5.2 CABLECOM-GENERAL INC.

			Motion Picture Theatres		CATV	
Year ending Nov. 30:	Revenue	Net Income	Revenue	Operating Income	Revenue	Operating Income
1977	$ 29.2	$ 4.0	$ 11.4	$ 1.5	$ 15.3	$ 3.8
1976	26.1	3.0	10.0	1.2	13.7	2.8
1975	23.8	2.7	9.2	.8	13.0	2.5
1974	22.2	1.1	8.4	.8	12.8	.3
1973	20.2	(4.4)	7.5	.4	12.1	(.3)
1972	19.0	(1.1)	8.0	1.0	10.4	(1.4)
1971	17.4	1.1	8.5	1.3	8.2	.1
1970	15.2	1.1	8.9	1.3	6.3	.6

Table A5.3 COLUMBIA PICTURES INDUSTRIES INC.

Year ending June 30:	Revenue	Net Income	Filmed Entertainment		Feature Films		TV Programs Revenue	Records and Music		Broadcasting	
			Revenue	Operating Income	Theatre Revenue	TV Revenue		Revenue	Operating Income	Revenue	Operating Income
1978	$574.6	$68.8	$437.0	$80.2	$269.0	$25.3	$95.0	$73.5	$3.6	$12.2	$3.2
1977	390.5	34.6	298.3	30.8	153.5	24.8	79.8	42.1	1.4	17.9	5.4
1976	332.1	11.5	272.1	28.3	152.2	19.3	67.8	35.4	1.1	24.6	5.5
1975	325.9	10.5	278.0	33.2	170.3	30.8	53.5	24.1	.9	23.8	4.2
1974	250.1	(2.3)	211.7	24.9	111.3	28.8	51.9	16.3	(.5)	22.1	4.4
1973	205.4	(50.0)	164.5	(61.5)	101.5	11.5	33.1	20.2	3.3	20.7	4.0
1972	223.5	(3.4)	182.2		110.0	34.4	37.8	17.8		15.7	1.9
1971	222.6	(28.8)	176.0		113.0	16.6	46.4	18.0		12.9	1.3
1970	242.1	(10.9)	196.6		137.9	20.5	38.2	45.4a			

a. Includes records, music, broadcasting and other.

Table A5.4 GENERAL CINEMA CORPORATION

Year ending Oct. 31:	Revenue	Net Income	Theatre Division		TV Broadcasting	
			Revenue	Operating Income	Revenue	Operating Income
1977	$465.1	$20.2	$213.8	$14.3	$10.9	$2.3
1976	365.3	17.1	168.4	13.4	8.0	1.9
1975	358.4	14.9	180.0	18.4		
1974	299.5	11.1	142.9	15.1		
1973	244.9	9.4	117.1	14.4		
1972	220.0	10.3	99.6	13.7		
1971	195.0	9.2	80.2	12.1		
1970	178.9	7.0	70.1	11.1		

Table A5.5 MCA INC.

Year	Revenue	Net Income	Filmed Entertainment[a]		Theatres	TV	Records and Music Publishing
			Revenue	Operating Income			
1977	$877.6	$95.1	$561.4	$107.4	$222.8	$289.4	$99.8
1976	802.9	90.2	506.9	100.6	213.4	249.7	112.4
1975	811.5	95.5	509.9	124.0	289.1	189.6	137.9
1974	663.2	59.2	387.5	68.0	205.1	158.5	126.7
1973	437.4	27.1	227.7	20.2	87.5	119.9	86.8
1972	345.9	20.9	204.6	19.9	61.9	127.3	61.4
1971	333.7	16.7	194.6	15.1	57.8	124.2	45.8
1970	333.5	13.3	220.0	32.4	96.7	110.0	36.0

a. Includes Studio Tours, Amphitheatre and other, as well as Universal.

Table A5.6 METRO-GOLDWYN-MAYER INC.

Year ending Aug. 31:	Revenue	Net Income	Filmed Entertainment[a]		Feature Films	TV Programs
			Revenue	Operating Income		
1978	$401.4	$49.3	$182.6	$39.0	$110.7	$43.8
1977	288.5	33.2	134.7	22.1	85.8	28.4
1976	266.6	35.6	123.3	19.7	77.2	27.8
1975	255.5	31.9	117.6	23.0	83.2	17.5
1974	234.4	26.8	145.8	17.9	111.1	20.7
1973	152.8	9.3	152.8	8.7	124.9	14.0
1972	148.2	10.7	148.2	15.3	120.4	13.7
1971	149.5	15.6	149.5[b]	19.0	136.1[a,b]	13.4
1970	149.4	(13.6)	149.3[b]	(7.8)	130.3[a,b]	19.0

a. Includes revenue from film processing laboratory.
b. Presumably includes revenue from theatre operation overseas.

Table A5.7 TWENTIETH CENTURY-FOX FILM CORPORATION

Year	Revenue	Net Income	Filmed Entertainment		Feature Films	TV Programs	Theatre Operation	Film processing	Broadcasting	Records and Music Publishing
			Revenue	Operating Income						
1977	$506.8	$50.8	$369.4	$69.7	$321.5	$48.0	$37.9	$30.7	$25.7	$22.7
1976	355.0	10.7	254.8	17.1	217.2	37.7	34.3	29.7	22.6	9.9
1975	342.7	22.7	242.1	28.9	210.8	31.3	44.3	26.3	9.9	17.9
1974	280.1	11.0	186.7	12.9	159.7	27.0	43.1	23.9	7.0	16.1
1973	250.4	10.7	180.0	12.1	152.6	27.4	34.6	20.0	6.6	7.7
1972	198.7	7.8	144.7	8.1	118.8	25.9	25.4	20.2	5.8	2.1
1971	222.5	9.7	171.5	12.4	143.2	28.3	20.8	23.2	5.0	2.0
1970	246.5	(80.4)	195.0	(77.2)	159.3	35.7	19.2	24.1	5.1	2.1

Table A5.8 UNITED ARTISTS THEATRE CIRCUIT INC.

Year ending Aug. 31:	Revenue	Net Income	Theatre Operations
1977	$147.0	$4.2	$143.5
1976	120.3	4.1	116.5
1975	123.9	4.1	121.3
1974	106.5	4.1	104.6
1973	85.2	3.1	83.6
1972	80.2	2.6	79.1
1971	74.4	1.5	73.2
1970	76.9	2.4	75.2

Table A5.9 WALT DISNEY PRODUCTIONS

| Year ending Sept. 30: | Revenue | Net Income | Motion Picture and Television Distribution | | Theatres | | TV | Records and Music | Publi- cations | Educa- tional Media |
			Revenue	Operating Income	Domestic	Foreign				
1978	$741.1	$98.4	$152.1	$54.1	$69.0	$57.9	$25.2	$17.2	$15.0	$24.8
1977	629.8	81.9	118.1	50.4	58.7	36.6	22.7	13.9	12.9	20.7
1976	583.9	74.6	119.1	57.9	60.5	39.8	18.8	12.2	11.1	17.7
1975	520.0	61.7	112.5	56.6	61.2	37.6	13.7	10.2	9.9	15.8
1974	429.9	48.5	90.4	45.8	48.6	29.9	11.9	15.2	8.6	12.5
1973	385.1	48.0	76.2	36.0	40.2	26.3	9.6	13.7	8.4	8.6
1972	329.4	40.3	70.8	35.7	35.5	26.2	9.1	10.8	5.0	7.5
1971	174.6	26.9	65.1	26.8	35.4	21.6	8.0	8.5	5.2	6.5
1970	167.1	21.8	63.3		33.9	22.0	7.4	7.0	4.0	5.4

Table A5.10 WARNER COMMUNICATIONS INC.

Year	Revenue	Net Income	Filmed Entertainment Revenue	Operating Income	Theatrical Revenue	Feature Films TV Revenue	TV Series	Recorded Music and Music Publishing	Publishing	CATV
1977	$1,143.8	$66.9	$353.0	$58.0	$253.6	$39.6	$60.0	$532.4	$52.2	$55.7
1976	826.8	57.5	285.2	42.2	221.6	42.5	21.0	406.1	48.4	51.6
1975	669.8	46.6	255.9	41.7	202.3	27.3	26.3	313.8	62.0	38.1
1974	720.1	42.9	319.0	57.7	275.5	18.9	24.6	291.7	78.7	30.8
1973	549.6	43.1	209.5	31.1	152.7	24.9	31.9	236.0	76.7	27.5
1972	498.6	43.1	193.4	22.7	144.3	17.7	31.4	214.5	66.5	24.3
1971	377.1	34.2	124.3	14.8	86.3	20.2	17.8	170.9	61.2	20.7
1970	304.2	33.6	114.9	6.8	64.2		50.7[a]	115.8	48.6	15.8

a. Includes revenue from distribution to television of feature films.

Source for all tables: Company annual reports, Form 10-K reports, prospectus for stocks and bonds.

6

Books

Any analysis of the book publishing industry is limited by the lack of useful, truly comparable statistics. Only since 1971 are industry data available from a single source, the Association of American Publishers, and even the work of that organization is affected by both questions of definitions and by partial reporting in certain categories. Only since 1977 have organized, consistent efforts been made to develop these statistics into useful industry forecasts by the not-for-profit Book Industry Study Group. Thus, more research is really needed to draw valid conclusions about the overall book industry in almost any of its aspects.

On the other hand, the book publishing industry is one of our oldest. Over the years, many of the industry's principal figures have been prolific writers, often concerned with developments in their field. Thus, there is a wealth of opinion, recorded experience, and incomplete data to draw upon, although the inferences from these may vary with the analyst.

BRIEF HISTORY

The very nature of the book publishing industry has changed over the years.

The first book publishers were primarily printers, at least in the United States. Presses required government sanction and did much of their work for the authorities, both secular and religious. Thus, they were considered primarily manufacturers, as they continue to be categorized to this day.

Most books to be found in the colonies were of English origin; the publisher-printers chiefly engaged in routine printing of useful documents for the church, the state and business. Lacking the economic incentive of the copyright, the author of the day wrote primarily for reasons of religious or patriotic fervor (with the blessings of the authorities). It is generally agreed that the first American press was established in Cambridge, Massachusetts, in 1638. The first item it printed was the *Freeman's Oath*, a government document, while its first best-selling book was *The Whole Booke of Psalmes* (1640).

English books appear to have been reprinted as well as imported, and some printers engaged in bookselling while some booksellers engaged in printing, apparently with little or no royalty to the English authors involved.

During the early part of the 18th century, as the colonists became more concerned with information about the communities in which they lived, weekly newspapers and almanacs appeared and flourished.

Perhaps illustrative of the industry's evolution was *The New England Primer*, the first widely used, American-printed textbook. Education was then largely conducted by religious groups with the sanction of government. The book was written by a Boston printer, Benjamin Harris, sometime between 1687 and 1690 and was first advertised for sale in 1691. It was mostly a compilation from contemporary English primers, with which Harris was familiar, as he also imported English books and ran a bookshop. Over the next hundred years it may have sold more than 3 million copies and certainly sold more than a million. The uncertainty as to its success is partly due to the fact that it was widely pirated by other printers and sold under differing names. Ben Franklin called his version *The Columbian Primer* and sold 37,100 copies between 1749 and 1756.

As late as the period from 1837 to 1849, about 100,000 copies of *The New England Primer* were sold.

The lesson of such blatant reprinting of the words of others was quickly recognized: if many publishers exist, capable of freely publishing anything, new authors may be discouraged from creating works and demonstrably successful works would tend to be pirated and reprinted at the expense of newer works for long periods of time.

The first English copyright law, "8 Anne, c. 9," was passed in 1709 and led to what has been called the "golden age of publishing" in England. By establishing a right to an intellectual property, it led to the separation of publishing functions from printing functions. Many of the new publishers, in fact, were booksellers rather than printers. They sought out authors in response to their perceptions of what would sell, usually bought manuscripts outright, arranged for their production and sold the results. Authors did not initially appreciate the advantages of the copyright which, as at present, reserved rights to them for a period of years. *Paradise Lost*, for instance, is said to have been sold to its publisher for ten pounds.

In the U.S., the comparatively lax state of the law and the comparatively high cost of transporting books appear to have been factors in the continuing dominance of English books reproduced by American printers until nationalism surfaced in the period of the American Revolution. Thomas Paine's *Common Sense* sold 100,000 copies following its publication in early 1776.

The Constitution was unique in its special provisions to ensure a thriving publishing industry. Key factors are not only the First Amendment, but also Section 8, Subsection (8) of Article I, which gives Congress the power:

> To promote the progress of science and useful arts, by securing for limited times to authors and inventors the exclusive right to their respective writings and discoveries.

These two provisions not only permit free speech but provide economic incentives for it.

It should not be dismissed too lightly that the Constitution, for all its bare bones format, had incorporated into it the explicit power to enact a federal copyright law. The existence of the copyright clause is in part due to lobbying efforts of one of this country's most successful author-publishers, Noah Webster. During 1781 and 1782, while teaching at Sharon, Connecticut, Webster wrote *The First Part of a Grammatical Institute of the English Language*, better known by shorter, simpler names and ultimately, following the 1829 revision, as the *Old Blue-Back Speller*. It has been said that, "No single book excepting the Bible ever approached the sales of this."[1] Using American pronunciations and spellings as distinct from the English ones commonly employed in textbooks of the time, the book was an instrument of nationalism. Familiar with English copyright law, Webster sought similar protection from Connecticut, financed the first printing, and then both sold it and lobbied for protection in other states and even before the Constitutional Convention in Philadelphia. Because of transportation difficulties, he granted reprint rights widely and, by 1783, the book was selling at the rate of 500 copies a week. By 1818, 5 million had been sold. At Webster's death in 1843, it was selling a million copies a year to a nation of 20 million. In 1840, D. Appleton and Company acquired publishing rights to the book and in 1880 reported, "We sell a million copies a year, and we have been selling it at that rate for forty years."

Distribution costs have always been a principal problem of the book industry and they played a role in the fragmentation, dispersion and lack of creativity of the earliest publishers. They also seem to have been significant in the establishment of the early publishing centers in Boston, New York and Philadelphia. The Yankee peddlers collected their wares in or near these manufacturing centers (e.g., at Hartford) and carried books along with them as they traveled into the hinterlands.

Thus, with a sense of national identity and interests to inspire American writers, with copyright protection to provide economic incentives for both authors and publishers, and with the formation of printing centers and distribution channels, the modern American book publishing industry began to form in the late 18th and early 19th centuries. A number of present-day publishers trace their origins to that period. However, the lack of an international copyright convention led to the continuing influence of English authors in the American market, for they could be pirated or paid nominal sums, thus reducing the attractiveness of American authors to publishers. At the same time, American authors frequently financed the first printings of their own works and rarely received advances. This condition persisted until 1891.

The early years of the 19th century were marked by improvements in transportation and production techniques as well as by the formation of a number of today's publishers. Gutenberg's version of movable type was still used well into the 19th century. Steel engravings appeared in 1814 and became dominant until superseded by photoengravings late in the century. In 1830 the first automatic, flat-bed power press was introduced. This was followed by the self-feeding rotary ("web") press after the Civil War. Publishers, as such, had seldom owned their own presses and had been quite willing to shift to newer, more economic production methods. This helped stimulate the evolution of the printing industry which, in turn, encouraged more publishers to dispose of their own presses.

Wars seem to stimulate sales by the book industry, perhaps because of greater household affluence, limitations on other pursuits and the needs of the military forces for recreation. The Civil War was no exception and marked another turning point in the book industry's fortunes. As World War II was to entrench today's mass market paperback in part through the distribution of such books to soldiers, so the Civil War spawned the "dime novel" of the late 19th century which, with rising education levels, may have helped expand the reading of original works.

Early Examples of Consolidation

The late 19th century was a period of rapid industrial growth, of the formation of many of today's larger publishers, of cutthroat competition and of the development of would-be monopolies, the "trusts."

In 1889 such a trust of publishers of inexpensive reprints was formed by publisher James W. Lovell at a time when distribution facilities seemed glutted, returns were very high and profits were minimal. His United States Book Company purchased the plates and stock of about

21 publishers who agreed either to join the organization or leave the field. By 1890 his organization was probably the largest publisher in the United States. But eight large reprinters had not joined him and, after 1891, many other regular publishers began to publish low-priced paperback editions of their own works, something like the trade paperbacks of today. Lovell soon went bankrupt, and he was removed by his directors in 1893. The subsequent liquidation of his inventories, coupled with the limitations of the 1891 copyright law, virtually ended this subsector of the industry.

A similar development took place in the textbook market. In 1870 the Schoolbook Publishers Board of Trade was launched by J. C. Barnes, one of the leading textbook publishers of the time. As that sector's chief concern was perceived to be unscrupulous tactics by local commission salesmen ("bookmen"), the Board's members agreed in 1870 to discontinue all direct selling and to sell by mail instead. But the use of bookmen continued surreptitiously, and the rules were amended to permit 15 per company in 1873. Board rules also limited discounts. But this amended program was also bypassed and the Board was dissolved in 1877. ˙

The limitation on discounts derived from the fact that at the time there was no uniform pricing of textbooks. This led Ohio to establish regulations: a 25% discount for manufacturers on sales to dealers or school boards and 10% for dealers on their sales. This seems to have been the origin of both the textbook industry's pricing structure and of the state adoption concept as other states rapidly passed laws requiring that they be offered the lowest prices at which textbooks were sold anywhere in the country. The school system adoption could be traced to Massachusetts in the 1840s, but the Ohio action tended to increase uniformity within a state.

In 1890, following the lead of The United States Book Company, the leading textbook publishers joined to form the American Book Company. It started with the merger of Ivison, Blakeman & Company of New York with Van Antwerp, Bragg & Company of Cincinnati, two of the five largest such companies, which then bought the textbook operations of two others of the big five. This "Syndicate of Four" took over the list of the fifth largest publisher. A few years later it bought out the textbook businesses of 10 other companies and eventually absorbed about 30. The largest non-joiner was the sixth-ranking firm, Ginn and Company. By the mid-1890s, American Book Company reportedly controlled 93% of the nation's textbook sales.

Although it did not subsequently go bankrupt (it survived to be acquired by Litton Industries early in 1967), the American Book Company seems to have been a failure as an attempt to monopolize a sector of book publishing through the consolidation of major factors in the industry. As with the United States Book Company, the emphasis in the merger was on assets rather than on people, on plates and inventory rather than on authors and editors. In both cases, a few independent companies survived the initial consolidation, and other companies with prior experience in the field were permitted to re-enter it after an initial waiting period. In both cases, competitors joined the field almost immediately upon the absorption of some of their former competition by the trusts. In each case, the markets appeared eager to support the proliferation of new suppliers with new ideas. Although there are no year-by-year data to study, and the segment of the industry led by the United States Book Company disappeared with its leader, we know that Ginn and Company went on to become one of the largest schoolbook publishers, while American Book Company's market share fell from 90% or more of industry sector sales in the 1890s to about 6.4% of textbook sales in the school field and perhaps 3.6% of all school and college sales by 1966, despite further acquisitions of its own.

Thus, history suggests that in book publishing it is difficult to create a monopoly with staying power, at least if the emphasis is placed on the consolidation of assets rather than on people.

TITLE OUTPUT AS GROWTH MEASURE

Lacking industry revenue data, it seems reasonable to examine the number of new titles produced annually as an indicator of the vitality of the book publishing industry. Table 6.1 shows that the industry grew explosively from 1880 to 1910, experienced an unsteady decline from 1910 to about 1945, and has been experiencing a new growth surge since 1945.

The statistics on new titles, however, may be more than measures of industry health. They may be also viewed as indicative of the industry's contribution to the spread of new ideas and information in the society. But they could readily be interpreted as signs of industry problems. For example, the late 19th century surge and the post-World War II expansion both coincided with the rapid expansion of low-priced reprint industries: that of the dime novel in the 19th century and the mass market paperback in the 20th. Also, it may not be coincidental that the 1890s and the 1960s were both periods of heightened merger activity. In any event, they certainly suggest increased competition in the world of ideas both from 1880-1910 and since 1945.

During the early 20th century, despite the essential flatness of industry title output, most of the major companies of today either were formed or grew in relative size. Some of the critics of the industry of the time would like those of more recent vintage. For example, some

Table 6.1   Output of New Book Titles, 1881-1977

Average for Years	New Titles and Editions	
1881-85	3,612	
1886-90	4,463	
1891-95	4,923	
1896-1900	6,439	
1901-05	8,048	
1906-10	10,077	
Compound Annual Growth, 1881-1910		3.5%
1911-15	11,200	
1916-20	9,352	
1921-25	8.883	
1926-30	10,129	
1931-35	8.880	
1936-40	10,877	
1941-45	8.496	
Compound Annual Growth, 1911-1945		−0.8%
1946-50	9,746	
1951-55	11,927	
1956-60	13,806	
1961-65	24,559	
1966-70	30,970	
1971-75	39,183	
Compound Annual Growth, 1946-1975		4.7%
1976[a]	35,141 (41,698)	
1977[a]	35,469 (42,780)	

a. Figures in parentheses represent new tabulation format, including titles recorded from January through July of the following year.

Source: Paine Webber Mitchell Hutchins, Inc. based on *Publishers Weekly* tabulations and U.S. Department of Commerce.

held that bankers had become inordinately involved in the industry and that too much emphasis was being placed on profits at the expense of the idealistic publishing presumed to have prevailed in the previous century. Price cutting by large stores with book departments led to the formation of the American Publishers Association and the American Booksellers Association, both in 1900, to attempt to maintain retail prices. Members refused to sell to discounters, most notable of which was R.H. Macy and Company. The dispute went up to the Supreme Court, where Macy won in 1913, leading to the dissolution of the publishers' trade association. The presumed problem posed to publishers in the emphasis by large retailers on the "big book" sold at a discount persists to this day.

Cheney Study

In 1931, during the depths of the Depression, the National Association of Book Publishers (formed in 1920) sponsored the publication of O.H. Cheney's *Economic Survey of the Book Industry 1930-1931*.[2] It was the first such study and remained the only one until recent years.

The Census of Book Manufacturers that year estimated industry revenues at $146 million, down from $199 million in 1929, with approximately 154 million books produced, down from 235 million in 1929. It was estimated that 217 publishers produced five or more titles in 1930.

Cheney found the industry's statistics "practically nonexistent." But he derived some conclusions as to the state of the industry nearly 50 years ago.

In examining publishers who had produced more than five titles apiece from 1925 through 1930, he found a very gradual increase in titles per house with some indication that larger houses rarely published more than 200 titles per year excluding reprints. In each year, he estimated that about 10% of the publishers (perhaps 17 to 22 as the period passed) accounted for 48% to 50% of titles published, while 17% to 22% of the companies (29 to 43) issued 50 titles or more. Each year, he reported, the 10 leading publishers accounted for 33% to 37% of total output of these publishers. During the period, the number of publishers in the group surveyed grew from 172 to 217; overall they accounted for 85% of the output of all publishers each year. Table 6.2 compares estimated industry concentration in the 1925-30 period based on title output with more recent data on value of shipments. If accurate, these estimates suggest almost no change in the industry's concentration ratios over a 50-year period.

Cheney observed that "mergers are the common remedy suggested for the troubles of the industry by lunch-table economics," but concluded:

There is no magic panacea in mergers to cure the economic ills of any industry and less magic in the case of the publishing industry than in almost any other. ... For every house which would be "eliminated" through merger, several new ones could — and would — easily spring up, because the capital need is so small and the "publishing urge" so great. The rate of increase in the number of houses by fission seems always to be at least equal to the rate of decrease by fusion.

Table 6.2   Concentration Ratios for the Overall Book Industry

Year	Number of Companies	Value of Shipments (millions)	Largest Companies				
			4	8	10	20	50
			Estimated Percent of Titles Accounted for:				
1925-30	N.A.	N.A.	20%	30%	35%	49%	73%
			Percent of Shipments Accounted for:				
1954	804	$ 665.4	18%	28%		47%	N.A.
1958	883	1,010.7	16	26		45	65
1963	936	1,547.8	18	29		52	73
1967	963	2,255.3	16	27		52	75
1972	1,120	2,915.4	16	27		52	75

N.A.   Not Available.
Sources: O.H. Cheney, *Economic Survey of the Book Industry 1930-1931;* Bureau of
the Census; Paine Webber Mitchell Hutchins, Inc.

Cheney may have reached this conclusion after observing the steady growth in the number of publishers in the 1925-1930 period, despite mergers.

The industry was hurt by the Great Depression, but few publishers went out of business and a number of new firms were started.

ACQUISITION DEVELOPMENTS

In the aftermath of World War II, the industry began to experience rapid growth, particularly in textbooks. Even so, leaders in the industry anticipated many of the problems being cited today. In 1949, Charles F. Bound concluded a study of the industry based largely on interviews with some familiar comments: [3]

- The good publisher today knows that no fortune is to be made in the business.

- Despite nearly record sales, the book industry is facing a crisis. Greatly increased costs for material and labor since the end of the war have virtually wiped out profit margins for publication of original trade books. ... The question quite naturally arises if the solution is not to be found in increased retail prices. The answer, unfortunately, seems to be no. Prices already have been advanced as far as the publisher dares raise them. These increases are by no means as great as is the case with most other consumer items; nevertheless it is generally agreed by all who are familiar with the industry that if prices are advanced much further the publisher is likely to price himself out of the market.

- The great problem facing the industry is not monopoly; it is failure to cooperate.

- Distribution of trade books is chaotic and one of the greatest problems and headaches facing the entire industry.

These same statements could be accepted as a current description of the industry. The industry's problems and concerns, as well as misperceptions about its strengths, seem to be as long-lived as the industry itself.

In retrospect, Bound was writing just as book publishing was beginning to experience one of its most profitable periods of growth. The surge was led by the textbook publishers, and many other publishers soon sought to expand through acquisitions of other textbook producers while, in turn, seeking public capital to grow further. On October 17, 1960, Bennett Cerf, president of Random House, which had just offered its stock to the public, spoke to the New York Society of Security Analysts and stated in part:

It is my belief that within the next few years, some five or six great publishing combines will dominate the publishing scene, much the way that a handful of companies today dominate steel, automobiles and other truly big industries. We intend that Random House will be one of these larger companies. . . .

That was also the period in which the economist Fritz Machlup published his seminal study, *The Production and Distribution of Knowledge in the United States* (1962), coining the term "knowledge industry" and embracing within it such sectors as education, the media, "information machines" and others.

Lyle Spencer, the late founder/president of Science Research Associates, has said, "There's nothing worse in publishing than being right too soon." A great many electronics companies made that mistake in the mid-1960s. Despite the mergers of publishers with publishers, perhaps the greatest wave of interaction was between electronics companies and publishers, anticipating that the rapid growth of both computers and educational funding presaged the acceptance of computer-based instruction in the schools. They believed that they would provide the hardware, the capital and the management skills; publishers would provide the raw materials for programs, the marketing skills and the acceptance. These have been inappropriately called conglomerate mergers. More accurately, they are, borrowing a term coined by Macmillan's president, Raymond Hagel, "congenerics": companies with perceived interrelationships that better meet the needs of common markets. The entrants included IBM, ITT, Litton, RCA, CBS, Raytheon, Xerox, General Electric, Westinghouse, Singer, General Telephone and many others, through acquisitions or interdevelopment. When this wedding proved unsuccessful (because teachers were unwilling to purchase their own replacements?) and both enrollments and discretionary funding declined in the schools, some of these marriages broke up (e.g., G.E.'s participation in General Learning) and others evidently approached the brink of dissolution (e.g., RCA's ownership of Random House).

Then a second type of congeneric merger, welding broad media companies, appeared; examples included Times Mirror, Time, The New York Times, MCA, Gulf + Western, Filmways, Billboard, Corinthian Broadcasting, Warner Communications and others.

Yet, a third, more recent, acquisition program has involved European publishers seeking to expand worldwide markets as well as greater political stability. Acquirers of this type have included Germany's Bertelsmann; Britain's William Collins, Howard & Wyndham, Longman, Morgan-Grampian, Penguin and Pitman; the Netherland's Elsevier; and Canada's Thomson.

Whether because of or despite the mergers of the 1960s and 1970s, the book publishing industry does not appear to have significantly altered with respect to trends long characteristic of it. These trends include: a consistent allocation of personal consumption expenditures to book purchases; a variable allocation of government expenditures to book purchases tied to such factors as the relative proportion of the population enrolled in schools; a steady growth in the numbers of new titles produced and in all titles in print with respect to the numbers of potential readers and writers (i.e., the population); a steady growth in the numbers of firms entering and comprising the book publishing industry; and relatively consistent shares of industry revenues in broad categories of book publishing held by its larger members. These observations will be substantiated by the following tables. It is true that these broad indications may obscure developments in detailed industry sectors and subsectors which will be discussed later, but as a generalization the industry appears to be performing its historic role without notable changes in trends nor in its usefulness to society.

Taking as an arbitrary base period the depths of the Great Depression, for example, the number of book publishing establishments appears to have been growing at about 2.6% per year (see Table 6.3).

Estimates vary of the number of companies engaged in book publishing, so that data in this and following tables should be taken as indicative rather than definitive. Still, they are enlightening.

Table 6.3 provides net figures: ongoing companies plus new formations less dissolutions. To get some idea of the rates of formation and dissolution of publishers, Table 6.4 tabulates the number of new

Table 6.3   Number of Book Publishing Companies and Establishments, Selected Years, 1933-1978

Year	Establishments	Companies
1933	410	N.A.
1935	505	N.A.
1939	706	N.A.
1947	648	635
1954	815	804
1958	903	883
1963	993	936
1967	1,024	963
1972	1,205	1,120
1978 (est.)	1,352	1,239

N.A.   Not Available.

Sources: U.S. Census of Manufacturers; 1978: Paine Webber Mitchell Hutchins, Inc.
An establishment is a single physical plant site or factory. It is not necessarily identical with a company, which may consist of more than one establishment.

publishers, including not-for-profit organizations, that published at least three books in 1977. Thus, of the 34 new firms started in 1968, in 1978 only four became inactive. Over the 10-year period, 414 new publishing entities were formed which were active in 1977, while 31 others formed in the same decade became inactive in 1977.

Table 6.4   Survival Rate of Publishers Formed Since 1968

Year Formed	Number Still Active in 1978	Number that Ceased Operations in 1977-78
1968	34	4
1969	64	3
1970	40	8
1971	50	3
1972	51	3
1973	35	3
1974	37	2
1975	46	3
1976	23	2
1977	34[a]	0
Average Per Year	41	3

a.   Includes organizations first listed in 1978 without founding date given.

Sources: *Literary Market Place,* 1978 and 1977/78; Paine Webber Mitchell Hutchins, Inc.

New companies are often not listed in *Literary Market Place*, the source for the table, until established, thus diminishing the numbers of companies reported founded in more recent years. Older organizations may be dropped for a number of reasons other than dissolution or may still be listed even if acquired if the organizations remain reasonably intact.

In combination, Tables 6.3 and 6.4 suggest that perhaps a hundred publishing enterprises are formed each year, of which about two-thirds may become inactive over 20 to 30 years, a period which would seem to approximate the founder's working lifetime.

ROLE OF BOOK PUBLISHING

Publishers, although treated in government compilations as manufacturers, are really service companies. They assess the information needs of society, locate sources of that information (authors), process it into forms suitable for the market (editing), arrange for its production (printing and binding) and market it (selling and distributing). In this sense, they function much like contractors, assembling and managing the necessary resources that may or may not be integral to their operations. In particular, book publishers are involved with information of more than transient value, which may be unique in its content, and which is intended for the use of individuals in small or large groups who wish easily accessible, relatively inexpensive, highly portable and readily understood information in a durable, relatively permanent format. Other characteristics are precision, the use of symbols for speed of communication and accuracy, and other factors that make the book preferable to alternative media for purposes of information dissemination.

In certain areas, these characteristics, as well as tradition, market acceptance, established distribution channels and/or other factors make it unlikely that the book will be replaced in the foreseeable future. It is difficult, for example, to conceive of the great religious books – the Bible, the Torah or the Koran – in other formats. Other types of books, however, such as collections of mathematical tables, are vulnerable to replacement, although in most cases publishers could themselves adapt the more acceptable formats.

With respect to the requirements of society, the book publishing industry should offer a reasonable opportunity to those with ideas to communicate, particularly those ideas that are intended to last and that require elaboration and interpretation. While it is difficult to determine what is "reasonable," presumably the concept implies ease of entry, a large number of potential publishers with differing viewpoints, and a rate of growth in titles published in excess of population growth so long as the proportion of literate citizens continues to rise. The title output growth as compared to population shows a steady long term increase in new titles per capita (see Table 6.5). Table 6.6 further shows that book industry sales, by growing faster than GNP, account for a greater percentage of the GNP today than in the 1930-1960 period. Thus, it could be the trends in these and previous tables that support the "reasonable opportunity" requirement for the book publishers' role in society.

Table 6.5   New Titles Produced and Relationship to Population, Aged 5-64, Selected Years, 1934-1977

Year	New Titles[a]	All Books in Print	Population Aged 5-64 (thousands)	New Titles per 1000 Population	Total Books in Print per 1000 Population
1934	6,788	—	108,461	0.0626	—
1940	9,515	—	112,512	0.0846	—
1945	5,386	—	116,455	0.0462	—
1950	8,634	—	112,991	0.0702	—
1955	10,226	—	132,319	0.0773	—
1960[b]	12,069	—	143,655	0.0840	—
1961	14,238	—	146,080	0.0975	—
1962	16,448	—	148,612	0.1107	—
1963	19,057	—	151,122	0.1261	—
1964	20,542	—	153,597	0.1337	—
1965	20,234	—	156,028	0.1297	—
1966	21,819	—	158,597	0.1376	—
1967	21,877	—	161,078	0.1358	—
1968	23,321	—	163,428	0.1427	—
1969	21,787	—	165,621	0.1315	—
1970	24,288	—	167,548	0.1450	—
1971	25,526	—	170,042	0.1501	—
1972	26,868	—	171,808	0.1564	—
1973	28,140	398,000	173,271	0.1624	2.2970
1974	30,575	418,000	174,825	0.1749	2.3910
1975	30,004	429,000	176,376	0.1701	2.4323
1976	26,983	450,000	178,395	0.1513	2.5225
1977	27,423	478,000	180,180	0.1521	2.6529

a. Does not include new editions.
b. Includes Alaska and Hawaii for the first time.

Sources: *Publishers Weekly,* U.S. Bureau of the Census, and Paine Webber Mitchell Hutchins, Inc.

Table 6.6   Book Sales and Book Industry Sales Related to Gross National Product, Selected Years, 1933-1977

Year	Gross National Product (billions)	Book Sales (AAP) (billions)	Percent of GNP	All Industry Book Sales (millions)	Percent of GNP	All Book Industry Sales (millions)	Percent of GNP
1933	$ 55.8	—	—	—	—	$ 81.7	0.146%
1935	72.2	—	—	—	—	113.0	0.157
1940	100.0	—	—	—	—	193.9	0.194
1945	212.5	—	—	—	—	293.4	0.138
1950	286.2	—	—	—	—	619.4	0.216
1955	399.3	—	—	—	—	732.8	0.184
1960	506.0	—	—	$1,282	0.253%	1,303.3	0.258
1961	523.3	—	—	1,365	0.261	1,382.3	0.264
1962	563.8	—	—	1,502	0.266	1,527.8	0.271
1963	594.7	$1,672	0.281%	1,547.7	0.260	1,534.6	0.258
1964	635.7	1,816	0.286	1,729.6	0.272	1,728.6	0.272
1965	688.1	2,000	0.291	1,817.6	0.264	1,767.1	0.257
1966	753.0	2,277	0.302	2,081.3	0.276	1,996.3	0.265
1967	796.3	2,380	0.299	2,255.3	0.283	2,134.8	0.268
1968	868.5	2,540	0.292	2,338.9	0.269	2,099.4	0.242
1969	935.5	2,673	0.286	2,521.8	0.270	2,417.2	0.258
1970	982.4	2,798	0.285	2,677.0	0.272	2,434.2	0.248
1971	1,063.4	2,917.8	0.274	2,814.1	0.265	2,739.3	0.258
1972	1,171.1	3,017.8	0.258	2,915.4	0.249	2,856.8	0.244
1973	1,306.6	3,268.4	0.251	3,160.2*	0.242	3,142.9*	0.241
1974	1,412.9	3,718.7	0.263	3,407.7*	0.241	3,348.8*	0.237
1975	1,528.8	4,105.7	0.269	3,789.3*	0.248	3,536.5*	0.231
1976	1,700.1	4,544.8	0.267	4,179.7*	0.246	3,967.5*	0.233
1977	1,887.2	5,127.8	0.272	4,975.5	0.264	4,881.9	0.259
1978	2,104.3	5,772.2	0.274	N.A.	N.A.	N.A.	N.A.

N.A.   Not Available.
*   Figures not revised by preliminary Census Bureau report for 1977.

Sources: *Publishers Weekly,* Bureau of the Census, Association of American Publishers and Paine Webber Mitchell Hutchins, Inc. estimates and calculations. Based on preliminary Census Bureau estimates for 1977.

MARKET SEGMENTS

Book publishing, with its tens of thousands of new titles each year and hundreds of thousands of titles in print, is the most specialized of present-day media industries. Wherever a need for information exists in our society, it is likely that one or more books have been or will be created to serve that need. However, the output of the industry may be categorized in two ways. Table 6.7 tabulates sales by channel of distribution, while Table 6.8 breaks sales down by type of book. More

Table 6.7 Book Industry Sales by Distribution Channel, 1972-1977 (millions)

Distribution Channel	1972	1973	1974	1975	1976	1977	Percent Share 1977	Growth Rate
Genl. Retail	$ 466.4	$ 539.8	$ 599.8	$ 688.8	$ 778.6	$ 894.7	20.5	13.7%
College Strs.	409.9	434.7	491.2	563.7	610.0	670.7	15.4	10.9
Librs./Insts.	284.8	283.5	276.3	313.2	330.7	358.3	8.2	5.1
Schools	610.5	649.2	696.7	728.0	729.3	801.8	18.4	5.1
Direct	802.9	854.5	970.1	986.3	1,144.2	1,227.9	28.2	9.0
Other	30.5	38.7	37.0	47.1	37.1	37.5	0.9	3.3
All Domestic	$2,605.0	$2,800.4	$3,071.1	$3,327.1	$3,629.9	$3,990.9	91.6	8.9
Export Sales	220.2	215.1	266.5	297.9	327.1	365.6	8.4	11.8
All Sales	$2,825.2	$3,015.5	$3,337.6	$3,625.0	$3,957.0	$4,356.5	100.0	9.2

Sources: Book Industry Study Group, plus Paine Webber Mitchell Hutchins, ihc. calculations.

books are sold directly to the consumer — as by direct mail — than any other mode. Schools buy primarily textbooks, while college stores sell textbooks as well as some trade books.

Table 6.8 shows book sales by industry category since 1971. It indicates that elementary and high school (el-hi) textbook sales are the largest single segment, with a 15.3% share in 1977 (but down from 17.0% in 1971), followed by trade books, with a 13.7% share. Of the major categories, mass market paperback books showed the greatest growth over the period, at 14.5%, followed by the mail-order segment. Book industry sales growth for the 1971 to 1977 period lagged somewhat behind increases in the GNP and personal consumption expenditures.

The Association of American Publishers has reported net income from operations from those publishers that report such information. The figures in Table 6.9, which show mail-order publishers to have the greatest margin, are based on AAP compilations, but have been modified to reflect estimates of other income (or expense). However, these calculations are representative at best of only the large publishers active in the industry trade association; they may be further distorted by the reallocation in 1977 of certain expenditures from mail-order to business and other professional book publishing operations by publishers engaged in both sectors, thereby increasing margins for mail order at the expense of professional books.

For some categories, there is also a breakdown of pretax operating margins by size of publisher. Here again the sample is small for many categories and may well be unrepresentative of the universe of publishers. Nonetheless, there is a certain pattern which emerges, seen most clearly in the el-hi textbook sample in Table 6.10. As might be expected, margins are greatest for large publishers. But the mid-range of publishers also display a tendency to lower margins than the smaller participants. One popular analysis of this phenomenon, which has appeared in other recent years, is that while the large publishers can be efficient with their large press runs and marketing forces and the small publishers can specialize in profitable niches selling relatively high priced books, the mid-range publisher (defined by one source as those with $8 to $25 million in el-hi sales)[4] are caught between both worlds and suffer most from the competition.

These trends in earnings by size in samples of larger publishers can be compared with trends in the overall industry using corporate income tax returns of the thousands of companies categorized as those of book publishers, publishers of greeting cards and miscellaneous publishers by the Internal Revenue Service. Table 6.11 is such an analysis. Returns are arrayed by asset size (not adjusted for inflation and the growth of the economy). Pretax income margins (Mar) consist of net income, less

Table 6.8 Book Publishing Market Sizes, Shares and Growth Rates, 1971-1977

	1971	1972	1977	1978	Share %	Growth %
GNP (billions)	$1063.4	$1171.1	$1887.2	$2107.6	—	10.3%
Personal Consumption Expenditures (billions)	668.2	733.0	1206.5	1340.1	—	10.5
All Books (millions)	2917.8	3017.8	5127.8	5772.2	100.0%	10.2
Textbooks	875.7	872.9	1409.7	1572.7	27.2	8.7
El-hi	496.6	597.6	747.3	823.5	14.3	7.5
College	379.1	375.3	662.4	749.2	13.0	10.2
Technical, Scientific, Professional	353.0	381.0	701.0	807.9	14.0	12.6
Tech/Science	122.3	131.8	248.9	277.0	4.8	12.4
Bus/Professional	178.3	192.2	288.8	336.2	5.8	9.5
Medical	52.4	57.0	163.3	194.7	3.4	20.6
Religious	108.5	117.5	249.0	273.8	4.7	14.1
Bibles, Hymnals, etc.	54.4	61.6	116.5	134.8	2.3	13.8
Other	54.1	55.9	132.5	139.0	2.4	14.4
General Trade	1075.6	1134.2	2150.5	2450.1	42.4	12.5
Book Clubs	229.5	240.5	404.3	460.1	8.0	10.4
Mail Order	194.6	198.9	397.3	441.4	7.6	12.4
Adult Hardbound	242.0	251.5	484.3	564.7	9.8	12.9
Adult Paperbound	69.6	79.6	171.6	205.4	3.6	16.7
Total Adult Trade	$ 311.6	$ 331.1	$ 655.9	$ 770.1	13.3	13.8

Juvenile Hdbd.	$ 108.9	$ 106.5	$ 126.5	$ 134.6	2.3	3.1
Juvenile Ppbd.	2.2	4.4	24.6	35.8	0.6	49.0
Total Juv. Trade	$ 111.1	$ 110.9	$ 151.1	$ 170.4	3.0	6.3
All Trade	$ 422.7	$ 442.0	$ 807.0	$ 940.5	16.3	12.1
Rack Size	$ 226.7	$ 250.0	$ 488.4	$ 544.9	9.4	13.3
Non-rack	2.1	2.8	53.5	63.2	1.1	62.6
Total Mass Market Paper	$ 228.8	$ 252.8	$ 541.9	$ 608.1	10.5	15.0
General Reference	$ 301.0	$ 278.9	$ 303.3	$ 351.5	6.1	2.2
Other books and pamphlets	64.6	67.9	100.8	114.2	2.0	8.5
Standardized tests	25.3	26.5	44.7	52.0	0.9	10.8
University Press	39.3	41.4	56.1	62.2	1.1	6.8
Not specified	152.0	165.4	213.5	202.0	3.5	4.1

Sources: Association of American Publishers; Paine Webber Mitchell Hutchins, Inc. and Knowledge Industry Publications, Inc. calculations. Based on preliminary Census Bureau estimates for 1977.

Table 6.9   Samples of Sector Publishers Ranked by Estimated 1977 Pretax Margins

Rank	Margin	Sector
1	21.5%	Mail Order Publications
2	18.1	College Textbooks
3	17.1	El-hi Textbooks
4	13.1	Professional (Total)
5	12.6	Adult Hardbound Trade
6	12.5	Book Clubs
7	12.4	Technical & Scientific
8	11.2	Medical
9	9.7	Trade (Total)
10	9.2	Juvenile Trade
11	8.5	Adult Paperbound Trade
12	5.5	Mass Market Paperbacks
13	4.4	Religious Trade
14	3.9	Business & Other Professional

Sources: Paine Webber Mitchell Hutchins, Inc. calculations based on Association of American Publishers 1977 statistical report.

Table 6.10   Estimated Pretax Margins for Different Size Publishers, by Selected Industry Segment, 1977

Segment	Size	Pretax Margin
Trade (Total)	Small	N.A.
	Medium	8.5%
	Large	6.2
	Very Large	12.4
Professional (Total)	Small	6.9
	Medium	6.7
	Large	14.2
El-hi Textbooks	Small	14.0
	Medium	0.7
	Large	19.9
College Textbooks	Small	4.3
	Medium	9.0
	Large	11.3
	Very Large	22.9

Source: Paine Webber Mitchell Hutchins, Inc. estimates based on Association of American Publishers 1977 statistical report.

deficits, divided by business receipts as reported. Return on equity (ROE) figures are obtained by dividing net income, less deficits, after tax by year-end net capital stock, surplus, plus retained earnings.

Industry pretax margins in 1974 appeared identical with those of 1965. The early estimate is that margins rose in 1975, eased in 1976 and were comparable with those of the 1965-67 period in 1977-78.

During the 1970s, both the number of books printed and the number of employees of the book publishing industry estimated by the Bureau of the Census have remained virtually constant, as shown in Table 6.12. On the other hand, the numbers of publishers, new titles and books in print have grown. These figures, therefore, do not clearly illustrate the precise direction of productivity in the industry.

However, it would appear that the average new title is selling fewer copies, that the average new firm is producing fewer new titles (i.e., that it is of smaller size) and has fewer employees, and that the industry's productivity is being achieved in terms of more titles per employee rather than more units per employee. In short, the industry is becoming more specialized.

The preceding data do not necessarily imply that the industry is also becoming less efficient. The longer-term consistency in margins (and probably in return on equity as well) argues otherwise. What the data do suggest is that the efficiency of publishing is not measured merely in units produced, but in the value of the information produced relative to associated expenses. More specialized information might logically be expected to be more valuable; productivity in this industry is indeed measured in part by the numbers of titles produced per worker and not by numbers of units per worker alone. Hence, the trend toward above-average inflation in book publishing is economically justified as demonstrated in the marketplace by industry margins. Furthermore, there is implied the indication that a small, highly specialized publisher with short production runs of very expensive titles can be as profitable as the very large publisher of titles with long production runs at very low prices.

INDICATORS OF CONCENTRATION

Early in 1979 American Express Co. made a bold cash bid for McGraw-Hill, Inc., which, if it had been consummated, would have been the largest acquisition ever of a company chiefly identified as a book publisher. The Chilton Company, publisher of books and trade magazines, was acquired by American Broadcasting Companies. Other participants in the industry are frequently identified as real or possible participants in other mergers. Thus, it appears that a great merger wave and resulting concentration is taking place. Yet closer study suggests

Table 6.11 Estimated Pretax Margins and Aftertax Return on Equity of Book Publishers, 1963-1974

Year Ending June 30		All	A	B	C	D	E	F	G	H	I	J
							Asset Category (thousands)					
1963	Mar	9.29	(3.42)	3.53	6.56	10.85	8.33	10.68	14.23	4.86	2.88	
	ROE	8.71	x	5.85	9.83	13.46	9.96	9.20	11.97	5.56	3.80	
1964	Mar	8.98	(2.21)	4.16	10.66	9.30	9.71	11.70	12.51	7.74	7.82	
	ROE	11.95	x	5.91	18.35	14.79	14.48	10.76	12.38	12.11	11.69	
1965	Mar	10.26	4.88	4.54	6.30	10.44	11.55	11.60	12.78	12.04	8.71	
	ROE	13.86	11.22	9.84	11.22	15.90	13.38	13.41	12.64	17.36	14.36	
1966	Mar	10.08	(6.35)	3.36	5.92	9.90	11.83	10.83	11.54	15.45	10.94	11.32
	ROE	13.35	x	8.02	10.87	14.43	19.05	11.53	11.17	19.78	28.66	5.25
1967	Mar	9.47	4.88	4.41	1.97	10.92	10.91	7.88	10.85	13.69	8.86	14.25
	ROE	10.00	13.61	9.90	x	12.46	10.34	7.15	9.29	11.82	8.28	16.43
1968	Mar	8.22	(8.02)	6.87	2.34	6.20	6.46	6.76	7.75	18.91		9.06
	ROE	8.48	x	11.08	x	8.55	8.42	5.96	6.46	15.23		9.48
1969	Mar	5.89	5.89	(1.69)	1.09	7.83	3.18	7.70	7.72	7.20	15.21	4.99
	ROE	5.58	5.58	x	x	x	2.22	7.21	7.24	6.70	11.24	5.06
1970	Mar	5.97	5.28	1.83	5.07	4.11	7.23	5.68	5.89	10.93		5.98
	ROE	7.13	12.27	2.35	x	2.97	10.49	5.71	5.81	9.89		6.17
1971	Mar	6.79	(4.69)	0.91	0.36	0.44	7.40	3.69	5.48	11.41	10.85	8.07
	ROE	7.22	x	0.85	x	x	9.15	3.15	4.47	10.01	12.26	7.64
1972	Mar	7.14	0.88	(0.71)	2.64	6.41	5.41	5.49	6.76	7.75	7.22	9.50
1973	Mar	6.59	0.69	4.44	7.84	4.76	2.47	3.74	8.42	8.26	10.03	6.41
1974	Mar	8.98	2.97	3.44	(0.42)	8.15	9.99	2.93	10.82	15.23	15.56	6.52

Mar   Pretax margin.
ROE   After tax return on equity.

x   Negative return on equity.
( ) Negative margin on sales.
Asset Categories (in thousands): A-$0-100; B-$100-500; C-$500-1000; D-$1000-5000; E-$5000-10,000; F-$10,000-25,000; G-$25,000-50,000; H-$50,000-100,000; I-$100,000-250,000; J-Over $250,000.

Source: Paine Webber Mitchell Hutchins, Inc. calculations based on Internal Revenue Service Data.

Table 6.12 Book Publishing Employees, Books Produced, New Titles and Establishments, 1972-1977

	1972	1973	1974	1975	1976	1977
Books Produced (millions)	1468.1	1524.1	1497.0	1452.0	1466.8	1525.4
Employees (thousands)	57.1	59.2	54.4	55.5	58.2	56
New Titles						
(Old series)	26,868	28,140	30,575	30,004	26,983	27,423
(New 18-month series)					32,352	33,292
Books in Print (thousands)		398	418	429	450	478
Total Publishers as measured by						
BIP	6,113					7,279
LMP	959					1,234
Census Bureau						
Establishments	1,205					1,326[a]
Companies	1,120					1,250[a]

a. Estimate.

Sources: Bureau of the Census; Book Industry Study Group, *Publishers Weekly, Books in Print,* (BIP), *Literary Market Place* (LMP).

that recent developments are not inconsistent with the longer-term trend in the industry and thus do not seem likely to lead a significant alteration in the industry's degree of concentration.

Table 6.13 presents a comparative history of recent merger activity. This table suggests that mergers with respect to known companies of size tend to take place at perhaps 3.5 times the rate in book publishing as in mining and manufacturing; that with respect to all mergers the number in the publishing and printing industries is a reasonably consistent 2.3%; that the number of book publishing mergers in the last four years (except for 1977) has actually been below the 16-year average rate of 1.92%. It also shows that the rate of acquisition is a small fraction of the rate of formation of new companies (perhaps 20%-25%) so that the industry continues to grow in the numbers seen previously; that cycles in publishing mergers appear to parallel cycles in other sectors and are therefore primarily tied to broad economic factors affecting all industry in all likelihood; and finally that the greatest period of merger activity was in the late 1960s.

Table 6.13 does not establish that there is no concentration taking place in the book publishing industry, merely that there is little indication that any current trends toward concentration are being significantly changed by recent merger activity. Historically, the book publishing industry has always been characterized by mergers and acquisitions, and virtually all current publishers of any size have made one or more along the way.

Table 6.13 Estimated Mergers and Merger Rates, 1963-1978

Year	Mining and Manufacturing			All Mergers			Book Publishing Industry		
	Mergers	Companies	Rate (Percent)	Total	Print/Publg.	Share (Percent)	Mergers	Companies	Rate (Percent)
1963	861	196.7	0.4377%	1,361	—	—	10	936	1.07%
1964	854	199.5	0.4281	1,950	—	—	8	943	0.85
1965	1,008	199.2	0.5060	2,125	—	—	23	949	2.42
1966	995	202.4	0.4916	2,377	—	—	25	956	2.62
1967	1,496	211.4	0.7077	2,975	—	—	29	963	3.01
1968	2,407	204.7	1.1759	4,462	—	—	47	993	4.73
1969	2,307	216.1	1.0676	6,107	172	2.82%	44	1,023	4.30
1970	1,351	212.3	0.6364	5,152	117	2.27	13	1,054	1.23
1971	1,011	213.6	0.4733	4,608	106	2.30	11	1,087	1.01
1972	911	217.4	0.4190	4,801	91	1.90	9	1,120	0.80
1973	874	222.1	0.3935	4,040	91	2.25	6	1,139	0.53
1974	602	217.3	0.2648	2,861	66	2.30	24	1,158	2.07
1975	439	N.A.	—	2,297	47	2.05	16	1,178	1.36
1976	559	N.A.	—	2,276	58	2.55	17	1,198	1.42
1977	N.A.	N.A.	—	2,224	57	2.56	28	1,218	2.30
1978	N.A.	N.A.	—	N.A.	65	—	14	1,239	1.13

N.A. Not Available.

Sources: Federal Trade Commission and Internal Revenue Service for mining and manufacturing; W.T. Grimm & Co. for all mergers; and *Publishers Weekly, U.S. Census of Manufacturers* and Paine Webber Mitchell Hutchins, Inc. for book publishing industry.

Every book is a unique information product with a unique niche to fill in society's information requirements. Most publishers have started with a single book or with very few books and rather quickly filled the target niche. Once that occurs, unit growth becomes modest or even negative while cash flow continues high. This provides the resources to create new information products or to acquire them in the form of "lists" (rights and inventories) or companies (with editorial staffs in particular, which seems to be the most successful approach). The continuing sale of "backlist" books, those few that prove to have longer-term appeal, is in fact the greatest difference between the unprofitable start-up publishing operation and the successful, profitable older company — or at least has been so historically. Thus, existing publishing operations with proven backlists have always been attractive to other publishers, in contrast to the uncertainties of publishing new and unproven titles.

But because it is still possible for many individuals to enter most sectors of book publishing with relatively limited funds, and because publishing is involved with the world of ideas and many people annually have ideas they consider worth publishing, the industry is also characterized by a relatively large number of new company formations each year. This is confirmed in Tables 6.3, 6.4 and 6.12. These new entrants, once established, but with a dearth of new capital or new ideas, have been those most often acquired in the past. As in the cases of the United States Book Company and American Book Company, the acquisition of lists or assets has tended to provide only temporary success in this industry. Thus, most successful acquirers tend to retain at least the key editorial staffs and often the entire publishing entities intact following their acquisitions. The key to successful publishing is people — and their ideas. Economies of scale through merger are most obvious in selling and distribution, to a lesser extent in manufacturing and may be nil in editorial.

In fact, in recent years many successful publishers have gone so far as to create new publishing subsidiaries from their own personnel, to hold on to key editors or key salesmen. There seem to be limits in either the market or in the successful management of publishing people to the growth or profitability of tightly integrated publishers above a certain size.

Thus, perhaps among all industries, publishing seems least likely to develop into a single, monolithic source of coherent opinion and information unless the industry's role is usurped or closely controlled by an institution such as a church or government.

These general opinions appear abundantly supported by the data on the growth and profitability of the largest publishing entities shown in Tables 6.3, 6.10, 6.11 and 6.15.

Concentration in Suppliers, Vendors and Customers

While, in general, the concentration of the overall book publishing industry does not appear to be changing greatly, its members might be affected by concentration trends among its suppliers, such as book manufacturers; its channels of distribution, such as book retailers; or its customers, such as schools and school districts (whose numbers are declining steadily). Table 6.14 compares the first two with publishing.

The growing concentration of the book manufacturing area does not presently pose a problem for the book publishing industry because it is being accompanied by the growing use by large printers of technology designed to handle short-run books more efficiently. Thus, for some time the smaller publishers may be able to reduce manufacturing costs for their products as a result of the trends in printing.

On the other hand, the concentration in the retailing area, combined with the relatively rapid increase of retailing channels in importance to book publishers (Table 6.7) does seem to pose potential problems for the book industry. Although the industry's distribution problems are being eased in part by the growth of such large bookstore chains as Walden and Dalton, the emphasis many chains tend to place on heavily-promoted "big books" may make it more difficult to obtain retail displays of the industry's more typical and specialized books by eroding the positions of traditional bookstores.

The Census Bureau concentration percentages for the industry segments in Table 6.15 suggest a loss of market share by the four largest publishing companies as well as those predominant in textbooks, general trade books and reference books. This may, however, reflect

Table 6.14 Concentration Ratios for Book Publishers, Manufacturers and Retailers

	Percent Value of Shipments Accounted for											
	4 Largest			**8 Largest**			**20 Largest**			**50 Largest**		
Year	Pubs.	Mfrs.	Rets.	Pubs.	Mfrs.	Rets.	Pubs.	Mfrs.	Rets.	Pubs.	Mfrs.	Rets.
1954	18	15	N.A.	28	24	N.A.	47	37	N.A.	N.A.	N.A.	N.A.
1958	16	15	10	26	22	13	45	34	16	65	48	19
1963	18	14	7	29	23	9	52	37	16	73	51	21
1967	16	15	7	27	23	10	52	38	17	75	53	21
1972	16	19	11	27	27	15	52	44	20	75	57	24
1978[a]	16	18	10	27	26	14	55	44	21	80	60	26

a. Statistical projection.

Sources: Bureau of the Census, *Publishers Weekly,* and Paine Webber Mitchell Hutchins, Inc.

trends in subordinate markets. For example, the schoolbook market is larger than the college textbook market but growing at a slower pace (Table 6.8); the mass market paperback sector is smaller than the trade sector but growing faster; and the Census recently redefined the reference book sector to include dictionaries and the like as well as the highly specialized encyclopedia field which has traditionally been centered in only four companies. Thus, the slower growth of the larger companies in each of these sectors may reflect technical factors rather than true conditions.

POSSIBLE FUTURE TRENDS IN CONCENTRATION

By analyzing the irregular samples of the AAP statistical reports, it appears that only in the textbook markets may the number of industry participants be declining. The number of book clubs may also be declining although the number of companies operating book clubs seems to be stable or rising. The mass market paperback industry appears to have had a relatively constant number of participants in the 1970s. In the trade, religious, mail order and professional book categories, the number of new, small competitors appears to be rising rapidly.

An indication of further consolidation through dissolution or mergers may be found in the margins of the various segments (Tables 6.9 and 6.10). Based on only sketchy data, margins over the 1971-77 period (and subject to change based on later data) appear to be falling in the fields of adult trade paperbacks, juveniles, mass market paperbacks and book clubs. In the cases of these industry categories, it is reasonable to expect mergers of necessity.

Margins may also be falling and concentration through mergers of necessity seem likely among: (possibly) very small adult trade publishers; (less likely) intermediate-size trade publishers; smaller mass market paperback publishers (in particular); and middle-sized el-hi textbook publishers.

Small mass market paperback publishers appear, as a group, to have incurred continuing losses throughout the 1971-77 period; it is thus not surprising that none is publicly held, and numerous mergers of such companies have been proposed or made in recent years. Their problem seems to be one of distribution — excessive returns — and it therefore seems desirable to permit mergers in this category, despite questions of concentration, retaining editorial teams while consolidating distribution functions. Although the Federal Trade Commission appears to oppose such mergers, they seem to make sense. This does not mean that no small mass market paperback publisher can survive. Good management, a good distribution arrangement, and specialization in the right areas

Table 6.15 Market Shares by Number of Companies and Type of Book, 1958-1972

Type of Book	1958 (billions)	1963 (billions)	1967 (billions)	1972 (billions)	Rate of Rev. Growth
All Book Publishing:					
Total Shipments	$1,010.7	$1,547.8	$2,255.3	$2,915.4	7.9%
Top 4 Companies	16%	18%	16%	16%	7.9
Top 8 Companies	26	29	27	27	8.2
Top 20 Companies	45	52	52	52	9.0
Top 50 Companies	65	73	75	75	9.1
Textbooks:					
Total Shipments	$ 281.7	$ 471.1	$ 733.6	$ 809.6	7.8
Top 4 Companies	33%	32%	29%	33%	7.8
Top 8 Companies	50	54	50	54	8.5
Top 20 Companies	76	81	79	80	8.4
Top 50 Companies	93	94	94	95	8.3
Technical, Scientific, Professional Books:					
Total Shipments	$ 116.0	$ 156.3	$ 240.2	$ 403.0	9.3
Top 4 Companies	27%	32%	38%	39%	12.2
Top 8 Companies	43	49	54	57	11.7
Top 20 Companies	71	68	74	76	10.1
Top 50 Companies	91	87	91	92	9.6
Religious Books:					
Total Shipments	$ 58.6	$ 81.1	$ 110.4	$ 131.2	5.9
Top 4 Companies	30%	22%	27%	36%	7.3
Top 8 Companies	45	37	46	51	6.9
Top 20 Companies	70	65	74	76	6.6
Top 50 Companies	90	89	96	97	6.7

General Trade Books:					
Total Shipments	$ 274.7	$ 458.2	$ 657.7	$1,006.7	9.7
Top 4 Companies	39%	30%	28%	29%	7.4
Top 8 Companies	53	46	46	47	8.8
Top 20 Companies	72	59	70	74	10.2
Top 50 Companies	90	89	91	92	9.9
General Reference Books*:					
Total Shipments	$ 163.6	$ 207.3	$ 216.3	$ 235.2	2.6
Top 4 Companies		87%	81%	71%	(0.5)
Top 8 Companies		96	91	82	(0.3)
Top 20 Companies				94	0.5
Top 50 Companies		100	100	99+	1.5
Other Books and Pamphlets:**					
Total Shipments	$ 96.0	$ 154.8	$ 200.1		N.A.
Top 4 Companies		37%	48%		N.A.
Top 8 Companies		48	61		N.A.
Top 20 Companies		68	78		N.A.
Top 50 Companies		85	92		N.A.
Book Publishing Not Specified:					
Total Shipments	$ 20.2	$ 18.9	$ 97.0	$ 155.6	N.A.

*Changed from Subscription Reference Books in 1972 to include dictionaries, etc.
**Omitted in 1972.

Sources: Department of Commerce (William S. Lofquist, in *Printing and Publishing*, July, 1976);
Paine Webber Mitchell Hutchins, Inc.

seem to permit rapid growth into the profitable upper tier of this sector. Harlequin (women's romances) and Ballantine (a strong science fiction list) are examples of the latter. Other specialties and other contenders can emerge if any information vacuum is left as the result of mergers, and there always seems to be another opening.

Pressures on El-hi Publishers

The pressures on middle-sized publishers in several categories, but notably the el-hi schoolbook sector, appear to be related to distribution in other aspects. In the schoolbook field, for example, there appears to be a natural maximum number of salesmen required to cover the national market in all subject areas: between 100 and 150 persons. Smaller firms need disproportionately large staffs and thus their marketing expenses can be much higher in relation to revenues. According to AAP reports, in 1977 marketing costs amounted to 23.3% of revenues for eight small el-hi publishers, 25.5% for 10 middle-sized publishers and 17.6% for nine large publishers in this sector.

The expense of sending sample books was comparable for all three groups at 3.4% to 3.7%; the larger the company the greater the outlay and the higher the inferred sampling effort with respect to a given series of books. Staff consultants' expenses were nearly proportional to sales for medium and larger publishers, as were selling departmental expenses. Thus, the larger the publisher the greater the indicated marketing, support and staff consulting effort, while still obtaining significantly higher margins and thus cash flow to improve the quality of major textbook series. Larger publishers thereby seem to be capturing greater shares of the more lucrative major textbook markets while allowing small textbook publishers to thrive in geographic or subject matter specialities.

For the medium-sized el-hi company, then, the available options seem to be: to merge to acquire significantly greater sales in short order; to arrange for sufficient financing to rapidly build a major internal product effort (which seems to be most common but riskiest); or to shift to specialty products or markets where the competition is smaller. As in the case of mass market paperback publishing, then, it seems likely that mergers would prove healthiest for the industry in the sense of maintaining large editorial staffs and a diversity of textbook offerings in all subject areas. The greater ease of entry in the smaller, specialized markets should encourage the continuing formation of new publishers in these fields if the medium-sized companies do not choose to devote their greater resources to these areas.

LEADING PUBLISHERS*

With its acquisition of Book-of-the-Month Club in late 1977, Time Inc. became the largest book publisher, as measured by revenue. Sales in 1978 were $361 million, the largest portion coming from the mail order Time-Life Books division. Trade publisher Little, Brown is also part of Time Inc. CBS Inc., which had reached the top of the list in 1977 after the Fawcett books acquisition that year, slipped to second, despite a revenue increase of 10%.

The third largest publisher, Reader's Digest Association, Inc., derives almost all of its book revenues from mail order sales of its condensed books series, home repair guides and other "how to" books. About half of Reader's Digest book sales are in foreign markets. McGraw-Hill, virtually even with Reader's Digest, is a leading textbook publisher, but also has extensive trade and professional book lists, all under its own imprint. Doubleday's estimated $275 million sales include its extensive book club operations (Literary Guild is the best known), but eliminate estimated bookstore and printing revenue from its 1978 total of $350 million. Doubleday's most recent publishing acquisition was mass market and trade publisher Dell.

Another leader listed in Table 6.16 is Scott & Fetzer, which became a publisher in 1978 with its acquisition of World Book/Childcraft from Field Enterprises.

As an indicator of the changing fortunes of publishers, as recently as 1974, Grolier was the leading publisher, having $240 million in sales that year. But a string of financial setbacks brought the mail order and encyclopedia publisher close to bankruptcy, and it has retrenched at the expense of some operations.

Harper & Row, an independent trade publisher, reached the top ranks having consummated its merger with J. B. Lippincott in 1978. Lippincott specializes in medical and college textbooks, with a separate religious imprint (Holman) and some trade sales.

In relative terms, book publishing is seen here to be a small enterprise, since even the largest publisher would not make it into the ranks of the *Fortune 500* on book sales alone.

Leading Trade Publishers

Trade books, the fiction and nonfiction titles that are addressed to the general consumer, are the most visible segment of the industry because they have distribution through bookstores across the country.

---

* This section provided by the editor, from data compiled by Knowledge Industry Publications, Inc.

Table 6.16 Leading Book Publishers, by Revenue, 1978

	Book Publishing and Related Revenue
	(millions)
1. Time Inc.	$ 360.9
2. CBS Inc.	332.0[a]
3. Reader's Digest Assn., Inc.	306.0[b]
4. McGraw-Hill, Inc.	305.3
5. Doubleday, Inc.	275.0[c]
6. Scott & Fetzer Co., Inc.	273.0[b,d]
7. Grolier, Inc.	242.8
8. Harcourt Brace Jovanovich, Inc.	236.0
9. Times Mirror Co., Inc.	214.2
10. Macmillan	207.9
11. Encyclopaedia Britannica	200.0[b]
12. Scott, Foresman	189.9[c]
13. Prentice-Hall, Inc.	189.0
14. Harper & Row	165.8[c,e]
Total	$3,497.8

a. Estimate, based on total Publishing Division revenue of $442.3 million.
b. Estimate.
c. Fiscal year ending April 30, 1978.
d. Fiscal year ending November 30, 1978.
e. Pro forma, not actual. Assumes Lippincott's 1977 revenues were included in Harper & Row figures for fiscal 1978.
Source: Company annual reports; 10-K reports; Knowledge Industry Publications, Inc.

Many would consider it the most glamorous segment of the industry, although it is not the largest.

In 1977 Random House edged out Harper & Row as the leading trade publisher, with less than half the number of new titles published by the latter. However, with the addition of Lippincott, Harper & Row may have surpassed Random House in 1978. Table 6.17 identifies the other leading trade publishers. In most cases the figures are estimates, since even publicly owned publishers do not report trade sales separately from other book sales.

Leading Mass Market Paperback Publishers

Mass market paperback publishing is one of the more concentrated segments of the industry, in large part because the ease of entry and low capital requirements that typify most other sectors are less applicable here. By its own terminology, this category requires considerable investment in printing as well as a massive distribution effort.

Table 6.17 Leading U.S. Adult Trade, Juvenile and Trade Paperback Publishers, 1977

Publishers	Parent	Titles	Sales (millions)	Percent of Domestic Market
1 Random House	RCA	345	$ 60.0	9.5%
2 Harper & Row		950	58.5	9.3
3 Grosset & Dunlap	Filmways	608	53.0	8.4
4 Doubleday		652	46.0	7.3
5 Crown/Outlet		546	40.0	6.3
6 Simon & Schuster	Gulf & Western	208	35.0[a]	5.5
7 Houghton Mifflin		333	20.1	3.2
8 ⎰ Little, Brown	Time, Inc.	272	20.0	3.2
⎨ Macmillan		N.A.	20.0	3.2
⎱ Putnam	MCA	234	20.0	3.2
1977 Sales, 10 largest trade publishers			373.0	60.0
1977 industry total			632.0	100.0

a. Includes Touchstone and Fireside but not Summit, Messner or Monarch juveniles.
N.A. Not available.

Source: *BP Report* (White Plains, N.Y.: Knowledge Industry Publication, Inc.), August 28, 1978, p. 1.

By definition, a publisher cannot be a short run, special subject participant in mass market paperbacks.

In 1977, Bantam continued its long time domination of the industry, with total revenue of nearly $95 million, about 12% of which was outside North America. Based even on domestic sales alone, Bantam had a sizeable lead over second-ranked Dell, now owned by Doubleday. The North American sales of the eight firms in Table 6.18 accounted for about 84% of total mass market sales in 1977.

Leading Textbook Publishers

Tables 6.19 and 6.20 provide rankings of leading college and el-hi textbook publishers, respectively. Although revenues for all would have increased by 1978, the relative position of the firms is estimated to be about the same as in the year for the data shown. Comparison of the two tables shows some overlap in participation, although the leading college textbook publisher, Prentice-Hall, is not a factor in the el-hi market. Many publishers find it easier to specialize in one market or the other, since the marketing requirements for each differ substantially.

Overall, many of the largest publishers in all segments have achieved their position through strong internal development as well as through acquisition of publishers with success lists, quality personnel and established marketing channels.

Table 6.18 Leading U.S. Mass Market Paperback Publishers, 1977

Company	Parent	Estimated Sales (millions)	Percent of Domestic Market
1 Bantam[a]	Bertelsmann	$ 95	18%
2 Dell[b]	Doubleday	55	12
3 CBS (Fawcett, Popular Library)		53	11
4 New American Library	Times Mirror	50	10
5 Ballantine	RCA	50	10
6 Pocket Books	Gulf & Western	47	10
7 Avon	Hearst	42	8
8 Warner	Warner Communications	23	5
North American paperback sales, 8 largest companies		$ 404	84
Industry total		$ 477	100

a. Bantam is the only one of the eight ranked mass market publishers that has substantial sales outside the U.S., through its ownership of Transworld (U.K.). U.S. and Canadian sales account for about $84 million of the company's $95 million in sales.

b. Sales quoted for Dell are only mass market paperbacks. Total Dell sales are actually around $75 million.

Source: *BP Report* (White Plains, N.Y.: Knowledge Industry Publications, Inc.), August 28, 1978, p. 1.

DISCUSSION

Before considering the newer types of mergers and diversifications, it might be well to reflect on the industry's history once again. Whereas publishers frequently began as printers — manufacturers — or booksellers, the industry changed with the advent of the copyright and national markets. First, few book publishers today do their own printing; the desirability of printing facilities closer to markets and the availability of a variety of manufacturing processes at competitive prices tend to separate these functions. Second, few book publishers today operate bookstores; those that do, such as Doubleday, carry the wares of a large number of competitors and not merely the publishers' own lines. Third, today, even the traditional editorial functions have been separated to some degree. Schoolbooks were usually prepared in-house in the past but now are sometimes prepared by outside firms. A number of independent or affiliated editor/author groups now serve the industry, particularly in textbooks and trade books.

It has thus become increasingly true that the publisher operates as a contractor, assembling the people, facilities and resources to best meet a particular market requirement for information, integrating only those people, facilities and functions that are particularly scarce or profitable

Table 6.19 Leading College Publishers, 1975

Rank	Company	College Revenues (millions)	Market Share
1	Prentice-Hall	$ 81.5	15.4%
2	McGraw-Hill	55.0	10.4
3	CBS/Publishing Group (Holt, Rinehart & Winston, W.B. Saunders)	41.8	7.9
4	Scott, Foresman	35.5	6.7
5	Harper & Row	34.3	6.5
6	Harcourt Brace Jovanovich	32.0	6.0
7	John Wiley & Sons	30.0	5.7
8	Macmillan	28.0	5.3
9	Richard D. Irwin	24.7	4.7
10	Addison-Wesley	22.0	4.1
11	Wadsworth Publishing Co.	17.5	3.3
12	Allyn & Bacon	15.8	3.0
13	Random House	14.0	2.6
14	Houghton Mifflin	13.9	2.6
15	W.W. Norton	11.0	2.1
16	William Brown	9.0	1.7
17	W.H. Freeman	7.9	1.5
18	Little Brown	7.5	1.4
19	Charles Merrill	7.0	1.3
20	D.C. Heath	7.0	1.3
	Total	495.4	93.0

Source: Knowledge Industry Publications, Inc.

and/or continually required. (However, typesetting, the transformation of manuscripts into finished print symbols, is making a comeback in the publishing industry on the strength of its new computer technology versatility and hence profitability.)

In the 19th century, acquisitions by book publishers seem to have been primarily of "lists" — books — in fields identical to those already served. In the early 20th century, the emphasis gradually shifted to the acquisition of companies — both people and books — in identical fields and then, as the differences between sectors became less distinct, to the acquisition of publishers in complementary fields.

Today, for a variety of reasons, the larger publisher (and many small ones) is being forced to take an even broader view of his function. Among the contributing factors are governmental limitations on acquisitions in fields in which one's stake is already large; the rapid proliferation of new methods of conveying information formerly considered the exclusive province of a well-defined book format; the continuing breakdown of distinctions among existing media (e.g. "instant" books, books from filmscripts); the growing interrelationships

Table 6.20 Estimated Revenues and Rank of Leading El-hi Publishers, 1976[a]

Rank based on 1976 Revenues	Rank based on 1970 Revenues		El-hi Revenues (millions)
1	3	Scott, Foresman	$129
2	4	Harcourt, Brace Jovanovich	115
3	2	Xerox (Ginn, XEP)	85
4	5	Scholastic Magazines, Inc.	80
5	6	CBS Educational Publishing[b]	72
6	7	Houghton Mifflin	72
7	1	McGraw-Hill	59
8	8	Macmillan	55
9	10	Doubleday[c]	40
10	10	IBM/Science Research Assoc.	33
11	NR	Encyclopaedia Britannica Educational Corp.	28
12	9	Litton Educational Publishing	25
12	NR	Esquire Education Group	25
14	NR	Addison-Wesley	23

a. Includes periodical and audio visual product sales to el-hi market.
b. Includes Holt, Rinehart & Winston and BFA Educational Media.
c. Includes Laidlaw and pro-rated revenues for Noble & Noble, acquired June, 1976.
NR   Not Ranked.

Source: Company annual reports; Knowledge Industry Publications, Inc.

of the media in appearance, distribution, content and the like; the explosion in the use of copying, undermining book sales in some areas and eroding the value of copyright on which the industry is based; rapid technological change within and without the industry; the growing affluence of society; changing popular tastes; the desirability of marketing expensive information to the largest possible audience; and many others.

It should not be surprising that, after centuries of habit, book publishers find it is difficult to adapt to change: to become media congenerics. They, like most of us, are used to thinking in one, two or three dimensions. Yet the larger publisher today must think of himself and his resources in a very much larger number of dimensions.

Consider but a few:

- Type of information: data, commentary, imagery, sensation, interpretation, analysis.

- Time requirement for the information: instantaneous; within minutes, hours, days, weeks, annual or indefinite.

- Place requirement for the information: anywhere; in the home, office, school, library, store or newsstand; or limited in other respects.

- Best method for conveying the information: visual or aural — through text or symbols; detailed or abstract; quickly or at length . . .

- Durability of the information: instantaneous, limited or permanent.

- Value of the information: very high, moderate, limited (or none).

- Purpose of the information: entertainment, instruction, reference. . . .

- Source of the information: authors, government, artists, accumulated data, files.

- Method of information preparation: editing, recording, computer transformation, photographing. . . .

- Method of information production: printing, pressing, xerography, binding, packaging, computer terminal, electronic.

- Channels of distribution: direct to consumers; through wholesalers, jobbers, retailers; through salesmen; through institutions.

- Markets for the information: doctors, consumers, governments, institutions. . . .

- Method of payment for the information: subscription, installment sale, consignment sale, direct purchase, advertising support.

As a result, some traditional book publishers have been acquired instead of growing into other areas of mass communications themselves. The starting point for any publisher is to determine the characteristics of the resources he already has at his disposal and can repackage without additions or with such limited additions as new mailing lists, new authors or new distribution or production arrangements. He must also determine which new packages would offer attractive new profit potentials or insurance against the loss of current profits with minimal additions: people or products.

The optimal combination is a complex of people, experience, products and management that can both benefit from the acquirer's resources and can benefit them with minimal duplication or waste.

Because the existing information producers have grown in an environment in which they were considered unique, with their own markets, channels of distribution, sources and processing techniques, in most cases a publisher planning to enter such an alternative information field needs an entity, an acquisition. This is as true of publishers of books as of publishers of magazines or newspapers, film producers, recording companies and so on. In addition, acquisitions reduce risks because of established product lines, economic histories and the like.

There are literally thousands of publishers of printed information products and additional thousands of producers of information in alternative forms. All face uncertainties, and many were created by entrepreneurs nearing the ends of their careers or forebears of families no longer engaged in their businesses so that their alternatives to merger may be limited.

It therefore seems logical to anticipate the continuing growth of a number of information congenerics, including book publishers. The formation of a large number of such organizations, indeed, should ensure continuing competition in the world of ideas, forestalling the possibility of government becoming the only source.

This trend should also enable a variety of information producers to compete, as the capital investments required by the future world of computers, data bases and interactive communications media continue to loom beyond the resources of many existing information specialists. This will ensure the continuing existence of some older information producing entities, book publishers, which might otherwise have been supplanted by the newer formats.

FOOTNOTES

1. *Textbooks in Education* (New York: American Textbook Publishers Institute, 1949).

2. (New York: R.R. Bowker Co., 1931).

3. *A Banker Looks at Book Publishing* (New York: R.R. Bowker Co., 1950).

4. Dantia Quirk, *The El-hi Market, 1978-83* (White Plains, N.Y.: Knowledge Industry Publications, Inc., 1977), p. 65.

Appendix A6
Personal Consumption Expenditures
Accounted for by Printed Materials
(Selected Years, 1934-1977)

Year	Personal Consumption Expenditures			
	Dollar Total (millions)	Books & Maps (Percent)	Newspapers & Periodicals (Percent)	Printed Total (Percent)
1934	$ 51,344	0.321%	0.859%	1.180%
1940	70,979	0.330	0.830	1.159
1945	119,493	0.436	0.808	1.243
1950	191,966	0.351	0.779	1.130
1955	253,665	0.342	0.737	1.079
1960	324,903	0.351	0.666	1.017
1961	334,995	0.362	0.605	0.967
1962	355,217	0.362	0.649	1.011
1963	374,578	0.377	0.659	1.036
1964	400,381	0.403	0.624	1.027
1965	430,154	0.383	0.619	1.002
1966	464,793	0.396	0.673	1.069
1967	490,358	0.377	0.654	1.030
1968	535,932	0.362	0.660	1.022
1969	579,711	0.359	0.613	0.972
1970	618,796	0.381	0.630	1.011
1971	668,171	0.368	0.635	1.003
1972	733,034	0.345	0.639	0.984
1973	809,885	0.342	0.733	1.064
1974	889,603	0.341	0.792	1.133
1975	979,070	0.368	0.766	1.139
1976	1,090,244	0.339	0.747	1.086
1977	1,206,507	0.365	0.749	1.114

Source: U.S. Department of Commerce.

Appendix B6
Imprints and Publishing Subsidiaries
of Leading U.S. Book Publishers

Parent Company	Imprints
CBS Inc.	Holt, Rinehart & Winston
	W.B. Saunders Co.
	Praeger Special Studies
	Dryden
	Fawcett Books: Crest, Gold Medal, Premier,
	Popular Library
Doubleday	Dell
	Delacorte Press
	Dial Press
	Laidlaw Brothers
	J.G. Ferguson
	Literary Guild and other clubs
Harcourt Brace Jovanovich	Academic Press
Harper & Row	J.B. Lippincott
	A.J. Holman
	Basic Books
	T.Y. Crowell
Encyclopaedia Britannica	G.&C. Merriam Co.
Grolier	Scarecrow Press
	Franklin Watts
Macmillan	The Free Press
	Collier
	Crowell-Collier
	Schirmer
	Glencoe Publishing
	Berlitz Publications
McGraw-Hill	Webster
	Schaum/Paperback
	Gregg
	Shepard's Citations
Prentice-Hall	Appleton-Century-Crofts
	Reston Publishing
	Goodyear Publishing
	Winthrop Publishers
	Spectrum Books
Scott, Foresman	South-Western Publishing
	Silver Burdett
	William Morrow
	Fleming H. Revell

Time Inc.	Little, Brown
	Time-Life Books
	Book-of-the-Month Club and other clubs
	Atlantic Monthly Press
	New York Graphic Society
Times Mirror	Southwestern
	New American Library
	New English Library
	Harry N. Abrams
	Matthew Bender
	C.V. Mosby
	Year Book Medical Publishers

7

Cable and Pay Television

Cable television initially benefited from, but later seemed cursed by, its original role as a support service to broadcast television. While the development of cable systems is nearly as old as television broadcasting, cable has become a medium of significant audience penetration — and thus policy concern — only in the past 10 to 15 years. The brief time period, relatively limited amount of detailed information, and fairly clearcut ownership regulatory position of the FCC all combine to force a comparatively brief treatment of the industry in this volume.

We are concerned here with concentration in cable television, or wired means of television reception. The industry today divides into two major segments — the larger and much older "traditional" cable industry built on carriage of broadcast television signals, and the much newer but rapidly growing business of pay cable television. While in fact subscribers naturally pay for either system, pay cable is almost always one or more premium channels for which there is an additional cost above the monthly charge for basic cable service. In this chapter, the discussion focuses first on the traditional industry, then on pay cable services, in each case briefly examining the industry's background to provide context to the discussion of ownership trends and regulatory efforts.

The literature on all aspects of cable is large and growing, and readers lacking background in the medium are directed to any of several good general introductions which are available.[1] Specialized material exists in profusion on such controversial issues not dealt with here as cable and copyright, the division of regulatory concern between federal and state/local governments, local origination and access rules, franchising problems (other than system ownership), pole attachment and other technical requirements, etc.[2] These subjects, as well as concentration of control, had all been regulated until the mid-1970s by the overriding concern of the FCC: to protect the primacy of broadcast television service by limiting the expansion of services provided by cable television.[3]

GENERAL CABLE TELEVISION

As a simple delivery system, cable television has existed for three decades. But over the years, cable has been seen more and more, both by those within the industry and by those who regulate that industry, as the central delivery element of a wide variety of communications formats and content to be delivered to the home. Debate has centered on whether cable is more than a mere delivery system of existing programming, or whether it creates opportunity for more options, more specialization, new and different ownership participation, and thus a real and substantive change in the media mix available to most Americans — the first such real change since television itself. That potential is a major underlying concern to regulatory interest in who owns cable.

Rise of Cable Television

Though it has been a brief time, and we are too close to it to allow any definitive approach, cable's short development appears to break into three periods which are divided primarily by changing federal regulatory positions on the medium.

Early Years to 1962. Cable, or community antenna, television systems began in the late 1940s as a means of delivering television signals to areas unable to receive over-the-air TV channels, either because of distance from the transmitters, or because of interference by intervening hills or mountains. A master receiving antenna on a hilltop picks up the air signals, which are then transmitted by means of cables to homes in the area. Typically, there is a one-time installation charge and then a monthly subscription fee. Well into the 1950s, cable systems could be characterized as: 1) quite small, running to just a few hundred homes in most cases, 2) carrying perhaps three or four broadcast TV signals, usually the closest stations, 3) generally confined to mountainous areas with little or no regular TV reception and 4) usually welcomed by broadcasters who knew the cable systems expanded their viewing audience. Ownership was typically a small local company often in some related primary line of business (such as selling receivers). Such "mom and pop" operations were often only marginally successful financially, though few records exist of the earliest years.[4]

Cable was but one of several industry responses to the limitations of localism-inspired television allocations (see chapter three). In the 1950s a proliferation of audience-extension facilities appeared: translator stations (which rebroadcast a weak signal on a higher UHF channel for immediate area reception), booster transmitters (which beefed up an incoming signal on the same channel), satellite stations (or "slave" stations which were merely secondary outlets for a station in a major community, though the satellite might be on a totally different channel) and cable. CATV was generally more expensive than the various broadcasting options, but it offered two important advantages: because it was a closed rather than broadcast delivery system, a charge could be made for the service, thus providing the key to support; and many channels could be carried at any one time. Still, cable grew very slowly for many years, as shown in Table 7.1, because it merely provided a different means of signal reception in rural, often sparsely populated, areas. Growth was strongest in Pennsylvania and many western states.

By the early 1960s, broadcasters began to have second thoughts about the role and effect of cable on over-the-air television. This was brought about by:

- increasing use of microwave relay facilities by cable systems to

Table 7.1   Growth of Cable Television Systems, Selected Years, 1952-1978

Year	Number of Systems	Number of Subscribers (thousands)	Percent of TV Homes with Cable	Average Number of Subscribers per System
1952	70	14	0.1%	200
1953	150	30	0.2	200
1954	300	65	0.3	217
1955	400	150	0.5	375
1960	640	650	1.4	1,016
1965	1,325	1,275	2.4	962
1966	1,570	1,575	2.9	1,003
1967	1,770	2,100	3.8	1,186
1968	2,000	2,800	4.4	1,400
1969	2,260	3,600	6.1	1,593
1970	2,490	4,500	7.6	1,807
1971	2,639	5,300	8.8	2,008
1972	2,841	6,000	9.6	2,112
1973	2,991	7,300	11.1	2,441
1974	3,158	8,700	13.0	2,755
1975	3,506	9,800	14.3.	2,795
1976	3,651	10,800	15.5	2,958
1977	3,800	11,900	17.3	3,132
1978	4,001	13,000	17.7	3,242

Sources: Sterling and Haight (1978), table 190-A, as taken from *Television Digest* information reprinted in annual issues of *Television Factbook,* and *Statistical Trends in Broadcasting.* 1978 data supplied by *Television Digest.* All figures are estimates as of January 1 of each year.

bring in distant stations — thus providing competition for local telecasters and further dividing up the audience;

• inception of urban cable systems, such as that in San Diego begun in 1961 to import Los Angeles signals to a market already well served with local television; in New York in 1966 to improve reception among the tall buildings; and Los Angeles in 1967;

• rising concern by broadcasters and producers over lack of payments by cable operators for material that cable thus carries free; and

• a slow trend to consolidation of cable system ownership from hundreds of small local companies to larger multiple system operators (MSOs), indicating the potential for cable's economic future. Rather than expanding broadcast audiences, cable began to be viewed by broadcasters and advertisers as a system for dividing the audience into smaller segments across a greater number of television channels — usually to the financial detriment of local TV stations.

Though pressure from broadcasters began to build on Congress and the Federal Communications Commission, initially there was little or no regulation of cable on any level of government. In 1959, for example, the FCC specifically declined to regulate cable, claiming it was neither broadcasting nor common carrier, and was thus outside of the scope of the Communications Act of 1934.[5] But this free-wheeling period finally came to an end.

Search for a Regulatory Formula, 1962-1972: Pressures from broadcasters combined with FCC concern over possible economic harm to television stations by cable operations brought about initial FCC regulation of cable in 1962.[6] Using the regulation of microwave under its jurisdiction the commission took over regulatory responsibility for cable systems using microwave to import distant signals and required all systems to carry any local stations in addition to distant signals. As an additional protection for local stations, any network service on a local station was not to be duplicated in an imported signal. In 1965 the FCC limited signal importation in the top 100 markets, required systems to carry local signals as well, and assumed regulatory control over common carriers providing cable service to local systems by means of microwave.[7] Just a year later, this federal regulation was expanded to cover all cable systems,[8] a decision upheld on review in a 1968 Supreme Court decision.[9] While the broadcast industry generally applauded this trend (and the clear statement by the FCC that cable was to be supplemental to broadcast television), they were frustrated by another 1968 Supreme Court decision that found cable systems were not infringing copyright by nonpayment for broadcast signals carried.[10] Despite such tight federal regulation, and increasing interest by some states (Connecticut had enacted the first state cable regulations in 1963),[11] the industry continued to expand.

One indication of cable's increasing importance in communications policy-making was the greatly increased rate of publication about cable in the late 1960s and early 1970s. In 1970-71, for example, came the first of a continuing series of Rand Corporation studies on the applications, technology, and regulation of cable.[12] It was followed late in 1971 by the report of the Alfred Sloan Foundation-funded commission on cable communications which conducted a number of detailed support studies to buttress its conclusion that cable should be allowed to develop in free competition with broadcasting.[13] It recommended retaining regulation to ensure development of the public service potential of cable (indeed, the report encouraged further establishment of state regulatory bodies), and requiring some kind of payment by cable operators for use of broadcast material. At the same time, behind the scenes, cable industry representatives, the National Association of Broadcasters, and some of the copyright holders (film and video producers) met in Washington and hammered out a compromise agreement to govern the forthcoming "definitive" FCC rules on cable which were subsequently issued in February 1972.[14] They were detailed and extensive, calling for limited importation of signals to the top 100 markets, a provision for local origination of programming for large cable systems, a complex system of access and community channels, system size and capacity regulations, etc. with existing cable systems having about five years to come to compliance. It appeared to many observers that with most issues resolved and a clear framework established, cable could then expand rapidly.

Deregulation since 1972: As will be shown later, the so-called definitive rules did not last long in their original state. In a series of both FCC decisions and court cases in the years since, the FCC's carefully constructed protectionist policy where cable was held subordinate to broadcast operations has become progressively eroded. The combination of seeming confusion on the federal level, varied activity on the state and local level by regulators, and a steadily worsening economic climate all served to hold down the expansion of cable penetration to a gradual evolution rather than explosion.

Indicators of Recent Growth

Table 7.2 illustrates the increase in size of individual cable systems. Mission Cable of San Diego, with well over 100,000 subscriber homes, has long held the distinction of being the largest system. The table also

Table 7.2   Characteristics of Cable Service, Selected Years, 1968-1978

	1968	1970	1972	1974	1976	1978
System Size by number of Homes Served						
20,000+ homes	N.A.	8	22	42	68	N.A.
10,000-19,999 homes	N.A.	50	83	142	181	N.A.
5,000-9,999 homes	N.A.	144	215	289	345	N.A.
2,000-4,999 homes	N.A.	402	566	644 }	1,407	N.A.
1,000-1,999 homes	N.A.	423	500	605 }		
500-999 homes	N.A.	427	514	577 }	1,688	N.A.
Under 500 homes	N.A.	776	843	851 }		
Unspecified size	N.A.	260	96	40	26	N.A.
Total systems		2,490	2,839	3,190	3,715	
Percent of Homes with Cable by County Population						
"A" Counties (most urban)	1.1%	1.7%	3.3%	4.3%	6.3%	8%
"B" Counties	3.9	5.1	7.5	9.5	14.1	17
"C" Counties	15.2	17.4	22.5	25.7	29.5	33
"D" Counties (most rural)	9.4	10.6	13.7	15.4	17.9	21
Average for all counties	4.4%	7.6%	9.6%	13.0%	15.5%	17%

Source: Sterling and Haight (1978), tables 190-B and 190-C taken from *Television Factbook* annually. County size information from A.C. Nielsen Co.

shows the varied rates of penetration into urban and rural counties. Although smaller towns and rural areas have the highest penetration, the most rapid growth in the 1970s has been in more urban areas. Table 7.3 details the increasing use of material originated by the local cable operator, which served to widen cable's appeal and subsequent broadcaster concern over competition. Whereas in 1970 most such local programming was of the automated variety (weather dials, news tickers, etc.), by 1976 the use of studio productions had nearly doubled to over a quarter of all systems, and nearly two-thirds of all cable systems provided some kind of local origination. Much of this local programming appeared first on newer systems with sufficient channel capacity to carry it and on larger systems with sufficient subscriber demand to make the cost worthwhile.

Information on the economic condition of the cable industry is much less common — and covers only a few recent years when the FCC began to collect financial data from cable "entities" (ownership units, regardless of how many systems are owned) to somewhat parallel that long gathered from broadcasters. The published results are summarized

Table 7.3   Cable Television Program Origination, Selected Years, 1970-1978

Category	1970	1972	1974	1976	1977	1978
Number Reporting Systems	2490	2839	3190	3715	3911	3997
% Systems with Origination	44	53	62	65	66	66
Channel Capacity of Systems:						
over 20	} 3%	13%	18%	{12%	13%	14%
13 to 20				{11	12	12
6 to 12	69	71	72	71	71	70
5 or fewer (incl. unspecified)	27	16	12	5	5	4
% Systems with Automated Origination	40%	46%	57%	60%	60%	65%
Systems with Studio Origination:	16	21	29	28	28	N.A.
local live	12	–	20	18	17	17
film and/or VTR	5	–	20	17	15	14
school channel	nil	–	3	5	6	6
public access channel	–	–	nil	3	5	5
advertising	nil	5	9	8	7	N.A.
other	–	–	2	2	5	6
Systems with Pay Cable	–	–	2	8	14	22

Sources: 1970-76, based on figures gathered by *Television Factbook* as reported in Sterling and Haight (1978), table 590-A. 1978: *Television Digest.* "Nil" indicates some systems carried that format, but under 1%.

on a national level in Table 7.4, and show cable systems to be increasingly profitable operations, with revenue growing faster than assets. No reliable employment figures exist on the cable industry, though a 1974 FCC estimate put the figure at about 25,000 persons, with about 9% minority and 15% female employment levels in "higher-paying" jobs. Given that something approaching 1000 additional cable systems have begun operation since that estimate, cable industry employment may be reasonably estimated to exceed 35,000.

The move to deregulate cable communications has received its impetus from a continuing series of policy papers following the pioneering Sloan Commission. Though some of its results, and indeed its very publication, got lost in the Watergate morass, the 1974 report of the Cabinet Committee on Cable Communications helped to nudge the FCC into softening some of the 1972 rules.[15] Assembled under the direction of Clay Whitehead, then director of the White House Office of Telecommunications Policy, the report advocated almost total deregulation of cable in the long run – but at the price of a "separations" policy discussed below. Just over a year later a generally conservative business research organization issued its analysis of cable and also called for a general loosening of government controls of cable.[16] The most incisive of the analyses came in January 1976 when staff members of the House Subcommittee on Communications issued a review of cable development, current status, and future options which scored the FCC

Table 7.4   The Economics of Cable Television: 1975-1977

	1975	1976	1977
Number of cable entities[1]	2,443	2,349	2,577
Average monthly subscriber rate	$6.21	$6.49	$6.85
Industry annual totals: (in millions)			
operating revenue	$894.9	$997.8	$1,205.9
pay cable revenue	N.A.	$41.1	$85.9
proportion of revenue from pay cable	N.A.	4%	7%
operating expenses	$567.4	$615.9	$716.9
income before tax	$26.9	$57.7	$133.7
profit margin[2]	37%	38%	40%
assets	$2,131.5	$2,515.7	$2,450.5

[1] Ownership units, including multiple system operators.

[2] Before interest, depreciation, amortization expenses, taxes, and extraordinary gains and losses.

Sources: FCC official figures as reported in "CATV Industry Financial Data for the Period Nov. 1975-Oct. 1976," FCC Mimeo 85210 (June 10, 1977); *Broadcasting* (June 26, 1978), pp. 25-26; and *Broadcasting* (January 1, 1979), p. 38.

for siding with the broadcast industry to hold down cable development.[17]   Both a 1977 publication made up during the Ford Administration, titled *Deregulation of Cable Television*,[18] and 1978-79 drafts of a rewrite of the Communications Act moved in the same direction. Clearly, public policy on cable TV was being debated at the end of the decade by more divergent and broad-based groups than had been the case when the broadcasters and cable system operators tried to settle their differences in 1971. One reason for the change was the passage in 1976 (effective 1978) of the new copyright act,[19] which partly resolved a prime conflict between copyright holders and cable system owners. Now, under compulsory license, cable operators simply carry the signals and pay an appropriate fee to a Copyright Tribunal, which is to handle processing for distribution to the copyright holders.

Just as the U.S. Court of Appeals for the District of Columbia has been overruling the Federal Communications Commission in many important broadcasting cases, so it has recently been contravening FCC rule-making concerning cable. While earlier decisions nibbled away at FCC pre-emptive jurisdictional decisions on cable, a 1978 decision set aside the Commission's access requirements and channel capacity rules. The decisions on these cornerstones to FCC limitations on cable were upheld in final adjudication before the Supreme Court in early 1979.[20] The FCC itself, however, in a series of decisions, loosened controls on cable by easing distant signal importation rules, ending formal franchise considerations (leaving this step almost totally to local and state regulators) and generally delaying imposition of rules on older grand-fathered systems.[21]

By the late 1970s, cable television growth appeared to be on the upswing, paced more than anything else by the potential of pay cable. The dismantling of the FCC's broadcasting-protective regulation was another inducement. Still, it was clear that grand assessments of cable's role in society made early in the 1970s were grossly optimistic, at least in their timing.[22] Part of the change was due to technology: the spread of home video recorders (and to a lesser extent, video games) provided some of the diversion from broadcaster-controlled transmissions that cable had promised. Many long-forecast cable services remained "blue sky" for economic reasons, and it was clear that development of cable's full potential would take years, perhaps a decade, longer than initially thought in the heady late 1960s and early 1970s.

Ownership Trends and Regulation

Having learned its lessons on ownership problems the hard way in radio and television broadcasting, the FCC made its important ownership regulations on cable early — and stuck to them. They have thus not caused anywhere near the controversy such regulation did in broadcasting.

Entry: Unlike the other mass media, cable systems are treated as natural monopolies in their coverage areas — much like electricity, telephone and water utilities. Cable systems are franchised on the local level and must meet such requirements as the local community establishes, such as minimal bonding, time limits on wiring the community, control on rates for installation and monthly service charges, a percentage of profits to be paid to the franchising body, and the like. Entry is thus controlled by economic cost (and cable is capital intensive at the construction stage)[23] and franchise requirements which may vary widely.[24] On the other hand, once entry is achieved, the system typically has sole rights in its area for 10 to 15 years on a renewable basis — a higher degree of "security" than the three years for broadcast licenses.

Trends in Ownership of Cable: Little or no detailed information on the ownership of cable systems exists for periods earlier than a decade ago. Table 7.5 summarizes ownership trends since that time, reporting only on some of the ownership categories (missing here until 1972 for example, is municipal ownership). Note the sizeable proportion of cable systems controlled by broadcasters — around a third of all systems for the 10-year period. The table also shows the increasing control of cable by newspapers and other publishers — from 7% in 1969 to one-fourth of all systems by 1977. Certainly important in policy consideration is

Table 7.5 Number of Cable (CATV) Systems in U.S. by Category of Ownership, 1969-1977

	1969 (February)		1970 (March)		1971 (March)		1972 (March)	
	Number of Systems	Percent of Systems Surveyed	Number of Systems	Percent of Systems Surveyed	Number of Systems	Percent of Systems Surveyed	Number of Systems	Percent of Systems Surveyed
Number of CATV Systems Surveyed	2300	—	2490	—	2578	—	2839	—
Category of Ownership:								
Broadcasters	741	32%	910	37%	766	30%	1077	38%
Newspapers	220	7	207	8	175	7	180	6
Publishers							75	3
TV Programming Prod. Distributors	N.A.	N.A.	N.A.	N.A.	N.A.	N.A.	217	8
Theater Owners	N.A.	N.A.	N.A.	N.A.	N.A.	N.A.	97	3
Telephone Companies	150	7	146	6	132	5	57	2
Community or Subscriber Ownership	N.A.	N.A.	N.A.	N.A.	N.A.	N.A.	81	3
TV Manufacturers	N.A.	N.A.	N.A.	N.A.	N.A.	N.A.	N.A.	N.A.

Table 7.5, continued. Number of Cable (CATV) Systems in U.S. by Category of Ownership, 1969-1977

	1973 (June)		1974 (June)		1975 (September)		1976 (September)		1977 (September)	
	Number of Systems	Percent of Systems Surveyed	Number of Systems	Percent of Systems Surveyed	Number of Systems	Percent of Systems Surveyed	Number of Systems	Percent of Systems Surveyed	Number of Systems	Percent of Systems Surveyed
Number of CATV Systems Surveyed	3032	–	3190	–	3405	–	3715	–	3911	–
Category of Ownership:										
Broadcasters	1048	35%	1178	37%	1090	32%	1183	32%	1179	30%
Newspapers	308	10	463	15	486	14	476	13	474	12
Publishers	221	7	230	7	247	7	492	13	501	13
TV Programming Prod. Distributors	604	20	744	23	772	23	729	20	772	20
Theater Owners	130	4	146	5	296	9	313	8	301	8
Telephone Companies	50	2	143	4	61	2	69	2	73	2
Community or Subscriber Ownership	75	3	83	3	88	3	96	3	106	3
TV Manufacturers	320	11	606	19	630	19	455	12	422	11

N.A.   Not Available.

Sources: 1969-76: Sterling and Haight (1978), table 290-A, as taken from annual issues of *Television Factbook*. 1977: *Television Digest*.

the degree of cross-ownership between cable and older existing media, although most systems owned by telephone or television firms are not in the same market as the other media properties, thus avoiding the local cross-media monopoly issue.

A more important trend in analyzing cable ownership is the increasing importance of the multiple system operator, or MSO. Table 7.6 provides a rough approximation of industry concentration by the four and eight largest MSOs over a decade. No clear trends are evident, with about 20% of the business controlled by the top four firms, and about 30% by the top eight firms. Approximate 1977 data show small declines from 1976. But, given the rapid increase in overall industry size, these top firms have had to grow accordingly just to maintain their position of control. Much of this growth has come about by a process of acquisition and merger rather than system building.[25]

Table 7.7 identifies the largest multiple system operators and their growth patterns. The growth of the long-time MSO leader, TelePrompter, has been from a process of acquisition as well as system construction. Note its dramatic spurts of growth in 1971, 1974, 1975 which all mark acquisitions, not all of which are detailed here. With one or two exceptions, system size rankings have changed only a little over the period included here. Overall concentration has also stayed level, with the largest eight firms accounting for 35.6% of all cable subscribers in 1978, down from the 39.0% of 1975.

Table 7.6 Four and Eight Largest Cable Systems Operations, Selected Years, 1965-1976

	Percent of all Cable Subscribers Accounted for by Largest:	
	Four Firms	Eight Firms
1965 (January 1)	19.6%	28.2%
1970 (January 1)	18.3	28.6
1972 (July 1)	23.3	35.0
1974 (June)	23.1	33.8
1976 (September)	22.9	36.8

Sources: 1976-72, based on Martin Perry, "Recent Trends in the Structure of the Cable Television Industry," (unpublished "discussion paper" at Stanford University, May 1974), pp. 5-11, updated with figures from Sterling and Haight (1978), table 290-B.

Table 7.7 Largest Cable Television MSOs, by Subscribers, 1970-1978 (subscriber figures in thousands)

Eight Largest Cable Operators, 1978	1978	1977	1976	1975	1974	1973	1972	1971	1970
1. Teleprompter	1,161	1,050	1,070	1,084	831	680	658	535	243
2. Time Inc. (American Television and Communications Corp.)[a]	750	N.A.	189	188	N.A.	N.A.	118	106	106
3. Warner Communications, Inc.	600	554	550	523	405	360	342	N.A.	N.A.
4. Tele-Communications, Inc.	572	557	551	539	400	320	249	142	N.A.
5. Cox Broadcasting[b]	560	437	413	375	240	245	242	197	190
6. Times Mirror Co.	412	82	78	N.A.	48	–	–	–	–
7. Viacom International, Inc.	359	324	304	290	254	190	183	150	150
8. Sammons Communications Corp.	322	286	286	271	245	200	200	N.A.	N.A.
Following were among top eight in years prior to 1978									
Communications Properties, Inc.	(sold to Times Mirror)	277	255	247	190	N.A.	154	N.A.	N.A.
American Television and Communications Corp. (ATC)	(sold to Time Inc.)	585	550	490	375	275	264	180	112
Cablecom General, Inc.	198	169	166	187	154	170	150	123	123
Cypress Communications Corp.	(sold to Warner Communications)							120	120
Jerrold Corp.	(sold to Sammons Communications)							100	N.A.
H & B Communications Corp.	(merged with TelePrompter)								242
Total, eight largest each year	4,632	4,070	3,979	3,819	2,940	2,440	2,292	1,873	1,286
Percent of Total Subscribers	35.6	34.2	36.8	39.0	33.8	33.4	38.2	35.3	28.6

a. Time Inc. sold its cable operation to ATC in 1973, then acquired ATC in 1978.

b. Sale to General Electric Co. pending in 1979. Combined with the 156,000 subscribers to General Electric Cablevision, the new MSO would be third largest in 1978 with about 720,000 subscribers.

Sources: 1970-76: Sterling and Haight (1978), table 290-B. 1977-78: Television Digest and press reports.

General Ownership Regulations: The FCC first expressed concern over system ownership in 1968 when it announced a series of overall limitations. The commission proposed a 50 system limit on ownership, assuming each system was made up of 1000 subscribers or more. If other media interests were held (one television station, two radio stations or two newspapers), the ownership limit would be cut in half, to 25 stations. As an option, the commission felt no single ownership entity should control more than about 2 million subscribers. The commission was clearly trying to control the situation before growth would force a policy of divestiture with a later rule-making.[26] Despite that feeling, however, no final action was ever taken on the proposal, and the question is still open. One reason for the lack of action has been the slower-than-expected growth of cable, and recognition of the fact that such large entities may be the best source of needed finance to enable such growth, especially in major urban areas. The House Subcommittee on Communications report of 1976 felt any action on such limits should be held off until a "separations" policy was clarified (see below) and that in the meantime, both the commission and the Department of Justice should maintain interest in and collect data on merger-acquisition activity in cable.[27]

Likewise, in 1976 the commission dismissed as premature any rules to limit or ban foreign ownership of cable systems — a distinct departure from the old and clear rules banning such ownership in broadcasting.[28]

More fundamental, but as yet only a proposal, is the "separations" approach to cable system ownership. Briefly stated, the idea is to separate ownership and control of the physical facilities of cable distribution from production of program material to be carried on those facilities. Entities could own one aspect of a given system or the other, but not both. The FCC's 1972 "definitive" rules raised this possibility for the future, contending that until cable grew to maturity, such a policy would only retard cable development.[29] Two years later, the Cabinet Committee on Cable Communications built its entire series of recommendations for cable around a separations principle, but again, only after cable reached a certain point (not made totally clear) of growth. The report of the committee made clear that other kinds of control of content and economics "would not be adequate to prevent anti-competitive behavior."[30] In 1976, the House Subcommittee report analyzed the issue, strongly recommending that Congressional action should formally require a separations policy no more than 10 years from such a law's enactment. Otherwise, the issue would be left to the FCC's discretion, which has only said it would re-examine the question at some unspecified time in the future, making it more difficult to demand divestiture at a later date.[31] If such a policy is put into effect, the various policy reports generally agree that cross-ownership of cable and other media would not necessarily need to be limited.[32] But for any separations policy to be made effective, some clear "trigger" event or date is needed in advance, such as 50% cable penetration in 50% of television households or a set future date.[33]

Cross-Ownership Concerns: Lacking any active separations approach, the commission has developed several rules limiting cross-ownership on both a national and local level, drawing from its experience with broadcasting. The question came up first in 1965 when the FCC considered, but rejected, a rule banning ownership of cable systems by television stations.[34] Five years later, the FCC reversed itself and banned local cross-ownerships of cable systems and TV stations (if the former was in any place within the B contour of the station) to "further the commission's policy favoring diversity of control over local mass communications media."[35] Existing cross-ownerships were not allowed to stand (a break with usual FCC practice), but were ordered to divest. But over the years, many waivers to this divestiture order were granted and the deadline was pushed back.

Finally, in 1975, the FCC decided waivers would be brought into line with newspaper-broadcast cross-ownership policy (see broadcasting chapter) by requiring divestiture only in very concentrated markets. The commission concluded: "While our concerns with economic competition and media diversity extend throughout a local television station's service area, the harshness of the divestiture remedy appears to us only warranted in those situations where there would otherwise be a virtual monopoly over local video expression."[36] Likewise, the commission has sometimes considered, but has not seen the necessity of, adopting rules banning local cross-ownership of radio stations and cable, or newspapers and cable systems.[37]

Two other types of cross-ownership, one local and the other national, have been banned, however. Since 1970 local telephone companies have been prohibited from gaining control of cable systems within their service areas.[38] Because telephone service is also a monopoly within a given area, the FCC expressed concern that phone firms could too easily pre-empt cable operation, especially as the telephone companies usually control the poles on which cable companies string their wires to their subscribers. Furthermore, "telephone company pre-emption [of cable service] in a community tends to extend, without need or justification, the telephone company's monopoly position to broadband cable facilities and the new and different services such facilities are expected to be providing in the future."[39]

A 1970 rule also banned television networks from control of cable systems anywhere in the country. The feeling here was that such ownership would hinder expansion of possible cable networks, there being a natural conflict of interest between network broadcast audiences and cable audiences, and that the networks were already clearly dominant in their own industry. Given the latter point alone, the FCC felt the networks might serve to hold back expansion of cable to protect their large broadcast role and investment.[40]

Further controls over cable system ownership do not appear likely as long as: 1) there is generally adequate channel capacity to allow for expansion of programming "voices" reaching the public, 2) there are sufficient separate firms providing program material to cable systems; 3) there are sufficient different means of cable networking (satellites, microwave lines, etc.) available; 4) examples of outright system abuse of the community monopoly position are absent; and 5) competing systems of pay cable are available for local carriage.

In cable as in broadcasting, however, there is a dearth of minority group owned systems. Late in 1977, of an estimated more than 7000 communities with cable service, only six were minority owned, not counting one cable-radio system begun that year. The first minority system had begun operations in Gary, Ind., in 1973.[41] Government policy to expand this role in cable closely parallels efforts in broadcasting.

PAY CABLE TELEVISION

Provision of a broadcast service requiring payment by the listener is not a new idea — pay radio schemes existed in the 1930s.[42] In the late 1940s and early 1950s, a major controversy in the growing television industry questioned whether over-the-air pay television stations should be authorized. Under strong pressure from broadcasters and the theatre industry, the pay threat was beaten back, at least long enough that by the time pay broadcast stations were authorized by the FCC in 1968, much of the initial rationale for such stations seemed to have passed and the threat was no longer important.[43] As it turned out, that long battle was merely over a side issue, for pay systems reappeared in the early 1970s in a totally different format.

Pay cable systems have been described as "old wine in new bottles,"[44] referring to the long history of the pay idea, combined with its more recent marriage with cable television systems as part of the delivery process. Pay cable, as discussed here, refers to a "premium" channel within a cable system. Viewers are required to pay a per-program, or extra per-month fee for reception of the premium service. As a rule, the pay service provides movies, sporting events, and other special programming not carried on either regular broadcasting or cable. There are no advertising interruptions on material presented on pay cable.

Pay Cable's Short History

The first regulatory actions taken on pay cable systems came long before any such systems existed. Until 1969 such operations were authorized by the FCC only on an experimental basis. Two such experiments had drawn strong broadcaster and theater opposition: a 1957 cable operation in Bartlesville, Ok., and a larger commercial operation in southern California in 1962-64 known as Subscription Television, which was ended by a state-wide referendum, itself later ruled unconstitutional.[45] Although the FCC issued an order in 1969 calling for unlimited programming approaches on cable, under continuing broadcast industry pressure the commission retreated to a 1970 rule severely limiting pay cable systems to the same kinds of content restrictions which had been placed on over-the-air pay television. The basis for the rules was the "anti-siphoning" principle intended to protect programming on free broadcast television from being purchased by the potentially greater buying power of a subscriber-supported system of broadcasting or cablecasting.[46] Although challenged on this decision, the commission did not come to any final decision for nearly five years. In the meantime the restrictions stood, while the pay cable industry became more than just a potential medium.

A parallel set of rules, the "definitive" 1972 cable rules discussed above, are thought by some to mark the real birth of pay cable, as they provided the important impetus to its growth. In the rules, the FCC encouraged local origination by cable systems to supplement signal importation, and allowed lease of extra cable channels to programmers other than the system operator, such outside firms including potential pay cable operations.[47] Late that same year, pay cable began regular operation when Home Box Office, a Time Inc. subsidiary, initiated service to Wilkes-Barre, Pa. Right at the start, HBO established four principles which guided operation:

1) a monthly per-channel fee, rather than the technically complex per-program fee most pay operators had used experimentally earlier;

2) affiliation with the local cable operator rather than an outright lease of a channel;

3) a commitment to a combination of live sports, informative and instructive material as well as entertainment — mainly feature films; and

4) transmission of the programming from a central studio by use of

common carrier microwave transmission facilities, rather than distribution by videotape.[48]

Over the next several months other systems began operation: Theater-Vision in Sarasota, Fla., Warner Communications "Gridtronic" system in four communities in the mid-Atlantic area, two systems in California, and several others. By August 1973, less than a year after pay cable had begun operations, the operating systems served about 35,000 subscribers with primarily sports and film entertainment, using a variety of distribution and payment systems.[49] By May 1974 there were some 45 pay cable operations serving about 67,000 subscribers — and Home Box Office had already emerged as the largest single pay cable distributor.[50]

In two important ways, 1975 turned out to be a pivotal year for pay cable. On March 20th, the FCC finally issued its final pay cable rules, which had been in limbo since 1970. Continuing on its protectionist approach (to make cable of all kinds clearly subsidiary to over-the-air broadcasting services), the commission issued detailed and complicated rules limiting what films and sporting events could be carried on pay systems. The rules were designed to protect what "free" television was then presenting in order to prevent siphoning by pay cable systems. The rules were broader and stricter than necessary in the eyes of some observers and were appealed.[51] The rules were overturned by the U.S. Court of Appeals on March 25, 1977, the Supreme Court declined to review in October, and thus any and all rules limiting pay cable content were lifted.[52] In retrospect, then, the seeds for the complete freeing of pay cable from content controls were sown by the strict FCC rules of 1975.

Table 7.8 clearly shows the impact of the court rulings. Although pay subscribers were growing in number up to 1977, the jump in 1978 was dramatic and such expansion is likely to be maintained in the early 1980s.

On April 10, 1975, just a few weeks after the FCC action, HBO announced it would be converting its distribution from land-based microwave systems to use of a domestic satellite, providing two channels of material 12 hours per day. Microwave was slow and expensive. Other options were a video-tape-exchange approach or reverting to several regional hubs rather than one center for a national pay cable system. HBO implemented the satellite system on September 30, 1975 in Florida, expanding to other systems over the next few years. That this was the key to freeing pay cable to expand beyond single systems or regions to true national distribution was made evident by the industry status late in 1975: 32 of the top 50 MSOs either already had or were planning to soon carry pay cable options, and 18 of the 35

Table 7.8   Growth of Pay Cable Systems and Penetration: 1973-1978

| | Pay Cable Systems | | | Pay Cable System Subscribers | |
	Estimated Number	Percent of all Cable Systems	Estimated Number	As Percent of Subscribers on Systems Offering Pay Cable	As Percent of all Cable Television Subscribers
1973	10	N.A.	18,400	N.A.	N.A.
1974	45	1%	67,000	N.A.	1%
1975	75	2	265,000	N.A.	3
1976	253	7	794,000	24%	7
1977	459	12	1,174,000	22	9
1978	790	21	2,352,000	31	18

Source: Knowledge Industry Publications, Inc., based on data published by Paul Kagan Associates, in census issues of *The Pay TV Newsletter.* All data as of June 30 except 1974 (May 15) and 1973 (April 1).

largest single cable systems were in a similar status.[53] The activation of the satellite option cleared the way for pay cable expansion — and helped revive general cable interest as well. Meanwhile, over-the-air pay television was undergoing something of a renaissance, with several in New Jersey (aimed at New York) and in Los Angeles.

Satellite competition for HBO came only in March of 1978, when Viacom's Showtime service (formed in mid-1976) began operations and quickly became the closest competitor to HBO's dominance of the industry. The rivalry was enhanced later in the year when TelePrompTer purchased a 50% interest in Showtime and switched its 280,000 HBO customers to Showtime in 1979. HBO itself had gone into the black financially only in the third quarter of 1977, evidence of the heavy start-up costs of pay cable systems using satellite. Rapid expansion of satellite distribution after 1977 was encouraged by changes in FCC requirements and mass production which helped to drop the cost of receiving earth stations from $100,000 each to about a third of that level, thus enabling cable systems of smaller size to partake of pay cable options. By late 1978, more than 800 earth stations were operating, carrying pay cable (and other) signals to cable systems across the country, serving some 5.4 million subscribers.[54]

Two important further regulatory developments came in 1978 and 1979, providing pay cable's final liberation. In April 1979 the U.S. Supreme Court upheld an Appeals Court ruling striking down the FCC mandatory access rules, thus freeing cable systems to provide their own premium channel programming as well as carry national or regional services. The commission was again judged by the court to have exceeded its authority — and in this case to have violated the First Amendment, because with cable the spectrum limitations of over-the-air broadcasting do not exist.[55]   Combined with the 1977 decision overturning the pay cable content regulations, the commission's controls on cable were substantially undermined. In a 1978 decision, the Appeals Court sustained FCC pre-emption of regulation of pay cable.[56] Given the dearth of supported national regulations, the effect of the decision was to ensure that no state or local rules could be made to limit pay cable expansion while federal rule-making was unlikely unless enacted by Congress.

Ownership Concentration in Pay Cable: The important ownership question in pay cable is on the regional or national level of control of the distributing services which supply the pay channels of local cable systems. Table 7.9 summarizes the development of the top distributors over the past four years highlighting several aspects of the business. First, Time Inc. clearly dominates the industry and has from the start — especially taking into account the fact that Telemation Program Services became a subsidiary of HBO (and thus of Time Inc.) in mid-1976. TPS operates on a tape basis supplementing the satellite-based HBO. Time Inc. thus controls about 80% of pay cable distribution. The second-largest distributing firm, Showtime, is also owned by two giants in this field. Begun by Viacom, in 1977, ownership of the service became a shared operation between Viacom (the sixth largest MSO) and TelePrompter (the largest MSO), when the former sold a 50% interest in late 1978. The ownership change pulled some 280,000 pay cable homes on 89 TelePrompter-owned systems out of HBO and into the Showtime network.[57]

But both systems continued to grow apace. By the beginning of 1979, HBO claimed over 2 million subscribers on 731 systems with coverage of nearly every state, while Showtime served about 600,000 subscribers on some 240 systems in 43 states.[58]   PRISM, operating primarily in the Philadelphia area, claimed some 50,000 subscribers in its three state coverage. On the other hand, the growth of these few firms was beginning to squeeze out others. Late in 1978, Optical Systems, a perennial money-loser with a shrinking proportion of the business, announced it was selling its cable interests to concentrate on over-the-air pay TV ventures.[59]   Similar consolidation may be expected of other marginal and local firms in the near future as the national satellite-based services expand their domination.

DISCUSSION

By the end of the 1970s, cable television was throwing off a decade-long lethargy, and predictions about its growth were the most optimistic since the mid-1960s. Paced by the profit potential of pay cable channels as well as by a broad loosening of regulatory constraints,

Table 7.9 Development of Leading Pay-Cable Distributing Companies: 1975-1978

Name of Distributor	June 30, 1978		June 30, 1977		June 30, 1976		April 1, 1975	
	Subscribers	Percent of all Pay Subscribers	Subscribers	Percent of all Pay Subscribers	Subscribers	Percent of all Pay Subscribers	Subscribers	Percent of all Pay Subscribers
1. Home Box Office (Time Inc.)	1,545,000	66%	1,046,400	64%	475,000	62%	90,000	48%
2. Telemation Program Services (owned by HBO since mid-1976)	284,157	12	239,300	15	176,000	23	33,000	17
3. Showtime (Viacom/TelePrompter)	154,900	7	91,600	6	not operating		not operating	
4. Optical Systems (Pioneer Systems Inc.)	27,000	nil	29,013	2	49,000	6	50,000	27
5. Pay TV Services	33,800	1	26,000	2	12,700	2	6,300	3
6. Warner Star Channel	N.A.		N.A.		34,000	5	8,000	4
7. Best Vision	33,400	1	25,145	2	4,600	1	not operating	
8. PRISM	34,000	1	23,700	1	not operating		not operating	
9. Hollywood Home Theatre	77,214	3	72,229	4	not operating		not operating	
System concentration (cumulative percentage of pay cable subscribers)	8 Systems	91%	8 Systems	96%	6 Systems	99%	5 Systems	99%

N.A. Not Available.

Source: Knowledge Industry Publications, Inc., based on data published by Paul Kagan Associates, in census issues of *The Pay TV Newsletter*. All figures are estimates.

frequently voiced predictions for cable penetration were on the order of 30% by the very early 1980s and half the country's homes by mid-decade. New applications of cable systems to two-way interactive options, once dismissed as excessively expensive and unrealistic, were being successfully experimented with in several communities — including the landmark QUBE operation of Warner Cable in Columbus, Ohio.[60]

The same localism issues that have been part of the underlying policies in broadcast regulation pervade the cable business. It was founded largely as a response to the limitations imposed by broadcast television allocations. Yet only two-thirds of the systems today have any local origination facilities and only 17% can provide live local programming. Clearly, cable has not been used to supplement local programming in areas that do not have their own broadcast stations.

Instead, the major developments appear to be in carrying more national programming, via pay channels, the traditional broadcast network programs, or new syndicated programming and "superstations" that are local in the area of origination but are transmitted by satellite to cable systems all over the country, such as Atlanta's WTCH-TV.

Ironically, Federal Communications Commission efforts to diversify ownership concentration in broadcasting may well be substantially undone by developments in cable television. For one thing, the expansion of cable, and especially the expansion of satellite-distributed pay cable systems, is already providing a potential "network" operation parallel to the broadcast networks. While ownership diversity in broadcasting is increasingly a matter of regulation, the only effective ownership controls in cable are limited to restrictions on local cross-ownership between TV and telephone companies and cable systems (with many waivers being granted even here) while national ownership control is limited to prevention of television network control of cable systems. There is no ownership limitation on MSO size, and no ownership limit on pay cable distribution — and those are the likely arenas where the control of cable's future will be decided.

As a result, many of the companies developing cable systems are also either current or potential suppliers of programming or information. Warner, UA-Columbia Cablevision, Viacom, TelePrompTer, Times Mirror, General Electric and Time Inc. are among the firms that have cable or pay television businesses and like the broadcast networks are also in a position to provide transmission facilities as well as content. Unlike the networks, however, which are limited to five VHF outlets, in the absence of cable regulation, MSOs can have extensive cable holdings around the country as well as supply the programming content. Potentially, then, they may accomplish what the broadcast networks have been prohibited from doing: controlling the distribution as well as the content. There are anticompetitive implications should this happen, not unlike the situation of the motion picture distributors owning chains of movie theatres, until they came under antitrust attack and sold off the outlet part of the combination. This potential was clearly recognized in the separations policy debate in Congress, but so far nothing has been done to implement it.

In just half a decade, the economic future of pay cable has become a game only giants can play — and others are easing out. While the small local cable system operator is still a force in this business, the profit potential of pay channels and other economic forces are converting cable into an MSO-dominated business just as television is group-owner dominated. It is possible that within a decade of renewed cable expansion we may really face the question of what early cable studies termed "The Wired Nation."[61] The dominance of commercial network television may be broken by the wired distribution system, which combining cable, microwave, and satellite delivery, provides more choice to viewers. What remains to be seen is whether the increased number of channels will actually provide a greater variety of programming, although logic says that this should be the case.

In a few markets, cable systems have devoted one or two channels to local access programming, although they can no longer be forced to do so. In effect, the cable operator in this mode serves as a common carrier, providing the means of transmission to anyone who cares to use it. As cable develops a greater national penetration, this common carrier function may develop into an altogether new means of communication. By setting up a tariff schedule, cable operators on a network basis may find a new source of revenue in selling time to individuals or businesses to transmit their messages to a national, regional or local cable market, but exercising no control over program content.

But whether overall ownership is diversified sufficiently to allow entry of important new ownership voices such that content diversity is truly increased remains in serious question. As the 1980s begin, the trend in cable and pay cable suggests that centralized control, and a resultant emphasis on the same kind of entertainment material of older film and television media, will continue for the immediate future.

FOOTNOTES

1. See, for example, Mary Louise Hollowell, ed. *Cable Handbook 1975-76* (Washington: Communications Press, 1975); Mary Louise Hollowell, ed. *The Cable/Broadband Communications Book 1977-1978* (Washington: Communications Press, 1977); and Walter S. Baer, *Cable Television: A Handbook for Decision-Making* (New York: Crane, Russak, 1974). The many earlier general guides, and

even some of the Baer book, are made obsolete by drastic changes in FCC regulations and developments in the cable industry which are briefly outlined here.

2. For one recent guide, see Felix Chin, *Cable Television: A Comprehensive Bibliography* (New York: IFI/Plenum, 1978). For a good annotated guide to the earlier literature, see Don R. LeDuc, *Cable Television and the FCC: A Crisis in Media Control* (Philadelphia, Temple University Press, 1973), pp. 265-282.

3. The best recent policy discussion, a bit out of date in spots, is U.S. Congress, House of Representatives, Committee on Interstate and Foreign Commerce, Subcommittee on Communications. *Cable Television: Promise versus Regulatory Performance*, 94th Cong., 2nd Sess. (January 1976), a staff report of 110 pp. (hereafter "House report"), and Bruce M. Owen, "Cable Television: The Framework of Regulation," in U.S. Senate, Committee on Governmental Affairs, *Study on Federal Regulation, Appendix to Volume VI, Framework for Regulation*, 95th Cong., 2nd Sess. (December 1978), pp. 349-389.

4. For the early history of cable, see Mary Alice Mayer Phillips, *CATV: A History of Community Antenna Television* (Evanston, Ill.: Northwestern University Press, 1972), and LeDuc (see note 2).

5. 26 FCC 403 (1959).

6. 32 FCC 459 (1962).

7. 38 FCC 683 (1965).

8. 2 FCC 2d 725 (1966).

9. *U.S.* v. *Southwestern Cable* 392 US 159 (1968).

10. *Fortnightly Corp.* v. *United Artists* 392 US 390 (1968).

11. House report, p. 12

12. Most of the Rand studies are listed and discussed in the bibliography in LeDuc.

13. *On the Cable: The Television of Abundance: Report of the Sloan Commission on Cable Communications* (New York: McGraw-Hill, 1971).

14. 36 FCC 2d 143 (1972).

15. The Cabinet Committee on Cable Communications. *Cable: Report to the President*. (Washington: GPO, 1974).

16. Research and Policy Committee of the Committee for Economic Development. *Broadcasting and Cable Television: Policies for Diversity and Change* (New York: CED, 1975).

17. See note 3.

18. Paul W. MacAvoy, ed. *Deregulation of Cable Television* (Washington: American Enterprise Institute for Public Policy Research, 1977), part of the series "Ford Administration Papers on Regulatory Reform."

19. Copyright Revision Act of 1976, P.L. 94-553 (also Title 17 of U.S. Code).

20. *Midwest Video* v. *FCC* F 2d (D.C. Cir. 1978). Often referred to as Midwest Video II. See also footnote 55.

21. Steven R. Rivkin. *A New Guide to Federal Cable Television Regulations* (Cambridge, Mass.: MIT Press, 1978).

22. See, for example, *On the Cable*, p. 2.

23. Charles C. Woodward Jr., *Cable Television: Acquisition and Operation of CATV Systems* (New York: McGraw-Hill, 1974).

24. See Walter S. Baer, et al. *Cable Television: Franchising Considerations.* (New York: Crane, Russak, 1974), and Rivkin, pp. 36-42 for an updating.

25. Martin Perry, "Recent Trends in the Structure of the Cable Television Industry," (unpublished discussion paper, Stanford University, May 1974), p. 11.

26. 33 FR 19028 (1968) as discussed in the House report, pp. 91-92.

27. House report, pp. 91-92.

28. 59 FCC 2d 723 as noted in Rivkin, p. 98.

29. House report, p. 89.

30. *Cable: Report to the President*, p. 30.

31. House report, p. 91.

32. See, for example, Cable: *Report to the President*, pp. 30-33.

33. Owen, p. 377.

34. House report, p. 93.

35. Ibid., p. 94.

36. 50 FCC 2d 1046 as reported in Rivkin, p. 97.

37. House report, p. 94.

38. 21 FCC 2d 307 as cited in House report, p. 94.

39. 21 FCC 2d at 324 as cited in House report, p. 95.

40. House report, p. 92.

41. White House press release on minority ownership of broadcasting and cable television, January 31, 1978, and Marion Hayes Hull, "Economic Potential for Minorities – Obstacles and Opportunities," in Hollowell (1977), p. 80.

42. Christopher H. Sterling and John M. Kittross, *Stay Tuned: A Concise History of American Broadcasting* (Belmont, Calif.: Wadsworth Publishing, 1978), p. 277.

43. 33 FR 19104 (December 21, 1968).

44. John R. Barrington, "Pay Cable – An Old Idea Whose Time Has Come," in Hollowell (1977), p. 119.

45. Walter S. Baer and Carl Pilnick, "Pay Television at the Crossroads," (Santa Monica, Calif.: Rand Corp. P-5159, April 1974), p. 4.

46. 23 FCC 2d 825 (1970) as in House report, pp. 62-63.

47. Richard Warren Rappaport, "The Emergence of Subscription Cable Television and its Role in Communications," *Federal Communications Bar Journal* 29:301-334 (1976), at 305.

48. Barrington, p. 122.

49. Baer-Pilnick, pp: 10-11.

50. See Christopher H. Sterling and Timothy R. Haight, *The Mass Media: Aspen Institute Guide to Communication Industry Trends* (New York: Praeger, 1978), table 190-D, citing information from Paul Kagan.

51. House report, pp. 64-68.

52. *The New York Times* (March 26, 1977), p. 1; and *Television Digest* (March 28, 1977), p. 1.

53. *Barrons* (November 24, 1975), p. 11.

54. Arthur Hill, "CATV and Satellites: The Sky is the Limit," *Satellite Communications* (December 1978), pp. 20-21.

55. See note 20. The Supreme Court decision was reported in "Justices Rule FCC Exceeds Authority in Requiring Public Access to Cable TV," *The Wall Street Journal*, April 3, 1979, p. 8.

56. *Brookhaven Cable TV Inc.* v. *Kelly* F 2d (Second Circuit, 1978).

57. *Videonews* (September 27, 1978), p. 6.

58. *Videonews* (December 20, 1978), p. 7.

59. *The Videocassette & CATV Newsletter* (November 1978), p. 10.

60. For analyses of Warner Cable's "Qube" system in Columbus, Ohio, see *Television Digest* (October 30, 1978), pp. 4-5; and *Broadcasting* (July 31, 1978), pp. 27-31.

61. Herman W. Land Associates. *Television and the Wired City* (Washington: National Association of Broadcasters, July 1968). The broader term was hinted at even more obviously in Ralph Lee Smith's *The Wired Nation: Cable TV – The Electronic Communications Highway* (New York: Harper & Row, 1972), part of which appeared as a special issue of *The Nation* in 1970.

8

Conclusion: How Few Is Too Few?

There are rarely simple solutions to complex questions. This is certainly true in dealing with the nature and concentration of ownership in the mass media. Part of the complexity is that there are at least three different types of combinations of firms taking place in the mass communications industry. First, there are horizontal mergers, creating chain owners of newspapers, magazines, cable systems, book publishers or broadcast stations. These clearly tend to reduce the number of direct competitors in a particular segment of the media. Second, there are vertical mergers, creating integrated producers, such as where a book publisher also owns a book distributor, a printer or an interest in a paper manufacturer. These have been the least frequent and may be fairly said to be of little concern to those watching the merger scene. Finally, there are the conglomerate mergers. Here, combinations of different media are brought together under a single entity or become part of a large firm that is engaged in many different types of businesses. Time Inc., Times Mirror Co. and CBS Inc. would be considered media conglomerates while Westinghouse and Gulf + Western are among the true cross-industry conglomerates.

It is the activity of the conglomerates that most alarms those who see a dangerous trend in media ownership patterns. Former journalist and articulate media critic Ben H. Bagdikian sees the pattern of control being compounded "by two new developments in media ownership. One is the inclusion of journalism and other media companies [sic] in large conglomerate corporations that are also in other industries, industries that regularly are reported — or not reported — by the same corporation's media properties." The other "is a pattern of several traditionally competing media coming under ownership by the same parent corporation,"[1] thus consolidating book, magazine, perhaps motion picture and television rights in a single firm.

NEED FOR NEW DEFINITIONS

Bagdikian's observations give rise to two central clarifications which must be made before it is possible to propose any conclusions about the nature or degree of this concentration in the mass communications industry. First, what is meant by "concentration"? Second, what are the relevant markets in determining concentration ratios?

What Is Concentration?

People use concentration in two ways when discussing media ownership. The more traditional understanding is that used in antitrust theory and serves as the basis for current standards and law. The second, broader, concept incorporates more general economic, political and social values.

The legal standard seeks to determine the degree to which the sales of an industry are attributable to a few, large sellers. It assumes that in instances of such concentration, the leading firms in the industry will earn higher profit than would firms in competitive industries. Kaysen and Turner, in a survey published in 1959, indicated that a type I oligopoly industry was defined by the eight largest firms having a 50% share of sales and the largest 20 firms at least 75%. A type II oligopoly was a 33% share by the eight largest and under 75% by the 20 largest.[2] By this definition, they said, two-thirds of all U.S. industries are concentrated. But except for motion picture production and distribution, the mass media industries would not be considered unduly oligopolistic by this standard. From an antitrust viewpoint, an industry that reaches the type I stage provides firms in that industry the ability to charge prices and make profits above competitive levels and to misallocate resources.

Those concerned with concentration in the media, however, are not as concerned with prices or profit levels. Rather, the issue here is more with the lessening of the number of persons who control the flow of information: the number of gatekeepers. There is the fear that the ideas that reach the public can be manipulated by a handful of executives in a few corporations.

The key question then becomes: How few is too few? Here, the traditional antitrust view of concentration and the broader social concerns are at loggerheads. Clearly, the acceptable number of gate-keepers would be far greater than the number that would trip antitrust action over control of prices and supply. To implement a policy taking into account the special concerns of society in maintaining a maximum number of diverse media voices would require a special set of standards unique to the mass communications industry.

What Is the Relevant Market?

It is misleading to suggest that all book publishers compete with one another, since they deal with many different types of books directed at various markets. Publishers of elementary and high school textbooks, for example, are not competing with publishers of mass market romance books nor are specialized professional publishers vying for consumer dollars with juvenile trade books producers. Similarly, much of the competition within each medium is less than the number of firms or titles would indicate. The existence of almost 1800 general interest daily newspapers itself says nothing about true competition since only a handful compete in any given geographic market. The 10,000 periodical titles published do not really overlap in the way that, say, toothpaste brands compete nationally head to head. In many ways, individual media properties are distinct enough from each other that each one has its own oligopolistic markets: news magazines readers really have a choice of only three national periodicals. Movie goers are limited by what the theaters in the area are showing. And an individual looking for a book on needlepoint is not concerned with the existence of the other 450,000 titles in print.

However, just as we may have to recast the operational definition of concentration from that of the objective standards of antitrust law, so may relevant markets for the media have to be reformulated in recognition of the changing nature of the mass communications industry. It is myopic to be concerned with concentration in the television business, the newspaper business or any given segment if what we are truly concerned with is promoting diversity of conduits for information and knowledge. We should be less concerned with deter-mining the threshold of concentration for each individual medium, while giving added emphasis to the number of owners in the mass communications industry overall. From this perspective, the news-weekly magazines have direct competition from all newspapers, as well as local and national television news programs and all news radio stations. Motion picture distributors clearly compete with television producers, but also with book publishers and certain periodicals. Special interest magazines, already knocking heads in price with mass market paperback books, may increasingly find themselves covering the same topics and even competing for advertiser dollars with video disc recordings and programs distributed by cable operators.

Perhaps no development serves to illustrate the increased and real intermedia competitiveness than the effects of the extended newspaper strikes in New York, Philadelphia, St. Louis and other cities in recent years. Before radio, no newspapers meant no regular news or advertising sources. Now, even a city like New York can lose the services of its three major newspapers for three months (August to early November 1978) and cause barely a ripple. Advertisers turned to television, radio, local magazines and zoned editions of national magazines. Consumers made use of all-news radio stations, the national news magazines, and the extended newscasts on local television. Retailers reported little impact on sales. This is not to say that people did not miss the unique features that newspapers provide, but with the wide array of media available, information kept flowing. Even residents of smaller towns and cities would find many of the same options.

TRENDS IN CONSUMPTION OF THE MASS MEDIA

Thus, a new definition of the media industry is called for because the industry itself has changed. For most of our history, the printed word was the only form of mass communications. First books, then newspaper-type publications and periodicals. Only in the 20th century have truly new and competing forms of mass communications technology been developed: film, radio and television broadcast, now distribution by cable, video tape and disc.

For those who create ideas, this profusion of alternatives has lessened their reliance on print media: some individuals whose creativity in the past would have found an outlet only in the printed word are now harnessing their ideas to visual media. This, then, reduces our reliance on newspapers, books or magazines and even radio for information. Perhaps it should not be surprising that many cities can only support a single newspaper, as the need for the newspaper, while still great, is mitigated by other media that did not exist in the heyday of the newspaper in 1900.

The development of new media has resulted in changing patterns of consumer and advertiser expenditures in their media purchases, although the relative amount of money expended by both sources has remained remarkably constant over the years. This phenomenon has given rise to what Charles Scripps calls the "constancy hypothesis,"[3] which is verified in Tables 8.1 and 8.2.

Since 1933, the amount of money that consumers have spent on media, in the form of purchases of newspapers, magazines, books; television and radio set purchases and repairs; and on movie admissions, has remained level as a percentage of personal consumption expenditures. But the composition of those expenditures has shifted along with the introduction of new media. The proportion of expenditures on newspapers and magazines has remained constant since 1940 and was greater in 1976 than in 1929. The rise in 1933 may well be an aberration caused by Depression-related declines in purchases of radios. Book expenditures have returned to the level of the 1950s after soaring in the 1960s, no doubt helped along by massive government programs for schools and libraries.

Although audio-visual media account for a similar percentage of expenditures in 1976 as in 1929, the overall trend since 1945 has been upward. Within this category, however, a drastic switch has taken place, as relative expenditures for movie admissions have dropped dramatically in concert with the sizeable increases on television and radio receivers. The most profound change came in the 1945 to 1950 period, as the end of the war and the introduction of television channeled funds away from movies and into the broadcast area. Another noticeable switch occurred in the 1960s, as color television produced a new wave of consumer investment. In the 1970s, movie admissions began to increase their share of expenditures as well, as spending for repairs of television and radio sets have been cut in half from their relative 1960 level.

Except for book publishers and theatrical film makers, advertisers provide all or most of the financial support for mass media businesses. As with consumer expenditures, advertising outlays have tended to remain at a constant proportion of the Gross National Product, staying near 2.00% of total goods and services. However, as seen in Table 8.2, the broadcast media have accounted for an increasing share, as first radio and then television drew a considerably greater share from the older print media.

Implications

Given the fixed proportion of consumer and advertiser expenditures that appear to be devoted to the media over an extended period, regardless of the condition of the economy and the number of mass

Table 8.1   Percentage of Consumer Spending on Print and Audio-Visual Media, Selected Years, 1929-1976

	Media Expend. as % of Per. Consump. Exp.	Newspapers, Magazines, Sheet Music	Books & Maps	Total Print	Radio, TV Recv'rs, Records, Instruments	Radio & TV Repairs	Movie Admis.	Total AV Media [a]
1929	3.37%	20.65%	11.86%	32.51%	38.85%	1.00%	27.64%	67.49%
1933	2.76	33.20	12.04	45.24	15.45	1.11	38.19	54.75
1940	2.94	28.26	11.23	39.43	23.70	1.53	35.27	60.50
1945	2.82	28.66	15.44	44.10	10.22	2.61	43.07	55.90
1950	3.25	23.92	10.78	34.70	38.74	4.53	22.02	65.29
1955	2.94	25.10	11.64	36.74	38.53	6.97	17.81	63.31
1960	2.67	25.32	15.06	40.38	39.39	9.25	10.98	59.62
1965	3.00	22.23	15.98	38.21	46.61	8.00	7.19	61.80
1970	2.97	22.33	18.75	41.08	45.38	7.20	6.33	58.91
1974	3.04	26.01	11.20	37.21	48.99	4.58	9.21	62.78
1975	3.00	25.49	11.54	37.03	49.53	4.80	8.62	62.95
1976	2.94	25.12	11.15	36.27	49.88	4.58	9.27	63.73

a. Total may not add to 100.00% due to rounding.

Source: U.S. Bureau of Economic Analysis.

media outlets, it may be reasonably assumed that such relationships will continue to hold. This means that if consumers devote large portions of their implicit media budgets to expensive video cassette, disc machines or monthly cable fees, they will have to cut back on other media expenditures, perhaps on magazines or books.

Similarly, as advertisers find new outlets for sponsorship, they will be spreading their budgets over more media, giving relatively less to the existing ones. For example, there is already some local advertising on cable channels in some communities from merchants, with a likely cutback in the proportion of funds available for newspapers. A truly national cable audience may further scatter the mass audience of network television and also create identifiable market segments that pull certain advertisers away from special interest magazines.

With this history and the implications for the future, it should not be surprising that owners of businesses in the mass communications industry would want to increase earnings by purchasing more properties or, even more to the point, get involved in the new media. This gives rise to a basic conflict of cross media ownership and conglomeration that this book addresses. Can the existing media be expected or even

Table 8.2 Share of Advertising in Major Print and Broadcast Media, Selected Years, 1935-1978

	Advertising Expenditures	Percent of GNP	Percent Broadcasting	Percent Newspaper & Magazines
1935	$1,690	2.34%	6.7%	53.1%
1940	2,088	2.09	10.3	48.5
1945	2,875	1.36	14.7	44.7
1950	5,710	2.00	13.6	45.4
1955	9,194	2.30	17.1	37.9
1960	11,932	2.36	19.1	38.9
1965	15,250	2.22	22.5	36.6
1970	19,550	2.00	25.1	35.8
1975	28,230	1.86	25.6	35.1
1976	33,720	1.99	26.8	34.7
1977	38,120	2.02	26.9	34.9
1978[a]	43,740	2.08	27.0	34.9

a. Preliminary.

Sources: 1935-1960 — *Historical Statistics of the United States, Colonial Times to 1970,* Series T444-471.
1965-1978 — *Advertising Age,* as prepared by McCann-Erickson, Inc., New York, for advertising; U.S. Bureau of Economic Analysis for GNP.

obliged to ignore developing media? Is a financially healthy media industry — necessary if we want variety and quality* — at odds with those who see greater diversity and broader access fostered by small enterprises, locally owned and controlled?

The activity of existing media firms broadening their operations into new media areas is consistent with a marketing philosophy popularized by Theodore Levitt's concept of "marketing myopia." This demands that a firm carefully determine its field of operations. Is a newspaper publisher in the business of manufacturing and selling newspapers, or in the business of gathering and disseminating information? Given that choice, the latter would be the logical response. Thus, it would be natural to seek other ways of disseminating the vast quantities of information a newspaper staff can gather: news services, radio and television outlets are several. Similarly, an expertise in assembling and publishing specialized information makes it reasonable to assume that a book publisher would find a natural kinship with magazine publishing or more recently programming for video cassette, disc or cable distribution. The producer of theatrical films finds it a short and necessary jump into production of television shows.

In essence, the recognition of a mass communications industry, as opposed to simply a newspaper, broadcast, magazine, book or film industry lends itself to what has been termed conglomeration.

OWNERSHIP CONCENTRATION IN MASS COMMUNICATIONS

Given the expanded nature of the available media and the apparent intermedia competition for consumer and advertiser expenditures, then the relevant market for measuring the diversity of ownership must be the broad mass communications industry. There are a total of 35,000-40,000 outlets for the mass communications media covered in this book. Clearly, not each outlet has equal weight in its ability to influence thought or present ideas, with *Time* magazine or a popular prime time television show at a different level than a scholarly journal or a local cable presented show. Granted this, however, there is an impressive array of diverse media voices. Nor does a media outlet need a large audience to be influential. An article in the *New England Journal*

---

*This is not to imply that a profitable industry necessarily provides the best quality at all times. Nonetheless, it is unlikely that a weakened industry will provide it.

of Medicine may be as noticed by its audience as any national television show with a wider viewership.

To what extent is the mass communications industry dominated by giant conglomerates?* Table 8.3 was compiled by taking all those companies that have been cited in this book as being one of the dominant firms in any of the six segments examined. Thus, it includes broadcast chains with the largest audiences, magazine and newspaper groups with the greatest circulations, book publishers with the highest revenues, cable operators with the most subscribers and the major film distributors. In all, the table identifies 58 firms. Of these, 11 are dominant in newspapers, 16 in broadcasting, 16 in magazines, 14 in book publishing, nine in cable and 10 in motion picture distribution.

Many of these firms participated in only one area of the industry. Most have holdings in several areas, making them media conglomerates.

When looked at in terms of being able to dominate across media segments, only one firm has a major position in as many as four segments of the industry — Times Mirror Co., with significant holdings in newspapers, magazines, cable and book publishing, and a minor interest in broadcasting. Three firms have dominant positions in three different media: Cox Enterprises (which had its sale of broadcast and cable properties to General Electric pending in 1979), CBS Inc. and Time Inc. Nine more firms had substantial positions in two areas. The other 45 companies had a major stake in only one medium, including such well-known names as RCA, Harcourt Brace Jovanovich, Gulf + Western, Transamerica Corp., and Gannett.

Recognizing this rather sizeable cast of media conglomerates and owners, in addition to the many smaller and yet substantial owners of media properties, it seems appropriate to expand on Walter Lippmann's 1965 warning to the American Press Institute: "A free press exists only where newspaper readers have access to other newspapers which are competitors and rivals. . . ." Today, the same sentiment must be expressed: "A free press exists so long as consumers of the mass media have access to a variety of media sources which are competitors and rivals. . . ."

---

*"Dominant" is used here to mean pre-eminent or a leading participant. It should *not* be construed as used in the antitrust terminology of "being so powerful that smaller companies hesitate to take independent action in trade policy."

Table 8.3 Companies Dominant in One or More Mass Media Segments, with other Media Holdings, 1979

	Newspaper	Broadcasting	Magazines	Books	Cable/Pay TV	Film[a]
DOMINANT IN FOUR MEDIA						
Times Mirror Co.	+	○	+	+	+	
DOMINANT IN THREE MEDIA						
CBS Inc.		+	+	+		
Cox Enterprises[b]	+	+			+	
Time Inc.	○	○	+	+	+	
DOMINANT IN TWO MEDIA						
Hearst	+	○	+	○		
McGraw-Hill		○	+	+		
Newhouse	+		+			
New York Times Co.	+	○	+	○	○	
Reader's Digest Assn.			+	+		
E.W. Scripps	+	+				
Tribune Co.	+	+				
Warner Communications				○	+	+
Washington Post Co.	○	+	+	○		
DOMINANT IN ONE MEDIUM						
American Broadcasting Companies		+	○			
Cablecom-General					+	
Capital Cities Communications	○	+	○			
Charter Co.		○	+	○		
Columbia Pictures Industries		○	○		○	+
Doubleday		○		+		
Dow Jones	+		○	○	○	
Encyclopaedia Britannica				+		

Table 8.3 Companies Dominant in One or More Mass Media Segments, with other Media Holdings, 1979 (cont'd.)

	Newspaper	Broadcasting	Magazines	Books	Cable/Pay TV	Film[a]
Field Enterprises	○					
Gannett	+	+				
Gaylord Broadcasting Co.	○	+				+
General Cinema					○	+
Grolier				+		
Gulf + Western			○	○		
Harcourt Brace Jovanovich			○	+		
Harper & Row				+		
Knight-Ridder	+	○				
McCall's			+	+		
Macmillan				○		+
MCA Inc.		(	○	○		+
Meredith	○	+	+	○		
Metro Goldwyn Mayer						(
Metromedia		+		○		
Playboy			+	○		
Prentice-Hall				+		
RCA				○		
RKO		○			○	
Sammons Communications Corp.					+	
Scholastic Magazines			+			
Scott & Fetzer				+		
Scott, Foresman				+		

Table 8.3   Companies Dominant in One or More Mass Media Segments, with other Media Holdings, 1979 (cont'd.)

	Newspaper	Broadcasting	Magazines	Books	Cable/Pay TV	Film[a]
Storer Broadcasting Co.		+			○	○
Taft Broadcasting Co.		+				
Tele-Communications Inc.					+	
Teleprompter Co.					+	○
Thomson Newspapers Ltd.	+					
Transamerica Corp.		○	+			+
Triangle Publishing						
20th Century Fox		○				+
United Artist Theatres Circuit [c]						+
Viacom International		○			+	○
Walt Disney Productions		+				+
WGN-Continental Broadcasting		+			○	
Westinghouse			+		○	
Ziff-Davis		○				

Key: + Area of Dominance
        ○ Area of other holdings

a. Production or distribution.
b. Includes all Cox holdings in separate companies. Sale of broadcast holding to General Electric pending in April 1979.
c. Has 28% ownership of UA-Columbia Cablevision, Inc.

Source: Knowledge Industry Publications, Inc. Current to April 15, 1979.

CONCERNS AND LIMITATIONS OF THE GOVERNMENT

There are, to be sure, legitimate concerns on the part of society, as represented by the government, about the preservation of diversity of ownership of the media, not just on economic grounds, but because of the special place the mass media hold in the political process and their special place under the First Amendment. To date, action in this area has been limited to traditional antitrust suits, primarily in the film business, with just a few forays into newspapers. The Federal Communications Commission places limits on broadcast holdings and cross media ownership. The Federal Trade Commission has been increasingly interested, as has Congress.

In considering new anti-merger legislation, the soundest approach for Congress must be one that covers all industry, rather than one that singles out the mass communications business for special standards. The revision of the antitrust laws, proposed by Senator Kennedy in 1979, although subject to criticism on its basic premise of bigness being bad, at least would treat the media business the same as any other. This limits the possibility of any action aimed specifically at the information media. The greatest danger of such targeted legislation is that it could be an entry into government control over content, if only indirectly.

The experience of the government in regulating the media has been primarily through Federal Communications Commission jurisdiction over broadcast licenses. As has been explained in chapter three, the traditional rationale for controls in this area was the scarcity of broadcast outlets, as defined by spectrum space. However, momentum appeared to be growing in 1979 for at least some amount of deregulation in the broadcast field. A measure introduced in the Congress by Representative Lionel Van Deerlin (D-Calif.) would abolish the FCC and phase out many controls, including cross-ownership of newspaper and broadcast properties in the same city.* Deregulation has become possible because satellite transmission and cable television have enhanced the opportunity of a diversity of viewpoints via the electronic media, thus eliminating the rationale for federal intervention. Although some curbs would remain on television broadcasters, such as the "fairness doctrine," almost all regulations for radio, other than some technical requirements, would be lifted. As part of the proposed

---

*In July 1979 Rep. Van Deerlin abandoned his attempt to rewrite the Communications Act. He was pursuing some amendments to the telecommunications section of the existing law.

legislation, there would be no limit on the number of radio stations owned by a single entity, save for only one am and one fm station in any market. The number of television stations would remain at the current level of seven.[4]

It would be ironic if new rules constraining mass communications firms were promulgated as the most regulated segment was being given back over to the marketplace. Indeed, former FCC Commissioner Margita E. White has warned of bringing newspapers "under the same kind of 'raised eyebrows' regulations as the FCC applies to broadcasters. If we have learned anything from the evolution of broadcast regulation over the past half century, it is when the government regulates the media, it also regulates the message."[5]

Granted, this viewpoint is subject to counterclaims. But as various government agencies explore the need for structural changes in the mass communications industry, they should consider the broad implications of proposed "remedies" as well as the assumptions they hold in making them. These would include:

• Does increased diversity and access imply greater quality? What happened when the FCC took 30 minutes of prime time programming from the three networks and forced this time on the individual stations? The prohibitive costs of single market productions has resulted in few quality shows and opened up the market to syndicators of low cost game shows of little substance.

• Who should be the arbiter of what type of programming or content is most desirable for society? Much of the criticism of the networks center on the supposedly mindless grade of the programming. However, when given a choice, the viewing public has "voted" by where it turns the dial. Excellent programs, such as *60 Minutes* and *Roots*, have received viewer support. But many of the top-rated shows have outperformed presentations of supposedly higher intellectual content. By the same reasoning, newspaper publishers, even those with no direct local competition, must still offer a content that entices consumers to buy the product each day. Thus, publishers, like programmers, must show some response to the needs of the audience. Government regulators must refrain from imposing their view of what is socially beneficial content into their rationale for any type of regulation.

• How much control by any firm or group of firms must be manifest before we are threatened with perceivable restraints on true access to a broad spectrum of opinion and information? Most crucially, how can this be measured? On the one hand, there is a point at which some combinations may have to be limited. On the other hand, there can be no credence given to the argument advanced by some that every opinion or creative idea has a right to be heard through the mass media (although anyone with a few dollars can make up a picket sign or hand out leaflets at City Hall. Often, such viewpoints get aired by becoming news.). There is a limit to the time available to broadcasters and the space for newspaper and magazine publishers. For-profit book publishers must be guided by commercial considerations in selecting titles, or else they would eventually go out of business.* Even not-for-profit university or other subsidized presses must employ some criteria of value to a specific market in determining which offerings to publish. Can concentration of ownership be measured by the total number of media properties? By the number of households reached by the media owned by a given firm? By the geographical concentration of the firm's properties?

• Besides the mass media companies themselves, are there other participants in the mass communications industry that play important roles in determining the ultimate nature of the range of diversity available? Among those that might be considered:

1) State and federal regulations affecting common carriers, especially those for telephone and satellite transmission, play a role in the mass media. The number of earth satellites, the number of circuits available, regulations concerning earth receiving stations, the tariff schedules may all affect the available, regulations concerning earth receiving stations, the tariff schedules may all affect the availability of information transmission. The ability of syndicators to set up simultaneous-feed networks to cable operators will depend on the access they have to satellite transponders, which in 1979 were already in short supply. What are the ownership relationships between the satellite firms and the mass media firms?

---

*This does not mean that every book must be a best-seller, just as every magazine title does not have to sell 1 million copies per issue to be profitable. Many book publishers make a good living publishing titles with sales of 1000 copies and less.

2) The policies of the U.S. Postal Service are being increasingly questioned in light of the rapidly escalating second class postal rates. Even if these do not force some smaller publications out of business, they may affect the entry of some new publications and have certainly contributed to higher subscription prices. This in turn can affect the number of periodicals to which consumers will choose to subscribe, indirectly reducing exposure to some sources of information.

3) As noted in chapter 2, almost all newspapers rely on two news services for the bulk of their state, national and international news. Therefore, would a reduction in chain ownership of newspapers result in any change in the access of communities to such news sources? Even adding a newspaper to a community, providing real competition, would not necessarily provide a radically different mix of news content. Large syndicators and supplementary news services also provide much of the feature material for newspapers, regardless of the extent of local competition or ownership type.

4) To what extent does the distribution system for mass market paperback books influence the number of publishers that could realistically operate in this segment of the market? About 250 wholesalers nationwide account for the bulk of paperback book distribution to newsstands, chain stores and the 80,000 other non-bookstore outlets for these books. In each geographic market, one wholesaler has a virtually exclusive franchise to deliver books and magazines, not so much out of conspiracy but due to the economics of supplying thousands of small outlets on a continuing basis. The volume of new books has been such that many mass market books already have a shelf life of a monthly magazine. What opportunity does this leave for additional entries into this mass market segment of publishing?

5) Most of the mass media are totally or largely advertiser supported. Cable, which today derives its support primarily from subscribers, is expected to become an advertising outlet as its penetration increases. As was just seen in the discussion on the relative level of advertiser expenditures, there is a limit to the number of media outlets that can expect to get a share of the advertising dollar. One reason for the demise of competing newspapers in many cities is the efficiency a single newspaper provides local merchants. Starting a new paper requires the support of advertisers, who do not necessarily see any benefit for themselves. New media will spread advertising dollars even thinner.

6) Finally, if we are to be concerned with a limited number of gatekeepers, perhaps we should pay more heed to the findings of Ben

Stein, author of *The View From Sunset Boulevard.*[6] In investigating television content, Stein found that a relative handful of scriptwriters and producers create the entertainment messages that are broadcast every day. He found that almost all of these people live in Los Angeles. "Television is not necessarily a mirror of anything besides what those few people think. The whole entertainment component of television is dominated by men and women who have a unified idiosyncratic view of life."[7]

Thus, whether the subject of the program is comedy or drama, about crime, military, police or business, it is the perception of this group that becomes the image. In particular, Stein was not prepared for the degree of animosity the writers and producers expressed against business and businessmen. " ... One of the clearest messages of television is that businessmen are bad, evil people, and that big businessmen are the worst of all. This concept is shared by a majority ... I spoke with."[8]

Stein does not recommend that any specific actions be taken to remedy this bias. But his findings do point once again to the complexity of the media ownership question. If Stein's findings are valid, would any change in the ownership structure of television broaden the range of attitudes expressed in entertainment programming? Presumably we already have large, billion dollar networks carrying programs that, among other things, are created by people who make business look bad, and police work appear romantic. It cannot be assumed that given the fixed number of hours for broadcasting, any change in ownership structure – other than opening up opportunities for additional national networks – would bring about greater diversity in the community of programmers.

CONCLUSION

In the perspective of history, we would be hard pressed to find argument with the forceful proposal of former FCC Commissioner Lee Loevinger that, far from being faced with lessening diversity of media ownership, we are blessed with the greatest variety of any society at any time in history.

In 18th century America, the populace of major cities in the United States had access to a few skimpy weekly newspapers. They were priced at levels placing them out of the reach of the ordinary citizen. A circulation of 3000 was impressive. The papers may each have been individually owned, but people still had access at best to just one or two local papers. In some cities, there began to appear public libraries with a few books. By 1900 the newspaper was flourishing, as were a few national magazines. Already there were chains and conglomerates, owned by Hearst, Munsey, Scripps and Pulitzer. Nonetheless, people had to get their information from a few daily newspapers (of questionable objectivity), a few magazines and books. Even with a wide range of ownership, it is not likely that individuals had the diversity of sources, from as great a variety of producers, as we have today.

We cannot take issue with the need to maintain a vigorous flow of varied ideas and information. Our form of government and way of life depend on this. We must be extremely careful, however, that we do not allow a concern for possible future concentration to lead us into making dangerous incursions into the First Amendment area. It is important to be able to separate occasional abuses of the right of the press and the freedom that goes along with private enterprise from an indictment of all media owners. Along with the right of freedom of individual action is the understanding that, in an imperfect world, there is the right to make mistakes and to take advantage of freedom. Our society will be in a tenuous position if we allow outspoken critics to drive government to curtailing freedom under the cover of preventing possible abuses, especially when the proposed remedy — smaller size, has never been validated as a cure or preventative. It may be argued that larger, more visible corporate owners must be more careful in their policies than less prominent owners.

The intent of this study has not been to propose what action should be taken, if any, although some of the authors have provided some suggestions to that end in their chapters. As noted in chapter 1, the primary objective of the book was to pull together the relevant data on the degree of concentration in each media segment, the leading participants and their market share, and, where possible, to report on the effects that ownership trends have had on content.

This final chapter, however, has attempted to indicate the complexity of the issue of concentration as well as the many variables that must enter into any policy-making decisions. First, we must decide on the critical definition of concentration. This involves not only the differentiation between the traditional antitrust standard and a broader social-economic-political concept, but an agreement on what the relevant market should be: each media segment or the mass communications industry. If, in fact, our concern is with diversity of media voices — that is the social-economic-political concept for defining concentration — then by the same reasoning we must support the broader mass communications industry as the proper designation of the market. This conclusion can only be bolstered by the trends in advertiser and personal consumption expenditures on the media. Both constituencies spend their dollars interchangeably on the media, but at a constant relative rate, despite the addition of new media into the mix of alternatives.

Given the vast array of separate entities with holdings in the mass communications industry, policy makers must avoid accepting at face value some assumed myths, such as that greater diversity yields higher quality. They must also discipline themselves not to impose their own values of what is good for society on the people in the form of moves to encourage the development of media with one kind of content over another. Finally, policy and law makers are faced with incorporating the effects of many non-media variables that affect the performance of the media: postal regulations, common carrier policies, limited number of syndicators, news services, distribution networks and program creators.

Much of the mass media is run by big business. There are greedy media company owners, just as there are greedy individuals in other areas. There are also those who will use their position to dictate content to promote their own interests (this can include a night city editor as well as the chairman of a television network). While their ability to cause harm is real, there are existing laws and regulations, such as those for libel or the fairness doctrine, that can overcome some of the worst actions. There is also the weight of public opinion, which can respond to frauds and tyrants in the private sector. By the same token, there are politicians, bureaucrats and lawmakers who are empire building and have self-interests that could be served by a weakened mass media. While not above the law, they are of the law, which carries authority. Neither are typical of their species. But for all the good intentions of those who would like to encourage specific regulations aimed at the mass media, even in the absence of any empirically substantiated threat to reasonable access and diversity of expression, the weight of the existing data must go against any precipitous action affecting the status of the media. Ironically, media ownership has come under attack just as the opportunity for a vast number of additional voices has become a reality through new technologies.

In the tension that tends to exist between government and the press, Thomas Jefferson is often cited: "Were it left to me to decide whether we should have a government without newspapers or newspapers without government, I should not hesitate to prefer the latter." Jefferson continued to subscribe to this priority despite being viciously attacked by the press during his Presidency. No one today is seriously proposing having to face the explicit choice Jefferson used to make his point.

Nonetheless, there are forces converging on the media as we enter the 1980s that could endanger the First Amendment. These include increased attention by the Federal Trade Commission, the interest of some regulators and legislators in structural reform of the communications industry and the tendency on the part of government to justify regulation of the media because of its impact on our moral, social and political values. Those who propose such regulation seem guided by the myth that it can be accomplished without trampling on the content. And that is not likely.

The danger is not that any single action in the name of promoting wider press ownership will cause harm: individual actions, for cause, may be necessary, such as the *Associated Press* case in 1945. Yet at the same time, we should keep in mind the warning of Lord Develin:

> If freedom of the press perishes, it will not be by sudden death.
> ... It will be a long time dying from a debilitating disease caused
> by a series of erosive measures, each of which, if examined singly,
> would have a good deal to be said for it.

Who owns the media? Thousands of firms and organizations, large and small. They are controlled, directly and indirectly by tens of thousands of stockholders, as well as by public opinion. The mass communications business is profitable — as it must be. It is an industry changing its boundaries from one defined by format (books, television, newspapers, etc.) to one defined by function — collecting and disseminating information. The industry is too crucial to our way of life to allow it to be dominated in any way that unreasonably limits access to a substantial variety of viewpoints. By the same token, the First Amendment was established to serve as a buffer between government and the press. The good intentions of those who wish to impose special limits on media ownership — and hence control — must not override the lack of empirical evidence that to date can show no existing or impending damage to the multiplicity of media voices. Those who are critical of media mergers — as well as media performance — serve us well by reminding owners and managers constantly of their responsibility and accountability. But a movement for substantial structural changes that go beyond those applicable to all business must be deliberated cautiously and with painstaking understanding of all their possible implications and outcomes.

FOOTNOTES

1. Ben H. Bagdikian, "Conglomeration Concentration and the Flow of Information." Paper presented to the Media Symposium Federal Trade Commission, Washington, D.C., Dec. 14, 1978. pp. 4-5.

2. Carl Kaysen and Donald F. Turner, *Anti-Trust Policy: An Economic and Legal Analysis* (Cambridge, Mass.: Harvard University Press, 1959) as cited by Richard E. Caves, *American Industry: Structure, Contrast and Performance*, 4th ed. (Englewood Cliffs, N.J.: Prentice-Hall, 1977).

3. McCombs, Maxwell E., "Mass Media in the Marketplace," *Journalism Monographs*, No. 24 (Lexington, Ky.: Association for Education in Journalism, 1972), pp. 5-6.

4. "Van Deerlin-Collins Enter Bill to End Broadcast Regulation, Abolish FCC," *Editor & Publisher*, April 7, 1979, p. 17; Richard L. Gordon, "Van Deerlin Proposes Ads on Public TV," *Advertising Age*, April 2, 1979, pp. 1, 95.

5. I. William Hill, "Ex-FCC Commissioner Says Government Will Try to Regulate Newspaper," *Editor & Publisher*, March 31, 1979, p. 10.

6. (New York: Basic Books, 1979).

7. Stein p. xiii.

8. Ibid., p. 15.

Bibliography

NEWSPAPERS

Books

Bleyer, Willard G. *Main Currents in the History of American Journalism.* Boston: Houghton Mifflin, 1927.

Commission on the Freedom of the Press. *A Free and Responsible Press.* Chicago: University of Chicago Press, 1948.

Compaine, Benjamin. *The Newspaper Industry in the 1980s: An Assessment of Economics and Technology.* White Plains, N.Y.: Knowledge Industry Publications, Inc., 1979.

Davison, W. Phillips, and Frederick T.C. Yu. *Mass Communications Research: Major Issues and Future Directions.* New York: Praeger Publishers, 1974.

Emery, Edwin and Michael Emery. *The Press and America*, 4th ed. Englewood Cliffs, N.J.: Prentice-Hall, 1978.

Gross, Gerald, ed. *The Responsibility of the Press.* New York: Simon & Schuster, A Clarion Book, 1966.

Mott, Frank Luther. *American Journalism.* 3rd ed. New York: Macmillan Co., 1962.

Owen, Bruce M. *Economics and Freedom of Expression.* Cambridge, Mass.: Ballinger Publishing Co., 1975.

Rivers, William L. and Wilbur Schramm. *Responsibility in Mass Communication.* rev. ed. New York: Harper & Row, 1969.

Tebbel, John. *The Compact History of the American Newspaper.* New York: Hawthorne Books, Inc., 1963.

Journals, Monographs and Other Serials

"The Big Money Hunts for Independent Newspapers." *Business Week*, February 21, 1977, pp. 58-62.

Bishop, Robert L. "The Rush to Chain Ownership." *Columbia Journalism Review*, November-December 1972, p. 14ff.

"A Bitter Family Squabble Put Oakland's *Tribune* on the Block." *Business Week*, February 21, 1977, p. 60ff.

"Booth Aims to Thwart a Newhouse Takeover." *Business Week*, March 22, 1976, p. 45ff.

Borstell, Gerald H. "Ownership, Competition and Comment in 20 Small Dailies." *Journalism Quarterly* 33 (Spring 1956): 220-22.

Carmody, Deirdre, and James P. Sterba. "Murdoch About to Take Over Post; Texas Papers Thrive on Violence." *The New York Times*, December 26, 1976, p. 49.

Dallos, Robert E. "Bidding Sends Prices Higher in Newspaper Acquisition Binge." *Los Angeles Times*, January 9, 1977, Sec. VI, p. 2.

"Dolly's Last Surprise." *Newsweek*, November 29, 1976, p. 84.

Doogan, Mike, "Anchorage Daily News Files Suit to Break Joint Operating Accord With Rival Paper." *The Wall Street Journal*, February 14, 1977, p. 19.

"Family Paper Faces Problems to Survive as an Independent." *Editor & Publisher* April 28, 1973, p. 11.

Fawcett, Denby. "What Happens When a Chain Owner Arrives." *Columbia Journalism Review*, November-December 1972, pp. 29-30.

"53 Dailies in 1978 Purchases; 46 of Them Go Into Groups." *Editor & Publisher*, January 6, 1979, p. 47.

"Half of Daily Circulation in 20 Newspaper Groups." *Editor & Publisher*, September 16, 1978, p. 12.

Hatfield, C. Donald. Letter to the Editor. *Columbia Journalism Review*, January-February 1973, pp. 65-6.

Hicks, Ronald G., and James S. Featherstone. "Duplication of Newspaper Content in Contrasting Ownership Situations." *Journalism Quarterly* 55 (Autumn 1978): 549-54.

Howard, Herbert H. "Cross-Media Ownership of Newspapers and TV Stations." *Journalism Quarterly* 51 (Winter 1974): 715-18.

Huenergard, H. Celeste. "Scripps Hoping for Quick Decision in Cincinnati Case." *Editor & Publisher*, February 6, 1979.

"Joint Ownership of Media Barred by Appeals Court." *The Wall Street Journal*, March 2, 1977, p. 4.

"Monopoly Claimed in U.S. Suit." *Editor & Publisher*, January 22, 1977, p. 40.

"Newhouse Buys Majority of Outstanding Booth Stock." *Editor & Publisher*, November 13, 1976, p. 14.

Nichols, Peter. "Check it with Bill." Review of Eric Veblen, *The Manchester Union Leader in New Hampshire Elections* (University Press of New England). *Columbia Journalism Review*, November-December 1975, p. 53.

Nixon, Raymond B. "Changes in Reader Attitudes Toward Daily Newspapers." *Journalism Quarterly* 31 (Autumn 1954): 421-33.

Nixon, Raymond B., and Tae-Youl Hahn. "Concentration of Press Ownership: Comparison of 32 Countries." *Journalism Quarterly* 38 (Spring 1978): 31ff.

Nixon, Raymond B., and Robert L. Jones. "The Content of Non-Competitive Vs. Competitive Newspapers." *Journalism Quarterly* 33 (Summer 1956): 299-314.

"Number of Dailies in Groups Increased by 100% in 3 Years." *Editor & Publisher*, February 23, 1974, p. 9.

"Press Lord Captures Gotham." *Newsweek*, January 17, 1977, pp. 48-53.

Rarick, Galen, and Barrie Hartman. "The Effects of Competition on One Daily Newspaper's Content." *Journalism Quarterly* 43 (Autumn 1966): 459-63.

Ray, Royal H. "Competition in the Newspaper Industry." *Journal of Marketing* 15 (April 1951): 444-56.

Rosse, James N. "Economic Limits of Press Responsibility." *Studies in Industry Economics,* No. 56. Stanford, Calif.: Department of Economics, Stanford University, 1975.

Rosse, James N., Bruce M. Owen and James Dertouzos. "Trends in the Daily Newspaper Industry 1923-1973." *Studies in Industry Economics,* No. 57. Stanford, Calif.: Department of Economics, Stanford University, 1975.

Schweitzer, John C., and Elaine Goldman. "Does Newspaper Competition Make A Difference to Readers?" *Journalism Quarterly* 52 (Winter 1975): 706-10.

Stempel, Guido H. III. "Effects on Performance of a Cross-Media Monopoly." *Journalism Monographs* 29 (June 1973): 10-28.

Sterling, Christopher. "Trends in Daily Newspaper and Broadcasting Ownership, 1922-1970." *Journalism Quarterly* 52 (Summer 1975): 247-56.

Villard, Oswald Garrison. "The Chain Daily." *The Nation* 130 (1930): 595-97.

Wackman, Daniel et al. "Chain Newspaper Autonomy as Reflected in Presidential Campaign Endorsements." *Journalism Quarterly* 52 (Autumn 1975): 417-20.

Weaver, David H., and L.E. Mullins. "Content and Format Characteristics of Competing Daily Newspapers." *Journalism Quarterly* (Summer 1975): 257-64.

Unpublished Dissertations and Papers

Dertouzos, James N. "Media Conglomerates: Chains, Groups and Cross Ownership." Discussion paper prepared for Federal Trade Commission Media Symposium. Washington, D.C. December 1978.

Grotta, Gerald L. "Changes in the Ownership of Daily Newspapers and Selected Performance Characteristics, 1950-1968: An Investigation of Some Economic Implications of Concentration of Ownership." Ph.D. Dissertation, Southern Illinois University, 1970.

Langdon, John Henry. "An Intra Industry Approach to Measuring the Effects of Competition: The Newspaper Industry." Ph.D. Dissertation, Cornell University, 1969.

U.S. Federal Communications Commission. *Second Report and Order, Docket No. 18110: Multiple Ownership of Standard, FM and Television Broadcast Stations.* FCC 74-104, Mimeo 29942, January 29, 1975.

Reference Works

Editor & Publisher International Year Book. Annual, New York: Editor & Publisher, Inc.

U.S. Department of Commerce. *Statistical Abstract of the United States.* Annual.

TELEVISION AND RADIO BROADCASTING

Books

Archer, Gleason L. *History of Radio to 1926.* New York: American Historical Society, 1938; reissued by Arno Press, 1971.

Banning, William Peck. *Commercial Broadcasting Pioneer: The WEAF Experiment 1922-1926.* Cambridge, Mass.: Harvard University Press, 1946.

Botein, Michael. *Legal Restrictions on Ownership of the Mass Media.* New York: Advanced Media Publishing Associates, 1977.

Bunce, Richard. *Television in the Corporate Interest.* New York: Praeger Special Studies, 1976.

Cherington, Paul W. et al. *Television Station Ownership: A Case Study of Federal Agency Regulation.* New York: Hastings House, 1971.

Current Developments in CATV, TV, and Pay Television. New York: Practicing Law Institute, 1978.

Emery, Walter B. *Broadcasting and Government: Responsibilities and Regulations.* 2nd ed. East Lansing: Michigan State University Press, 1971.

Ginsburg, Douglas H. *Regulation of Broadcasting: Law and Policy Towards Radio/ Television and Cable Communications.* St. Paul, Minn.: West Publishing, 1979.

Head, Sydney W. *Broadcasting in America.* 3d ed. Boston: Houghton Mifflin, 1976.

Kahn, Frank J., ed. *Documents of American Broadcasting.* 3d ed. Englewood Cliffs, N.J.: Prentice-Hall, 1978.

Kittross, John M., ed. *Documents in American Telecommunications Policy.* Vol. 1. New York: Arno Press, 1977.

McAlpine, Dennis B. *The Television Programming Industry.* New York: Tucker Anthony and R.L. Day, 1975.

Noll, Roger G. et al. *Economic Aspects of Television Regulation.* Washington, D.C.: Brookings Institution, 1973.

Owen, Bruce M. *Economics and Freedom of Expression: Media Structure and the First Amendment.* Cambridge, Mass.: Ballinger, 1975.

Owen, Bruce M. et al. *Television Economics.* Lexington, Mass.: Lexington Books, 1974.

Quinlan, Sterling. *The Hundred Million Dollar Lunch.* Chicago: J. Philip O'Hara, Inc., 1974.

Sterling, Christopher H., and Timothy R. Haight. *The Mass Media: Aspen Institute Guide to Communication Industry Trends.* New York: Praeger Special Studies, 1978.

Sterling, Christopher H., and John M. Kittross. *Stay Tuned: A Concise History of American Publishing.* Belmont, Calif.: Wadsworth Publishing, 1978.

Journals, Monographs and Other Serials

Avery, Robert K. "Public Broadcasting and the Duopoly Rule." *Public Telecommunications Review* 5 (January-February 1977): 29-37.

Baer, Walter S. et al. *Concentration of Mass Media Ownership: Assessing the State of Current Knowledge.* R-1584-NSF. Santa Monica, Calif.: Rand Corporation, September 1974.

___ *Newspaper-Television Station Cross-Ownership: Options for Federal Action.* R-1585-MF. Santa Monica, Calif.: Rand Corporation, September 1974.

Barnett, Stephen R. *Cross-Ownership of Mass Media in the Same City: A Report to the John and Mary R. Markle Foundation.* Santa Monica, Calif.: Rand Corporation, September 1974.

Baudino, Joseph E., and John M. Kittross. "Broadcasting's Oldest Stations: An Examination of Four Claimants." *Journal of Broadcasting* 21 (Winter 1977): 61-83.

Broadcasting, September 30, 1957; January 8, 1968; May 11, 1970; April 17, 1972; November 22, 1976; March 7, June 27, December 12, 1977; March 6, October 9, December 11, December 18, 1978; January 1, 1979.

Christians, Cliff. "Home Video Systems: A Revolution?" *Journal of Broadcasting* 17 (Spring 1973): 223-34.

Busterna, John C. "Diversity of Ownership as a Criterion in FCC Licensing Since 1965." *Journal of Broadcasting* 20 (Winter 1976): 101-10.

Gormley, William T. Jr. "How Cross-Ownership Affects News-Gathering." *Columbia Journalism Review,* May-June 1977, pp. 38-46.

Howard, Herbert H. "The Contemporary Status of Television Group Ownership." *Journalism Quarterly* 53 (Autumn 1976): 399-405.

___. "Multiple Broadcast Ownership: Regulatory History." *Federal Communications Bar Journal* 27 (1974): 1-70.

Manning, Willard G., and Bruce M. Owen. "Television Rivalry and Network Power." *Public Policy* 24 (Winter 1976): 33-57.

Media Decisions. October 1978.

The New York Times, 11 December 1974; 18, 24 November 1976; 15 December 1978.

Park, R.E. *New Television Networks.* Santa Monica, Calif.: Rand Corporation, 1973.

Phillips, Kevin. "Busting the Media Trusts." *Harpers,* July 1977, pp. 23-24.

Publishers Weekly, December 25, 1978.

Sandman, Peter M. "Cross-Ownership on the Scales." *More,* October 1977, pp. 21-24.

Sarno, Edward F. Jr. "The National Radio Conferences." *Journal of Broadcasting* 13 (Spring 1969): 189-202.

Smith, Robert R. "Duopoly and ETV." *NAEB Journal,* May-June 1966, p. 42.

Smith, Robert R., and Paul T. Prince. "WHDH: The Unconscionable Delay." *Journal of Broadcasting* 18 (Winter 1974): 85-96.

Spalding, John W. "1928: Radio Becomes a Mass Advertising Medium." *Journal of Broadcasting* 8 (Winter 1963-1964): 31-44.

Toohey, Daniel W. "Newspaper Ownership of Broadcast Facilities." *Federal Communications Bar Journal* 21 (1966): 44-57.

The Wall Street Journal, 29 April 1975; 24 November 1976; 2 November 1978.

The Washington Post, April 23, 1976.

Wirth, Michael O., and James A. Wollert. "Public Interest Program Performance of Multimedia-Owner TV Stations." *Journalism Quarterly* 53 (Summer 1976): 223-30.

Government Publications

U.S. Congress. House. Committee on Interstate and Foreign Commerce. *Network Broadcasting.* Report 1297, 85th Cong., 2nd sess., January 27, 1958.

___. *Television Network Program Procurement.* Report 281, 88th Cong., 1st sess., May 8, 1963.

U.S. Congress. Senate. Committee on Interstate and Foreign Commerce. *Investigation of Television Networks and the UHF-VHF Problem,* by Robert F. Jones. Committee Print, 84th Cong., 1st sess., 1955.

____. *The Television Inquiry: Television Network Practices.* Committee Print No. 2, 85th Cong., 1st sess., 1957.

____. *Television Network Regulation and the UHF Problem,* by Harry M. Plotkin. Committee Print, 84th Cong., 1st sess., 1955.

U.S. Congress. Senate. Committee on the Judiciary. *Possible Anticompetitive Effects of Sale of Network TV Advertising. Hearings before a subcommittee of the Senate Committee on the Judiciary.* 89th Cong., 2nd sess., 1966.

U.S. Federal Communications Commission. *Public Service Responsibility of Broadcast Licensees.* 1946; reprinted by Arno Press, New York, 1974.

____. *Report of the Committee Appointed by the Commission to Supervise the Investigation of Chain Broadcasting, Commission Order No. 37, Docket No. 5060.* 1940.

____. *Report on Chain Broadcasting.* 1941. Reprinted by Arno Press, New York. 1974.

____. *Report and Order on Docket No. 20520, FCC 76-540.* June 18, 1956.

____. *Second Interim Report by the Office of Network Study: Television Network Program Procurement, Part 2.* 1965.

____. *Second Report and Order on Docket No. 18110, FCC 75-104.* January 31, 1975.

____. *Sixth Report and Order on Dockets 8736, 8975, 9175, and 8976; FCC 52-294.* April 14, 1952.

U.S. Federal Trade Commission. *Report of the Federal Trade Commission on the Radio Industry.* 1924; reprinted by Arno Press, New York, 1974.

U.S. President. Office of Telecommunications Policy. *Analysis of the Causes and Effects of Increases in Same-Year Rerun Programming and Related Issues in Prime-Time Network Television.* March 1973.

MAGAZINES

Books

Compaine, Benjamin M. *Consumer Magazines at the Crossroads: A Study of General and Special Interest Magazines.* White Plains, N.Y.: Knowledge Industry Publications, Inc., 1974.

Ford, James L.C. *Magazines for Millions.* Carbondale, Ill.: Southern Illinois University Press, 1969.

Mott, Frank Luther. *A History of American Magazines.* 5 vols. Cambridge, Mass.: Harvard University Press, 1968.

Peterson, Theodore. *Magazines in the Twentieth Century.* Urbana, Ill.: University of Illinois Press, 1964.

Quirk, Dantia. *The Library Market for Publications and Systems, 1979-1983.* White Plains, N.Y.: Knowledge Industry Publications, Inc., 1978.

Servan-Schreiber, Jean-Jacques. *The Power to Inform.* New York: McGraw-Hill, 1974.

Tebbel, John W. *The American Magazine: A Compact History.* New York: Hawthorne Books, 1969.

Periodicals and Other Serials

Advertising Age, September 26, 1977.
Folio, January and December 1977.
Media Decisions, June 1978.
Media Industry Newsletter, February 12, 1979.

Reference Works

Ayer Directory of Publications. Annual. Philadelphia: Ayer Press.
Bowker Annual of Library and Book Trade Information. New York: R.R. Bowker Co., 1971 and 1979.
U.S. Department of Commerce. *U.S. Industrial Outlook, 1979.*

THEATRICAL FILM

Books

Association of Cinematograph, Television and Allied Technicians. *Nationalising the Film Industry*. London: Association of Cinematograph, Television and Allied Technicians, 1973.
——. *Patterns of Discrimination Against Women in the Film and Television Industries*. London: Association of Cinematograph, Television and Allied Technicians, 1975.
Bächlin, Peter. *Der Film als Ware*. Basel: Burg Verlag, 1947.
Batz, Jean-Claude. *A Propos de la Crise de l'Industrie du Cinéma*. Bruxelles: Université Libre de Bruxelles, 1963.
Berton, Pierre. *Hollywood's Canada: The Americanization of Our National Image*. Toronto: McClelland and Stewart Ltd., 1975.
Bonnell, René. *Le Cinéma Exploité.* Paris: Editions du Seuil, 1978.
Conant, Michael. *Antitrust in the Motion Picture Industry*. Berkeley: University of California Press, 1960.
Degand, Claude. *Le Cinéma, Cette Industrie*. Paris: Editions Techniques et Economiques, 1972.
Gianelli, Enrico. *Economia Cinematografica*. Rome: Reanda Editore, 1956.
Guback, Thomas H. *The International Film Industry*. Bloomington: Indiana University Press, 1969.
Hampton, Benjamin B. *History of the American Film Industry*. New York: Dover Publications, Inc., 1970; previously published as *A History of the Movies*, New York: Covici, Friede, 1931.
Huettig, Mae D. *Economic Control of the Motion Picture Industry*. Philadelphia: University of Pennsylvania Press, 1944.
Kelly, Terence. *A Competitive Cinema*. London: Institute of Economic Affairs, 1966.
Kennedy, Joseph P., ed. *The Story of the Films*. Chicago: A.W. Shaw Company, 1927.

Klingender, F.D., and Stuart Legg. *Money Behind the Screen.* London: Lawrence and Wishart, 1937.

Lewis, Howard T. *The Motion Picture Industry.* New York: Van Nostrand Co., 1933.

Mercillon, Henri. *Cinéma et Monopoles.* Paris: Librarie Armand Colin, 1953.

Minority Employment in Daily Newspapers. Prepared by the Frank E. Gannett Urban Journalism Center, Medill School of Journalism. Evanston: Northwestern University, 1978.

Political and Economic Planning. *The British Film Industry.* London: Political and Economic Planning, 1952.

Schmidt, Georg; Werner Schmalenbach; and Peter Bächlin. *The Film – Its Economic, Social and Artistic Problems.* London: The Falcon Press, 1948.

Spraos, John. *The Decline of the Cinema.* London: George Allen and Unwin Ltd., 1962.

Journals, Monographs and Other Serials

The British Film Industry 1958 24 (June 1953).

Crandall, Robert W. "The Postwar Performance of the Motion Picture Industry." *The Antitrust Bulletin* 20 (Spring 1975).

Guback, Thomas. "Les Relations Cinéma-TV aux Etats-Unis Aujourd'hui." *Film Exchange* 2 (Spring 1978).

Guback, Thomas and Dennis Dombkowski. "Television and Hollywood – Economic Relations in the 1970s." *Journal of Broadcasting* 20 (Fall 1976).

Harmetz, Aljean. "Orion's Star Rises in Hollywood." *Warner World* 2 (1978).

Hennessee, Judith Adler. "Gross Behavior: How to Get Your Percentage Back." *Action* 2 (January-February 1978).

The Hollywood Reporter, 4, 5, 8 January 1979.

The Pay-TV Newsletter, Paul Kagan Associates, 30 November 1976; 8, 22 November 1977; 19 October, 17 November 1978.

Variety, 8 January 1975; 4 January, 15 February, 21 June, 6 September 1978; 3, 10 January 1979.

Reference Works

National Association of Theatre Owners. *Encyclopedia of Exhibition 1978.*

Roeber, Georg, and Gerhard Jacoby. *Handbuch der Filmwirtschaftlichen Medienbereiche.* Munich: Verlag Dokumentation, 1973.

Standard and Poor's Industry Surveys. *Leisure Time, Basic Analysis.* August 31, 1978.

Government Publications

Great Britain. The Monopolies Commission. *Films, A Report on the Supply of Films for Exhibition in Cinemas.* London: Her Majesty's Stationery Office, 1966.

Great Britain. Prime Minister. *Future of the British Film Industry.* Report of the Prime Minister's Working Party. London: Her Majesty's Stationery Office, 1976.

U.S. Commission on Civil Rights. *Behind the Scenes: Equal Employment Opportunity in the Motion Picture Industry.* Report prepared by the California Advisory Committee to the U.S. Commission on Civil Rights, 1978.

U.S. Congress. House. Committee on Education and Labor. *Impact of Imports and Exports on Employment, Part 8.* Hearings before the Subcommittee on the Impact of Imports and Exports on American Employment of the Committee on Education and Labor, 87th Cong., 1st and 2d sess., 1962.

———. *Unemployment Problems in American Film Industry.* Hearings before the General Subcommittee on Labor of the Committee on Education and Labor, 92nd Cong., 1st sess., 1972.

U.S. Congress. House. Committee on Interstate and Foreign Commerce. *Cable Television Regulation Oversight, Parts 1 and 2.* Hearings before the Subcommittee on Communications of the Committee on Interstate and Foreign Commerce, 94th Cong., 2d sess., 1977.

U.S. Congress. House. Committee on the Judiciary. *Consent Decree Program of the Department of Justice.* Report of the Antitrust Subcommittee (Subcommittee No. 5) of the Committee on the Judiciary, 86th Cong., 1st sess., 1959.

———. *Investigation of Conglomerate Corporations, Parts 1 to 4.* Hearings before the Antitrust Subcommittee (Subcommittee No. 5) of the Committee on the Judiciary, 91st Cong., 1970; and report by the staff of the Antitrust Subcommittee, 92d Cong., 1st sess., 1971.

U.S. Congress. House. Committee on Post Office and Civil Service. *Self-Policing of the Movie and Publishing Industry.* Hearings before the Subcommittee on Postal Operations of the Committee on Post Office and Civil Service. 86th Cong., 2d sess., 1960.

U.S. Congress. House. Committee on Small Business. *Movie Ratings and the Independent Producer.* Hearings before the Subcommittee on Special Small Business Problems of the Committee on Small Business, 95th Cong., 1st sess., 1977; and Report of the Subcommittee on Special Small Business Problems of the Committee on Small Business, 95th Cong., 2nd sess., 1978.

U.S. Congress. Senate. Committee on Finance. *Multinational Corporations.* Hearings before the Subcommittee on International Trade of the Committee on Finance, 93d Cong., 1st sess., 1973.

U.S. Congress. Senate. Committee on Foreign Relations. *International Communications and Information.* Hearings before the Subcommittee on International Operations of the Committee on Foreign Relations, 95th Cong., 1st sess., 1977.

———. *Overseas Information Programs of the United States, Part 2.* Hearings before a subcommittee of the Committee on Foreign Relations, 83d Cong., 1st sess., 1953.

———. *U.S. Informational Media Guaranty Program.* Hearings before the Committee on Foreign Relations, 90th Cong., 1st sess., 1967.

U.S. Congress. Senate. Committee on Government Operations. *Disclosure of Corporate Ownership.* Report by the Subcommittee on Inter-governmental Relations and the Subcommittee on Budgeting, Management and Expenditures of the Committee on Government Operations, 93d Cong., 1st sess., 1973.

U.S. Congress. Senate. Committee on the Judiciary. *Communications – Pay Cable Television Industry.* Hearings before the Subcommittee on Antitrust and Monopoly of the Committee on the Judiciary, 94th Cong., 1st sess., 1975.

——. *Economic Concentration, Parts 1 to 8.* Hearings before the Subcommittee on Antitrust and Monopoly of the Committee on the Judiciary, 88th Cong., 2d sess., to 91st Cong., 2d sess., 1964-1970.

U.S. Congress. Senate. Select Committee on Small Business. *Motion Picture Distribution Trade Practices.* Hearings before a subcommittee of the Select Committee on Small Business, 83d Cong., 1st sess., 1953; and 84th Cong., 2d sess., 1956.

——. *Motion Picture Distribution Trade Practices – 1956.* Report of the Select Committee on Small Business, 84th Cong., 2nd sess., July 27, 1956.

——. *Problems of Independent Motion Picture Exhibitors.* Report of the Select Committee on Small Business, 83d Cong., 1st sess., August 3, 1953.

U.S. Department of Commerce. *U.S. Industrial Outlook, 1978.*

——. *U.S. Service Industries in World Markets,* 1976.

U.S. Department of Commerce. Bureau of the Census. *1972 Census of Selected Service Industries: Motion Picture Industry.*

——. *Census of Selected Service Industries, 1972. Vol. 1, Summary and Subject Statistics.*

——. *Statistical Abstract of the United States, 1977.*

U.S. Department of Commerce, Bureau of Labor Statistics. *Employment and Earnings* 25 (October 1978).

U.S. Federal Trade Commission. *Paramount Pictures, Inc. et al. Consent Judgments and Decrees Investigation.* Report, February 25, 1965.

——. *Webb-Pomerene Associations: A 50-Year Review.* 1967.

U.S. Temporary National Economic Committee. *Investigation of Concentration of Economic Power. Monograph 43, The Motion Picture Industry – A Pattern of Control.* 1941.

BOOK PUBLISHING

Books

Bound, Charles F. *A Banker Looks at Book Publishing.* New York: R.R. Bowker Co., 1950.

Burlingame, Roger. *Endless Frontiers: The Story of McGraw-Hill.* New York: McGraw-Hill Book Company, Inc., 1959.

Cheney, O.H. *Economic Survey of the Book Industry: 1930-1931.* New York: R.R. Bowker Co., 1960.

Compaine, Benjamin. *The Book Industry in Transition: An Economic Study of Book Distribution and Marketing.* White Plains, N.Y.: Knowledge Industry Publications, Inc., 1978.

Comparato, Frank E. *Books for the Millions.* Harrisburg, Pa.: The Stackpole Company, 1971.

Dessauer, John P., Paul D. Doebler and E. Wayne Norberg. *Book Industry Trends 1977.* Darien, Conn.: The Book Industry Study Group, Inc., 1977.

——. *Book Industry Trends 1978.* Darien, Conn.: The Book Industry Study Group, 1977.

Duke, Judith S. *Children's Books and Magazines: A Market Study.* White Plains, N.Y.: Knowledge Industry Publications, Inc., 1979.

Ehrlich, Arnold W., ed. *The Business of Publishing: A PW Anthology.* New York: R.R. Bowker Co., 1976.

Foresman, Hugh A. *These Things I Remember.* Chicago: Scott, Foresman and Co., 1949.

Gross, Gerald, ed. *Publishers on Publishing.* New York: Grosset and Dunlap, Inc., 1961.

Irwin, John W. *Schoolbooks.* Columbus, Ohio: School and College Service, 1956.

Lawler, Thomas Bonaventure. *Seventy Years of Textbook Publishing: A History of Ginn and Company 1867-1937.* Boston: Ginn and Company, 1938.

Machlup, Fritz. *The Production and Distribution of Knowledge in the United States.* Princeton, N.J.: Princeton University Press, 1962.

Madison, Charles A. *Book Publishing in America.* New York: McGraw-Hill Book Company, 1966.

Miller, William. *The Book Industry.* New York: Columbia University Press, 1949.

Oswald, John Clyde. *Printing in the Americas.* New York: Hacker Art Books, 1937; reprinted 1963.

Pratt, John Barnes. *A Century of Book Publishing: 1838-1938.* New York: A.S. Barnes and Company, 1938.

Quirk, Dantia. *The College Publishing Market, 1977-1982.* White Plains, N.Y.: Knowledge Industry Publications, Inc., 1976.

———. *The El-Hi Market, 1978-1983.* White Plains, N.Y.: Knowledge Industry Publications, Inc., 1977.

Tebbel, John. *A History of Book Publishing in the United States.* New York: R.R. Bowker Co., vol. 1, 1972; vol. 2, 1975; vol. 3, 1978.

Textbooks Are Indispensable. New York: American Textbook Publishers Institute, n.d. (ca. 1955-1956).

Textbooks In Education. New York: American Textbook Publishers Institute, 1949.

Yankelovich, Skelly, and White, Inc. *The 1978 Consumer Research Study on Reading and Book Purchasing.* Darien, Conn.: The Book Industry Study Group, Inc., 1978.

Periodicals

Book Production Industry; and predecessors, *Book Production* and *Book Industry.* Northbrook, Ill.: BPI Publishing Co., monthly.

BP Report. White Plains, N.Y.: Knowledge Industry Publications, Inc., weekly.

Educational Marketer. White Plains, N.Y.: Knowledge Industry Publications, Inc., semi-monthly.

Publishers Weekly. New York: R.R. Bowker Co., weekly.

Reference Works

Annual Survey of the Textbook Publishing Industry. New York: The American Textbook Publishers Institute.

The Bowker Annual of Library and Book Trade Information. New York: R.R. Bowker Co.

Industry Statistics. Annual. New York: Association of American Publishers.
Literary Market Place. Annual. New York: R.R. Bowker Co.

Government Publications

U.S. Department of Commerce. *Printing and Publishing.* Monthly.
——. *Survey of Current Business.* Monthly.
——. Bureau of the Census. *Annual Survey of Manufactures.* Annual except in census years.
——. Bureau of the Census. *Census of Manufactures.* Census years.
——. Bureau of the Census. *Historical Statistics of the United States: Colonial Times to 1970.* 1975.
——. Bureau of Economic Analysis. *The National Income and Product Accounts of the United States, 1929-1974: Statistical Tables.* 1976.
U.S. Department of Health, Education and Welfare. *Biennial Survey of Education in the United States.* Biennial.
U.S. Department of the Treasury. Internal Revenue Service. *Corporation Source Book of Statistics of Income.* Annual.
U.S. Office of the President. *Economic Report of the President.* Annual.

CABLE AND PAY TELEVISION

Books

Baer, Walter S. et al. *Cable Television: Franchising Considerations.* New York: Crane, Russak, 1974.
Land, Herman W. Associates. *Television and the Wired City.* Washington, D.C.: National Association of Broadcasters, 1968.
LeDuc, Don R. *Cable Television and the FCC: A Crisis in Media Control.* Philadelphia: Temple University Press, 1973.
On the Cable: The Television of Abundance. Report of the Sloan Commission on Cable Communications. New York: McGraw-Hill, 1971.
Phillips, Mary Alice Mayer. *CATV: A History of Community Antenna Television.* Evanston: Northwestern University Press, 1972.
Research and Policy Committee of the Committee for Economic Development. *Broadcasting and Cable Television: Policies for Diversity and Change.* New York: Committee for Economic Development, 1975.
Rivkin, Steven R. *A New Guide to Federal Cable Television Regulations.* Cambridge: MIT Press, 1978.
Smith, Ralph Lee. *The Wired Nation: Cable TV — The Electronic Communications Highway.* New York: Harper & Row, 1972.
Sterling, Christopher H., and Timothy R. Haight. *The Mass Media: Aspen Institute Guide to Communication Industry Trends.* New York: Praeger, 1978.
Sterling, Christopher H., and John M. Kittross. *Stay Tuned: A Concise History of American Broadcasting.* Belmont, Calif.: Wadsworth Publishing, 1978.
Woodward, Charles C. Jr. *Cable Television: Acquisition and Operation of CATV Systems.* New York: McGraw-Hill, 1974.

Journals, Monographs and Other Serials

Baer, Walter S., and Carl Pilnick. *Pay Television at the Crossroads.* P-5159. Santa Monica, Calif.: Rand Corporation, April 1974.

Barrons, November 24, 1975.

Broadcasting, July 31, 1978.

Hill, Arthur. "CATV and Satellites: The Sky is the Limit." *Satellite Communications,* December 1978, pp. 20-21.

MacAvoy, Paul W., ed. *Deregulation of Cable Television.* Ford Administration Papers on Regulatory Reform. Washington, D.C.: American Enterprise Institute for Public Policy Research, 1977.

The New York Times, March 26, 1977.

Rappaport, Richard Warren. "The Emergence of Subscription Cable Television and its Role in Communications." *Federal Communications Bar Journal* 29 (1976): 301-34.

Television Digest, 28 March 1977; 30 October 1978.

The Videocassette & CATV Newsletter, November 1978.

Videonews, 27 September 1978; 20 December 1978.

Reference Works

Baer, Walter S. *Cable Television: A Handbook for Decision-Making.* New York: Crane, Russak, 1974.

Chin, Felix. *Cable Television: A Comprehensive Bibliography.* New York: IFI/Plenum, 1978.

Hollowell, Mary Louise, ed. *The Cable/Broadband Communications Book 1977-1978.* Washington, D.C.: Communications Press, 1977.

____. *Cable Handbook 1975-1976.* Washington, D.C.: Communications Press, 1975.

Government Publications

Copyright Revision Act of 1976. P.L. 94-553, U.S. Code Title 17 (1976).

U.S. Cabinet. Committee on Cable Communications. *Cable: Report to the President.* 1974.

U.S. Congress. House. Committee on Interstate and Foreign Commerce. *Cable Television: Promise versus Regulatory Performance.* Report of the Subcommittee on Communications of the Committee on Interstate and Foreign Commerce, 94th Cong., 2d sess., January 1976.

U.S. Congress. Senate. Committee on Government Affairs. *Study on Federal Regulation, Appendix to Volume VI, Framework For Regulation.* 95th Cong., 2d sess., December 1978.

CONCLUSION

Bagdikian, Ben H. "Conglomeration, Concentration and the Flow of Information." Discussion paper prepared for Federal Trade Commission Media Symposium. Washington, D.C. December 1978.

Caves, Richard E. *American Industry: Structure, Contrast and Performance.* 4th ed. Englewood Cliffs, N.J.: Prentice-Hall, 1977.
McCombs, Maxwell E. "Mass Media and the Marketplace." *Journalism Monographs.* No. 24. Lexington, Ky.: Association for Education in Journalism, 1972.
Stein, Ben. *The View from Sunset Boulevard.* New York: Basic Books, 1979.

INDEX

About the Authors . . .

Benjamin M. Compaine, executive director of the media and allied arenas at Harvard's Program for Information Resources Policy, was director of books and studies for Knowledge Industry Publications, Inc. when *Who Owns the Media?* was compiled. He is the author of *The Book Industry in Transition: An Economic Analysis of Book Distribution and Marketing, The Newspaper Industry in the 1980s: An Assessment of Economics and Technology*, and other studies and articles on magazines and mass communications. A graduate of Dickinson College, he has an M.B.A. from Harvard Business School and a Ph.D. in mass communications from Temple University.

Christopher H. Sterling is associate professor of communications at Temple University's School of Communications and Theater. He is the co-author (with John M. Kittross) of *Stay Tuned*, a text on the history of broadcasting, and (with Timothy Haight) of *The Mass Media: Aspen Institute Guide to Communications Industry Trends*. A past editor of *Journal of Broadcasting*, he has a Ph.D. from the University of Wisconsin.

Thomas Guback is research professor of communications at the University of Illinois at Champaign-Urbana, where he also earned his Ph.D. He is the author of *The International Film Industry*, as well as numerous articles on the motion picture business.

J. Kendrick Noble, Jr. is a frequent contributor of articles on the book publishing business to *Publishers Weekly, Book Production Industry*, and other publications. He is vice president of Paine Webber Mitchell Hutchins, Inc., where he is a leading analyst of publicly owned firms in the mass media business. He holds an M.B.A. from New York University.

Other Titles in the Communications Library Series . . .

The Book Industry in Transition: An Economic Study of Book
Distribution and Marketing
by Benjamin M. Compaine
LC 78-7527   ISBN 0-914236-16-4   hardbound $24.95

Children's Books and Magazines: A Market Study
by Judith S. Duke
LC 78-24705   ISBN 0-914236-17-2   hardbound $24.95

Trends in Management Development and Education: An Economic Study
by Gilbert J. Black
LC 79-4435   ISBN 0-914236-24-5   hardbound $24.95

Available in Fall 1979

Videotext: The Coming Revolution in Home/Office Information Retrieval
edited by Efrem Sigel
ISBN 0-914236-41-5   hardbound $24.95

The Newspaper Industry in the 1980s: An Assessment of Economics
and Technology
by Benjamin M. Compaine
ISBN 0-914236-37-7   hardbound $24.95